HAMLET

The third edition of *Hamlet* offers a completely new introduction to this rich, mysterious play, examining Shakespeare's transformation of an ancient Nordic legend into a drama whose philosophical, psychological, political, and spiritual complexities have captivated audiences world-wide for over 400 years. Focusing on the ways in which Shakespeare reimagined the revenge plot and its capacity to investigate the human experiences of love, grief, obligation, and memory, Heather Hirschfeld explores the play's cultural and theatrical contexts, its intricate textual issues, its vibrant critical traditions and controversies, and its history of performance and adaptation by celebrated directors, actors, and authors. Supplemented by an updated reading list, extensive illustrations, and helpful appendices, this edition also features revised commentary notes explicitly designed for the student reader, offering the very best in contemporary criticism of this great tragedy.

D0140223

THE NEW CAMBRIDGE SHAKESPEARE

All's Well That Ends Well, edited by Russell Fraser
Antony and Cleopatra, edited by David Bevington
As You Like It, edited by Michael Hattaway
The Comedy of Errors, edited by T. S. Dorsch
Coriolanus, edited by Lee Bliss
Cymbeline, edited by Martin Butler
Hamlet, edited by Philip Edwards
Julius Caesar, edited by Marvin Spevack
King Edward III, edited by Giorgio Melchiori
The First Part of King Henry IV, edited by Herbert Weil and Judith Weil
The Second Part of King Henry IV, edited by Giorgio Melchiori
King Henry V, edited by Andrew Gurr
The First Part of King Henry VI, edited by Michael Hattaway
The Second Part of King Henry VI, edited by Michael Hattaway
The Third Part of King Henry VI, edited by Michael Hattaway
King Henry VIII, edited by John Margeson
King John, edited by L. A. Beaurline
The Tragedy of King Lear, edited by Jay L. Halio
King Richard II, edited by Andrew Gurr
King Richard III, edited by Janis Lull
Love's Labour's Lost, edited by William C. Carroll
Macbeth, edited by A. R. Braunmuller
Measure for Measure, edited by Brian Gibbons
The Merchant of Venice, edited by M. M. Mahood
The Merry Wives of Windsor, edited by David Crane
A Midsummer Night's Dream, edited by R. A. Foakes
Much Ado About Nothing, edited by F. H. Mares
Othello, edited by Norman Sanders
Pericles, edited by Doreen DelVecchio and Antony Hammond
The Poems, edited by John Roe
Romeo and Juliet, edited by G. Blakemore Evans
The Sonnets, edited by G. Blakemore Evans
The Taming of the Shrew, edited by Ann Thompson
The Tempest, edited by David Lindley
Timon of Athens, edited by Karl Klein
Titus Andronicus, edited by Alan Hughes
Troilus and Cressida, edited by Anthony B. Dawson
Twelfth Night, edited by Elizabeth Story Donno
The Two Gentlemen of Verona, edited by Kurt Schlueter
The Two Noble Kinsmen, edited by Robert Kean Turner and Patricia Tatspaugh
The Winter's Tale, edited by Susan Snyder and Deborah T. Curren-Aquino

THE EARLY QUARTOS

The First Quarto of Hamlet, edited by Kathleen O. Irace
The First Quarto of King Henry V, edited by Andrew Gurr
The First Quarto of King Lear, edited by Jay L. Halio
The First Quarto of King Richard III, edited by Peter Davison
The First Quarto of Othello, edited by Scott McMillin
The First Quarto of Romeo and Juliet, edited by Lukas Erne
The Taming of a Shrew: The 1594 Quarto, edited by Stephen Roy Miller

HAMLET, PRINCE OF DENMARK

Third Edition

Revised with a new introduction by
HEATHER HIRSCHFELD

Edited by
PHILIP EDWARDS

CAMBRIDGE
UNIVERSITY PRESS

CAMBRIDGE
UNIVERSITY PRESS

University Printing House, Cambridge CB2 8BS, United Kingdom

One Liberty Plaza, 20th Floor, New York, NY 10006, USA

477 Williamstown Road, Port Melbourne, VIC 3207, Australia

314–321, 3rd Floor, Plot 3, Splendor Forum, Jasola District Centre, New Delhi – 110025, India

79 Anson Road, #06–04/06, Singapore 079906

Cambridge University Press is part of the University of Cambridge.

It furthers the University's mission by disseminating knowledge in the pursuit of education, learning, and research at the highest international levels of excellence.

www.cambridge.org
Information on this title: www.cambridge.org/9781107152977
DOI: 10.1017/9781316594117

© Cambridge University Press, 1985, 2003, 2019

First published 1985
Tenth printing 2001
Updated edition 2003
Thirteenth printing 2012
Third edition 2019

Printed in the United Kingdom by TJ International Ltd. Padstow Cornwall

A catalogue record for this publication is available from the British Library.

ISBN 978-1-107-15297-7 Hardback
ISBN 978-1-316-60673-5 Paperback

CONTENTS

List of Illustrations   *page* vi

Preface   ix

List of Abbreviations and Short Titles   x

Introduction   1

  Welcoming the Stranger   1

  Staging Revenge   2

  Staging the Stage   6

  Staging the Text   12

  Critical Responses   18

  The Play's the Thing   32

  Stages and Screens   52

Note on the Text   76

List of Characters   78

The Play   81

Reading List   250

Appendices (*Philip Edwards*)

  1 Textual Analysis   253

  2 Names   278

v

ILLUSTRATIONS

1 'Do you not come your tardy son to chide?' (3.4.106). Redrawn by
   Du Guernier for the 1714 edition of Rowe's Shakespeare (Folger
   Shakespeare Library)   *page* 46

2 John Philip Kemble as Hamlet, after Sir Thomas Lawrence, early
   1880s (Folger Shakespeare Library)   55

3 Edwin Booth as Hamlet *circa* 1870 (Library of Congress / Corbis /
   VCG via Getty Images)   56

4 Ellen Terry as Ophelia and Henry Irving as Hamlet (Time Life
   Pictures / Mansell / The LIFE Picture Collection / Getty Images)   57

5 'Go on, I'll follow thee' (1.4.86). Johnston Forbes-Robertson as Hamlet
   in a 1913 film (Mander and Mitchenson Theatre Collection)   58

6 John Gielgud as Hamlet (Hulton Archive / Getty Images), 1934,
   New Theatre   59

7 Laurence Olivier as Hamlet and Eileen Herlie as Gertrude, 1948
   (ITV/Shutterstock)   60

8 Mark Rylance as Hamlet and Peter Wright as Claudius at the Royal
   Shakespeare Theatre, Stratford-upon-Avon, 1989 (© John Bunting /
   ArenaPAL)   62

9 Kenneth Branagh as Hamlet, 1996 (Castle Rock Entertainment /
   Kobal / Shutterstock)   63

10 David Tennant as Hamlet and Patrick Stewart as Claudius in the 2008
   Royal Shakespeare Company production directed by Gregory Doran
   (© Robbie Jack / Corbis / Getty Images)   64

11 Benedict Cumberbatch as Hamlet at the Barbican, London, 2015
   (© Johann Persson / ArenaPAL)   65

12 Paapa Essiedu as Hamlet at the Royal Shakespeare Theatre, Stratford-
   upon-Avon, 2016 (courtesy of the Royal Shakespeare Company)   66

13 The Mousetrap scene, Berlin, 1926, directed by Leopold Jessner (courtesy
   of Theaterwissenschaftliche Sammlung, University of Cologne)   68

14 Sebastian Schwarz as Horatio/Gueldenstern, Lars Eidinger as Hamlet,
   and Robert Beyer as Polonius/Osrik in the 2008 Schaubuehne Berlin
   production directed by Thomas Ostermeier (Lieberenz / Ullstein Bild /
   Getty Images)   69

15 Innokenti Smoktunovsky as Hamlet in the 1964 film *Hamlet*, directed by
    Grigori Kozintsev (Sovfoto / Universal Images Group / Getty Images)   70

16 *Al-Hamlet Summit* – Sulayman Al Bassam as Hamlet, Mariam Ali as
    Ophelia, Nicolas Daniel as Claudius, 2005, Kronborg Castle, Elsinore/
    Helsingor, Denmark; director: Sulayman Al Bassam (courtesy of
    SABAB Theatre)   72

17 Sarah Bernhardt as Hamlet in the 1900 film directed by Clément
    Maurice (Bettmann / Getty Images)   74

18 Angela Winkler as Hamlet and Evia Mattes as Gertrude at the Royal
    Lyceum Theatre, Edinburgh, 2000 (© Clive Barda / ArenaPAL)   75

PREFACE

One of the consequences of the enduring, and global, appeal of *Hamlet* is the nearly limitless commentary on the play. This edition thus cannot but be selective in its presentation of the play's critical tradition and performance history. Its new Introduction and revised commentary aim to provide robust accounts of influential early approaches to the play as well as persuasive recent treatments of it.

All editions of *Hamlet* must grapple with the play's significant textual challenges. These challenges result from the existence of three distinct early editions of the play: the quarto of 1603 (Q1), the quarto of 1604/5 (Q2), and the text supplied in the 1623 First Folio (F). Q2 has over 200 lines not in F; F has over 80 lines not in Q2. Q1, half the size of the other two texts, has stage directions and an entire scene that appear neither in Q2 nor in F, as well as a linguistic sensibility that differs markedly in places from the others.

This state of affairs demands that editors have a coherent explanation for the existence of these distinct texts, the connections between them, and their relationships to what Shakespeare might have written and what his acting company might have performed. In the first edition of the *New Cambridge Shakespeare* (*NCS*) *Hamlet*, Philip Edwards provided such an explanation, offering a consistent theory of the three copies and clarifying how his theory determined the various choices he made for his text. His account remains seminal for other editors and scholars considering the textual problem.

Edwards's explanation, roughly twenty-five pages, was thoroughly integrated into his Introduction. This is not the case in the new Introduction. Instead, this Introduction outlines the play's complex textual status, the questions that arise from it, and the various answers, both old and recent, that scholars have formulated for it. Edwards's account, upon which the text of the revised *NCS Hamlet* remains almost entirely based, is preserved in the 'Textual Analysis' at the end of the volume, distinct from the rest of the Introduction.

I am grateful to A. R. Braunmuller and Brian Gibbons for asking me to undertake this revision and for their careful reading of the manuscript, and to Emily Hockley at Cambridge University Press for her advice and patience. I was greatly assisted by the enthusiasm of the talented students in my undergraduate honours seminar, '*Hamlet* 24/7', at the University of Tennessee: Peter Cates, Savannah DeFreese, Emily Ferrell, Taylor Gray, Brenna Hosman, Noreen Premji, Bridget Sellers, Sophia Shelton, Logan Sutherland, Gage Taylor, and Courtney Whited. I am especially thankful for the support of Anthony Welch.

H. H.

Knoxville, Tennessee
2018

ABBREVIATIONS AND SHORT TITLES

All quotations and line references to plays other than *Hamlet* are to G. Blakemore Evans (ed.), *The Riverside Shakespeare*, 1974.

Adams	*Hamlet*, ed. Joseph Quincy Adams, 1929
N. Alexander	*Hamlet*, ed. Nigel Alexander, 1973 (Macmillan Shakespeare)
P. Alexander	*William Shakespeare, The Complete Works*, ed. Peter Alexander, 1951
Bullough	Geoffrey Bullough (ed.), *Narrative and Dramatic Sources of Shakespeare*, 8 vols., 1957–75
Cambridge	*The Works of William Shakespeare*, ed. William George Clark, J. Glover and William Aldis Wright, 1863–6, viii; 2nd edn, 1891–2, vii (Cambridge Shakespeare)
Capell	*Mr William Shakespeare, His Comedies, Histories and Tragedies*, ed. Edward Capell, 1767–8, x
Clark and Wright	*Hamlet Prince of Denmark*, ed. William George Clark and William Aldis Wright, 1872 (Clarendon Press Shakespeare)
Collier	*The Works of William Shakespeare*, ed. J. Payne Collier, 1842–4, vii
conj.	conjectured
CR	David Farley-Hills, *Critical Responses to 'Hamlet' 1600–1900*, 4 vols. (New York: AMS Press, 1996–2006)
Dowden	*The Tragedy of Hamlet*, ed. Edward Dowden, 1899 (Arden Shakespeare)
Duthie	George Ian Duthie, *The 'Bad' Quarto of 'Hamlet': A Critical Study*, 1941
Dyce	*The Works of William Shakespeare*, ed. Alexander Dyce, 1857, v
f	*Mr William Shakespeares Comedies, Histories, and Tragedies*, 1623 (First Folio)
F2	*Mr William Shakespeares Comedies, Histories, and Tragedies*, 1632
Hanmer	*The Works of Shakespear*, ed. Sir Thomas Hanmer, 1743–4, vi
Hoy	*Hamlet*, ed. Cyrus Hoy, 1963 (Norton Critical Editions)
Jenkins	*Hamlet*, ed. Harold Jenkins, 1982 (Arden Shakespeare)
Johnson	*The Plays of William Shakespeare*, ed. Samuel Johnson, 1765, viii
Kittredge	*Hamlet*, ed. George Lyman Kittredge, 1939
Knight	*The Pictorial Edition of the Works of Shakspere*, ed. Charles Knight, 1838–43, i, 'Tragedies'
MacDonald	*The Tragedie of Hamlet*, ed. George MacDonald, 1885
Malone	*The Plays and Poems of William Shakespeare*, ed. Edmond Malone, 1790, ix
MLN	*Modern Language Notes*
MSH	J. Dover Wilson, *The Manuscript of Shakespeare's 'Hamlet'*, 2 vols., 1934; reprinted 1963
N & Q	*Notes and Queries*

NV	*Hamlet*, ed. Horace Howard Furness, 2 vols., 1877; reprinted 1963 (A New Variorum Edition of Shakespeare)
OED	*The Oxford English Dictionary*, 1884–1928, reprinted 1933
PMLA	*Publications of the Modern Language Association of America*
Pope	*The Works of Shakespear*, ed. Alexander Pope, 1723–5, VI
Pope²	*The Works of Shakespear*, ed. Alexander Pope, 2nd edn, 1728, VIII
Q1	*The Tragicall Historie of Hamlet Prince of Denmarke*, by William Shakespeare, 1603 (first quarto)
Q2	*The Tragicall Historie of Hamlet, Prince of Denmarke*, by William Shakespeare, 1604, 1605 (second quarto)
Q 1611, Q 1676	Quarto editions of those dates
RES	*Review of English Studies*
Ridley	*Hamlet*, ed. M. R. Ridley, 1934 (New Temple Shakespeare)
Rowe	*The Works of Mr William Shakespear*, ed. Nicholas Rowe, 1709, V
RQ	*Renaissance Quarterly*
Schmidt	Alexander Schmidt, *Shakespeare-Lexicon*, 2 vols., 1874–5; 2nd edn, 1886
SD	stage direction
SH	speech heading
Shakespeare's Words	David Crystal and Ben Crystal, *Shakespeare's Words: A Glossary & Language Companion* (London: Penguin Books, 2002).
Spencer	*Hamlet*, ed. T. J. B. Spencer, 1980 (New Penguin Shakespeare)
SQ	*Shakespeare Quarterly*
Staunton	*The Plays of Shakespeare*, ed. Howard Staunton, 1858–60, reissued 1866, III
Steevens	*The Plays of William Shakespeare*, ed. Samuel Johnson and George Steevens, 1773, X
Steevens²	*The Plays of William Shakespeare*, ed. Samuel Johnson and George Steevens, 2nd edn, 1778, X
Steevens³	*The Plays of William Shakespeare*, ed. Samuel Johnson and George Steevens, 4th edn, 1793, XV
Sternfeld	F. W. Sternfeld, *Music in Shakespearean Tragedy*, 1963
Taylor, Jowett, Bourus, and Egan	*The New Oxford Shakespeare*, ed. Gary Taylor, John Jowett, Terri Bourus, and Gabriel Egan (Oxford University Press, 2016)
Theobald	Lewis Theobald, *Shakespeare Restored*, 1726
Theobald²	*The Works of Shakespeare*, ed. Lewis Theobald, 1733, VII
Theobald³	*The Works of Shakespeare*, ed. Lewis Theobald, 1740, VIII
Thompson and Taylor	*Hamlet*, ed. Ann Thompson and Neil Taylor, rev. edn (Bloomsbury Arden, 2016)
Tilley	Morris Palmer Tilley, *A Dictionary of the Proverbs in England in the Sixteenth and Seventeenth Centuries*, 1950 [references are to numbered proverbs]
TLS	*The Times Literary Supplement*
Walker	William Sydney Walker, *A Critical Examination of the Text of Shakespeare*, 3 vols., 1860
Warburton	*The Works of Shakespear*, ed. William Warburton, 1747, VIII
White	*The Works of William Shakespeare*, ed. Richard Grant White, 1857–66, XI
Wilson	*Hamlet*, ed. J. Dover Wilson, 1934; 2nd edn, 1936, reprinted 1968 (New Shakespeare)

INTRODUCTION

Welcoming the Stranger

'And therefore as a stranger give it welcome', Prince Hamlet instructs his friend Horatio at the close of the play's first act. Hamlet is speaking of the ghost of his dead father, whose 'wondrous strange' appearance the men have just witnessed. The welcome, however, expands in the moment of delivery to invite into Hamlet's story a wider audience. When Shakespeare's play was first performed, that audience included the men and women assembled for an afternoon performance at the Globe Theatre on the south bank of the Thames. By now, in a tradition that extends over 400 years, the protagonist's line beckons to actors, spectators, readers, and adapters around the world, bidding them to detect themselves in its address.

As with so many aspects of the play, that address is a complicated one. Hamlet's hospitality, with its echoes of the Hebrew Bible and the New Testament,[1] gives way to hesitation; his tenderness towards the ghostly stranger, to suspicion. His attitude is informed, surely, by his own identification with the 'outsider': in the wake of the death of his royal father and the remarriage of his mother, Gertrude, to his uncle Claudius, who has assumed the throne, Hamlet understands himself as a kind of foreigner, an alien in his native Denmark and its court at Elsinore. But he also feels a stranger to himself, absorbed in the kinds of tortured self-reflection seen today as a model of modern consciousness.

Recipients of his welcome, then, face an interpretive challenge. Does Hamlet's invitation summon them into the narrative in order for them to discover that they, like the Romantic poet Samuel Taylor Coleridge, 'have a smack of Hamlet' in themselves?[2] Or does it usher them into the world of the play only to remind them, as it does T. S. Eliot's Prufrock ('I am not Prince Hamlet, nor was meant to be'), that they are different and distant from him?[3] Or does it ask them to see the whole drama as something strange, and to welcome it into their lives with both interest and trepidation?

At the turn of the seventeenth century, when Shakespeare's *Hamlet* was first played, it may have seemed as familiar as it did strange on the London stage. Its story was not new: a dramatic version – what scholars call the Ur-*Hamlet* – had been performed as early as the late 1580s, when it was mentioned by the prolific writer Thomas Nashe in

---

[1] Naseeb Shaheen gives the New Testament allusions (2 Heb. 13.2 and Matt. 25.35) in *Biblical References in Shakespeare's Plays* (Newark: University of Delaware Press, 1999), 545. Consider also Lev. 19.34, Deut. 10.17–19.

[2] Samuel Taylor Coleridge, *The Collected Works of Samuel Taylor Coleridge: Table Talk*, ed. Carl Woodring (Princeton University Press, 1990), 14.2: 61.

[3] T. S. Eliot, 'The Love Song of J. Alfred Prufrock', in *Collected Poems, 1909–1962* (New York: Harcourt, Brace & World, Inc., 1963), 7.

a scornful attack on contemporary dramatists. And its dramatic events and concerns were guaranteed to resonate for its audience with familiar, topical issues: the ageing of the female ruler, Queen Elizabeth I; the question of her successor; the declining fortunes of the charismatic figure of the Earl of Essex and with him a model of chivalric honour; the deep challenges to religious belief and practice as a result of Reformation religious change; and the revival of philosophical stoicism and its concerns with liberty and tyranny. In addition, viewers would have recognized in the play ancient themes and narratives of intimate violence, adultery, and retaliation. These include the biblical accounts of Adam and Eve, and Cain and Abel – Judaeo-Christian culture's primal scenes of marital betrayal, fraternal hatred, and death – as well as Greek and Roman drama and epic by Aeschylus, Euripides, Seneca, and Virgil.[1]

Staging Revenge

WHAT DO REVENGERS WANT?

Perhaps most strikingly, the play – which takes shape around a son's pursuit of vengeance for his father – would have echoed for its audience the concerns and conventions of the popular dramatic genre of revenge tragedy. Although the term 'revenge tragedy' is a modern invention, plots of vengeance and vendetta – like Thomas Kyd's *The Spanish Tragedy* (1588–90) and Christopher Marlowe's *The Jew of Malta* (1589–90) – captured the dramatic imagination in the late sixteenth and early seventeenth centuries. These plots were characterized by a flexible set of conventions. A protagonist discovers a fatal or destructive deed that wrecks his or her sense of justice and order. He or she wants the violation addressed – wants balance restored – but recognizes that social institutions are unable to deal with the outrage. Therefore, the protagonist, often urged by a ghost or other soliciting spirit, takes upon him- or herself the burden of personally and privately avenging the wrong. His or her efforts, pursued to the edge of the protagonist's sanity, involve tactics of delay, disguise, and theatrical display before they end in a final retaliation that exceeds the destructiveness of the original crime.[2]

Shakespeare had been interested in these tropes since early in his career: he used them in the abundantly gory *Titus Andronicus* (1592); he put issues of the vendetta and talionic justice at the core of mid-1590s plays like *Romeo and Juliet* (1595) and *The Merchant of Venice* (1595); and he haunted both *Richard III* (1592) and *Julius Caesar* (1599) with ghosts. Vengeance for Shakespeare and his audience was not novel, but its dramatic allure remained potent. Both the topic and structure of revenge offer, as John Kerrigan has noted, 'a compelling mix of ingredients: strong situations shaped by violence; ethical issues for debate; a volatile, emotive mixture of loss and agitated grievance'.[3]

---

[1] For the biblical allusions, see Hannibal Hamlin, *The Bible in Shakespeare* (Oxford University Press, 2013), 154–61. For the classical allusions, see Robert Miola, *Shakespeare and Classical Tragedy* (Oxford: Clarendon Press, 1992), esp. 33–67; Colin Burrow, *Shakespeare and Classical Antiquity* (Oxford University Press, 2013), 173–6.

[2] Fredson Bowers, *Elizabethan Revenge Tragedy* (Princeton University Press, 1945).

[3] John Kerrigan, *Revenge Tragedy: Aeschylus to Armageddon* (Oxford: Clarendon Press, 1996), 3.

Early modern audiences would have appreciated the ways in which those 'ingredients' could be fashioned to speak to their own moment and investment in revenge scenarios. Past scholars such as Eleanor Prosser claimed that Shakespeare and his contemporaries condemned retaliation as barbaric and contrary to divine law (as in Deuteronomy 32.35 and Romans 12.19, 'Vengeance is mine, sayeth the Lord'). Revenge plays, according to this reading, reinforced this message.[1] But more recent scholarship has challenged this conclusion, suggesting that the early modern drama offered more complex approaches to the morality and legality of revenge.[2] Revenge plays, that is, did not simply condemn vengeance; they dramatized the human desire to match crime with crime, exploring it in connection with classical, Christian, and Elizabethan principles of justice, honour, stoicism, obedience, resistance, and suffering.

Plots of revenge accommodated issues that fascinated contemporary dramatists and their audiences. Death, sexuality, and bodily violation lie at the heart of stories of vendetta, and when these involve murder or rape at the highest levels, they become political as well as personal challenges to honour and liberty. Similarly, the human capacities to mourn, remember, and repent are all scrutinized in relation to the pursuit of revenge. These were urgent topics for Shakespeare's period, particularly as they were inflected by the social, cultural, and religious changes associated with the sixteenth and seventeenth centuries. The genre's concern with crime, punishment, and atonement provided a structure for exploring both developments in sixteenth-century jurisprudence and doctrinal changes associated with the English Reformation and its competing theologies of death, sin, the afterlife, and the sacraments. Some scholars have seen a special relationship between the blood and gore of revenge drama and Catholic–Protestant debates about the Eucharist.[3] Michael Neill has argued that revenge tragedy, with its extraordinary fixation on a dead loved one, functioned as a substitute for rejected (but longed-for) Catholic memorializing practices grounded in a belief in Purgatory. The genre, he writes, supplied 'a fantasy response to the sense of despairing impotence produced by the Protestant displacement of the dead'.[4] And although religious belief and practice provided the 'matrix for explorations of virtually every topic' during this time, revenge tragedy trafficked in realms other than the strictly devotional.[5] Lorna Hutson has suggested that early modern revenge tragedy dramatized legal thought and practice by representing on stage 'the protracted processes of detection, pre-trial

---

[1] Eleanor Prosser, *Hamlet and Revenge* (Stanford University Press, 1971).

[2] Linda Woodbridge offers the most thorough-going account in *English Revenge Drama: Money, Resistance, Equality* (Cambridge University Press, 2010). For discussions of the complementarity, rather than the opposition, between revenge and early modern law, see Ronald Broude, 'Revenge and Revenge Tragedy in Renaissance England', *RQ* 28 (1975), 38–58; and Derek Dunne, *Shakespeare, Revenge Tragedy and Early Modern Law: Vindictive Justice* (Houndmills: Palgrave Macmillan, 2016).

[3] Huston Diehl, *Staging Reform, Reforming the Stage: Protestantism and Popular Theater in Early Modern England* (Ithaca, NY: Cornell University Press, 1997), 94–123.

[4] Michael Neill, *Issues of Death: Mortality and Identity in English Renaissance Tragedy* (Oxford: Clarendon Press, 1997), 244, 246.

[5] Debora Shuger, *Habits of Thought in the English Renaissance: Religion, Politics, and the Dominant Culture* (University of Toronto Press, 1997), 6.

examination, trial, and evidence evaluation'.[1] The genre also gave fictional shape to the sorts of real-life 'systemic unfairness' its audience might encounter at a time that 'witnessed severe disproportion between crime and punishment, between labor and its rewards'.[2] And, insofar as its plots were focused on the pursuit of justice in the face of political corruption by an individual called upon to strategize and plan, revenge tragedy gave dramatic space to a host of long-standing philosophical dilemmas around identity, intention, and agency.[3] Finally, revenge plays seized on ideological assumptions about women and uncontrolled violence to 'tap into fundamental fears about women ... maternal power and female agency'.[4]

HAMLET AND THE RESOURCES OF REVENGE

Hamlet participates in these concerns and the revenge conventions to which they are attached. It relies for its core narrative on the Nordic legend of Amleth, the clever, as well as vengeful, son of a valiant father slain by his own brother. The story, set in pre-Christian Denmark, was chronicled in Saxo Grammaticus's late-twelfth-/early-thirteenth-century compendium *Gesta Danorum*, or 'Deeds of the Danes', which was printed for the first time in Paris in 1514 as *Historiae Danicae*. It was translated by François de Belleforest in the fifth volume of his collection *Histoires Tragiques* (1570); Shakespeare's play ultimately derives from this version.[5] (Belleforest's account was translated into English as the *Hystorie of Hamblet* in 1608, well after Shakespeare's play was in the repertory.) Saxo and Belleforest's accounts differ in important ways,[6] but they agree on most of the elements of the plot. In both, Amleth's uncle takes over as ruler of the province of Jutland and marries his widowed sister-in-law. Amleth, the betrayed son, feigns madness in order to protect himself from his spying, murderous uncle and to implement his revenge, which he accomplishes with great relish, teasing the court with seemingly nonsensical riddles and grotesque behaviour (including the murder of a councillor whom he feeds to pigs) before burning down the palace hall and decapitating his uncle. He then appeals to the startled populace with a powerful oration, defending his revenge as the only way to preserve the people's liberty against the depredations of the tyrant.[7]

---

[1] Lorna Hutson, *The Invention of Suspicion: Law and Mimesis in Shakespeare and Renaissance Drama* (Oxford University Press, 2008), 9.

[2] Woodbridge, *English Revenge Drama*, 7.

[3] Christopher Crosbie, *Revenge Tragedy and Classical Philosophy on the Early Modern Stage* (Edinburgh University Press, 2018).

[4] Alison Findlay, *A Feminist Perspective on Renaissance Drama* (Oxford: Blackwell Press, 1999), 49.

[5] Bullough, VII: 15; Margrethe Jolly, '*Hamlet* and the French Connection: The Relationship of Q1 and Q2 *Hamlet* and the Evidence of Belleforest's *Histoires Tragiques*', *Parergon* 29.1 (2012), 83–105.

[6] Bullough, VII: 10–15. For the ideological use of Saxo by Belleforest during the religious conflicts of the sixteenth century, see Julie Maxwell, 'Counter-Reformation Versions of Saxo: A New Source for *Hamlet?*" *RQ* 57.2 (2004), 518–60.

[7] Bullough gives Oliver Elton's translation of Saxo in Bullough, VII: 60–79, and of *The Hystorie of Hamblet* in *ibid.*, 81–124. For a more contemporary translation of Saxo, with Latin on facing pages, see Saxo Grammaticus, *Gesta Danorum: The History of the Danes*, ed. Karsten Friis-Jensen and trans. Peter Fisher (Oxford: Clarendon Press, 2015), I: 178–221.

Hamlet takes this ancient fable of the north, absorbs the warrior practices and ideals it represents, and transforms them ethically, psychologically, politically, and theatrically. There are three distinct texts of *Hamlet* – the first quarto (Q1, 1603), the second quarto (Q2, 1604/5), and the First Folio (F, 1623) – but they are all informed by this kind of global adaptation. (The different texts are discussed below, pp. 12–17, and in the Textual Analysis.) Shakespeare gives his play a cosmic frame, with frequent references to the heavens, earth, and the underworld. He portrays as an unsolved mystery the killing by Claudius of his brother Hamlet, making the play an early instance of detective fiction or even a 'precursor' of cinema.[1] He introduces the ghost of the murdered King Hamlet, a deliberately mysterious presence, who urges his namesake to avenge his death and who reappears when the demand has not been fulfilled. Shakespeare uses the conventional revenge delay – mistakenly cited by some critics as a sign of Hamlet's failure as an avenger – to present the young Hamlet as a grief-stricken son who, in the play's signature soliloquies, contemplates suicide and castigates himself for his own doubts and fears of death.

At the same time, Shakespeare develops in Hamlet Amleth's wit, giving his protagonist extended opportunities to riddle and perform in ways that reflect the kind of philosophical scepticism associated with Michel de Montaigne, a favourite of the dramatist. Shakespeare introduces the characters of Laertes and young Fortinbras, who function as Hamlet's foils, and he portrays a unique male friendship between Hamlet and Horatio. Shakespeare enlarges and complicates notions of the feminine and female sexuality in the role of Ophelia, whose conflicts and desires are given dramatic space for their own sake, and in the role of his mother Gertrude, whose own seemingly selfish need for erotic attachment gives way over the course of the play to concern for her son. He furnishes a troupe of travelling players who fuel Hamlet's sense of humour and who provide a play-within-a-play that rehearses the original crime. And he complicates the end of the story in two significant ways. First, he brings Hamlet into a graveyard, where he faces death in its most literal form when he holds the skull of the dead jester Yorick. And then, in the play's final scene, he brings Hamlet to a duel at court, where he kills his uncle only after his mother has been poisoned and he himself fatally injured by Laertes. (Is his revenge, then, for himself, his father, or his mother? Or some combination of the three? Are these even different?) Finally, Shakespeare substitutes for Saxo's and Belleforest's pre-Christian world a moment closer to his own, setting the play in a Renaissance Danish court coloured by humanist and Christian principles and alert to key symbols of the different Christian confessions (Hamlet returns to Elsinore from Wittenberg, seat of Lutheranism; his father's Ghost seems to return from Purgatory, a distinctly Catholic otherworld).

With these kinds of changes, Shakespeare refashions the legendary source material into an early modern revenge tragedy. In so doing, his play 'updates' the form, reinvigorating his colleagues' models according to his own interests and dramatic

---

[1] Courtney Lehmann, *Shakespeare Remains: Theater to Film, Early Modern to Post-Modern* (Ithaca, NY: Cornell University Press, 2002), 90.

priorities.[1] These priorities give the play what Maynard Mack calls its distinctly 'interrogative mood', its presentation of a 'world where uncertainties are of the essence'.[2] Hamlet's response to these uncertainties distinguishes him from his vengeful predecessors. He is certainly disgusted by Gertrude and Claudius, but he is a conflicted, resistant avenger – the opposite not only of the Nordic Amleth but also of single-minded Renaissance characters such as Kyd's Hieronimo, Marlowe's Barabas and even his own foils, Fortinbras and Laertes. Of course, some critics and performers have portrayed Hamlets who are keen on exacting revenge; their approaches are justified textually by Hamlet's pledge to the Ghost to 'sweep to [his] revenge' and by his declaration that he 'could . . . drink hot blood' (1.5.31, 3.2.351). But at significant moments he also voices reluctance about his task, as it seems to him to require not only the talionic killing of his uncle but also the spiritual rescue of his mother and the restoring to health of his entire country, now an 'unweeded garden / That grows to seed' (1.2.135–6). We hear this reluctance in his lament, for instance, that 'The time is out of joint: O cursèd spite, / That ever I was born to set it right' (1.5.189–90), and in the famous 'To be or not to be' soliloquy, where the problem of not being is woven through with the dilemma of not revenging.

The impact of his hesitation is only intensified by his 'antic disposition', the feigned madness that he assumes as a strategy for protection. But if Hamlet adopts his antic disposition as a cagey disguise, at times it actually seems to express – to be – his true, broken emotional state. This complication of appearance and reality, of exterior and interior, pervades the play so completely that even – perhaps especially – an audience familiar with revenge plays would see Shakespeare's version as something 'strange'.

Staging the Stage

Hamlet's revenge plot, in other words, opens onto a persistent conundrum of human experience: the problem of seeming and being. The conundrum has a long philosophical and theological history that predates *Hamlet* by two millennia. But, as Katherine Maus has explained, 'in late sixteenth- and early seventeenth-century England the sense of discrepancy between "inward disposition" and "outward appearance" seem[ed] unusually urgent and consequential for a very large number of people'.[3] Hamlet presents this dilemma at the play's outset, when he announces to the Danish court that 'I have that within which passes show' (1.2.85). Hamlet testifies here to a personal crisis, the painful distance between his internal grief and the modes available for him to express it publicly. Hamlet's lament thus presents his onstage and offstage audiences with an epistemological challenge, a reminder of how difficult it is to assess another person's interior feelings or essence according to what they do or say. For the rest of the play, we will experience this predicament

---

[1] For the play's 'updating' of the revenge genre, see Allison K. Deutermann, '"Caviare to the general?" Taste, Hearing, and Genre in *Hamlet*', *SQ* 62.2 (2011), 230–55.

[2] Maynard Mack, 'The World of *Hamlet*', *The Yale Review* 41 (1951–2), 504.

[3] Katherine Maus, *Inwardness and Theater in the English Renaissance* (University of Chicago Press, 1995), 13.

most powerfully during Hamlet's signature soliloquies, since they encourage us to believe, despite their obvious construction for performance, that they give us 'unimpeded contact with Hamlet's mind'.[1] But Hamlet's statement also refers to a political crisis, the radical fracture between appearance and reality at the now-corrupt Danish court. After Claudius's murder of King Hamlet and assumption of the throne, Elsinore 'seems' one way but 'is' another. Claudius can 'smile, and smile, and be a villain' (1.5.108).

METADRAMA

The theatre serves as a rich analogue for this kind of existential confusion. The theatre is all about appearances: on a purpose-built stage, actors perform pre-scripted narratives, playing characters other than themselves and pretending to do things they don't truly accomplish (falling in love, killing an enemy). At the same time, those appearances have a special relation to reality. They may voice truths that can be spoken only at a slant. They may inculcate behaviour on stage that becomes a model for activity off stage (this was a particular fear of the anti-theatricalists, civic and religious leaders opposed to the professional drama). Or they may remind spectators of the influential commonplace that 'all the world's a stage' – that earthly life itself is a fiction or performance in comparison to the reality of eternal life. Human beings, according to this notion, play roles for one another as well as for a divine audience.

The imaginative reach of the theatrical metaphor explains *Hamlet*'s fascination with plays, players, and playing. *Hamlet* is full of metatheatrical moments, scenes that 'stage the stage'. These scenes remind audience members that they are watching a play, that they occupy the time-honoured role of spectator and thus are subject to both the rewards and dangers associated with playgoing. Such moments also highlight the disjunction between seeming and being, feigned action and genuine action, or feigned action and genuine effect. The supreme instances of this kind of metatheatre are the arrival of a travelling troupe of actors at Elsinore in the second act and their performance of an inset play in the third. In the first instance, the lead player delivers Aeneas' account of the fall of Troy in a speech that, to Hamlet's wonder, moves the player himself to tears. In the second instance, the group performs at court a fully realized play that recapitulates a royal marriage and the murder of the king by an interloper who seizes his crown. Both reflect, from different angles, recent events in Denmark, and both are meant to affect the audience ('The play's the thing', Hamlet says, 'Wherein I'll catch the conscience of the king' (2.2.557–8)).

Additional gestures in these scenes also reflect recent events in Shakespeare's immediate theatrical landscape. For example, just before the play-within-the play in Act 3, Hamlet quizzes Polonius about his acting experience:

---

[1] Harley Granville-Barker, *Prefaces to Shakespeare: 'Hamlet'* (Princeton University Press, 1946), 53.

HAMLET ... My lord, you played once i'th'university, you say.
POLONIUS That did I my lord, and was accounted a good actor.
HAMLET And what did you enact?
POLONIUS I did enact Julius Caesar. I was killed i'th'Capitol. Brutus killed me.
HAMLET It was a brute part of him to kill so capital a calf there. (3.2.87–93)

This is a shout-out to Shakespeare's *Julius Caesar*, and alert audience members then and now are rewarded with the gratifying sense of being 'in the know' about Shakespeare's canon. But in Shakespeare's time, it was also a warning: if the same actor who played Caesar played Polonius, and the same actor who played Brutus played Hamlet, Polonius is setting himself up to die at Hamlet's hands, just as Caesar died at Brutus'.

THE POETS' WAR

There is a similar, though more complex, dynamic at work in the 'tragedians of the city' scene in Act 2 (present, though with significant variations, in all three early texts). It offers a fictionalized glimpse into early modern performance conditions, gesturing imaginatively to events and pressures within the entertainment industry. In Q1, Hamlet is told that the players visiting Elsinore have left their residence in the city because 'noveltie carries it away', and audiences are 'turned' 'to the humour of children'. In F, Rosencrantz elaborates a similar complaint (2.2.313–33), when he tells Hamlet (in lines often referred to as the 'little eyases' passage) that:

there is sir an eyrie of children, little eyases, that cry out on the top of question and are most tyrannically clapped for't. These are now the fashion, and so be-rattle the common stages (so they call them) that many wearing rapiers are afraid of goose-quills, and dare scarce come thither.

These moments in Q1 and F have long been linked to developments in the theatre industry at the turn of the century, specifically the revival of two children's companies, Paul's Boys and the Children of the Chapel, in 1599–1600. According to the traditional narrative, a so-called 'War of the Theatres' pitted the boy players, who performed in smaller, indoor playhouses and dominated the market by exploiting the satiric and erotic potential of adolescent performers, against the adult troupes, which suffered financially. Rosencrantz seems to affirm this situation when he admits to Hamlet, who has asked if the boys 'carry it away', that indeed they do. 'Ay', says Rosencrantz, with an allusion to the Globe Theatre emblem, 'Hercules and his load too' (332–3).

   Recent scholarship has challenged this adversarial scenario in various ways. James Bednarz has suggested that the 'Poetomachia', as one dramatist called it – or 'Poets' War' – was not a commercial battle between adult and boy companies but a theoretical, and perhaps mutually beneficial, debate between individual playwrights about the 'social function of drama'.[1] Dramatists such as Ben Jonson, John Marston, and

[1] James Bednarz, *Shakespeare and the Poets' War* (New York: Columbia University Press, 2001), 7. Suspicion that the whole affair was a 'contrived situation' for publicity purposes is expressed by W. Reavley Gair, *The Children of Paul's: The Story of a Theatre Company, 1553–1608* (Cambridge University Press, 1982), 134.

Thomas Dekker put caricatures of one another on stage in order to showcase their different ideas about effective playwrighting and performance. The 'little eyases' passage, Bednarz explains, represents Shakespeare's 'distress over the vituperative tenor of the Poets' War', as well as his concern for the fates of both adult and boy companies as a result of the theatrical skirmishing.[1] Roslyn Knutson, in contrast, has argued that F's 'little eyases' passage was a later addition to the manuscript, and that it does not comment on both boy companies at the turn of the century. Rather, it was added between 1606 and 1608, and it gestures to Children of the Revels (formerly the Children of the Chapel) and their politically charged Jacobean plays performed between 1604 and 1608.[2]

As we shall see, these distinct metatheatrical references can help us to date the composition of the play. But they also work thematically, showcasing Shakespeare's ability to reinforce events happening in the fictional world of the play with the real world of the theatre. Here, he glances at the generational rivalries between contemporary London playing companies in order to illuminate the generational rivalries at the Danish court. Both sets of rivalries, Shakespeare makes clear, are intimately bound up with the issues of professional and political inheritance. In F, his Hamlet enquires of the children: 'Will they not say afterwards, if they should grow themselves to common players – as it is most like if their means are no better, their writers do them wrong to make them exclaim against their own succession?' (2.2.322–5).

In Q2, the corresponding passage lacks explicit references to boy actors, stressing instead the more general precariousness of theatrical success. When Hamlet asks why the players have left the city to tour, Rosencrantz submits in the second quarto that 'their inhibition comes by means of the late innovation'. His response may invoke the popular novelty of the boy companies. Or it may refer to immediate political contexts: scholars have suggested the regulation by the Privy Council in June 1600 to limit the number of London playing companies, or the Essex rebellion of February 1601. Or it may refer to events a couple of years later: Elizabeth I's death, the accession of James I, and the plague which shut down the theatres in 1603.[3] But the pleasingly alliterative line also makes sense entirely within the fiction itself: the players have left the city because of the 'innovation' that is King Hamlet's death. The troupe, similar to Hamlet, has been displaced by Claudius. Hamlet himself, in fact, makes the comparison as he remarks upon the oddity of the new regime: 'Is it not very strange, for my uncle is king of Denmark, and those that would make mouths at him while my father lived give twenty, forty, fifty, a hundred ducats apiece for his picture in little' (2.2.334–6).

DATING HAMLET

Metadramatic scenes call attention to the play's status as a play, inviting the audience to reflect on the relationship between the stage and the world. Metadramatic scenes

---

[1] Bednarz, *Poets' War*, 30.
[2] Roslyn L. Knutson, 'Falconer to the Little Eyases: A New Date and Commercial Agenda for the "Little Eyases" Passage in *Hamlet*', *SQ* 46.1 (1995), 1–31.
[3] See Richard Dutton, *Shakespeare, Court Dramatist* (Oxford University Press, 2016), 226–44.

that are as topical as the little eyases passage call attention to the play's immediate historical moment. They – along with other kinds of internal and external evidence – thus seem to give scholars interpretive access to *when* the play was composed and first performed. In other words, various elements of the play seem to give us access to the complex personal, social, political, and literary contexts that spoke to Shakespeare, and to which he spoke back in the *Hamlet* we know today. But, as with other strange or estranging aspects of the drama, the evidence is multivalent and scholarly interpretations complex, recursive, and often in conflict.

Given this caveat, however, we can locate other important signposts for dating the play. *Hamlet* is not included in the list of Shakespeare's tragedies mentioned in Francis Meres's famous catalogue in his *Palladis Tamia* (entered in the Stationers' Register in September 1598). Claims from omission are never conclusive, but the absence makes a date earlier than 1598 unlikely. So, although a marginal note about *Hamlet* by Gabriel Harvey in his copy of Speght's Chaucer, which was published and purchased by Harvey in 1598, has often been taken to suggest an early date, we should be more circumspect. The notation, which groups *Hamlet* with Shakespeare's narrative poems of 1593–4, is a compelling instance of early modern literary evaluation: 'The younger sort takes much delight in Shakespeares Venus, & Adonis, but his Lucrece, & his tragedy of Hamlet, Prince of Denmarke, have it in them, to please the wiser sort.'[1]

But as a means of dating the composition and performance of the play, the note is inconclusive, as the date of the note itself is subject to debate. A recent study suggests that it is likely a series of five notes composed over a number of years after Harvey purchased the volume', and that the comment on *Hamlet* was probably 'written … after the Second Quarto of the play was published in late 1604'.[2]

As opposed to the vagaries of the Harvey note, the play has a definitive entry for publication – 26 July 1602 – in the Stationers' Register, the official record book of the Stationers' Company that was essential for regulating the book trade. The entry documents the right of the printer James Roberts to print 'The Revenge of Hamlet Prince [of] Denmark as it was lately acted by the Lord Chamberlain his men'. It thus reinforces a date before the summer of 1602, suggesting that Shakespeare's *Hamlet* had been on the stage both recently ('lately') and for enough time to make the prospect of printing it (a significant investment for stationers) appear worthwhile.

The Poets' War has been used routinely to fix the date of *Hamlet*'s composition and performance. Since the children's troupes were revived in 1599–1600, and since the playwrights were staging barbs at one another well into 1601, the allusions discussed above suggest that the play was taking shape around the turn of the century, from roughly 1599 to 1601. But this evidence is neither transparent nor unequivocal. Bednarz, for instance, suggests that the 'little eyases' passage was added in 1601 to

[1] *Gabriel Harvey's Marginalia*, ed. G. C. Moore Smith (Stratford-upon-Avon: Shakespeare Head Press, 1913), 232.
[2] Michael J. Hirrel, 'When Did Gabriel Harvey Write His Famous Note?' *Huntington Library Quarterly* 75.2 (2012), 292. See also Jenkins, 3–6 and 573–4; E. A. J. Honigmann, 'The Date of *Hamlet*', *Shakespeare Survey* 9 (1956), 24–6.

a play that had been on the stage for some time.[1] Richard Dutton agrees with this dating of the 'little eyases' passage, but suggests, based on Q2's 'late innovation', that the play was substantively revised – rewritten into the canonical version we know today – in mid- to late 1603 for court performance.[2]

Additional metatheatrical nods also orient the play to the turn of the century. In late 1599, Shakespeare's company, the Chamberlain's Men, had relocated from their previous home, the Theatre in Shoreditch, to the Globe Theatre, on the south side of the Thames. Hamlet's lamentation on 'this distracted globe' (1.5.97) seems to glance at the new amphitheatre, a reference that makes the most dramatic sense if the play was scripted and performed in the immediate wake of the move. The same applies to his mention of 'Hercules and his load': the emblem of the new theatre was Hercules carrying the celestial globe on his shoulders. And so too do many of the play's thematic preoccupations, which resonate with the popular concerns of the end of the sixteenth century: the downfall of the Earl of Essex, fears about the ageing Queen Elizabeth and who would succeed her as monarch.[3]

At the same time, the play has been seen to resonate more directly with topical events of mid- to late 1603, including the death of Elizabeth I and the accession to the English throne of King James I of Scotland. (James's own father had been murdered and his mother, Mary Queen of Scots, had remarried the putative assassin. James's queen, Anne, was Danish, the sister to the current King of Denmark, Christian IV.) Stylistic and linguistic evidence places it near *Henry V* (1599) and *Troilus and Cressida* (1600–1), but also near his major Jacobean tragedies: *Othello* (1603), *King Lear* (1606), and *Macbeth* (1606).[4]

Hamlet himself struggles with dates and temporality. In his first soliloquy, he accuses his mother of remarrying within two months of King Hamlet's death; he then remeasures: 'nay not so much, not two ... within a month ... A little month' (1.2.138–47). At an equally critical juncture, the protagonist, having seen and spoken with the ghost of his father, realizes that 'The time is out of joint' (1.5.189). In the world Hamlet inhabits, that is, even the routine flow of days, months, and years has been rendered unstable and untrustworthy. That sense of instability seems most appropriate for a composition and performance date at the turn of the century: 'later than mid 1599 ... and ... earlier than July 1602'.[5] *Fins de siècle*, Elaine Showalter has written, are particularly charged moments, when 'crises ... are more intensely experienced, more emotionally fraught, more weighted with symbolic and historical meaning, because we invest them with the metaphors of death and rebirth that we

[1] Bednarz, *Poets' War*, 225–54.   [2] Dutton, *Shakespeare, Court Dramatist*, 226–44.
[3] See Stuart M. Kurland, '*Hamlet* and the Scottish Succession?' *Studies in English Literature* 34.2 (1994), 279–300.
[4] Stanley Wells and Gary Taylor, *William Shakespeare: A Textual Companion* (repr. New York: Norton, 1997), 122. Taylor has more recently argued for a mid- to late 1603 date for the composition and first performances of the canonical *Hamlet*; see The New Oxford Shakespeare: Authorship Companion, ed. Gary Taylor and Gabriel Egan (Oxford University Press, 2016), 544.
[5] Philip Edwards, 'Introduction', in *Hamlet*, ed. Philip Edwards, 2nd edn (Cambridge University Press, 2003), 7–8.

project onto [them]'.[1] *Hamlet* may challenge us to mistrust our instincts to give it any precise date; but there is a poetic justice in locating its 'questionable shape' in such a moment.

Staging the Text

Towards the end of his interaction with the travelling players in Act 2, Hamlet asks whether, for their performance the following night, they could 'study a speech of some dozen or sixteen lines, which I would set down and insert in't' (2.2.493–5). The request offers a theatricalized rendition of textual practice in Shakespeare's theatre, where revisions of various kinds were routinely made to playscripts: older scripts were rewritten by different playwrights, working scripts were cut or supplemented for performance – sometimes by their original dramatists, sometimes by a new writer.[2] Shakespeare's *Hamlet* was fashioned in this environment. It helps to account for other aspects of the play's strangeness: its relation to an earlier Hamlet play and the shape of its earliest printed editions.

HANDFULS OF HAMLETS?

A reference by Thomas Nashe indicates that by the late 1580s there was on the London stage a pre-Shakespearean *Hamlet*, which we now refer to as the Ur-*Hamlet*. The reference is not complimentary. In a dedicatory epistle at the start of his friend Robert Greene's *Menaphon* (1589), Nashe complains about a group of ambitious, blustering playwrights for whom 'English *Seneca* read by candlelight yields many good sentences, as *Blood is a beggar*, and so forth, and if you entreat him fair in a frosty morning he will afford you whole Hamlets, I should say handfuls, of tragical speeches.'[3] Another reference to a play of *Hamlet* dates to 1594, from the account book (known now as *Henslowe's Diary*) of the theatrical entrepreneur Philip Henslowe. He records the performance (likely by Shakespeare's company, the Chamberlain's Men) of a play called *Hamlet* on 9 June 1594, at the Newington Butts playhouse on the south side of the Thames.[4] This reference may or may not be to the same play mentioned by Nashe. And in his 1596 *Wit's Misery*, the writer Thomas Lodge invoked the character of Hamlet to describe a type of slanderous devil who 'walks for the most part in black under cover of gravity, and looks as pale as the vizard of the ghost who cried so miserably at the Theatre like an oyster-wife, *Hamlet, revenge!*'[5] Lodge's description may point to the play recorded by Nashe or by Henslowe.

These references to a putative early *Hamlet* play (or plays) raise multiple questions. Some are questions about authorship: who wrote the Ur-*Hamlet*? Because Nashe's epistle of 1589 seems to include three swipes at the playwright Thomas Kyd, Kyd has

---

[1] Elaine Showalter, *Sexual Anarchy; Gender and Culture at the Fin de Siecle* (New York: Penguin Books, 1990), 2.

[2] Grace Ioppolo, *Revising Shakespeare* (Cambridge, MA: Harvard University Press, 1994).

[3] Thomas Nashe, Preface to R. Greene's *Menaphon*, in *Works*, ed. Ronald B. McKerrow (London: A. H. Bullen, 1905), III: 315, spelling modernized.

[4] *Henslowe's Diary*, ed. R. A. Foakes and R. T. Rickert, 2nd edn (Cambridge University Press, 2002), 21.

[5] Thomas Lodge, *Wits Miserie* (London, 1596), h4v, spelling modernized.

been seen as a candidate for penning the play. Kyd is an attractive option since he is the author of another play preoccupied with revenge, *The Spanish Tragedy*, which features a ghost and a character named Horatio. But Nashe, whose references come in the form of puns and allusions, never explicitly states that Kyd is the 'afforder' of 'whole Hamlets'. More cautious approaches, then, resist naming a specific writer, suggesting instead that the hand behind the early *Hamlet* be identified simply as one among a group of playwrights that had earned Nashe's scorn. Shakespeare himself may be implied in Nashe's critique, and some scholars have suggested that he was the author of an early *Hamlet* play that he subsequently revised around the turn of the century. A related, but not inevitable, position is that the first quarto (see p. 17) is what we now call the Ur-*Hamlet*.

Additional questions concern the relationship between an earlier version and Shakespeare's drama. Grace Ioppolo has argued forcefully that Shakespeare was a dedicated reviser of his own work.[1] But how might he have refashioned an earlier play? Did he work from a manuscript, from memories of the other play, or from some combination of the two? To what extent did he follow the earlier play's structural and linguistic patterns? A long line of criticism tended to accept the idea that Shakespeare rewrote his *Hamlet* in one fell swoop, making it into an entirely different text from the play Nashe and Lodge mocked. But more recent scholarship has challenged this model of 'radical substitution'. Instead, some scholars have argued, Shakespeare's *Hamlet* was the product of his 'incremental' revision over many years, rather than the result of the replacement of a primitive play by Shakespeare's brilliant script.[2] Others have questioned the existence of an Ur-*Hamlet* altogether, seeing it as a scholarly invention or 'phantom play' to which textual bibliographers have attributed a 'surprising corporeality'.[3]

All of these claims remain unsettled, subject to further debate. For now, the most reliable – though not indisputable – account may be summarized as follows: Kyd or one of his fellow-dramatists wrote an early version of *Hamlet* at the end of the 1580s; shortly after that, Kyd capitalized on its success in his revenge play *The Spanish Tragedy*; and Shakespeare had both earlier plays in mind when he pursued his own drama of a Danish prince. His pursuits, as we shall see, come to us in three distinct printed versions, yet another aspect of the play's complexity or 'strangeness'.

THE THREE TEXTS OF HAMLET

There exist three distinct early versions of the play: the first quarto, published in 1603; the second quarto, published in 1604/5; and the text in the Folio, published in 1623. Differences between them, both large and small, abound. Q2 has over 200 lines not in

---

[1] 'Shakespeare's authorial revisions in character, theme, plot, structure, and setting, made for changed theatrical or political conditions, censorship, publication, or private transcription (and for his own artistic demands) infuse the canon of his plays' (Ioppolo, *Revising Shakespeare*, 133).
[2] James Marino, *Owning William Shakespeare: The King's Men and Their Intellectual Property* (Philadelphia: University of Pennsylvania Press, 2011), 79.
[3] Emma Smith, 'Ghost Writing: *Hamlet* and the Ur-Hamlet', in *The Renaissance Text: Theory, Editing, Textuality*, ed. Andrew Murphy (Manchester University Press, 2000), 177, 179.

F (including Hamlet's soliloquy 'How all occasions do inform against me' in 4.4 and the dialogue with the Lord in 5.2), and F has over 80 lines not in Q2 (including the little eyases passage in 2.2).

Q1 is a text substantially distinct from both Q2 and F; the latter two look much more similar in comparison to the first quarto. (The title page of Q2 announces this difference by proclaiming that it is 'Newly imprinted and enlarged to almost as much againe as it was, according to the true and perfect Coppie'.) Q1, at about 2,200 lines, has roughly half the number of lines of Q2 (around 3,800) and F (around 3,700).[1] Q1 has some different names (Polonius is Corambis) as well as detailed stage directions not in Q2 or F. Interestingly, Q1 gives more attention to Gertrude. In dialogue not in Q2 or F's closet scene (3.4), Hamlet tells his mother that her new husband murdered her former one, at which point she promises to assist Hamlet in his plans for revenge. Q1 also includes an entirely novel scene between Gertrude and Horatio in which Horatio delivers, in abbreviated form, the news of Hamlet's return to Denmark (4.6) and of Claudius's intent to kill him (5.2). Q1 also places the famous 'to be or not to be' speech significantly earlier than the other two texts: before the arrival of the players in Elsinore. Differences in language are also worth noting: Q1 is significantly less poetic and more garbled at numerous points than Q2 or F.[2] Finally, there are noticeable irregularities in the print history of the quartos. The 1602 entry of *Hamlet* in the Stationers' Register licenses the play to James Roberts. Roberts's name, however, does not appear on the title page of Q1, which was published the next year by Nicholas Ling and John Trundle and printed by Valentine Simmes. Roberts returns to the scene with the enlarged Q2, which he printed for Nicholas Ling.

Hamlet's complex textual situation has long been known to scholars. Although Shakespeare's eighteenth-century editors were unaware of the survival of the first quarto (it was not found until 1823), they grappled with the differences between the second quarto and the Folio. Such grappling, made thornier by the discovery of Q1 and its significant differences from Q2 and F,[3] still continues. It often takes the form of a transmission history, a bibliographical and editorial strategy founded by scholars in the early to mid-twentieth century in order to explain the process by which a play moved from script to stage to print. The job of a transmission history of *Hamlet* is to establish the temporal and substantive relationships between the three editions by determining the type of manuscript or copy-text 'behind' each of them. These types include Shakespeare's autograph draft; transcriptions or

---

[1] See Thomas Clayton, 'Introduction: Hamlet's Ghost', in *The 'Hamlet' First Published (Q1, 1603): Origins, Form, Intertextualities*, ed. Thomas Clayton (Newark: University of Delaware Press, 1992), 22.

[2] The differences between versions of 'to be or not to be' are often cited: Q1 reads 'To be, or not to be – ay, there's the point: / To die, to sleep – is that all? ay, all'; Q2/F: 'To be, or not to be, that is the question – / Whether 'tis nobler in the mind to suffer / The slings and arrows of outrageous fortune'. The best way to observe the differences is with Paul Bertram and Bernice Kliman, *The Three-text Hamlet: Parallel Texts of the First and Second Quartos and the First Folio*, 2nd edn (New York: AMS Press, 2003).

[3] Zachary Lesser provides an important account of the 'uncanny' effects of the discovery of Q1. See *Hamlet After Q1: An Uncanny History of the Shakespearean Text* (Philadelphia: University of Pennsylvania Press, 2015).

revisions of that draft – by Shakespeare or another scribe, in preparation for performance; and written recollections of performance. (It is important to note that no manuscript of a Shakespeare play survives – though some do for other Renaissance dramatists, and these inform bibliographers' categories.) Once the category of manuscript underlying the printed edition has been surmised and its connection to the others established, scholars can then advocate for that edition's status as the most 'authoritative' in relation to other versions. But in another twist, scholars do not necessarily agree on which kind of printer's copy represents the most 'authoritative' text. Some champion printed editions that derive from manuscripts closest to Shakespeare's own papers. Others champion texts that seem closest to the play as it was performed.

As might be anticipated when the evidence is both scarce and subject to multiple interpretations, scholars have proposed competing transmission theories for *Hamlet*. Philip Edwards's comprehensive Textual Analysis (pp. 253–77) provides such a theory, and it governs the text of the *New Cambridge Shakespeare Hamlet*. In brief, Edwards suggests printers set Q2 from an early authorial copy ('foul papers'), perhaps with reference to Q1; F from a revision of those foul papers as they were readied for performance, perhaps with reference to Q2; and Q1 from a memorial reconstruction, probably by an actor or actors, of the play in performance. In a nutshell, Q2 is closer to the page and F is closer to the stage. In terms of a timeline of composition, the manuscript behind Q2 was the first to be written, the manuscript behind the Folio the second, and the manuscript behind Q1 the last. Edwards's persuasive account, from 1985, was published at roughly the same time as three other major editions: Harold Jenkins's for Arden 2, G. R. Hibbard's for Oxford, and Gary Taylor and Stanley Wells's for the Oxford *Complete Works*. All four editions from the 1980s concur, with qualifications, on the nature of the manuscripts behind the *Hamlet* editions. And they all agree that the complexity of the play's textual situation reverberates in the complexity, even ineffability, of its central character. But they disagree in crucial ways about how the status of the texts should influence the editing of the play. Their editions, then, reflect conflicting views on which version should be used as the basis (the 'copy-text') for an edition and on how to choose between variants. In general, Edwards's careful choices for the body of this *NCS* edition represent what he believes Shakespeare intended when composing *Hamlet*. (Variants are printed under the main text, so readers can see the alternative versions.) Often Edwards chooses Folio readings over Q2 readings. Such choices may seem paradoxical for Edwards, since he maintains that Q2 was printed from an authorial manuscript and thus putatively closer to Shakespeare's original intentions than F, which was printed from a transcript prepared for performance. But Edwards proposes that Shakespeare had made significant revisions to the manuscript behind Q2. These revisions, he explains, confused the printers of the second quarto. But they were accurately included in the transcription for performance that stands behind the Folio version. In those cases, then, the Folio represents the text closest to Shakespeare's designs.

THE THREE TEXTS TODAY

Later 20th- and early 21st-century scholars have inherited these and other disagreements. In response, they have fashioned their own approaches to the three-text problem, challenging or correcting with fresh intellectual energy many of the suppositions of earlier bibliographical scholarship. One of the salient characteristics of this kind of work is its critical self-reflexivity. That is, it makes explicit not only its methodological principles, as previous scholarship does, but also the assumptions behind, and stakes of, those principles.[1] So, although these approaches often echo proposals from earlier decades, they reflect recent theoretical and practical developments in bibliography, editorial theory, theatre history, and performance studies. And, insofar as they are embedded in more comprehensive arguments about the structure and sociability of the early modern theatre, they put pressure on inherited assumptions about authorial intention, about strategies of revision, about the status of page versus stage, even about the definition of a Shakespeare play itself.

For instance, some scholars of *Hamlet*'s complex transmission history do not seek to establish Shakespeare's authorial aims and motives (they contest that very notion). Rather, they study the textual situation as an example of the collaborative nature of the early modern theatre, where actors, scribes, printers, and publishers all contributed to the shaping of the drama in its various forms. In contrast, other scholars see the three texts as a measure of Shakespeare's intentionality as well as his commitment to the revision and publication of his plays. Grace Ioppolo maintains that Shakespeare himself, and not his acting company, is responsible for variations between Q2 and F. And Lukas Erne has upended the commonplace that Shakespeare composed only for performance. He argues that Q2 was written specifically for print – that Shakespeare was thinking of readers as well as spectators for his plays. In Erne's account, Q1 represents a reconstructed version of an abridgement for the London stage; looked at together, the two texts offer 'access . . . to the difference between the writing practice of Shakespeare the dramatist, on the one hand, and the performance practice of Shakespeare and his fellows, on the other'.[2]

Erne's discussion hints at a significant tendency in recent studies of the textual problem: they often involve reassessments of Q1 as an object of literary, dramatic, and cultural interest. Since the 1930s, the orthodox (though not the only) explanation of Q1 was that it was the debased product of 'memorial reconstruction': the report by an actor or actors of recollected dialogue. Assumed to be a performance text, Q1 had usually been treated as an editorial afterthought, even an embarrassment to the cultural meaning of Shakespeare, and of interest only for the stage directions it supplied. But the new scholarly priorities of the late twentieth and early twenty-first centuries have allowed Q1 to be evaluated according to criteria that privilege it as a record of playing conventions, and actors and directors, as well as scholars, have

---

[1] Gabriel Egan, *The Struggle for Shakespeare's Text: Twentieth-Century Editorial Theory and Practice* (Cambridge University Press, 2010).
[2] Lukas Erne, *Shakespeare as Literary Dramatist* (Cambridge University Press, 2003), 192.

championed its appeal on stage.[1] Q1, the director Peter Guiness explains, 'has an energy and an edge that the Folio in all its refinement . . . doesn't have'.[2] At the same time, other scholars have challenged these very categories of 'performance' and 'literary', arguing that Q1 is indeed 'a literary publication' – but because of, rather than in spite of, its 'origins in the professional theaters'.[3]

The fresh appreciation of Q1 has also altered approaches to *Hamlet*'s transmission history. Essays in the 1992 *'Hamlet' First Published*, for instance, offer multiple positions on Q1's origins: (1) Q1 represents an early Shakespearean draft of the play or even a 'stage-worthy version of the tragedy from the 1590s' brought out in 1603 to capitalize on turn-of-the century performances; (2) Q1 is the product of an 'intermediate' copy between Q2 and F, made as Shakespeare and his company revised an earlier draft for performance; and (3) Q1 is an abridgement of the play reflected in F, recollected by an actor (probably the one who played Marcellus).[4] More recent work has challenged this idea of actorly 'piracy', suggesting that multiple note-takers in the audience collaborated in getting the performance on paper and then to the printing house.[5] And Terri Bourus, arguing against this thesis, has revived interest in earlier theories that Q1 is the Ur-*Hamlet*, written by a young Shakespeare in the late 1580s, about a Hamlet in his late teens to be performed by a young Richard Burbage, Shakespeare's company's leading man. According to her account, the manuscript behind Q1 gave rise to the script behind the Folio, which in turn gave rise to the text behind Q2.[6] Dutton, in contrast, maintains that Q1 is not the Ur-*Hamlet*. But he does view it as an earlier version of the play, the one acted around the turn of the century until Shakespeare substantially revised it in late 1603 into the play we know from Q2 and F. These analyses are discussed in more recent editions, including the 2016 *New Oxford Shakespeare Complete Works*, which is based on Q2, and the 2016 Arden 3 revised edition. Arden editors Ann Thompson and Neil Taylor endorse a chronology of Q2 to F to Q1, and they publish the three texts as independent entities, since 'they have a claim to be regarded as separate plays as well as separate versions of the same play'.[7]

---

[1] Leah Marcus, *Un-editing the Renaissance: Shakespeare, Marlowe, Milton* (New York: Routledge, 1996), 132–76.

[2] Quoted in Brian Loughrey, 'Q1 in Recent Performance: An Interview', in Clayton, *The 'Hamlet' First Published*, 125.

[3] Zachary Lesser and Peter Stallybrass, 'The First Literary *Hamlet* and the Commonplacing of Professional Plays', *SQ* 59.4 (2008), 409. Paul Menzer also calls Q1 the most 'literary' of the three texts; looking at the 'preservation of cues' in the different editions, he proposes that Q2 is based on an early authorial draft, F on a manuscript modified over time, probably by players rather than Shakespeare, and Q1 on a new script by 'a person or persons unknown . . . solely for publication' (*The Hamlets: Cues, Qs, and Remembered Texts* (Newark: University of Delaware Press, 2008), 21).

[4] See the following, all in Clayton, *The 'Hamlet' First Published*: Alan Dessen, 'Weighing the Options in *Hamlet* Q1', 65–78; G. R. Hibbard, 'The Chronology of the Three Substantive Texts of Shakespeare's *Hamlet*', 79–89; Kathleen Irace, 'Origins and Agents of Q1 *Hamlet*', 90–122.

[5] Tiffany Stern, 'Sermons, Plays and Note-takers: *Hamlet* Q1 as a "Noted" Text', *Shakespeare Survey* 66 (2013), 1–23.

[6] Terri Bourus, *Young Shakespeare's Young Hamlet: Print, Piracy, and Performance* (New York: Palgrave Macmillan, 2014).

[7] Thompson and Taylor, 95.

Critical Responses

It is probably safe to say that no single work of literature has been so extensively discussed, adapted, and appropriated as *Hamlet Prince of Denmark*. The play has become a phenomenon of intercultural exchange and analysis, a cultural icon that various thinkers, writers, and performers have used to understand their own work and worlds. Critical responses to *Hamlet* have thus become an object of study in their own right, as they provide clues to their own culture's values and assumptions. At the same time, they share a set of interpretive paradigms that have become standard concerns for studying the play. In looking at just a sample, we will see them treating again and again, in their distinct ways, the spiritual status of the ghost; the question of Hamlet's interior life (and whether he is playing, or truly, mad with his antic disposition); the causes of Hamlet's so-called delay; Gertrude's and Ophelia's sexuality (Was the former sleeping with Claudius before the murder of King Hamlet? Did the latter intentionally drown herself?); and the political as well as personal valences of the play (is this more a domestic drama or a tragedy of state?).

SHAKESPEARE'S CONTEMPORARIES

Commentary on *Hamlet* began as early as its arrival on stage at the Globe Theatre. Allusions to the play in the period's poetry and drama suggest that Shakespeare's contemporaries intuited (and thus helped to generate) what would become *Hamlet*'s abiding appeal. But what later generations appreciate as the play's philosophical and psychological complexities they tended to parody, singling out Hamlet's madness for special mockery. Anthony Scoloker, in his verse romance *Daiphantus* (1604), compares his own poem to '*Friendly Shake-speares Tragedies*' and hopes that it will 'please all, like Prince *Hamlet*'. But he worries that, as a result, his own protagonist (who falls in love with three different women) will 'runne mad'.[1] The city comedy *Eastward Hoe* (1605) is even more sardonic: it gives the name Hamlet to an ancillary character, a footman who serves Gertrude, the daughter of a social-climbing goldsmith. As he dashes across the stage '*in haste*', the other characters call out: 'Sfoote *Hamlet*; are you madde?'[2]

Eastward Hoe burlesques the serious foundations of Shakespeare's tragedy by turning the hero into a comic servingman. Two other plays closely associated with *Hamlet* operate differently, as they use *Hamlet* as a blueprint for revenge plots fuelled by court corruption. John Marston's *Antonio's Revenge*, performed by 1601, shares many of *Hamlet*'s premises, though it rehearses them with a self-conscious excess and refusal of ambiguity unknown to Shakespeare. In Marston's play, the envious, corrupt Piero poisons his brother, the Duke of Genoa, and plans to marry his sister-in-law and to kill his nephew, Antonio. The ghost of his father appears to Antonio, who follows his command to revenge with delighted, gruesome relish. He murders Piero's own son, and then, as part of an elaborately orchestrated court masque of fellow avengers, he plucks out Piero's tongue and stabs him to death. *The Revenger's Tragedy*

[1] Anthony Scoloker, *Daiphantus* (London, 1604), A2r.
[2] George Chapman, Ben Jonson, and John Marston, *Eastward Hoe* (London, 1605), D1r.

(published 1607) also takes Shakespeare's themes and conventions and appropriates them with maniacal, parodic energy. Its protagonist, Vindice, has been waiting for nine years to exact his revenge (a poke at Hamlet's hesitations), and he now has two objects of vengeance: the venal Italian duke who murdered his fiancée (and caused his father's demise), as well as the duke's son, who wants to sleep with his sister. In a literalization of Hamlet's 'antic disposition', he takes on an alter-ego, Piato, which he abandons midway through the play and which he (as Vindice) is hired to kill. He actively tempts his mother to sin and then castigates her for it; he murders a 'nest of dukes' with outrageous, and theatrical, violence; and he scoffs at, rather than submits to, a sense of providential design. But *The Revenger's Tragedy*'s most ostentatious parody of *Hamlet* depends upon its use of a skull, which scholars speculate may have been the same one used for Yorick in the graveyard scene.[1] Vindice arrives onstage with the skull of his dead beloved, Gloriana, and he addresses it throughout his first speech. In the *coup de théâtre* of the third act, Vindice uses the skull to exact revenge, dressing it up and putting poison on its lips so that the lecherous duke is killed with its kiss.

We know that *The Revenger's Tragedy* was written and performed after *Hamlet*, as it rescripts Shakespeare's play for the preoccupations of the developing Jacobean stage. But scholars continue to debate the direction in which artistic influence runs between *Hamlet* and *Antonio's Revenge*: from Marston to Shakespeare, from Shakespeare to Marston, or from the Ur-*Hamlet* to both, independent of one another. (Solutions to this question are interwoven with solutions to the puzzle of *Hamlet*'s date.)[2] More crucial for us, however, is that, in their meticulous engagement with *Hamlet*'s narrative details, *Antonio's Revenge*, together with the other texts mentioned above, attest to the play's gravitational pull in its own moment.

THE EIGHTEENTH AND NINETEENTH CENTURIES

The long eighteenth century saw the making of Shakespeare as Britain's 'national poet'.[3] (He also became an international poet: it was at this time that Shakespeare's plays and poetry were first translated into French, German, Italian, and Russian.) He was beloved by his early editors and commentators as the natural, genius creator of expressive, realistically human characters.

This kind of appreciation did not necessarily translate into affection for Hamlet and *Hamlet*. The great literary scholar and poet Dr Samuel Johnson (1765) found the prince a failure in his filial obligations (he is 'rather an instrument than an agent', and 'makes no attempt to punish' Claudius after he has confirmation of his guilt), and he spoke of the 'useless and wanton cruelty' of his treatment of Ophelia. Of the speech in the prayer scene, when Hamlet refrains from killing Claudius for fear he will go to heaven, Johnson famously said it was 'too horrible to be read or to be uttered'.[4]

---

[1] See *The Revenger's Tragedy*, ed. Brian Gibbons (London: New Mermaids, 2008), 70, fn. for 1.1.100.
[2] See Charles Cathcart, '*Hamlet*: Date and Early Afterlife', *RES* 52.207 (2001), 341–59.
[3] See Michael Dobson, *The Making of the National Poet: Shakespeare, Adaptation, and Authorship, 1660–1769* (Oxford: Clarendon Press, 1992).
[4] NV II: 145–6.

Johnson's novelist friend Charlotte Lennox, the author of *Shakespeare Illustrated*, was unimpressed by the play's ending: 'he stabs the King immediately upon the Information of his Treachery to himself! Thus his Revenge becomes interested, and he seems to punish his Uncle rather for his own Death, than the Murder of the King, his Father.'[1] The novelist Tobias Smollett labelled the famous 'To be or not to be' soliloquy a 'heap of absurdities, whether we consider the situation, the sentiment, the argumentation, or the poetry'.[2] And, in his edition of 1778, George Steevens condemned what he considered Hamlet's violence and callousness, pointing out the 'immoral tendency of his character'.[3]

Not all eighteenth-century critics concurred. Nicholas Rowe (1708) compared the play favourably to Sophocles' *Electra*, praising Shakespeare for representing a protagonist 'with the same piety towards his father, and resolution to revenge his death, as *Orestes*; he has the same abhorrence for his mother's guilt, which, to provoke him the more, is heighten'd by incest: But 'tis with wonderful art and justness of judgment, that Poet restrains him from doing violence to his mother.'[4] Rowe's appreciation echoes in other accounts, particularly those that stress Hamlet's filial piety. The Earl of Shaftesbury, in his philosophical compendium *Characteristicks of Men, Manners, Opinions, Times* (1710), wrote approvingly that the play 'appears most to have affected *English* Hearts', describing it as 'almost one continu'd *Moral*; a Series of deep Reflections, drawn from *one* Mouth, upon the Subject of *one* single Accident and Calamity, naturally fitted to move Horrour and Compassion'.[5] Laurence Sterne treated the play with comic affection in *Tristram Shandy* (1752–67). Hannah More, the gifted writer, philanthropist, and educator, composed verses on Shakespeare's ability to conjure a range of emotions for Hamlet, 'to draw characters most justly bright, / To contrast light with shade and shade with light: / To trace up passions to their inmost source'.[6] And Henry Mackenzie (1780), known himself as a writer of 'feeling', acknowledged Hamlet's exquisite sensibility and virtue. He saw the protagonist as a man 'placed in a situation in which even the amiable qualities of his mind serve but to aggravate his distress and to perplex his conduct'. He was not perfect, but he was possessed of an 'indescribable charm ... which attracts every reader and every spectator'.[7]

This emphasis on Hamlet's emotional and intellectual sensitivity became a consistent focus in the first half of the nineteenth century. His princely gentleness, and with it his reluctance to take immediate revenge, made Hamlet, in the eyes of critics, the representative of a troubled, self-divided, specifically *modern* consciousness. In perhaps the most influential European Romantic view of the play, Johann Wolfgang von Goethe depicted *Hamlet* as the story of a noble, dignified prince shocked by the crudeness of his situation, his courteous soul inadequate for or unequal to the stern demands of action. Goethe's metaphor for Hamlet's suffering in his *Wilhelm Meister's Apprenticeship* (1795–6; translated into English by Carlyle, 1812) has become a standard of criticism: an oak tree has been planted in a precious vase

---

[1] *CR*, I: 178. [2] *Ibid.*, I: 181. [3] NV II: 147. [4] *CR*, I: 31.
[5] *Ibid.*, I: 36. [6] *Ibid.*, I: 194. [7] NV II: 148.

fitted to receive beautiful flowers; as the tree's roots spread out, the vase is shattered into pieces. 'A beautiful, pure, noble, and most moral nature, without the strength of nerve which makes the hero, sinks beneath a burden which it can neither bear nor throw off; every duty is holy to him, – this too hard.'[1] The staying power of Goethe's analogy is matched by August Wilhelm von Schlegel's claim in his *Lectures on Dramatic Art and Literature* (1809–11; translated into English, 1815): that *Hamlet* is a 'tragedy of thought' (*Gedankentrauerspiel*). By 'thought', Schlegel implies a profound scepticism, in the face of 'the dark perplexity of the events of this world', that questions the value of action. His Hamlet is a doubter and not an amiable dreamer – a restless sceptic of uncertain principles:

> Hamlet has no firm belief either in himself or in anything else: from expressions of religious confidence he passes over to skeptical doubt . . . The stars themselves, from the course of events, afford no answer to the questions so urgently proposed to them. A voice, commissioned as it would appear by Heaven from another world, demands vengeance for a monstrous enormity, and the demand remains without effect. The criminals are at last punished, but, as it were, by an accidental blow . . . The less guilty or the innocent are equally involved in the general destruction.[2]

In the English Romantic tradition, in which it was preferable to read rather than watch the play, Hamlet is again an anguished thinker. According to Samuel Taylor Coleridge in his lectures on Shakespeare (1808–12), the protagonist's thought renders him incapable of action. And action, Coleridge maintained, was the message of Shakespeare's play: it is 'the chief end of existence'. Coleridge sketches the scene:

> The poet places him in the most stimulating circumstances that a human being can be placed in. He is the heir apparent of a throne; his father dies suspiciously; his mother excludes her son from his throne by marrying his uncle. This is not enough; but the Ghost of the murdered father is introduced, to assure the son that he was put to death by his own brother. What is the effect upon the son? Instant action and pursuit of revenge? No: endless reasoning and hesitating – constant urgings and solicitations of the mind to act, and as constant an escape from action; ceaseless reproaches of himself for sloth and negligence, while the whole energy of his resolution evaporates in these reproaches.[3]

For Coleridge, Hamlet is plagued not by doubt, as Schlegel suggested. Rather, Hamlet is too meditative – he has what Coleridge calls 'an overbalance in the contemplative faculty'. Hence the 'great, enormous, intellectual activity, and a consequent proportionate aversion to real action'.[4]

Despite Coleridge's disdain for Hamlet's lack of action, he confessed that 'I have a smack of Hamlet myself, if I may say so.'[5] The critic William Hazlitt (1817) identified himself similarly, only he included others in the experience. 'It is *we* who are Hamlet', he wrote, democratizing the prince into a version of an Everyman.[6] Thomas Carlyle,

---

[1] *Ibid.*, II: 273–4.   [2] *Ibid.*, II: 279–80.   [3] *Ibid.*, II: 59, 54.
[4] *Ibid.*, II: 61, 62.   [5] NV I: 152–5.
[6] NV II: 114. For democratization, see R. A. Foakes on the Romantic treatment of Shakespeare that 'established him as a figure of enormous cultural authority, yet at the same time democratized him as a representative consciousness' (*'Hamlet' Versus 'Lear': Cultural Politics and Shakespeare's Art* (Cambridge University Press, 1993), 12).

writer and translator of Goethe, extended the identification with Hamlet to Shakespeare himself: 'How could a man travel forward from rustic deer-poaching to such tragedy-writing, and not fall in with sorrows by the way? Or, still better, how could a man delineate a Hamlet . . . if his own heroic heart had never suffered?'[1] Across the Atlantic Ocean, Edgar Allen Poe noted that, in *Hamlet*, Shakespeare 'wrote of Hamlet as if Hamlet he were'.[2]

Identification with characters was not limited to the protagonist – or to male authors, as the above formulas might imply. Writers such as Anna Jameson, an advocate for women's rights and economic improvement, were interested in *Hamlet*'s females. Jameson's *Characteristics of Women: Moral, Poetical, and Historical* (1832), which came to be known as *Shakespeare's Heroines*, offered a 'program of female education through empathetic encounters with Shakespeare's female characters'.[3] Jameson championed in Ophelia the essentially feminine qualities associated with her own period's domestic ideology – innocence, grace, and tenderness – at the same time as she sketched, in a way that effectively captures the heart of the drama, the threats to those qualities: 'the situation of Ophelia in the story, is that of a young girl who, at an early age, is brought from a life of privacy into the circle of a court . . . at once rude, magnificent, and corrupted'.[4] Mary Cowden Clarke, in her *Girlhood of Shakespeare's Heroines* (1850–2), invented for Ophelia a fictional 'backstory' in which, having learned of the betrayal of two other young women by a crude suitor, she dreams of their deaths as well as King Hamlet's and her own. The story ends where *Hamlet* begins for Ophelia: with instructions from her brother Laertes.

The commentary that we have just traced contributed to the emergence of what writers call 'Hamletism' – the idea that the protagonist models a particular approach to life. The concept sees Hamlet as 'well-intentioned but ineffectual, full of talk but unable to achieve anything, addicted to melancholy and sickened by the world around him'. It named a complete 'attitude to life, a philosophy as we say':[5] one of withdrawal or disengagement from the social world into the private realm of thought. It could be embraced, but it also could be derided, as it was by the German writer Ferdinand Freilgrath. His accusation 'Deutschland ist Hamlet' (Germany is Hamlet) was meant to draw 'a rude and bitter parallel between the vacillating dreamer's political inefficiency and the Hamletian German liberal intellectual'.[6] The cultural purchase of Hamletism in the second half of the nineteenth century only expanded as the play became a centrepiece for 'all of the major discourses of the age: literary, historical, psychoanalytical, religious, and political'.[7] Thus, in addition to being the focus of major literary commentaries by scholars such as Edward Dowden and F. J. Furnivall, *Hamlet* and its protagonist made cameo appearances in the work of novelists on both

---

[1] *CR*, II: 215.   [2] Quoted in Foakes, *'Hamlet' Versus 'Lear'*, 12.
[3] Cheri L. Larsen Hoeckley, 'Introduction', in Anna Jameson, *Shakespeare's Heroines: Characteristics of Women: Moral, Poetical, and Historical* (Peterborough, Ont.: Broadview Press, 2005), 24.
[4] Jameson, *Shakespeare's Heroines*, 177.   [5] Foakes, *'Hamlet' Versus 'Lear'*, 20.
[6] *Shakespeare on the German Stage: The Twentieth Century*, ed. Wilhelm Hortmann (Cambridge University Press, 1998), 90.
[7] *CR*, IV.1: xvii–xviii.

sides of the Atlantic, including Herman Melville's *Pierre* (1852), Charles Dickens's *Great Expectations* (1860), George Eliot's *The Mill on the Floss* (1860), and Mark Twain's *Huckleberry Finn* (1885). The play was of similar interest internationally, though often treated with a sceptical or sinister twist. The literary historian Hippolyte Taine described Hamlet as a 'delicate soul' who, once introduced to death, begins to see, in himself and others, 'an evil-smelling and grinning skull'.[1] His fellow Frenchman, the poet Stéphane Mallarmé, who saw the protagonist as 'a symbol of himself as poet',[2] wrote at the close of the century that Hamlet's thinking makes him a killer: 'The black presence of this doubter causes this poison.'[3] These interpretations are not far removed from that of Friedrich Nietzsche, who used Hamlet to define his vision, figured in 'Dionysian man', of tragic awareness. As Nietzsche puts it in *The Birth of Tragedy* (1872): 'Both [Dionysian man and Hamlet] have gazed into the true essence of things, they have *acquired knowledge* and they find action repulsive, for their actions can do nothing to change the eternal essence of things; they regard it as laughable or shameful that they should be expected to set to rights a world so out of joint. Knowledge kills action; action requires one to be shrouded in a veil of illusion – this is the lesson of Hamlet.'[4]

Nietzsche's comments, as we can see, revisit the question of Hamlet's delay. For Nietzsche, the failure to act was a philosophical matter. But for others during this period it was a distinctly political one. In tsarist Russia in particular, where through the century the play served functions 'more social and political than aesthetic', Hamlet's plight represented for writers such as Ivan Turgenev and Anton Chekhov a type of aristocratic self-indulgence and retreat from social responsibility that they rejected rather than admired.[5]

THE TWENTIETH AND TWENTY-FIRST CENTURIES

In 1898, the Danish Shakespeare scholar Georg Brandes remarked that Hamlet 'represent[s] the genius of the Renaissance'. But he quickly added that, because of 'his creator's marvelous power of rising above his time', the character 'covers the whole period between him and us'. Hamlet thus 'has a range of significance to which we, on the threshold of the twentieth century, can foresee no limit'.[6]

Well into the twenty-first century, that limitlessness has become only more apparent. We can see it in the incorporation of the play in the works of major figures of literary modernism (including James Joyce, D. H. Lawrence, and Franz Kafka), who

[1] *Ibid.*, 168, 172.
[2] Martin Scofield, *The Ghosts of 'Hamlet': The Play and Modern Writers* (Cambridge University Press, 1980), 11.
[3] "La noire présence du douteur cause ce poison, que tous les personnages trépassent: sans même que lui prenne toujours la peine de les percer, dans la tapisserie": Mallarmé, *Oeuvres complètes* (Paris: Gallimard, 1945), 1564.
[4] Friedrich Nietzsche, *The Birth of Tragedy and Other Writings*, ed. Raymond Geuss and Ronald Speirs, trans. Ronald Speirs (Cambridge University Press, 1999), 40.
[5] Peter Holland, "'More a Russian than a Dane": The Usefulness of *Hamlet* in Russia', in *Translating Life: Studies in Transpositional Aesthetics*, ed. Shirley Stead and Alistair Stead (Liverpool University Press, 1999), 316.
[6] *CR*, IV.2: 788.

took *Hamlet* and its protagonist as 'symbols for the perplexing, fragmented experience of modern life'.[1] We can also observe the play's reach in post-modern novels such as Thomas Pynchon's *The Crying of Lot 49*, with its long riff on Elizabethan revenge tragedy, or Ian McEwan's *Nutshell*, in which Hamlet, a foetus in his mother's womb, overhears her plotting with his uncle, Claude, to murder his father. In an even more accessible vein, entertaining YouTube 'mash-ups' offer clips of Hamlet references from popular culture.[2] And with the institutionalization of English literature as an academic discipline at the end of the nineteenth century – and, more recently, with the explosion of web-based means for research – the scholarly study of *Hamlet* has increased exponentially. It has been fuelled by new methodological and theoretical approaches to the play's perennial questions.

Psychoanalytic Approaches
Sigmund Freud announced his theory of the unconscious in 1900 in his *Interpretation of Dreams*. *Hamlet* serves Freud simultaneously as an object of study and as proof of concept. His brief account of the play returned to the riddle of Hamlet's delay, proposing to solve it with the language of psychoanalysis. Freud suggested that the protagonist hesitates because his unconscious desires – his Oedipal wish to supplant his father and sleep with his mother – make him feel as guilty in mind as Claudius is in deed. In other words, if for Schlegel *Hamlet* was a tragedy of thought, for Freud it is a tragedy of unconscious thought.

Hamlet is able to do anything – except take vengeance on the man who did away with his father and took that father's place with his mother, the man who shows Hamlet the repressed wishes of his own childhood realized. Thus the loathing which should drive him to revenge is replaced in him by self-reproaches, by scruples of conscience, which remind him that he himself is no better than the sinner whom he is to punish.[3]

Ernest Jones expanded this idea in 1949 in his *Hamlet and Oedipus* ('[Hamlet's] uncle incorporates the deepest and most buried part of his own personality, so that he cannot kill him without killing himself'). Jacques Lacan, in his linguistically inflected return to Freud, explained that Hamlet's desire to be the object of Gertrude's desire renders him unable to act. But Freud provided the best gloss in his essay on 'Mourning and Melancholia' (1914). Here he suggests that Hamlet suffers from the kinds of self-recrimination that follow the loss of his father, an idealized other: 'the shadow of the object fell upon the ego, and the latter could henceforth be judged'.[4]

For the next few decades, psychoanalysis, as the theory and study of the unconscious, asserted an interpretive claim over Hamlet, the prince of inwardness as well as Denmark. Early psychoanalytic criticism of the play elaborated it in Freudian terms. But with changes in both analytic theory and literary practice, the hermeneutic angles shifted. Psychoanalytic interpretations of the 1970s, 1980s, and 1990s had to counter

---

[1] Scofield, *The Ghosts of 'Hamlet'*, 6.   [2] www.youtube.com/watch?v=DDTAn6r4HpQ.
[3] Sigmund Freud, *Standard Edition of the Complete Psychological Works*, ed. and trans. James Strachey (London: Hogarth Press, 1953), IV: 265.
[4] *Ibid.*, XIV: 249.

objections to the theory's patriarchal and anachronistic assumptions (Francis Barker's Foucauldian critique of *Hamlet* as inaugurating the bourgeois subject that psycho-analysis takes for granted is a prime example).[1] They also had to incorporate new, non-Freudian understandings of the ego and the unconscious. Some scholars used object relations theory or ego psychology in order to shift the interpretive emphasis from Hamlet's Oedipus complex to the challenges to his identity occasioned both by the death of his father and by corruption in the Danish court. Others, suspicious of the primacy afforded the ego in these accounts, combined Lacanian and other poststructuralist approaches to focus on the radical instability of the self as it is presented in the play, so that Hamlet, after his confrontation with the ghost of his father, becomes caught in 'compulsive behavior of a kind that translates *him* into a daemon, into a ghost'.[2]

In one of the most influential psychoanalytic readings of the play to date, Janet Adelman grounded her reading of *Hamlet* on the premise that the protagonist's goal is the assumption of an adult male identity based on the model of his father. Gertrude, however, disables this identification when she remarries: she 'fails to differentiate' between Hamlet Sr and Claudius, forcing Hamlet to idealize his dead father in a way that sacrifices his own sense of self. In this scenario, revenge is not only a dramatic principle or an effect of a violent culture, but also a form of memory designed to preserve the idealized image of the father undercut and threatened by the malevolent, 'suffocating' mother:

Even at the start of the play, before the ghost's crucial revelation, Gertrude's failure to differentiate has put an intolerable strain on Hamlet by making him the only repository of his father's image, the only agent of differentiation in a court that seems all too willing to accept the new king in place of the old. Her failure of memory – registered in her undiscriminating sexuality – in effect defines Hamlet's task in relation to his father as a task of memory: as she forgets, he inherits the burden of differentiating, of idealizing and making static the past; hence the ghost's insistence on remembering and the degree to which Hamlet registers his failure to avenge his father as a failure of memory.[3]

Readings such as Adelman's, for all their extraordinary sensitivity to *Hamlet*'s language and its place in Shakespeare's oeuvre, nevertheless treat the play's characters as creatures in a timeless psychodrama, unaffected by their social or cultural environments. More recent psychoanalytic studies of the play, in contrast, have accommodated these environments either by exploring the effect on Hamlet's unconscious experience of various historical and ideological contexts, or by establishing the place of the play at the origins of psychoanalysis itself.[4]

[1] Francis Barker, *The Tremulous Private Body: Essays in Subjection* (London: Methuen, 1984).
[2] Marjorie Garber, *Shakespeare's Ghost-writers: Literature as Uncanny Causality* (New York: Methuen, 1987), 162. See also Julia Reinhard Lupton and Kenneth Reinhard, who explain Hamlet's melancholy as the collapse of the 'crucial distinction between self and world ... Hamlet's world has become a "sterile promontory" because he has fashioned it in the image of his own ego' (*After Oedipus: Shakespeare in Psychoanalysis* (Ithaca, NY: Cornell University Press, 1993), 20).
[3] Janet Adelman, *Suffocating Mothers: Fantasies of Maternal Origin in Shakespeare's Plays, 'Hamlet' to 'The Tempest'* (New York: Routledge, 1992), 13.
[4] See, for instance, Heather Anne Hirschfeld, 'Hamlet's "first corse": Repetition, Trauma, and the Displacement of Redemptive Typology', *SQ* 54.4 (2003), 424–48; Susan Zimmerman, 'Psychoanalysis and the Corpse', *Shakespeare Studies* 33 (2005), 101–8; Andrew Barnaby, 'Tardy Sons: Hamlet, Freud, and Filial Ambivalence', *Comparative Literature* 65.2 (2013), 220–41; Philip Armstrong, *Shakespeare in Psychoanalysis* (London and New York: Routledge, 2001).

Historicist Approaches

In his seminal 1905 account of the play, A. C. Bradley described Hamlet as an example of the tragic hero: he is an exceptional character, divided within himself, whose downfall is imbued with a sense of mystery as well as great waste. Like earlier critics, Bradley tried to tease out the source of Hamlet's hesitation; unlike his predecessors, he denied that it was the result of a delicate spirit or intellectual scepticism. Rather, he insisted, it was Hamlet's predisposition to melancholy, a passion that overwhelms him after the shock of his father's death and his mother's remarriage.

> Suppose that under this shock, any possible action being denied to him, he began to sink into melancholy, then, no doubt, his imagination and generalising habit of mind might extend the effects of this shock through his whole being and mental world. And if, the state of melancholy being thus deepened and fixed, a sudden demand for difficult and decisive action in a matter connected with the melancholy arose, this state might well have for one of its symptoms an endless and futile mental dissection of the required deed.[1]

Bradley is best known for his treatment of characters – in a way often considered anachronistic – as though they were 'real' people with backstories in excess of the text and the times. But, for his discussion of *Hamlet*, he referred to a range of early modern discussions of melancholy and its causes and symptoms. Bradley, that is, recognized the use of archival documents for studying the play's persistent concerns.

Bradley's historicist impulse, rehearsed in the following decades in essays such as William Empson's '*Hamlet* When New', was thoroughly, methodically developed in the 1980s and 1990s by the interpretive schools of New Historicism and Cultural Materialism. Their approaches have become the dominant principle of contemporary literary study. Both schools follow the critical demand to 'always historicize!' – that is, to examine literary works not as transcendent creative achievements independent of their conditions of production but as texts in conversation with ideas and events of their moment. For some scholars, that moment is the early modern one. (Roland Mushat Frye's lucid *Renaissance Hamlet* provides a thorough discussion of it.)[2] For others who follow Jan Kott's approach to Shakespeare as 'our contemporary', that moment is now, our own: '*Hamlet* is like a sponge . . . it immediately absorbs all the problems of our time'.[3]

Politics

Historicist and materialist scholars have assessed *Hamlet* as both a reflection of and an active intervention in its contexts. Some have focused on the political determinants of the play, including its engagement with issues of royal succession or its republican overtones in demystifying monarchical authority.[4] Or they have diagnosed Hamlet's

---

[1] A. C. Bradley, *Shakespearean Tragedy: Lectures on Hamlet, Othello, King Lear, Macbeth* (London: Macmillan and Co., 1905), 100.
[2] Roland Mushat Frye, *The Renaissance Hamlet: Issues and Responses in 1600* (Princeton University Press, 1988).
[3] Jan Kott, *Shakespeare, Our Contemporary* (Garden City, NY: Doubleday, 1964), 64.
[4] Andrew Hadfield, *Shakespeare and Republicanism* (Cambridge University Press, 2005), 203, 198.

melancholy inwardness as a political condition that, when pressed upon by external and internal circumstances, can become treasonous.[1] Or they have seen in the play's revenge plot an engagement with geopolitics rather than domestic affairs, so that in *Hamlet* 'the thematics of the revenge tragedy are bound together with the dynamics of state-building' and the protagonist's success 'is contingent on his cunning as a diplomat'.[2]

Religion

Others have addressed the play's religious contexts. Of course, studying *Hamlet*'s Christian orientation has long been part of the critical tradition, particularly in assessing the play's perspective on revenge and sin. But contemporary scholars have become increasingly sensitive to the influence of Reformation religious change on the tragedy. That is, they focus on the ways in which the play is infused with the theological as well as ecclesiastical conflicts that characterized the shift from Catholicism to Protestantism in England over the course of the sixteenth century and into the seventeenth. The Reformation context has allowed scholars to formulate the play's signature concerns – with the interior life, with death and the afterlife, memory, mourning, guilt, and the relation of self and other – in discerning ways: in terms of Protestantism's commitment to scripture and print culture; in terms of the geography of heaven and hell; in terms of a specific breed of religious melancholy that followed from the loss of Catholic sacraments and customary rituals for the dead; and in terms of competing theologies of justification, predestination, free will, and sectarian resistance.[3]

Perhaps the most significant of these studies has been Steven Greenblatt's *Hamlet in Purgatory*, a comprehensive exploration of the Protestant attack on Purgatory and the effect of this attack on Shakespeare's drama. The Catholic doctrine of Purgatory as a 'middle space' between hell and heaven promised believers an end to post-mortem punishment as well as a tangible, memorializing link between the living and the dead. Protestants rejected it, and the institutions that developed around it, opening a gap for mourners worried about lost relatives and for sinners worried about their own fates. This gap – the 'disruption or poisoning of virtually all rituals for managing grief, allaying personal and collective anxiety, and restoring order' – preoccupied

---

[1] Karin S. Coddon, '"Suche Strange Desygns": Madness, Subjectivity, and Treason in *Hamlet* and Elizabethan Culture', *Renaissance Drama* 20 (1989), 51–75.

[2] Timothy Hampton, *Fictions of Embassy: Literature and Diplomacy in Early Modern Europe* (Ithaca, NY: Cornell University Press, 2009), 147, 161.

[3] See, for instance, Jennifer Rust, 'Wittenberg and Melancholic Allegory: The Reformation and Its Discontents in *Hamlet*', in *Shakespeare and the Culture of Christianity in Early Modern England*, ed. Dennis Taylor and David N. Beauregard (New York: Fordham University Press, 2003), 260–86; Kristen Poole, *Supernatural Environments in Shakespeare's England: Spaces of Demonism, Divinity, and Drama* (Cambridge University Press, 2011), 93–135; Thomas Rist, *Revenge Tragedy and the Drama of Commemoration in Reforming England* (Burlington, VT: Ashgate Press, 2008), 60–74; John Gillies, 'The Question of Original Sin in *Hamlet*', *SQ* 64.4 (2013), 396–424; Heather Hirschfeld, *The End of Satisfaction: Drama and Repentance in the Age of Shakespeare* (Ithaca, NY: Cornell University Press, 2014).

Shakespeare throughout his career, Greenblatt explains. But the preoccupation took its most concentrated form in *Hamlet*, which entertains even as it challenges and doubts the Ghost's claim to come from the Catholic realm of Purgatory. As Greenblatt wryly observes, the play represents a prince with 'a distinctly Protestant temperament troubled by a distinctly Catholic ghost'. For Greenblatt, then, Hamlet's 'corrosive inwardness' finds its source in the pressures of Reformation doctrinal change, which Shakespeare in turn used to fuel his plays. In fact, for Greenblatt, the Renaissance stage assumes for its audience Purgatory's function as a place of mourning. As he concludes, 'The Protestant attack on the 'middle state of souls' and the middle place those souls inhabited destroyed this method [of remembering the dead] for most people in England, but it did not destroy the longings and fears that Catholic doctrine had focused and exploited. Instead . . . the space of purgatory becomes the space of the stage where Old Hamlet's ghost is doomed'.[1]

Culture

Still other historicist scholars have been concerned with the broader cultural contexts that help to make sense of the play's treatment of madness, marriage, and mourning – even its use of fictional space. Attention to early modern humoral theory, for instance, has allowed us to see Hamlet's failure to kill Claudius not only as a psychological problem but also as a physiological one: a 'lack of gall'.[2] Attention to early modern laws governing incestuous relationships has allowed us to see that the real threat to Hamlet from the marriage of Claudius and Gertrude is not that they were sexually involved before Hamlet Sr's death but that they have disabled his succession to the crown.[3] Attention to the cultural construction of early modern emotions has allowed us to see the ways in which Hamlet models for his audience a particular kind of grief associated with their witnessing the ageing of Queen Elizabeth.[4] And attention to early modern architecture has allowed us to see the public, theatrical dimensions of what we assumed were the play's private spaces, so that we understand Hamlet's consummate expressions of selfhood as 'tableau[x] of interiority meant for display'.[5]

Feminist Approaches

In 1919, T. S. Eliot described *Hamlet* as a play 'dealing with the effect of a mother's guilt upon her son'. Unlike the psychoanalytic critics, however, he saw this focus as a threat to the aesthetic success of the play, rendering it an 'artistic failure' (though interesting precisely for its problems). According to Eliot's logic, Hamlet's obsession with his mother's sexuality – and thus his neglect of his duty to revenge – is in excess of

---

[1] Stephen Greenblatt, *Hamlet in Purgatory* (Princeton University Press, 2001), 240, 257.

[2] Gail Kern Paster, *Humoring the Body: Emotions and the Shakespearean Stage* (University of Chicago Press, 2004), 25–60.

[3] Lisa Jardine, *Reading Shakespeare Historically* (London: Routledge, 1996), 35–47.

[4] Steven Mullaney, 'Mourning and Misogyny: *Hamlet*, *The Revenger's Tragedy*, and the Final Progress of Elizabeth I, 1600–1607', *SQ* 45.2 (1994), 150, 153.

[5] Mimi Yiu, *Architectural Involutions: Writing, Staging, and Building Space, c. 1435–1650* (Evanston, IL: Northwestern University Press, 2016), 108.

what her character should solicit. Gertrude is not, he explained, a satisfactory 'objective correlative' for Hamlet's feelings: 'Hamlet is up against the difficulty that his disgust is occasioned by his mother, but that his mother is not an adequate equivalent for it.'[1]

A rich tradition of feminist scholarship – scholarship that prioritizes women's experience and the social, cultural, and political institutions that structure that experience – has responded to, and then moved beyond, Eliot's 'reproach against the character of a woman'.[2] Jacqueline Rose interrogated Eliot's dependence on femininity as the basis for his aesthetic theory, recalling in the process the protagonist's own – disavowed – female side: 'Hamlet becomes Renaissance man only to the extent that he reveals a femininity which undermines that fiction.'[3] Other scholars have pursued alternative angles to understand the place of the female in the play and its reception. Elaine Showalter's 'Representing Ophelia' investigates how Ophelia has served for centuries as an iconic representation of female madness and its link to female sexuality, perhaps most famously in the art of the pre-Raphaelites. On the stage as well as in popular and medical discourses, Showalter explains, the image of Ophelia 'carr[ied] specific messages about femininity', messages that ranged from ideas that female madness is innate, natural, and biologically determined to ideas that it is caused by familial or societal double-standards and their ultimate realization in physical or emotional trauma.[4] More recent studies of Ophelia have similarly developed the ways in which the representation of Ophelia is always implicated in cultural fantasies about women, sexuality, and madness.[5] Of particular interest are studies that examine the confessional implications of Ophelia's language and behaviour, especially in Act 4. Her songs, with their echoes of medieval Catholic piety, have been seen to reflect either 'the costs – especially to women – of the English Reformation' or the possibility that Ophelia was 'capable of a kind of performance that . . . was unique to early modern girls, and to Catholic girls especially'. In other words, 'If Hamlet can put on an antic disposition, why can't [Ophelia]?'[6]

Other feminist studies have laid bare the early modern political and social structures that conditioned the ways in which the women act and are acted upon. (Even the textual issue can be studied from a feminist perspective; Q2 and F, it has been noted, take the more active, sympathetic women of Q1 and 'effectively reduce [them] to the

---

[1] T. S. Eliot, 'Hamlet and His Problems', in *The Sacred Wood: Essays on Poetry and Criticism* (London: Methuen, 1964), 98, 101.

[2] Jacqueline Rose, '*Hamlet* – the Mona Lisa of Literature', *Critical Quarterly* 28.1 & 2 (1986), 35.

[3] *Ibid.*, 44.

[4] Elaine Showalter, 'Representing Ophelia: Women, Madness, and the Responsibilities of Feminist Criticism', in *Shakespeare and the Question of Theory*, ed. Patricia Parker and Geoffrey Hartman (London: Methuen, 1985), 77–94.

[5] See Carol Thomas Neely, 'Documents in Madness: Reading Madness and Gender in Shakespeare's Tragedies and Early Modern Culture', *SQ* 42.3 (1991), 315–38; Carol Chillington Rutter, 'Snatched Bodies: Ophelia in the Grave', *SQ* 49.3 (1998), 299–319.

[6] Alison A. Chapman, 'Ophelia's "Old Lauds": Madness and Hagiography in *Hamlet*', *Medieval and Renaissance Drama in England* 20 (2007), 112; Caroline Bicks, 'Instructional Performances: Ophelia and the Staging of History', in *Performing Pedagogy in Early Modern England: Gender, Instruction, and Performance*, ed. Kathryn M. Moncrief and Kathryn R. McPherson (Aldershot: Ashgate, 2011), 210, 211.

body'.)[1] Additional scholarship has discussed period assumptions about femininity that generate Hamlet's attachments to as well as contempt for women – and for the aspects of himself (his vulnerability, his passivity) that he understands as female. And recent studies, taking masculinity as a subject for investigation rather than a transhistorical given, have studied the changing models of manhood so central to the play's plot and language, including Hamlet's grief, his friendship with Horatio, and his duel with Laertes. Indeed, we might say that most contemporary accounts of the play, whether implicitly or explicitly, take gender and sexual difference as a category of analysis. Even the play's sources in classical drama have been suggestively rethought through a feminist lens. In her work on *Hamlet* and Greek drama, for instance, Tanya Pollard argues that what Shakespeare takes – and revises – from Greek drama is the centrality of the grief-stricken, vengeful female protagonist: 'Hamlet is no Hecuba, but the role that he constructs for himself, and in many ways for a generation of English stage revengers, grows directly out of his confrontation and negotiation with her iconic power.'[2]

Comprehensive Studies

We have been surveying articles, essays, and chapters that offer particular arguments about specific aspects of *Hamlet*. But some of the most influential criticism comes in the form of books devoted entirely to the play. Their scope often defies the methodological categories above. In a format imitated by later writers and editors, John Dover Wilson in 1935 chronicled the play act by act, finding a through-line in the burdens placed on Hamlet – and by Hamlet on others. But he rejected any single conclusion about the play. 'We were never intended to reach the heart of the mystery', he wrote in *What Happens in Hamlet*. Instead, we were meant to appreciate Shakespeare's development of tragic mystery, observing the 'technical devices he employed to create this supreme illusion of a great and mysterious character, who is at once mad and the sanest of geniuses, at once a procrastinator and a vigorous man of action, at once a miserable failure and the most adorable of heroes'.[3] (Two important works of roughly the same period found nothing mysterious or adorable in Hamlet: G. Wilson Knight preferred the virile Claudius to the protagonist, whom he found morbid, and Salvador de Madariaga decried Hamlet's egotism.)[4]

A clutch of subsequent monographs also pursued the play's dramaturgical as well as artistic and rhetorical designs. Harry Levin, in *The Question of Hamlet*, charted the play's depiction of both the primitive and the civilized sides of Elsinore, the background for Hamlet's interrogations and doubts.[5] Nigel Alexander studied the ways in which Shakespeare uses revenge conventions to dramatize philosophical and

---

[1] Tony Howard, *Women as Hamlet: Performance and Interpretation in Theatre, Film, and Fiction* (Cambridge University Press, 2007), 19.

[2] Tanya Pollard, 'What's Hecuba to Shakespeare?' *RQ* 65.4 (2012), 1081.

[3] *What Happens in Hamlet* (New York: Macmillan, 1935), 229.

[4] G. Wilson Knight, *The Wheel of Fire: Interpretations of Shakespearian Tragedy* (London: Routledge, 1930); Salvador de Madariaga, *On Hamlet*, 2nd edn (London: Frank Cass & Co. Ltd, 1964).

[5] Harry Levin, *The Question of Hamlet* (New York: Oxford University Press, 1959).

psychological problems (such as the protagonist's relationship to revenge).[1] William Kerrigan has shown how the arc of the revenge plot affords Hamlet an opportunity for self-purification, the purging of an imagination 'as foul / As Vulcan's stithy' into one that can, with equanimity, announce that 'the readiness is all' (3.2.73–4, 5.2.194–5).[2] More recently, Andras Kiséry has argued that *Hamlet* offered its early modern audiences training in 'political competencies', while Rhodri Lewis has studied *Hamlet* as thorough-going critique of the orthodoxies of Renaissance humanism, which the play reveals as a 'set of doctrines that distorts reality and constrains all human beings to obscure their true natures'.[3]

Margreta de Grazia's '*Hamlet' without Hamlet*, which anchors the play in early modern preoccupations with land ownership and inheritance, demands special attention. The title is an ironic shout-out to Bradley's assertion that 'the tragedy of *Hamlet* with Hamlet left out has become the symbol of absurdity', and it sets the stage for de Grazia's challenge to *Hamlet* scholarship that, since the eighteenth century, has emphasized the protagonist's 'intransitive inwardness'. De Grazia wishes to 'do without . . . the modern Hamlet, the one distinguished by an inner being so transcendent that it barely comes into contact with the play from which it emerges'. She thus works to put the protagonist back into his 'plot' – that is, back into the story of his dispossession of land and crown. In a sequence of chapters that weave through the play's associations with the Bible, the medieval morality play, classical and sixteenth-century world histories, and epics of the Trojan War, de Grazia examines the ways in which the play's language reinforces connections between Hamlet, the earth, inheritance customs, and global politics. The 'old mole' – Hamlet's appellation for the Ghost in 1.5, for instance – emphasizes the 'overlays between man and clay' that culminate in the graveyard scene, while the setting in Elsinore links Hamlet to the Danish invasion of England in the early eleventh century, and thus to 'what might be called a premodern imperial schema'. Hamlet's insistence on having 'that within which passes show' would not have been mysterious to Elizabethan audiences: 'the Prince cannot utter his expectation of succession during the reign of the king who pre-empted him, not because the disappointment is beyond the reaches of language or the ken of his auditors' but because it would be treason; Ophelia's deadly garlands, like Hamlet's references to Niobe and Jephthah, signal the play's concern with 'spoiled genealogy': 'the play instances what may be the bleakest moment of a civilization: the extinction of a bloodline, that of a family, dynasty, or race'. Such readings, de Grazia promises, preserve the 'centrality and complexity' of Hamlet, but they do so by paying attention not to his interior life but to 'his worldliness'.[4]

---

[1] Nigel Alexander, *Poison, Play and Duel: A Study in Hamlet* (Lincoln: University of Nebraska Press, 1971), 19. See also James Calderwood, *To Be and Not To Be: Negation and Metadrama in Hamlet* (New York: Columbia University Press, 1983); Peter Mercer, *Hamlet and the Acting of Revenge* (London: Macmillan, 1987).

[2] William Kerrigan, *Hamlet's Perfection* (Baltimore, MD: Johns Hopkins University Press, 1994).

[3] Andras Kiséry, *Hamlet's Moment: Drama and Political Knowledge in Early Modern England* (Oxford University Press, 2016); Rhodri Lewis, *Hamlet and the Vision of Darkness* (Princeton University Press, 2017), 10.

[4] Margreta de Grazia, '*Hamlet' without Hamlet* (Cambridge University Press, 2007), xiii, 1, 31, 65, 89, 126, 5.

'The Play's the Thing'

The following analysis explores the worldliness of both protagonist and play – how they stretch imaginatively from Elsinore to Wittenberg to Norway to Poland to England. It also explores the events and situations that have made this world a 'distracted globe' (1.5.97), one that has become confused, conflicted – strange and estranging. Thus, it also explores the effects of such distraction, on Hamlet and on us, in body, mind, and soul.

1.1: THE WATCH ON THE BATTLEMENTS

Like Hamlet, 'crawling between earth and heaven', *Hamlet* is framed by, and deeply concerned with, the regions of the afterlife. But the worldly space it stages is Denmark. Another island (or peninsular) nation, Denmark was one of England's closest geographical neighbours, and there was a 'pervasive sense of the closeness' between the countries in Shakespeare's time.[1] Scholars have noted the playwright's 'achievement' in giving a 'subtle' impression of the actual environment of early modern Elsinore: cold, windswept, dominated by a castle that was '"unequalled in Europe for situation, magnificence, force, and revenues"'.[2]

The first scene opens on the castle ramparts, and it is full of a perturbation and anxiety that never truly leaves us. The replacement sentry, rather than the one on guard, asks in the play's first line, 'Who's there?'. It is a seemingly simple question that heralds the play's profound concern with identity and personhood. For the moment, though, the concern is with the appearance of a ghost – 'this dreaded sight' – a spectre that signals some kind of danger or crisis. Indeed, we learn quickly that the Danish state is under threat, on the alert for an invasion by young Fortinbras of Norway. At issue is the 'king that's dead', in whose 'fair and warlike form' the Ghost now emerges. The past actions of this king, the 'valiant Hamlet', motivate the present preparation for war. As Horatio explains, a generation ago, King Hamlet defeated in single combat the former King of Norway, winning the lands which Fortinbras now seeks to recover in the name of his father. Shakespeare lavishes considerable effort on Horatio's narration of the combat between the two kings, emphasizing King Hamlet's warrior status so that his recent death seems particularly momentous, as if marking the end of an era. He also introduces young Fortinbras as a significant presence in the play, setting him up as a foil to 'young Hamlet', who is invoked only at the very end of the scene, when Barnardo, Marcellus, and Horatio agree to inform the prince of what has passed. Until this moment, then, the name Hamlet is associated with the dead king; the protagonist, that is, will always be seen and heard in the shadow of his father.

---

[1] Lisa Hopkins, *Shakespeare on the Edge: Border-crossing in the Tragedies and the Henriad* (Aldershot: Ashgate, 2005), 35.

[2] For the achievement, see Gunnar Sjögren, 'The Danish Background in *Hamlet*', *Shakespeare Studies* 4 (1968), 221–30. Quotation from *Calendar of State Papers Foreign*, July–Dec. 1588, 75, cited in Cay Dollerup, *Denmark, 'Hamlet', and Shakespeare*, 2 vols. (Salzburg: Institut fur Englische Sprache, 1975), I: 153.

I.2: 'I KNOW NOT SEEMS'

That shadow lingers over the second scene, despite the efforts of the new monarch, Hamlet's uncle Claudius, and the queen, Hamlet's mother, Gertrude, King Hamlet's widow, to erase it. Superficially, they appear to have succeeded: 1.2 – set indoors, in the midst of a crowd, around a feast celebrating Claudius and Gertrude's marriage – appears a great contrast with the opening scene. (Even the relatively 'empty space' of the Elizabethan stage would have made that difference come to life with ornate props and sparkling costumes.) But, as *Hamlet* will prove so often, this appearance or 'seeming' belies reality, what 'is'. Prince Hamlet, dressed conspicuously in black mourning garb, serves as an active reminder to all around him not only of the death of his father but of the indecent, and indecently hasty, remarriage of his mother to his uncle. As a 'near personification of night', Hamlet recalls for the court its failure to remember, its failure to observe sufficiently his royal father's death.[1] This neglect of ritual (linked now by scholars to Reformation challenges to traditional observances for the dead) preoccupies the prince and contributes to the 'rottenness' of Denmark. As a kind of rebuke, Hamlet insists on expressing his grief. He does so to mock the oily, effective Claudius but also to insult Gertrude and to distinguish himself from the rest of the court. As opposed to them, he 'know[s] not seems'. His emotions, unlike theirs, are authentic. In fact, they are so authentic that no rituals could ever accommodate them. 'I have that within which passes show' (1.2.85), Hamlet says. He thus initiates the great riddle of the character's interiority, the possibility that he harbours an inner life so complicated that it defies expression, an inner life that is an enigma even to himself. This is the riddle that, as we have seen, has energized so much of the play's commentary, including even commentary that diagnoses Hamlet's inner life as a 'hollow void'.[2]

Hamlet stages the riddle with more focus when the protagonist is alone on stage. Scholars remain divided about what precisely Hamlet *does* in this and the other famous soliloquies. For some, a soliloquy represents a character's 'inner monologue', his or her silent thoughts; for others, it represents a character talking to him- or herself aloud, capable of being overheard if intruded upon.[3] And in one clever configuration, the convention of the soliloquy gives Hamlet an opportunity to 'speak to an onstage audience of one [and] delight in his own discourse'.[4] Given these uncertainties, it becomes difficult to determine precisely what Hamlet *reveals* in his soliloquies. A long tradition saw the soliloquy as 'mak[ing] audible the personal voice ... of an individual speaker'. But, as scholars have challenged, Hamlet may not necessarily be revealing his true beliefs or feelings. Rather, he may be 'engag[ing] in self-deception' or 'giv[ing] voice to differing points of view'. Or he may be revealing not just the different viewpoints of an individual but the conflicting viewpoints of a divided self: 'Hamlet cannot be fully present to himself or to the audience in his own speeches and *this* is the heart of his mystery, his

---

[1] Kerrigan, *Perfection*, 43.
[2] Terry Eagleton, *William Shakespeare* (Oxford: Basil Blackwell, 1986), 72.
[3] James Hirsh, 'Shakespeare and the History of Soliloquies', *Modern Language Quarterly* 58.1 (1997), 1–26.
[4] Deutermann, '"Caviare to the general"', 254.

interiority, his essence.'[1] Or, in a recent formulation, Hamlet's soliloquies may be like prayer, the 'fragmentary repository of alternative selves'.[2]

But, whether or not Hamlet's reverie on his 'too too solid flesh' gives us access to an 'inexhaustible interiority', it communicates to us with great feeling a sense of despair, disillusionment, sexual nausea, and, most of all, a sense of personal, familial, and even universal taint (a sense made more palpable in Q2's reading of 'sallied [sullied] flesh'). In the aftermath of his father's death and his mother's quick remarriage to his uncle, the world appears to him to be entirely corrupt, tempting him to a suicide that he knows divine law prohibits. Hamlet traces this corruption to the Fall in Eden – the 'unweeded garden / That grows to seed' – the origin of human sin. He goes on, however, to enumerate the evidence of that sin which he considers most glaring: the disloyalty of his mother in wedding his uncle, his father's brother, and thus her brother-in-law. Hamlet explicitly names this incest, the 'ultimate breach' of natural and divine law that had become in the literature of Shakespeare's time a 'powerful metaphor for other forms of social or political corruption'.[3] (The issue of incest had also played a critical role in Henry VIII's divorce from his first wife, Catherine of Aragon, the widow of his deceased brother, and thus in the origin story of English Reformation.)

But the remarriage represents additional violations for Hamlet, as he tells us in vivid terms. It threatens his idealized image of his father, of Hamlet Sr's majesty as well as his chivalric solicitousness of Gertrude. It turns his mother into something worse than a 'beast that wants discourse of reason', an appropriate match for the uncle he calls a 'satyr', unfit to rule in comparison to so 'excellent a king'. And it implicates him, Gertrude's child, in the general depravity, so he cannot help but draw parallels between himself and Claudius: 'My father's brother, but no more like my father / Than I to Hercules'. In accepting Claudius as Hamlet Sr's substitute, Gertrude fails to observe the distinctions and differences upon which her son's identity, as well as the nation's social and cultural relations, depend. In sum, the remarriage endangers Hamlet's memories, makes them intrusive rather than sustaining: 'must I remember?'

1.3–5: THE GHOST AND OTHER FATHERS

Hamlet is galvanized into activity by the news of the appearance of a ghost that resembles his dead father. He promises to join Horatio and the others on the platform, where he will speak to the spectre, whatever happens. But before he stages that meeting, Shakespeare pauses the pace to dramatize other fathers and children. The third scene features the offspring of Claudius's councillor Polonius: Laertes, the courtier whom we have already seen asking to return to Paris, and the innocent Ophelia, whom we quickly learn is in Hamlet's 'favour'. Polonius arrives to give both son and daughter advice, cautioning Ophelia in particular against

[1] Catherine Belsey, *The Subject of Tragedy: Identity and Difference in English Renaissance Drama* (London: Routledge, 1985), 42, 50.
[2] Brian Cummings, *Mortal Thoughts: Religion, Secularity, and Identity in Early Modern Culture* (Oxford University Press, 2013), 180.
[3] Richard McCabe, *Incest, Drama, and Nature's Law, 1550–1700* (Cambridge University Press, 1993), 5.

believing the prince's claims of love. Polonius can be played as wily and calculating; he can also be portrayed as good-natured and well-intentioned, though obtuse and bumbling. But his suspicion of Hamlet as well as his brusque treatment of his daughter, in addition to his association with Claudius, announce him as another authority or father figure that the audience – like Hamlet – would do well not to trust.

The interlude with Polonius heightens our anticipation of Hamlet's meeting with the Ghost. He appears in the following scene, prompting an outcry from the prince that will reverberate through the rest of the play: 'Be thou a spirit of health, or goblin damned, / Bring with thee airs from heaven or blasts from hell.' Hamlet's address, in other words, offers competing interpretations of the moral and theological status of the Ghost, interpretations that would have represented to his first audiences different early modern models of thinking about ghosts. Strict Protestant doctrine, rejecting the Catholic position that souls could return from Purgatory, maintained that ghosts existed but were demons sent by the devil. Yet records show entrenched popular belief in the return of the dead as ghosts. At the same time, a number of sceptics dismissed the entire prospect of spirits, whether human or demonic.[1] Hamlet's lines invite the audience to 'share [his] doubts', even if they favour one conclusion over the other.[2]

Drawing Hamlet away from his friends, the Ghost declares that he is the spirit of the dead Hamlet Sr, and he makes it abundantly clear that he suffers now in Purgatory for sins unsatisfied during his lifetime. The Ghost's desperation is poignant: he wants Hamlet both to listen to him and, as a sign of filial love and obedience, to '[r]evenge his foul and most unnatural murder'. The Ghost gives details of that murder meant to inspire retribution, but even as he introduces the new information that Claudius is the killer, his speech resembles the language and fixations we have already heard from Hamlet's in 1.2. The Ghost recalls – conflates, really – the Fall in Eden and the slaying of Abel by Cain that was one of its consequences: 'know, thou noble youth, / The serpent that did sting thy father's life / Now wears his crown'. He dwells on Claudius's extraordinary perfidy, including the treacherous way he poisoned the sleeping, vulnerable Hamlet Sr, destroying the inside and the outside of his perfect martial body. But the Ghost is most concerned by Claudius's usurpation of crown and wife. Indeed, it is the latter that preoccupies the Ghost, who considers the remarriage adulterous as well as incestuous: 'that incestuous, that adulterate beast', he says of Claudius. The implication may be only that the Ghost sees remarriage itself as an act of infidelity. But he opens up the possibility – for Hamlet as well as for the audience – that Gertrude had been unfaithful even before his death.[3] Either way, he conveys his betrayal:

---

[1] Frye, *The Renaissance Hamlet*, 19–24; Keith Thomas, *Religion and the Decline of Magic* (New York: Charles Scribner's Sons, 1971), 587–605.

[2] Graham Bradshaw, *Shakespeare's Scepticism* (London: Harvester, 1987), 118.

[3] This is the implication in Belleforest, in which Fengon is accused of marrying 'with her whom hee used as his concubine during good Horvendiles life' (Bullough, VII: 88).

> O Hamlet, what a falling off was there,
> From me whose love was of that dignity
> That it went hand in hand even with the vow
> I made to her in marriage, and to decline
> Upon a wretch whose natural gifts were poor
> To those of mine.
> But virtue as it never will be moved,
> Though lewdness court it in a shape of heaven,
> So lust, though to a radiant angel linked,
> Will sate itself in a celestial bed,
> And prey on garbage.
>
> (1.5.47–57)

The Ghost's image, so expressive of moral and sexual disgust with Gertrude, under-mines his subsequent injunction to Hamlet: 'Taint not thy mind, nor let thy soul contrive / Against thy mother aught. Leave her to heaven'. King Hamlet was poisoned through the ear literally; Prince Hamlet has been poisoned figuratively, even as his suspicions about Claudius and the corrupt state of Denmark are confirmed.[1] Later, he will acknowledge that, despite the Ghost's warning, his 'imaginations are as foul / As Vulcan's stithy' (3.2.73–4).

The Ghost exits after one last message for Hamlet: 'Remember me.' The command poses a crucial question for the play – and for revenge drama more generally – about the relationship between retribution and memorialization. Are they one and the same thing? Or are they distinct but mutually compatible undertakings, with the pursuit of revenge a means for remembering a lost loved one (or remembering a lost loved one a means of revenge)? Or does vengeance detract from, even vitiate, remembrance, redirecting attention from the dead to the enemy, or even to the self? Or does the play suggest a more complex mixture of possibilities, influenced in crucial ways by different religious and cultural assumptions about memory, mourning, and the status of the dead?

In a sweeping pledge, Hamlet promises both to remember and to avenge: he will replace all of his previous knowledge and experience so that

> thy commandment all alone shall live
> Within the book and volume of my brain,
> Unmixed with baser matter.
>
> (1.5.102–4)

Recording the command as though he were his father's secretary, Hamlet may indeed pursue 'revenge as a task of creative remembrance'.[2] Such a commitment, however, comes at a cost and with complications. Scholars have demonstrated that Hamlet would have had as a prop a literal book – an erasable 'table' – to record his thoughts about Claudius ('My tables – meet it is I set it down / That one may smile, and smile, and be a villain').[3] But insofar as he also 'wipe[s] away' the metaphoric 'table

---

[1] Alexander, *Poison*, 56.

[2] For Hamlet as his father's secretary, see Yiu, *Involutions*, 135. For creative remembrance, see Edwards, 'Introduction', in *Hamlet, Prince of Denmark*, 45.

[3] Peter Stallybrass, Roger Chartier, T. Franklin Mowery, and Heather Wolfe, 'Hamlet's Tables and the Technologies of Writing in Renaissance England', *SQ* 55.4 (2004), 379–419.

of my memory', he swaps the words of the ghost of his father for those of his own 'youth and observation'. In other words, Hamlet may become half-ghost, even half-dead, himself. Or, as Michael Neill remarks, 'Hamlet's solemn rite of memory after his first encounter with the Ghost [is] also an act of oblivion, in which the memories installed by the Ghost expunge' all former recollections.[1]

1.5: THE ANTIC DISPOSITION

The verbal exchange between the Ghost and prince continues when Horatio and Marcellus rejoin Hamlet. In a comic imitation of the Ghost's injunctions, Hamlet swears his comrades to silence, with the Ghost echoing from under the stage – the conventional habitation of devils. Hamlet also hints to his friends that he plans to assume an 'antic disposition': he will 'bear [him]self' in 'strange or odd' ways that he, as well as the other characters, go on to label specifically as *mad*.

Madness was an essential element in the source story – Amleth's feigned frenzy kept him alive – but it was also a critical aspect of Shakespeare's more recent model, *The Spanish Tragedy*. The difference between the three works is revealing. In Saxo and Belleforest's account, the hero clearly preserves his sanity beneath a disguise of idiocy, a disguise that allows him to accomplish his revenge effectively. But in Kyd's play, Hieronimo yields to a real, palpable insanity, the psychological effect of the murder of his son and the inaccessibility of justice. And it seems as much a hindrance as a help to his pursuit of retribution. Hamlet's madness in Shakespeare's version blends these models in complex ways. Hamlet makes clear that he will '*put on*' his antic disposition, outfitting himself in the conventional costume of the stage malcontent and thus enabling himself to express in a safe fashion his distance from and contempt for the court. But as the play unfolds he seems to inhabit – or to be inhabited by – a madness that exceeds both his control and the boundary between pretended and genuine, so that the costume has become real. With the antic disposition, Harley Granville-Barker has noted, pretence and reality are no longer easily distinguished.[2] This instability inheres in the very word 'disposition', which denotes both external and internal structure. That is, the term refers to the arrangement or order of a material thing – like a building or a garden or even a human body – and the arrangement or order of its personality, 'a frame of mind or feeling; mood, humour' (*OED*).

This instability also puzzles – at times threatens – not only Hamlet and the other characters but also the audience. The latter must wonder not simply whether Hamlet is mad or not, but about the connection between acting and being: whether *acting* mad ends up *producing* authentic madness. (Such a transformation – of becoming in reality what you play on stage – was a great fear of the period's anti-theatricalists, churchmen, and other moralists who were opposed to the existence of the professional drama.) The questions raised by Hamlet's antic disposition, then, are part of the play's larger meditation on the relationship between the world and the stage.

---

[1] Neill, *Issues of Death*, 254.   [2] Granville-Barker, *Prefaces*, 62.

But Hamlet's final words in the first act seem far from feigned. Alone again on stage, he acknowledges that 'The time is out of joint', his own version of Marcellus's oft-cited comment that 'Something is rotten in the state of Denmark'. Only, for Hamlet, the recognition demands that he take personal and political responsibility for 'set[ting] it right'. This is the all-encompassing obligation of the revenger, the restoration of familial and social harmony, balance, and justice through potentially unjust and extrajudicial punishment and pain.

2.1–2: BAIT OF FALSEHOOD, CARP OF TRUTH

As if enacting Hamlet's note that 'The time is out of joint', Shakespeare makes a temporal jump of roughly one month to Act 2. The court now seems more claustrophobic than before, as all the characters are spying on one another. Polonius is in the centre of much of this activity: Reynaldo is licensed by him to pry into Laertes's life in Paris, and the obedient Ophelia reports to him about Hamlet's behaviour in her closet. She gives a striking narration of the protagonist's appearance before her:

> with his doublet all unbraced,
> No hat upon his head, his stockings fouled,
> Ungartered, and down-gyvèd to his ankle,
> Pale as his shirt, his knees knocking each other,
> And with a look so piteous in purport
> As if he had been loosèd out of hell
> To speak of horrors.   (2.1.76–82)

The report leads to more surveillance. Shakespeare's England had seen the growth of a multi-pronged spy network, designed to ferret out, both at home and abroad, religious and political threats to the monarch and the state. Indeed, Claudius and Gertrude's growing concern with – paranoia about – 'Hamlet's transformation' echoes these contexts, reminding us that Hamlet's inwardness represents a danger to the political nation. But Hamlet's threat is also deeply intimate, striking directly at family members. So Claudius and Gertrude have hired Hamlet's old friends Rosencrantz and Guildenstern to investigate the situation. They in turn team up with Polonius, who believes Hamlet has gone mad because of his rejection by Ophelia. Polonius is willing to sacrifice Ophelia to the plan – he promises to 'loose my daughter to him' – so that Claudius can watch the two from behind an arras. The scheme becomes the occasion and the setting for the famous 'to be or not to be' soliloquy in 3.1.

But, as thorough as these plans seem, the most effective spy – or counterspy – is Hamlet himself. The antic disposition, certainly, gives him cover to scrutinize every-one at court, as he does with Polonius in their grotesque conversation about maggots, his daughter, conception, and crabs. But he is overt in his own suspicion about, and investigation of, Rosencrantz and Guildenstern, whom he pointedly challenges: 'Were you not sent for? . . . You were sent for – and there is a kind of confession in your looks which your modesties have not craft enough to colour'. Hamlet's wariness informs, and thus gives an ironic twist to, all of his exchanges with the two friends, which include some of his most pointed statements – 'Denmark's a prison' – and his most noble formulations:

indeed it goes so heavily with my disposition that this goodly frame, the earth, seems to me a sterile promontory; this most excellent canopy the air, look you, this brave o'erhanging firmament, this majestical roof fretted with golden fire – why, it appeareth no other thing to me but a foul and pestilent congregation of vapours. What a piece of work is a man! How noble in reason, how infinite in faculties, in form and moving how express and admirable, in action how like an angel, in apprehension how like a god! The beauty of the world, the paragon of animals – and yet to me, what is this quintessence of dust?   (2.2.281–90)

The force of this monologue lies in its articulation of both the most optimistic claims of Renaissance humanism about human capacities and the most pessimistic claims of Reformation theology about human sinfulness. But its philosophical appeal must be understood in the context of Hamlet's performance for the duo he distrusts, and whom he will later indict for attempting to 'pluck out the heart of my mystery' (3.2.331).

2.2: THE PLAYERS

Hamlet's interactions with the troupe of players, newly arrived at Elsinore, also cannot be separated from this act's general climate of surveillance. Hamlet clearly delights in the actors, welcoming them to court and requesting from them a 'passionate speech'. He suggests 'Aeneas' tale to Dido' – that is, a narration based on the account of the destruction of Troy in Book II of Virgil's *Aeneid*. Hamlet himself initiates the oration, focusing on Pyrrhus, the son of the Greek warrior Achilles. The passage – its metre, diction, and syntax – are meant to make the speech 'audibly different from the rest of the play':[1]

> 'The rugged Pyrrhus, he whose sable arms,
> Black as his purpose, did the night resemble
> When he lay couchèd in the ominous horse,
> Hath now this dread and black complexion smeared
> With heraldy more dismal. Head to foot
> Now is he total gules, horridly tricked
> With blood of fathers, mothers, daughters, sons,
> Baked and impasted with the parching streets,
> That lend a tyrannous and a damnèd light
> To their lord's murder. Roasted in wrath and fire,
> . . .
> With eyes like carbuncles, the hellish Pyrrhus
> Old grandsire Priam seeks –'   (2.2.410–22)

At this point, the Player takes over the narration, elaborating a scene of gore and violence. According to the Player, Pyrrhus hesitates for a moment over the toppled but still living Trojan king. But then '[a] rousèd vengeance sets him new a-work', and his 'bleeding sword / Now falls on Priam'. The Player then describes the response of

---

[1] Burrow, *Classical Antiquity*, 66.

Hecuba – the 'mobled queen' – to the disaster, which he depicts as a spectacle for the gods:

> But if the gods themselves did see her then,
> When she saw Pyrrhus make malicious sport
> In mincing with his sword her husband's limbs,
> The instant burst of clamour that she made,
> Unless things mortal move them not at all,
> Would have made milch the burning eyes of heaven,
> And passion in the gods. (2.2.470–6)

Although the Player's speech suspends the momentum of the play, it is deeply connected to its broader concerns. Pyrrhus, like Laertes and Fortinbras, offers an additional foil for Hamlet: he is a son proving his martial valour on behalf of his heroic father. And Hecuba serves as a model for Gertrude: she is a wife who knows how to mourn her husband properly. With its Latinate structure and Homeric/Virgilian content, the speech can also be seen as an explicit instance of what Patrick Cheney calls Shakespeare's 'engagement with the epic tradition', which he uses to record the loss of heroic values to 'a mercenary post-epic culture'.[1] Finally, the speech provides a meta-commentary on the emotional effects of oratory, when the Player, during his description of Hecuba, is moved – moves himself – to tears.

This capacity of the theatre serves as a kind of taunt to Hamlet. Calling himself a 'rogue and peasant slave', he notes that the Player, 'in a fiction, in a dream of passion', can generate real, concrete emotion in himself and his audience, while he, '[a] dull and muddy-mettled rascal', can neither say nor do anything. What he should be doing, he says, is seeking vengeance; in fact, if he weren't 'pigeon-livered', he already 'should ha' fatted all the region kites / With this slave's offal'. Hamlet's concern here, Steven Mullaney suggests, is not only that he delays *per se*, but that the delay 'cast[s] doubt on the authenticity of his own grief. Is his grief real or sincere if he can't respond appropriately – by killing Claudius?'[2] The Player's speech thus functions as a means for Hamlet to spy on himself. The result is a self-interrogation by which Hamlet is convinced of his own wrong-doing, a failure he equates with prostitution. 'This is most brave,' he complains, 'That I ... Must like a whore unpack my heart with words, / And fall a-cursing like a very drab' (2.2.535–9).

His solution, famously, is to direct the power that he associates with the theatre back onto the entire court, onto his entire situation. He had already asked the Player to perform *The Murder of Gonzago* the next day; now he explains:

> I'll have these players
> Play something like the murder of my father
> Before mine uncle. I'll observe his looks,
> I'll tent him to the quick. If a do blench,
> I know my course. The spirit that I have seen

---

[1] Patrick Cheney, *Shakespeare's Literary Authorship* (Cambridge University Press, 2008), 61.
[2] Steven Mullaney, *The Reformation of Emotions in the Age of Shakespeare* (University of Chicago Press, 2015), 60.

May be a devil . . .
                                . . . I'll have grounds
More relative than this. The play's the thing
Wherein I'll catch the conscience of the king.   (2.2.547–58)

The plan, in other words, involves scrutinizing both Claudius and the Ghost. Hamlet
will test the latter's veracity by observing the former's response to the play. He does this,
he says, to protect his own soul from damnation. (He does not seem to realize that the
Ghost could be a devil out to damn him *and* still tell the truth.) He will also be examining
his own conscience – the conscience of a king-in-waiting – in the scenarios that follow.

3.1: 'TO BE OR NOT TO BE'

The celebrated soliloquy of 3.1, which has generated vast layers of commentary,
participates in this pattern of self-scrutiny. Hamlet, of course, is being 'seen unseen'
by Claudius and Polonius, but he is also observing, prying into, himself. Without ever
using the first person pronoun, he nevertheless discovers his fascination with both the
lure of non-existence and the sturdiness of the self. In 1.2, reeling from his father's
death and his mother's remarriage, Hamlet had desired that his flesh 'resolve itself into
a dew' (1.2.130). Now, with the heavy burden of revenge placed on his shoulders, he
returns to these kinds of thoughts as an issue of both body and soul. 'To be or not to be,
that is the question', he begins: the line is so well known that, taken out of context, it
can become an occasion for theatrical delight. (In April of 2016, for instance, to
celebrate the 400th anniversary of Shakespeare's death, a BBC Shakespeare Live
presentation at Stratford featured a renowned cast of Hamlets – including Benedict
Cumberbatch, Dame Judi Dench, Paapa Essiedu, Rory Kinnear, Ian McKellen, Tim
Minchin, and David Tennant – who performed distinct emphases of the line, with
a cameo by Prince Charles.) In the play's moment, however, it leads Hamlet into
a painful, if riveting, consideration of suicide.

To be or not to be, that is the question –
Whether 'tis nobler in the mind to suffer
The slings and arrows of outrageous fortune,
Or to take arms against a sea of troubles,
And by opposing end them. To die, to sleep –
No more; and by a sleep to say we end
The heart-ache and the thousand natural shocks
That flesh is heir to – 'tis a consummation
Devoutly to be wished.   (3.1.56–64)

When Hamlet had presented the problem in his first soliloquy, he had dismissed it
quickly by noting that God forbids self-slaughter. Here he considers the issue in far
greater detail, attracted as he is to suicide as something honourable, the one action he
can take against a 'sea of troubles' that preserves his nobility.[1] The alternative is to go

---

[1] See Philip Edwards, 'Tragic Balance in *Hamlet*', *Shakespeare Survey* 36 (1983), 43–52. Eric Langley
offers a useful discussion of the period's competing views of suicide as either noble or damnable, in
Narcissism & Suicide in Shakespeare and His Contemporaries (Oxford University Press, 2009).

on living, to see, from a Stoic or Christian perspective, suffering as noble, a form of self-mastery of emotions and passions. (Hamlet will praise this sensibility in 3.2, when he congratulates Horatio as a 'man / That is not passion's slave'.) Hamlet's debate, Frye has pointed out, takes the form of a school rhetorical exercise, arguing *in utramque partem*, on both sides of a topic. But, as the soliloquy proceeds, Hamlet weighs suicide not against patient endurance but against the threat of a Christian afterlife, the 'dread of something after death, / The undiscovered country from whose bourn / No traveller returns'. He is concerned not with death but with the uncertainty of death as more life, in a strange, 'undiscovered' realm. Invoking conscience – the still small voice of God's judgement implanted in every human – Hamlet widens the scope of concern:

> Thus conscience does make cowards of us all,
> And thus the native hue of resolution
> Is sicklied o'er with the pale cast of thought,
> And enterprises of great pitch and moment
> With this regard their currents turn awry
> And lose the name of action.   (3.1.83–8)

'[E]nterprises of great pitch and moment': Hamlet now must be thinking not only about killing himself but also killing Claudius. (Jan Kott suggests, in fact, that the whole soliloquy is about such a murder: '"To be" means for [Hamlet] to revenge his father and to assassinate the king; while "not to be" means – to give up the fight.')[1] So it is worth noting the intimate relation for Hamlet between suicide and revenge: both are forms of punitive violence, the first directed at himself and the second at his uncle. For a revenger like Hieronimo, they were distinct impulses: Hieronimo, tempted as he was, refused to commit suicide in order to pursue revenge for his son. For Hamlet, they are versions of one another: 'The desire to kill Claudius keeps metamorphosing into an impulse to suicide', Gordon Braden explains. The result is that Hamlet can only 'contemplate [their] unactability with new rigor'.[2] Indeed, contemplation is precisely what makes them unactable.

3.1: 'GET THEE TO A NUNNERY'

The impasse of thought generated in the soliloquy can be seen as either a cause or an effect of Hamlet's sense of personal and global sinfulness. In the interview with Ophelia that follows, he unleashes the brunt of his outrage for this situation on her, challenging her chastity and attributing to her the infidelity he associates with Gertrude and, by misogynist analogy, with all women. Of course, his accusations – which he also directs at himself – may be a ruse, an element of his antic disposition or a response to his suspicion that they are being watched. (Hamlet asks pointedly, 'Where's your father?') But even if meant as a show, the accusations are grounded in Hamlet's governing sense of a moral and sexual taint that inheres in individuals and

---

[1] Kott, *Shakespeare, Our Contemporary*, 62.
[2] Gordon Braden, *Renaissance Tragedy and the Senecan Tradition: Anger's Privilege* (New Haven, CT: Yale University Press, 1985), 219.

the world. Even Claudius makes this inference: 'There's something in his soul / O'er which his melancholy sits on brood.' It is possible, then, to hear in his demand 'Get thee to a nunnery' not only bitterness but also protectiveness. A convent is the only place where Ophelia will be safe from him and other men: 'We are arrant knaves all, believe none of us.' So Ophelia's lament after the meeting is unironic. It serves as an index of what both she and he have lost over the course of the play, another 'falling off' on the model of Hamlet Sr's replacement by Claudius:

> Oh what a noble mind is here o'erthrown!
> The courtier's, soldier's, scholar's, eye, tongue, sword,
> Th'expectancy and rose of the fair state,
> The glass of fashion and the mould of form,
> Th'observed of all observers, quite, quite down,
> And I of ladies most deject and wretched.   (3.1.144–9)

Claudius takes Hamlet's activity seriously, for it is at this point that he decides to send Hamlet to England to exact a tribute from its king.

3.2: 'SPEAK THE SPEECH'

Hamlet's Senecan and Elizabethan predecessors in the genre of revenge – including Shakespeare's own *Titus* – saved their inset spectacles (plays or banquets) for the end of their dramas, where they are often used to accomplish the vengeance at which the plot has aimed. Hamlet's 'Mousetrap' operates differently. Here the play-within-a-play, orchestrated in the middle of the drama, functions as a strategy of surveillance. Hamlet and Horatio will 'observe my uncle' during the performance in order to assess not only Claudius's but the Ghost's guilt.

It also serves as an opportunity for Hamlet to enunciate his own dramatic aesthetic, one that prizes 'naturalness' over the kinds of excess – the 'dumb-shows and noise' – that Hamlet both associates with earlier dramatic forms and connects to Claudius's violence.[1] 'Suit the action to the word', he tells the players, 'the word to the action, with this special observance, that you o'erstep not the modesty of nature'. Such a theory of acting seems to indict Hamlet's own behaviour, since it insists that the actors maintain a control over their emotions that the prince has shown himself unable to do. The entertainment that follows seems to ignore Hamlet's orders. It begins with a dumb-show, in which a king is poisoned and his wife, the queen, is whisked away by the poisoner. It proceeds to a highly stylized dialogue, notable for its elliptical syntax and rhyming couplets, between the original king and queen. Claudius cuts off the play when he sees 'one Lucianus, *nephew to the king*' (my italics) prepare to poison him. For Graham Bradshaw, Claudius's timing makes the 'Mousetrap' a 'lamentable failure', since we cannot be certain whether he was seized by guilt or by fear that his nephew might be coming after him.[2] But Hamlet declares himself assured of the reliability of

---

[1] Lee Sheridan Cox, *Figurative Design in Hamlet: The Significance of the Dumb Show* (Columbus: Ohio State University Press, 1973), 46–7.
[2] Bradshaw, *Shakespeare's Scepticism*, 117.

the Ghost: 'I'll take the ghost's word for a thousand pound', he tells Horatio, and he confirms his role as revenger:

> 'Tis now the very witching time of night,
> When churchyards yawn, and hell itself breathes out
> Contagion to this world. Now could I drink hot blood,
> And do such bitter business as the day
> Would quake to look on.   (3.2.349–53)

It also confirms for Claudius the need to send his nephew abroad to the King of England: 'I your commission will forthwith dispatch / And he to England shall along with you', he instructs Rosencrantz and Guildenstern. That commission, we will learn, is to have Hamlet slain.

3.3: 'NOW A IS A-PRAYING'

Claudius is intent on exiling (and, the audience will learn in 4.3, executing) Hamlet. At the same time, he feels remorse for his actions, as his soliloquy in 3.3 reveals. Indeed, we might consider this scene as the exact response, only delayed until *after* the 'Mousetrap', that Hamlet had hoped the inset play would prompt. Claudius recognizes the horror of his crime, an inheritance that reaches back to Adam and Eve and Cain and Abel: 'O my offence is rank, it smells to heaven; / It hath the primal eldest curse upon't, / A brother's murder.'

The rest of his speech, more reminiscent of an Elizabethan morality play than a revenge tragedy, enacts the difficulty of Christian repentance, the struggle for Claudius of 'aligning his internal state with his external gestures'.[1] The problem is not only the obvious, explicit one: that Claudius is reluctant to give up the rewards of his 'foul murder'. It is also that Claudius is uncertain of the efficacy of his repentance. In other words, he suspects that his impulse to repent may only be an element of his sinfulness, may only 'lime' – entrap – his soul further. But Hamlet, who discovers Claudius on his knees, alone, is not privy to his uncle's supplication, and he thus does not doubt the status of his uncle's remorse. We might say, then, that Hamlet *misreads* this scene. So, although this moment might seem a perfect opportunity to slay his enemy, Hamlet hesitates, reluctant to send 'this same villain ... To heaven'. He wants Claudius damned. He will wait for the opportunity to make his revenge more complete and Claudius's damnation more certain.

> Then trip him that his heels may kick at heaven,
> And that his soul may be as damned and black
> As hell whereto it goes.   (3.3.93–5)

Such savage intent disgusted some of *Hamlet*'s early critics. But it is a hallmark of Elizabethan revenge fiction; it answers to the great Senecan insight in *Thyestes* that

---

[1] Ramie Targoff, 'The Performance of Prayer: Sincerity and Theatricality in Early Modern England', *Representations* 60 (1997), 49.

'Thou never dost enough revenge the wronge / Exept [*sic*] thou passe'.[1] Here 'doing enough' (which in the world of revenge is always doing *more*) extends retaliatory violence into the afterlife. While this goal may be an unstated assumption of other revengers, Hamlet makes it explicit: he wants Claudius not only dead but in a Christian hell. Hamlet's articulation of his desire – as either a genuine reason or as an excuse for postponing revenge – marks another way in which the play refashions the genre.

3.4: THE CLOSET SCENE

Hamlet's encounter with the praying Claudius had interrupted his passage to Gertrude's closet. Elizabethan closets were not bedrooms *per se* but built spaces for either prayer, or study, or storage of treasures, or even for the gathering of small sets of people – different functions that all implied 'possessiveness ... exclusivity ... privacy ... [and] secrecy'.[2] Hamlet had promised that he would speak, rather than use, daggers when he met his mother, but the scene is pervaded by real as well as metaphoric violence. In a scenario adapted from the sources, Hamlet stabs at the noise he hears coming from behind an arras – only to discover that it is Polonius he has killed and not the King: 'Thou wretched, rash, intruding fool, farewell. / I took thee for thy better.' In Belleforest, Hamlet's treatment of Fengon's spy was ostentatiously grotesque: he chopped up the dead body and fed it to hogs. Hamlet is not as disrespectful, and he acknowledges that the deed makes him susceptible to divine punishment for murder. But he humiliates the corpse at the end of the scene, 'lug[ging] the guts' into another room and, in what can be seen as a parody of the Eucharist, telling Rosencrantz and Guildenstern that Polonius is at supper '[n]ot where he eats, but where a is eaten'.

Some consider the murder of Polonius the catastrophe of the play, as it 'sends the plot off in a violent new direction, from which everything else flows in ugly consequence'.[3] But Hamlet is less concerned about it than his mother, whom he goes on to castigate in a flurry of accusations that repeat both his own and the Ghost's earlier sense of her 'falling off'.

Hamlet, who calls himself both 'scourge and minister', may understand his chastisement of Gertrude as a form of shrift, prompting her to examine her conscience and to repent. He is thus, as the Ghost had earlier demanded, leaving her to heaven but at the same time encouraging her to feel contrite, to experience the 'thorns that in her bosom lodge' in order to save her soul. There is self-interest at work in this effort: a chastened Gertrude would give to Hamlet a purified sense of self and restore for both him and his father the difference between Hamlet Sr and his fratricidal brother. But the extraordinary vehemence and eroticized energy with which he recounts her sins call these goals into question, turning Hamlet's supposed supervision of his mother's penitence into a form of revenge, one in which he takes a kind of pleasure. He offers an

---

[1] See Prosser, *Hamlet and Revenge*, 261–75. Quotation from *Seneca His Tenne Tragedies, translated into Englysh* (London, 1581), D8v.
[2] Lena Cowen Orlin, 'Gertrude's Closet', *Shakespeare Jahrbuch* 134 (1998), 65.
[3] Cummings, *Mortal Thoughts*, 228.

Figure 1 'Do you not come your tardy son to chide?' (3.4.106). Redrawn by Du Guernier for the 1714 edition of Rowe's Shakespeare (Folger Shakespeare Library)

extended comparison between Hamlet Sr as Hyperion or Mars or Mercury, and Claudius as a 'mildewed ear';[1] he then imagines Gertrude's sexual desire and her coupling with Claudius:

> but to live
> In the rank sweat of an enseamèd bed,
> Stewed in corruption, honeying and making love
> Over the nasty sty.   (3.4.91–4)

Hamlet's fixation summons, for the last time, the Ghost, who comes to 'whet thy almost blunted purpose' – to urge Hamlet against Claudius and not his mother. But perhaps the most significant effect of the Ghost (who remains invisible to Gertrude) is that his appearance seems to redefine the relationship between Hamlet and Gertrude. When Hamlet asks his mother to keep secret the fact that he is only 'mad in craft', she agrees, taking his side against the court:

> Be thou assured, if words be made of breath,
> And breath of life, I have no life to breathe
> What thou hast said to me.   (3.4.198–200)

He also reveals to Gertrude that he has potentially deadly plans for Rosencrantz and Guildenstern – whom he 'will trust as ... adders fanged' – when they sail off to England. Hamlet has already tasted the blood of Polonius; now he imagines that, for his former friends, he 'will delve one yard below their mines / And blow them at the moon'.

4.1–7: ENGLAND, POLAND, ELSINORE

The prince's trip to England is a key component of the earlier tale. But it would have had special meaning to Shakespeare's earliest audiences. It included them in the story. It might have recalled for them their island's past thralldom to Danish invasion and rule in the ninth, tenth, and eleventh centuries. Or it might have reminded them of their present-day commercial and diplomatic relationships with Denmark. After 1603, it would have gestured to another significant relationship between England and Denmark, since the new English Queen, Anne, was born in Denmark, a member of the Danish royal family.

The fourth act rotates around Hamlet's journey, which, as he narrates in a letter to Horatio (4.6), is cut short by pirates, and he returns to Elsinore. The trip out and back is mirrored or foiled in other characters' 'travels': Fortinbras's invasion of Poland, Laertes's return to Denmark from Paris, and Ophelia's fatal slip into a 'weeping brook'. In a brief scene, Fortinbras leads a march through Denmark on his way to the continent; in Q2, but not in Q1 or F, Hamlet observes the Norwegian prince, weighs himself in the balance, and finds himself wanting. His soliloquy retards the action and contains striking inconsistencies (Hamlet proposes that 'from this time forth, / My thoughts be bloody or be nothing worth', although he has already stabbed

---

[1] For the possibility that while making the comparison Hamlet gestures to the tapestries that were a feature of Kronborg, see Dollerup, *Denmark*, 84–5.

Polonius and is plotting the ends of Rosencrantz and Guildenstern), and it may have been cut between Shakespeare's first draft and the script prepared for performance. But the fifty-five or so lines missing from F serve a crucial purpose: they show Hamlet still mired in the self-contempt he has exhibited earlier, still seeking models of himself in other figures, and still attracted to the unreflective martial tendencies that they exhibit and that he lacks: 'to be great / Is . . . greatly to find quarrel in a straw / When honour's at the stake'.

Hamlet does not get a chance to observe Laertes, who comes roaring back to Elsinore seeking vengeance for his murdered father. But the audience does. And it witnesses in him a model neither of warrior honour nor of chivalric magnanimity but rather of easily manipulable – if sympathetic – passion. For when he learns, with Claudius, that Hamlet has returned to England in mysterious circumstances, Laertes colludes with the king in plotting the fatal deception of the prince by envenomed, unbated sword.

His willingness to conspire is enhanced on account of what he has seen of the maddened Ophelia. Having lost father and lover, Ophelia lives the lunacy that Hamlet has been feigning. Her eroticized ballads express both desire and innocence: she has become the 'green girl' Polonius foreshadowed in the first act, sick from unrequited sexual longing. Her distribution of flowers is a pantomime of defloration. But it is also part of a mourning ritual for her father, a ritual she brings – or is reported by Gertrude in 4.7 to have brought – to her own drowning: 'she chanted snatches of old lauds / As one incapable of her own distress'.

Ophelia's death is the real version of Hamlet's imagined one, and its status – suicide or accident? – is notoriously tricky. Gertrude's narration, syntactically careful as it is not to cede any agency to Ophelia, does not offer a definitive answer:

> There on the pendant boughs her cronet weeds
> Clamb'ring to hang, an envious sliver broke,
> When down her weedy trophies and herself
> Fell in the weeping brook. (4.7.172–5)

An answer is of great consequence, since it determines whether or not she will be afforded a Christian burial, in the churchyard and with the rituals appropriate to a woman of high status. And yet, as Michael Macdonald points out, Shakespeare seems deliberately to keep the question unresolved, to 'exploit' a 'new ambivalence about suicide' that began in his lifetime.[1] These attitudes ranged from treating suicide as a terrible crime to seeing it as an honourable deed, from considering it to be the result of insanity to insisting that it was a deliberate, sane action. (The gravedigger mocks all of these options, suggesting in a parodically scholastic appeal that Ophelia's drowning was an act of self-defence, a notion that, knowing the moral condition of Elsinore, we would do well to take seriously.) These distinct attitudes inform Ophelia's funeral and the characters' responses to it, which in turn would have been

---

[1] Michael Macdonald, 'Ophelia's Maimèd Rites', SQ 37.3 (1986), 315.

refracted by considerations of status, wealth, and gender.[1] Laertes is furious, while the priest, who authorized the burial on Christian ground, nevertheless hedges his bets, limiting the ceremonies to 'maimèd rites' since her 'death was doubtful'.

5.1: GRAVEYARD

What is not doubtful is that Ophelia's death moves the action to the graveyard, where Hamlet's thoughts have been tending since his first appearance. In 5.1, standing over the grave being dug (without his knowledge) for Ophelia, Hamlet confronts the materiality of death and its levelling power over all classes of people (peasant, courtier, lawyer, emperor). The scene fits the poetic and artistic tradition of *memento mori*, of meditating on the inevitability and omnipresence of death. But it gives the tradition decisive twists. First, this late-in-the-play scene brings us back to the beginning, since the gravedigger – whose literalism is the play's only match for Hamlet's wit – explains that his first day on the job was the same day that old King Hamlet defeated old King Fortinbras. He thus harks back to Horatio's account in the opening scene of the mortal combat between the now-dead warrior kings. (The gravedigger also folds Hamlet into this origin story, announcing for the first time that the prince was born on this very day (5.1.123–4).) Next, the gravedigger throws up a skull – likely the first on the English stage – which he claims is that of Yorick, a former court jester.[2] Looking at the skull, Hamlet speaks of Yorick as a kind of surrogate father – 'he hath borne me on his back a thousand times' – whose remains now nauseate him: 'how abhorred in my imagination it is! My gorge rises at it.' Like the ghost of his father, the prop takes on a second life of its own, exerting an influence over Hamlet that reflects its dual function as subject and object, person and thing.[3]

That influence turns Hamlet's thoughts away from himself and his own individual mortality to humans' shared destiny in the dust. He mocks women, for whom the skull should serve as a reminder that their use of cosmetics cannot prevent their death and decay; and he lingers on the transience even of emperors and their empires: 'Alexander died, Alexander was buried, Alexander returneth to dust.' But his musings are interrupted by the entrance of Claudius, Gertrude, Laertes, and the rest of the funeral procession. In a famous stage direction, Laertes '*Leaps in the grave*', professing his affection for Ophelia with a flamboyance that seems both an expression of genuine feeling and an effort to compensate for the 'no more done' about which he has complained to the priest.[4] Hamlet responds with similar ostentation. He advances himself with the epithet reserved for the monarch – 'This is I, / Hamlet the Dane' – and he asserts that he loved Ophelia in a way that 'forty thousand brothers / Could not with all their quantity of love / Make up my sum'. A stage direction in Q1 but not in Q2 or F has the prince jump into the grave along with Laertes. The notion, even if not standard theatrical practice (see commentary), is consistent with Hamlet's

---

[1] Janet Clare, '"Buried in the Open Fields": Early Modern Suicide and the Case of Ofelia', *Journal of Early Modern Studies* 2 (2013), 241–52, www.fupress.com/bsfm-jems.

[2] Frye, *Renaissance Hamlet*, 206.

[3] See Andrew Sofer, *The Stage Life of Props* (Ann Arbor: University of Michigan Press, 2003), 89–115.

[4] The stage direction is in F and Q1 but not Q2; Shakespeare may or may not be responsible for it.

competitive, even vengeful, ranting. His exhibition may signal a return to his 'antic disposition' or perhaps a sincere – if inappropriate and unsympathetic – demonstration of grief over Ophelia's death. It also underscores his special relationship with Laertes, his adversary but also, as he says in the next scene, his 'brother'.

5.2: 'THE READINESS IS ALL'

The Hamlet of the final scene sounds not at all like the Hamlet of the graveyard face-off with Laertes. He recounts his sea-journey in detail to Horatio (in Q1, these details are given in an entirely distinct scene between Horatio and Gertrude). In the retelling, Hamlet demonstrates an unprecedented calm and objectivity, as well as a sense of providential design, of God's shaping presence: 'There's a divinity that shapes our ends, / Rough-hew them how we will.' He has come to this sense, for which he has been accused of fatalism or resignation, based on his experience aboard the ship to England. During the trip, he tells Horatio, he discovered that Rosencrantz and Guildenstern had been given written instructions from Claudius to have him executed. Hamlet explains that his instincts took over, and before he 'could make a prologue to my brains / They had begun the play'. He rewrote the letter, directing the English king to have the letter-bearers killed. It is at this point, as Horatio already knows, that the ship was boarded by pirates, and Hamlet escaped. In his retrospective narration to Horatio, then, Hamlet describes his actions as rooted in his own fortunate impulses and as guided by an omniscient power.[1] Such an understanding marks a literal and figurative 'sea-change' in Hamlet, emblematized by his use of his father's signet to seal his letter. He is now prepared to seize the opportunity to duel with Laertes: 'we defy augury. There is special providence in the fall of a sparrow. If it be now, 'tis not to come; if it be not to come, it will be now; if it be not now, yet it will come – the readiness is all' (5.2.192–5).[2]

The fencing contest at the end of Act 5, balanced against the opening description of Hamlet Sr's judicial combat, provides a 'frame' for the play; it also offers 'a means of performance acceptable' to a character who has been so queasy about acting and action.[3] But even as he agrees to fight with Laertes, his real target is Claudius. Fuelled by his discovery of the king's treachery, Hamlet has returned to Denmark committed to killing him. Hamlet may be asking for assurance from Horatio or seeking it from himself when he poses the matter:

> Does it not, think thee, stand me now upon –
> He that hath killed my king, and whored my mother,
> Popped in between th'election and my hopes,
> Thrown out his angle for my proper life,
> And with such cozenage – is't not perfect conscience
> To quit him with this arm? And is't not to be damned

---

[1] For the connection between luck or chance and Providence, see Cummings, *Mortal Thoughts*, 208–35.
[2] The allusion is to Matthew 10.29.
[3] John Kerrigan, *Shakespeare's Binding Language* (Oxford University Press, 2016), 221; Jennifer Low, 'Manhood and the Duel: Enacting Masculinity in *Hamlet*', *The Centennial Review* 43.3 (1999), 508.

To let this canker of our nature come
In further evil?   (5.2.63–70)

Hamlet rehearses the situation as we have heard it repeated many times, but with some important variations. He is now concerned explicitly with the political nature of his uncle's crime: Claudius has not only usurped the throne from Hamlet Sr but also taken Hamlet's own rightful place in the 'hope' – if not the guarantee – of election to the crown, the expectation of a son in an elective monarchy such as Denmark.[1] And although he returns to the problems of conscience and damnation, his perspective on the two has shifted: conscience is no longer an obstacle to action, but an encouragement to it, and the threat of damnation no longer hovers over his killing of Claudius but over his failure to do so.

5.2: 'THE REST IS SILENCE'

The 'excitement of the fencing match' that ends the play brings us back to its beginning, to poison.[2] Shakespeare provides unusually detailed stage directions for '[a] *table prepared, with flagons of wine on it*' – suggestive of a Communion service. Only this is a perversion of the sacrament, since Claudius taints the cup of wine he will offer Hamlet, the 'back-up' plan he has devised should Laertes not stab Hamlet successfully. After three passes, Laertes lands an unscrupulous strike, but in the scuffle he loses the rapier to Hamlet and is 'justly killed with mine own treachery'. In the meantime, Gertrude has drunk from the poisoned cup meant for Hamlet; her death, as well as Laertes's revelation of the 'foul practice', give Hamlet the opportunity for his revenge. The staged duel has become real vengeance. He wounds Claudius with the deadly sword and forces the poisoned liquid down his throat: 'Here, thou incestuous, murderous, damnèd Dane, / Drink off this potion.' This double strike is the 'superfluous death' Claudius had feared in Act 4, and it goes a long way towards Hamlet's mission, since the third act, to damn Claudius in an 'act / That has no relish of salvation in't' (3.3.91–2).

Unlike most revenge protagonists, Hamlet does not orchestrate the tragedy's final spectacle; he is a player in Claudius's design who improvises effectively to exact his revenge. (Indeed, one scholar has called his blow against Claudius 'almost a posthumous act'.)[3] But he is like his predecessors in that he is a victim of the conclusion's carnage. His dying speech carries all the more weight given his characteristic introspection. He makes sure to ask Horatio to stay alive to report his story – one of personal vendetta but also action on behalf of his country. He thus makes sure to confirm the nation's successor: 'I do prophesy th'election lights / On Fortinbras; he has my dying voice.' The rest is silence – both from and for Hamlet. The silence stuns all until Fortinbras arrives to assume the crown. He gives Hamlet a final commendation: 'he was likely, had he been put on, / To have proved most royal'.

---

[1] Andrew Gurr, 'Hamlet's Claim to the Crown of Denmark', *Critical Essays on Hamlet* (1988), 92–9.
[2] Dover Wilson, *What Happens in Hamlet*, 266.   [3] Scofield, *The Ghosts of 'Hamlet'*, 103.

Fortinbras's words affirm for the play what Bradley asked of great tragedy, that it 'involve the waste of [the] good'.[1] Fortinbras steps in to fill the gap left by this waste, and the irony is obvious: the son of a Norwegian king defeated by King Hamlet now wears the Danish crown. But it is Hamlet's story, not Fortinbras's, that Shakespeare wanted told – told again and again according to the prince's demand that Horatio remain alive and 'draw thy breath in pain / To tell my story'. That story, at its heart, is a revenge tale, but one with an essential, deeply Shakespearean sensibility. For it is the story of a revenger doubtful of, divided by, and resistant to the retaliation that his foils (Fortinbras, Laertes) seem so easily to embrace. Whatever the source of this resistance – and, as we have seen, scholars have offered many accounts – it fuels the play's plot and language, and these in turn generate audiences' endless fascination with his tragedy.

Stages and Screens

Fascination with *Hamlet* is manifest in its enduring, worldwide popularity in performance. Behind this popularity, Robert Hapgood suggests, is the play's 'exceptional responsiveness to changing times and places'.[2] As Hamlet wished to welcome the stranger, the play seems to invite different cultures, over the centuries and across the globe, to enter its ambit: to see their own psychological and political predicaments in Hamlet's situation in Elsinore, and to use the play as a means of expressing urgent existential dilemmas – about power, action, generational decline, authenticity, theatricality – that might otherwise 'pass show'. (Though the welcome is double-edged: as much as actors aspire to the role, several have found it too much to bear and have broken down before, during, or after a performance run.) Far beyond what Hamlet requested of Horatio, the prince's story has been told repeatedly, in venues and with technologies that Shakespeare could hardly have imagined.

This performance history is richly chronicled and, now more than ever, studied in terms not only of Shakespeare's theatrical legacy but also of its implications for social and cultural history. Its documents tell of the invention and reinvention of signature practices, including those to do with scenery and settings, costume, stage-business, the cutting of scenes, and the delivery and styling of individual lines and passages. They also tell of the interpretations and reinterpretations of the play's political dimensions and the prince's tragic status. Marvin Rosenberg has usefully generalized two camps of performance: the 'sweet' Hamlet or the 'power' Hamlet.

The following review provides the broad outlines of this history, calling attention to a few widely regarded, striking, or innovative treatments and adaptations of the play and its characters – most often Hamlet. It traces first an Anglo-American stage and

[1] Bradley, *Shakespearean Tragedy*, 39.
[2] Hapgood, 'Introduction', in *Hamlet, Prince of Denmark*, Shakespeare in Production Series (Cambridge University Press, 1999), 3. In this section, I rely heavily on Hapgood; Marvin Rosenberg, *The Masks of 'Hamlet'* (Newark: University of Delaware Press, 1992); Anthony Dawson, *Shakespeare in Performance: 'Hamlet'* (Manchester University Press, 1995); David Bevington, *Murder Most Foul: Hamlet Through the Ages* (Oxford University Press, 2011); Andy Lavender, *Shakespeare in Pieces: Peter Brook, Robert La Page, Richard Wilson* (London: Nick Hern, 2001), 1–50.

screen tradition before turning to global performances, adaptations, and the tradition
of female actors in *Hamlet* and as Hamlet.

EARLY STAGES

Hamlet's first performances around 1600 were by the Lord Chamberlain's Men, who
would become the King's Men at the accession of James I in 1603, at the Globe
Theatre on the south side of the Thames. Theatre historians have illuminated the
standard conventions of the early modern theatre – all-male casts, bare platform stage,
trap door for ghosts, devils, and burials, central opening in the tiring house for royal
entries – from which we can infer the embodied movement of the play. (Andrew Gurr
and Mariko Ichikawa propose a blueprint for *Hamlet* in *Staging in Shakespeare's
Theatres*.)[1] Q1 supplies information specific to the play: from it we learn that the
Ghost appears in 3.4 'in his nightgown', that Ophelia 'play[s] on a lute, and her hair
down, singing' in 4.5, and Hamlet jumps into the grave with Laertes in 5.1. Other
evidence makes clear that the role of Hamlet was first performed by Richard Burbage,
the leading tragic actor in the Chamberlain's/King's Men and Shakespeare's long-
time fellow. An elegy upon his death in 1619 mourned: 'No more young Hamlet . . . /
That lived in him'.[2] And we have hints – though more circumstantial – that
Shakespeare himself played the Ghost in the earliest performances.

The professional theatre was closed by the government during the Interregnum or
Commonwealth period (1642–60). *Hamlet* survived this period in the droll
The Grave-Makers, a short comic piece that, like other drolls, had been excerpted
and adapted from an earlier play.[3] When professional playing began again in London
at the start of the Restoration, the play returned to the stage under the aegis of the
Duke of York's Company, helmed by William Davenant. The theatre scene was
different now, more modern and continental, featuring a proscenium arch, perspective
scenery, artificial lighting, and, most striking, women actors playing female parts.
In 1663, the Duke's Men's star actor Thomas Betterton took over the role of Hamlet,
which he was to play until 1709, when he was in his seventies. (His wife, Mary
Saunderson, played Ophelia.)

A 1676 quarto of *Hamlet* (known as the Players' Quarto) gives us a good sense of
how extensively the play was cut for these early performances. (The 1676 edition
follows the quarto of 1637; it identifies passages to be cut with inverted commas.)
Substantial chunks of dialogue were eliminated, from Horatio's account of Hamlet
Sr's combat with the King of Norway to much of Hamlet's self-reproach in 2.2, from
Rosencrantz and Guildenstern's musing on the 'cess [cease] of majesty' to Hamlet's
sober reflection on the 'death of a sparrow'. Perhaps most significant, however, was the
reduction of the Norwegian element: the account of Fortinbras's 'revenge' in 1.1 is

[1] Andrew Gurr and Mariko Ichikawa, 'The Early Staging of *Hamlet*', in *Staging in Shakespeare's Theatres* (Oxford University Press, 2000), 121–62.
[2] In Edwin Nungezer, *A Dictionary of Actors and of Other Persons Associated with the Public Representation of Plays in England Before 1642*, reprint (New York: Greenwood Press, 1968), 74.
[3] Dale Randall, *Winter Fruit: English Drama, 1642–1660* (Lexington: University Press of Kentucky, 1995), 155.

truncated and the embassy to Norway (1.2 and 2.1), as well as Fortinbras's parade across Denmark on his way to Poland (4.1), were omitted. Cuts shape the meaning and impact of the play; reading and listening for them can be a revelatory interpretive experience. The key outcome of the Players' Quarto's cuts, specifically the diminution of Fortinbras's role, was to downplay the international quality of the tragedy, circumscribing within the realm the threats to Hamlet and to Denmark. This move presaged a related trend that dominated performance well into the nineteenth century: a concentration on the portrayal of Hamlet's emotional over his political condition.

THE EIGHTEENTH AND NINETEENTH CENTURIES

A focus on Hamlet's personality was developed in distinct ways by the great actors of the eighteenth and nineteenth centuries. David Garrick, who occupies a central place in the institutionalization of Shakespeare at the heart of the British literary canon, assumed the role in 1742. He captivated his audience with a naturalistic style that emphasized Hamlet as a man of action and feeling; he was known for conveying his palpable terror at his first sight of the Ghost. John Philip Kemble's performance style, in contrast, was studied and stately, offering a Hamlet less active, more solemn, than Garrick's.

Edmund Kean, who began playing the role in 1814, portrayed the Romantic Hamlet of Goethe and Coleridge (see pp. 20–1): he was brooding rather than active (like Garrick) and self-involved rather than grand (like Kemble). But he also conveyed Hamlet's potential for impetuosity and cruelty: one of his signature contributions was to crawl, during the 'Mousetrap' play, towards Claudius to observe and frighten him.

In 1820 Kean, following a tradition of English actors touring the United States, performed major Shakespearean roles – including Hamlet – at the 'best playhouses in New York, Philadelphia, Baltimore and Boston'.[1] At the same time, another English actor, Junius Brutus Booth, had arrived in the United States – unlike Kean, to stay. Booth performed in venues as far west as San Francisco, but he is better known for having established a family theatrical dynasty: his three sons Junius Brutus, Jr; Edwin Thomas; and John Wilkes (now known not for his acting but for his assassination of President Abraham Lincoln).

Edwin Booth famously played Hamlet from 1853 to 1891, and he was celebrated for his tender approach to the role. His first biographer, the drama critic William Winter, praised him for 'the spiritualised intellect, the masculine strength, [and] the feminine softness' he demonstrated in the role.[2] On the other side of the Atlantic, Henry Irving demonstrated some of this tenderness and vulnerability, coupled with a nervous, introspective intensity, in performances that spanned the years 1871 to 1902.

Booth and Irving bring us to the close of the nineteenth century and thus to *fin-de-siècle* rethinkings of *Hamlet* for the stage. These reconsiderations went in tandem with changes in theatrical practice, changes that become even more conspicuous in the

[1] Alden T. Vaughan and Virginia Mason Vaughan, *Shakespeare in America* (Oxford University Press, 2011), 41. The first known performance of *Hamlet* in America was in Philadelphia in 1759.
[2] Quoted in *Shakespeare in America: An Anthology from the Revolution to Now*, ed. James Shapiro (New York: Literary Classics of the United States, 2013), 232.

Figure 2 John Philip Kemble as Hamlet, after Sir Thomas Lawrence, early 1880s (Folger Shakespeare Library)

Figure 3   Edwin Booth as Hamlet *circa* 1870 (Library of Congress / Corbis / VCG via Getty Images)

twentieth century. Victorian productions of Shakespeare were highly pictorial, with expensive, elaborate set designs and a proscenium arch that separated audience from actor. Practitioners such as William Poel wanted to dispense with these customs in order to recover the original practices of Elizabethan performance, with its limited stage trappings and fast pace. In 1881, Poel oversaw an amateur performance of Q1 *Hamlet* on a bare platform stage in London; this initiated an interest in the staging of the first

Figure 4   Ellen Terry as Ophelia and Henry Irving as Hamlet (Time Life Pictures / Mansell / The LIFE Picture Collection / Getty Images)

Figure 5 'Go on, I'll follow thee' (1.4.86). Johnston Forbes-Robertson as Hamlet in a 1913 film (Mander and Mitchenson Theatre Collection)

quarto that continues today. In 1897, Johnston Forbes-Robertson tried to get closer to the original *Hamlet* by restoring Fortinbras to the play's conclusion. And in 1899–1900, at the Shakespeare Memorial Theatre in Stratford-upon-Avon, F. R. Benson produced a complete *Hamlet* – the whole play as it appears in standard editions (Q2 combined with F). It took six hours to play.

THE TWENTIETH AND TWENTY-FIRST CENTURIES
1900–1965

The kind of oversight and vision observed in Poel and his colleagues became increasingly important, and increasingly commonplace, in the twentieth-century theatre. The period is known for the rise of the director and designer, and with them an emphasis on unified stagings in which all the elements of performance contributed to a deliberate concept or interpretation of the play. The collaboration between Gordon Craig and Konstantin Stanislavski for the Moscow Art Theatre in 1912, with Vasili Kachalov as the prince, represented a striking international effort, joining Craig's commitment to stylization and symbolism with Stanlislavski's investment in

Figure 6   John Gielgud as Hamlet, 1934, New Theatre (Hulton Archive / Getty Images).

psychological realism. The famous production used abstract, movable screens and lighting to delineate stage space, while Kachalov played Hamlet as an innocent prince who could still offer a serious challenge to Claudius.

Productions of *Hamlet* in the 1920s responded to the social and political quandaries that followed the trauma of the First World War. In the Birmingham Repertory's modern-dress performance of 1925, Colin Keith-Johnston portrayed the prince as a rebellious but regular, contemporary young man. This was a political as well as an aesthetic choice; the break with tradition, Anthony Dawson suggests, made Hamlet 'recognizably ordinary', helping to 'move his dilemmas and crises into the arena of the audience's actual concerns, reducing his remoteness'.[1] (John Barrymore's aristocratic prince, also from the 1920s, thus served as a ballast to Keith-Johnston's.) Important performances of the 1930s (and into the early 1940s) include John Gielgud's acclaimed

---

[1] Dawson, *Shakepeare in Performance: 'Hamlet'*, 89.

Figure 7   Laurence Olivier as Hamlet and Eileen Herlie as Gertrude, 1948 (ITV/Shutterstock)

portrayal of Hamlet as both elegant hero and bitter satirist, and Laurence Olivier's performance, directed by Tyrone Guthrie, of Hamlet as an athletic, energetic prince psychologically fractured by Oedipal desire.

In the 1940s actors, directors, and audiences found in the crises of *Hamlet* ways of approaching the horrors of the Second World War. In 1944, the actor and director Maurice Evans, who had directed the play in London and New York in the 1930s, developed a *G.I. Hamlet*, to be performed by and for American soldiers in the Pacific theatre. The pared-down script presented a heroic, action-oriented Hamlet who could serve as both mirror and model for young men 'on the eve of going into battle or . . . staggering with fatigue and confusion after their first encounter with the enemy'.[1] In contrast, a de-politicized *Hamlet*, given a Victorian setting in a 1948 performance at the Shakespeare Memorial Theatre in Stratford-upon-Avon under the direction of Michael Benthall, was meant to celebrate English cultural achievement even as the country's imperial power was in obvious decline. The same year saw the release of the influential film version of the play, directed by and starring Olivier. The version hewed closely to the Freudian sensibilities of the 1937 performance, intensifying them with camera-work, and setting 3.4 in Gertrude's bedroom.

1965 to the Present

The counter-cultures of the 1960s, 1970s, and 1980s saw the play and the prince as a standard for – and against – a different set of values. Directors and actors saw *Hamlet* as especially apt for channelling Vietnam-era disillusionment with both heroic ideals and cynicism about social and economic conditions on both sides of the Atlantic. In their deliberately polemical aesthetic engagements, these productions were influenced by the work of prominent twentieth-century theatre theorists and practitioners: Stanislavski, as well as Antonin Artaud, Bertolt Brecht, Jerzy Grotowski, and Jan Kott. The visions of these theorists are radically different (from realist to expressionist to Marxist) but they all attest to the place of the stage as a shaping historical and cultural force. Peter Hall's 1965 production for the Royal Shakespeare Company (RSC; founded in 1961) at its home base in Stratford-upon-Avon spoke to the times, featuring the 24-year-old David Warner as an alienated, unprincely Hamlet – an 'angry young man' – whose absurdist humour could do little to oppose the power structure at Elsinore. Joseph Papp directed the play in 1968 for the Public Playhouse in New York City; his Hamlet, played by Martin Sheen as nearly mad, shook hands with and sold trinkets to the audience. (Papp toured another, shorter *Hamlet*, with a bi-racial cast, in city parks that summer.) Richard Eyre's 1980 production at the Royal Court in London was set in a Renaissance palace whose architecture emphasized the play's concern with the power of state surveillance. But its most spectacular innovation was to make the broken-hearted Hamlet, played by Jonathan Pryce, be literally possessed by the ghost of his father. In 1.5, the prince himself, rather than a paternal spirit on stage, choked out the Ghost's lines. Mark Rylance, in a 1989 production for the RSC, portrayed Hamlet as truly mad, particularly when he delivered 'to be or not be' in soiled pyjamas and then accosted Ophelia during the nunnery scene. The set, with off-kilter window and walls, was meant to simulate the atmosphere of a mental institution.

Appropriately, given the *fin-de-siècle* origins of the script, the turn of the twenty-first century was characterized by a range of experiments on both film and stage.

---

[1] *Maurice Evans' G.I. Production of Hamlet by William Shakespeare* (Garden City, NY: Doubleday & Company, Inc., 1947), 17.

Figure 8   Mark Rylance as Hamlet and Peter Wright as Claudius at the Royal Shakespeare Theatre, Stratford-upon-Avon, 1989 (© John Bunting / ArenaPAL)

In 1996, Kenneth Branagh, who had played Hamlet on stage in 1992 (for the fourth time), translated the performance into a film version, which he also directed. Uncut and running over four hours, the film made sumptuous use of the resources of the medium, with impressive wide-angle shots that convey the size and grandeur of the great hall and throne that Hamlet comes to understand have been stolen from him. Branagh's Hamlet was multi-faceted, alert, and energized as well as self-lacerating; his

Figure 9   Kenneth Branagh as Hamlet, 1996 (Castle Rock Entertainment / Kobal / Shutterstock)

delivery of 'to be or not to be' in front of a spread of mirrored walls turned introspection into highly self-conscious performance.

Michael Almereyda's far shorter, modernized film version, *Hamlet 2000*, substituted the skyscrapers and streets of Manhattan – the symbol of the heights and depths
of international capitalism – for Elsinore, 'using corrupted wealth as a surrogate for
stained royalty'.[1] Ethan Hawke's Hamlet performed 'to be or not to be' in
a Blockbuster video store in the 'Action' aisle, and Julia Stiles, as Ophelia, was
'wired' in order to record and transmit her conversation with Hamlet in the nunnery
scene.

Stage versions from this period offer an embarrassment of riches, illuminating the
play's psychological, political, and theatrical possibilities (or, perhaps more accurately,
using the play to illuminate period insights about society, politics, and theatre). Simon
Russell Beale's notably plump Hamlet, at London's National Theatre in 2000, was
praised as a callback to the sensitive, gentle, wounded prince of Irving and Booth.
The same year, renowned director Peter Brook, who at age 75 had already produced
both the play and his own adaptation of the play, *Qui Est Là* (see below), relied on
a multicultural cast of just eight (with Adrian Lester in the lead role) to perform first in
Paris and then on tour in the United States and London. The heavily cut, minimalist
version emphasized the play's theatricality as well as Hamlet's inquisitiveness and

---

[1]   *New York Times*, 12 May 2000.

Figure 10   David Tennant as Hamlet and Patrick Stewart as Claudius in the 2008 Royal Shakespeare Company production directed by Gregory Doran (© Robbie Jack / Corbis / Getty Images)

playfulness: in the graveyard scene, Lester 'treated the swivelling skull as if it were a ventriloquist's dummy'.[1] The RSC's 2008 high-profile, modern-dress production featured David Tennant, best known at the time for playing the Time Lord in the popular BBC television show *Dr Who*. Tennant's smooth, elegant Hamlet crumpled to

---

[1]   *The Guardian*, 22 August 2000.

the floor while considering 'to be or not to be', but he was ultimately 'more than up to his task, a man whose behavior ... marked him as the most exemplary member of a brilliant and cunning court circle'.[1]

Jude Law was a similar 'celebrity' Hamlet the following year at the Donmar Warehouse (and was praised for his moving presentation of 'moody solitude and moral disgust' and his commitment to a death-wish).[2] In 2015, Lyndsey Turner directed Benedict Cumberbatch as an alternately exuberant and deeply thoughtful – though never paralysed – prince. The production opened not on the ramparts but with Hamlet, alone, looking through a family picture album; for the scene with the Players, he cheerfully wore the costume of a toy soldier and manned a toy castle.

The RSC's 2017 production, with a set-design of oil-cloths painted with brightly coloured graffiti, featured a predominantly black cast; the young Paapa Essiedu played Hamlet as 'young, quick-witted, and ... sportive'.

Figure 11   Benedict Cumberbatch as Hamlet at the Barbican, London, 2015 (© Johann Persson / ArenaPAL)

---

[1] *Shakespeare Bulletin* 26.4 (2008), 119.   [2] *The Guardian*, 3 June 2009.

Figure 12   Paapa Essiedu as Hamlet at the Royal Shakespeare Theatre, Stratford-upon-Avon, 2016 (courtesy of the Royal Shakespeare Company)

The prize for most ambitious undertaking may belong to members of Shakespeare's Globe who, under the direction of Dominic Dromgoole, took the play on a worldwide journey from 2014 to 2016, with final performances in London at the Globe to coincide with the 400th anniversary of Shakespeare's death.

Dromgoole's vision was to visit every country on the planet with a spare company (sixteen actors and technicians) and a lean, original-practices version meant to honour both the plot and the situation of the characters. (When conditions did not allow entry, as with Syria, the company performed in refugee camps; they were unable to go to North Korea.) The tour represents a triumph of planning and perseverance fed by a deep love for the play and a sense of its mystery.[1]

AROUND THE GLOBE

Hamlet, of course, is shaped by fictive as well as real travelling performers. Hamlet's one delight is the visit of the touring 'tragedians of the city', and Shakespeare's knowledge of Elsinore and the castle, scholars believe, comes from information he could have gleaned from fellow players, including Will Kemp, who played there in the 1580s with Leicester's Men.[2] The journal of William Keeling, captain of the East India Company's *Red Dragon*, records a performance by English sailors off the coast of Sierra Leone as early as 1607.[3] And English players had *Hamlet* in their repertory for performance on the continent by 1626, when it was performed in Dresden.[4] But *Hamlet*'s role as an object of intercultural exchange quickly developed beyond these instances of early touring. Over time, the play has become a part of national and regional performance traditions, engaging actors' and audiences' most pressing moral and political convictions.

This is especially true in Germany; *Hamlet* has long occupied a significant place in the German cultural landscape. It was staged first by touring English players, followed by a considerably shortened – to the point of burlesque – German prose version of the play, *Der Bestrafte Brudermord oder Prinz Hamlet aus Dannemark* (commonly translated as *Fratricide Punished*).[5] Performed by a German company who toured with it between 1660 and 1690, *Der Berstrafte* follows roughly the plot of Shakespeare's work but with curious differences of its own invention: its Ophelia, for instance, shows her madness after her father's death by chasing another courtier. Over the course of the nineteenth century, Shakespeare was seen by Germans as one of their national poets; *Hamlet* in particular 'occupied a central position in German national discourse'.[6] It was thus available for different kinds of theatrical and political uses, as Wilhelm Hortmann so thoroughly demonstrates in *Shakespeare on the German Stage*. A provocative instance of political experimentation was Leopold Jessner's 1926 Berlin production which, in the wake of the First World War, aimed to present

---

[1] Dominic Dromgoole, *Hamlet Globe to Globe: Two Years, 190,000 Miles, 197 Countries, One Play* (New York: Grove Press, 2017).

[2] See Dollerup, *Denmark*, 177–80.

[3] Though see Bernice Kliman, who believes the letter is a forgery: 'At Sea About *Hamlet* at Sea: A Detective Story', *SQ* 62.2 (2011), 180–204.

[4] See E. K. Chambers, *The Elizabethan Stage* (Oxford: Clarendon Press, 1923), II: 286; Jerzy Limon, *Gentlemen of a Company: English Players in Central and Eastern Europe, c. 1590 – c. 1660* (Cambridge University Press, 1985), 22.

[5] Bullough prints the text, VII: 128–58. It was first published in its entirety in 1781.

[6] Peter W. Marx, "Challenging the Ghosts: Leopold Jessner's *Hamlet*', *Theatre Research International* 30.1 (2005), 78.

Figure 13   The Mousetrap scene, Berlin, 1926, directed by Leopold Jessner (courtesy of Theaterwissenschaftliche Sammlung, University of Cologne)

what Jessner considered the 'essence' of the play, the rottenness of Denmark (and not the melancholy of the prince).[1] All aspects of the production's design were meant to reinforce this vision and its potential to critique both the pre-war imperial and the post-war Weimar regimes. It culminated in the set for the Mousetrap scene, which included elaborate boxes for Claudius and Gertrude that mirrored the real interior of the Staatstheater.

During the Third Reich, Hamlet was portrayed as the 'fair-haired Saxon son of a brave Nordic prince'.[2] After the Second World War, such treatment was countered, in both West and East Germany, from a variety of angles. Some performances were characterized by a 'calculated aestheticism', with stage designs, for instance, modelled on Renaissance painting. Others challenged the play's humanist themes as well as its canonical status in German culture – one, for instance, was set in a circus tent.[3] Thomas Ostermeier's 2008 Berlin production offers a striking 21st-century treatment of such a challenge, offering a darkly comic version, bordering at times on the anarchic. The performance opened with 'to be or not to be' announced over a loudspeaker, as a video of Hamlet's head was projected onto a screen hung in the middle of the stage.

[1] Hortmann, *Shakespeare on the German Stage*, 58–9.   [2] Bevington, *Murder Most Foul*, 150.
[3] Hortmann, *Shakespeare on the German Stage*, 300; Maik Hamburger, 'Shakespeare on the Stages of the German Democratic Republic', in Hortmann, 410–13.

Figure 14   Sebastian Schwarz as Horatio/Gueldenstern, Lars Eidinger as Hamlet, and Robert Beyer
as Polonius/Osrik in the 2008 Schaubuehne Berlin production directed by Thomas Ostermeier
(Lieberenz / Ullstein Bild / Getty Images)

(Hamlet would go on to videotape a number of later scenes, adding fresh dimensions to
the play's concerns with surveillance and introspection.) The set was constructed
around a pit of soil-turned-to-mud, which served as a kind of omnipresent graveyard
and into which Hamlet flopped during the second scene. A rolling platform provided
space above the mud, where the banquet and other court scenes unfolded. A cast of only
six actors made the doubling of roles especially intense; perhaps most remarkable, the
same actor played both Gertrude (with a blond wig and sunglasses) and Ophelia, turning
the two women into one another on stage in the same way Hamlet does in his mind and
speech. Lars Eidinger, who played the prince in a fat suit and attempted to rape Ophelia
during the nunnery scene, was deliberately un-classical, a 'nasty Hamlet whose energy
and aggression [were] almost perversely fascinating'.[1]

Russia has had a similarly extensive engagement with the play: 'Not only has *Hamlet*
been the most popular and influential of Shakespeare's plays in Russia; its hero, more
than any other literary figure, has captured the imagination of the Russian people.'[2]
The play was performed in St Petersburg as early as 1750. The collaboration between
Gordon Craig and Konstantin Stanislavski for the Moscow Art Theatre in 1912 was,

[1] John Rouse, 'Jurgen Gosch's *The Seagull* and Thomas Ostermeier's *Hamlet* in Berlin, Dec. 2008',
     Western European Theatre 2 (2009), 11.
[2] Eleanor Rowe, *Hamlet: A Window on Russia* (New York University Press, 1976), viii.

Figure 15 Innokenti Smoktunovsky as Hamlet in the 1964 film *Hamlet*, directed by Grigori Kozintsev (Sovfoto / Universal Images Group / Getty Images)

as we observed above, a signature moment in the history of the play's performance, announcing its affiliation with trends in both theatrical abstraction and psychological realism. In 1954, Grigori Kozintsev directed a production in Leningrad (now St Petersburg again) using a translation by the novelist Boris Pasternak; his film version of 1964 advanced his vision of a Hamlet beset by external sources and for whom thinking itself was an act of political resistance.[1]

At the beginning of the film, Hamlet, played by Innokenti Smoktunovsky, races on horseback up rocky sea-side slopes to Elsinore; after he greets his mother, the iron gates of the castle are shut like a prison. The opulent but uninviting interior teems with people; Hamlet moves among the crowds silently while his 'How weary' soliloquy is delivered as a voice-over. The Ghost appears on the ramparts in armour, huge, majestic, and terrifying. He towers over Hamlet, but his voice is a poignant whisper, even when he intones 'O horrible, horrible'. Hamlet never explicitly adopts an 'antic disposition', which shifts the play's interpretive focus away from the protagonist's psychic conflict and towards his political clash with the new guardians of power in Elsinore.

[1] *Ibid.*, 154.

Kozintsev's political *Hamlet* was widely influential across the globe, including in the post-colonial Arab world.[1] As Margaret Litvin has discussed in her important book, *Hamlet's Arab Journey*, in the second half of the twentieth century Arab artists and audiences found in *Hamlet* a crucial model for engaging with the challenges of political agency. The introspective but also anti-tyrannical Hamlet 'encapsulates a debate coeval with and largely constitutive of modern Arab identity: the problem of self-determination and authenticity'. Since the middle of the twentieth century, then, a wide range – a 'kaleidoscope' – of *Hamlet*s has appeared on the Arab stage, presenting the play in ways that accommodated various political needs and aspirations. Mohamed Sobhi's production, first staged in 1971 and filmed in 1977, offered Hamlet as a 'visionary activist, a fighter for justice', whose goals were communal as well as personal.[2] The production starts where the script ends, with Hamlet's dead body borne in a funeral procession; we thus know the conclusion and can concentrate on the causal logic that brought it to pass. Hamlet displays fearlessness as well as shock and anger in his interview with the Ghost, and he demonstrates suspicion of, as well as cruelty towards, Ophelia in the nunnery scene, glancing towards stage doors and pillars looking for spies. A version of the 'to be or not to be' soliloquy, with Hamlet holding Yorick's skull, is moved to the end of the play, so that it seems to express not doubt so much as conviction.

Hamlet's extensive global reach makes a full survey impossible for any Introduction. But one additional regional tradition commands our attention here: performance in Helsingor, Denmark, at Kronborg Castle, the sixteenth-century fortress noted by English travellers and on which Shakespeare's Elsinore is based. The play was staged around the castle precincts for the first time in 1816, in a Danish translation, in honour of the 200th anniversary of Shakespeare's death. A century later it was performed by actors from Copenhagen, but this time on the castle's ramparts. The performers, in other words, knew that they could exploit the castle's imposing architecture in order to accentuate the play's sense of foreboding, danger, and mystery. International companies have continued to do this over the last century, using either the courtyard or the precincts to give the sense that Denmark really is a prison.[3] As Ralph Berry suggests, at Kronborg the setting itself becomes 'a political fact of the first order. It radiates upon the play its own stage directions. The highlighted words in the text become living realities close to the actors' space . . . The play is made for the castle.'[4]

ADAPTATIONS

Part of the performance history of *Hamlet* is the history of *Hamlet* adaptation – that is, the reworking of elements of the play's characters or plots into fresh fictions. These new pieces diverge from, at the same time as they hark back to, their source, allowing authors

[1] Margaret Litvin, *Hamlet's Arab Journey: Shakespeare's Prince and Nasser's Ghost* (Princeton University Press, 2011), 10, 77–9. See also her blog 'Arab Shakespeare': http://arabshakespeare.blogspot.com.
[2] Litvin, *Hamlet's Arab Journey*, 36.
[3] See Niels Bugge Hansen, 'Be As Ourself in Denmark: *Hamlet* in Performance at Kronborg Castle, Elsinore', *Angles on the English Speaking World*, 10 (1997): 5–16.
[4] Ralph Berry, 'Hamlet's Elsinore Revisited', *Contemporary Review*, 279.1631 (2001), 365.

Figure 16 *Al-Hamlet Summit* – Sulayman Al Bassam as Hamlet, Mariam Ali as Ophelia, Nicolas Daniel as Claudius, 2005, Kronborg Castle, Elsinore/Helsingor, Denmark; director: Sulayman Al Bassam (courtesy of SABAB Theatre)

and actors to channel the concerns – as well as to capitalize on the cultural authority – of the tragedy to speak to their own interests. The long trajectory of *Hamlet* adaptations could be said to reach back to *The Revenger's Tragedy*; it certainly includes Victorian burlesques such as *Hamlet Travestie* (1849), *A Thin Slice of Ham let!* (1863), and *Hamlet Revamped: A Travesty Without a Pun* (1879). In the twentieth and early twenty-first centuries, it embraces an even wider range of revisions. They include Tom Stoppard's tour-de-force *Rosencrantz and Guildenstern Are Dead* (1967), a blend of Shakespeare and Samuel Beckett that both pays homage to and mocks the canonicity of the model play. They also include Charlotte Jones's *Humble Boy* (2001), as well as the multi-media experiments of Robert La Page's *Elsinore* (1995), Robert Wilson's *Hamlet: A Monologue*, and Peter Brook's *Qui Est Là*. Adaptation is not limited to the Anglo-American world. Heiner Muller's *Hamletmachine* (1977), a radical reconceptualizing that sought to eliminate any vestiges of the heroic from the play, has proven especially influential. More recently, Sulayman Al Bassam's *Al-Hamlet Summit* uses the architecture of the play to create a dynamic, cross-cultural investigation of geopolitics and terrorism, 'show[ing] the inevitable consequences of an alliance between native Arab despotism and the economic machinations of the West'.[1] In it, Ophelia becomes perhaps the most radical and violent of all the characters.

[1] Graham Holderness, 'Introduction', in Sulayman Al Bassam, *Al-Hamlet Summit* (Hatfield: University of Hertfordshire Press, 2006), 19.

Indeed, other adaptations have reframed the play entirely from Ophelia's perspective and with a sense of her potential for insight and action. These include Jean Betts's *Ophelia Thinks Harder* (1993), Kim Kwang-bo's *Ophelia: Sister Come to My Bed* (1995), and Ujin Sakuram's *Ophelia-Noh*, for the Koh Lo Sha company, which debuted at the Shakespeare Festival at Kronborg Castle in 2017.

WOMEN AS HAMLET

These latter, feminist adaptations serve as a reminder of the crucial performance choices demanded of Ophelia and Gertrude: choices about Gertrude's maternal relationship to Hamlet, her complicity with Claudius, her intentions when taking the poisoned cup at the play's end, and choices about Ophelia's collaboration with her father, her intimacy with Hamlet, her disintegration into madness. It is also worth emphasizing the presence of women directors of the play, from Buzz Goodbody, whose signature use of the small studio space of the RSC's The Other Place for her production of *Hamlet* was lauded in 1975, to Lyndsey Turner, who used the cavernous setting of the Barbican to great effect in 2015.

Of special interest is the tradition of women playing Hamlet. The gender of the prince perplexes even the prince, who rails at what he perceived to be his feminine – whorish – grief and inaction. From its inception, then, the character – alternately thoughtful and aggressive, meditative and energetic – has been a challenge to rigid gender assumptions and paradigms, a creature whose femininity may be part of his masculinity, or whose complicated impulses may defy categories entirely. Cross-casting, as Tony Howard explains in his indispensable account *Women as Hamlet*, intensifies these concerns:

Women who take the role pose recurrent questions. Is Hamlet a 'universal' figure whose dilemmas everyone shares, male or female? Is Hamlet a 'female' character whose words invite a woman's voice? What is the relation between Shakespeare's all-male theatre and the conventions that have succeeded it? How may the sexual and state politics of an English Renaissance play relate to the time and place of its reenactment?[1]

The tradition begins with Charlotte Clarke, who played an 'explicitly oppositional and carnivalesque' prince in the first half of the eighteenth century, and it extends across centuries and countries as female actors responded to the appeal of the role. Sarah Siddons, who performed the role throughout Great Britain (though not in London) in the late eighteenth century was 'mold-breaking', according to Howard, in that she 'prioritis[ed] an androgyny not of the eroticized body but of the mind'. By the mid-nineteenth century, female Hamlets were 'common' in the United States; Charlotte Cushman (who had already played Gertrude) was especially remarked for eliminating melodramatic effects and 'stress[ing] the painful intensity of the bond between mother and bereaved child'.[2]

---

[1] Howard, *Women as Hamlet*, 9.   [2] *Ibid.*, 36, 39, 48.

Figure 17 Sarah Bernhardt as Hamlet in the 1900 film directed by Clément Maurice (Bettmann / Getty Images)

When the renowned French actor Sarah Bernhardt addressed the role at the turn of the twentieth century, there had been some fifty travesti performances in England and abroad (including France, Italy, Austria, and Germany).

But Bernhardt's vision for her Hamlet was the most encompassing: she produced and directed, as well as played the lead role in, the French production. And she did so not only with the belief that women are better suited for the role but also with the deliberate intent to challenge the 'Hamletism' of nineteenth-century Romantic

Figure 18   Angela Winkler as Hamlet and Evia Mattes as Gertrude at the Royal Lyceum Theatre, Edinburgh, 2000 (© Clive Barda / ArenaPAL)

princes, in favour of a 'determined avenger whose roots were to be found in the Elizabethan theater'.[1] The production debuted in Paris and then toured England, including London and Stratford, exciting audiences with Bernhardt's dignified and intellectual Hamlet, who was bold when meeting with the Ghost and tender when dealing with Ophelia in the nunnery scene. Her portrayal of Hamlet's death, by falling back into Horatio's arms, was 'instantly famous'.[2] A century later, Angela Winkler was heralded for her performance in a German production; her Hamlet seemed designed for the new century, an 'emotionally raw and unprotected' prince whose child-likeness was tinged with a sense of the anarchic.

Winkler thus embodied Howard's striking description of the travesti Hamlet, in which 'the paradoxes and dissident intensities of Hamlet's beliefs and language become sharper through the figure of an actress/prince whose very presence exposes artifice ... The female Hamlet is a walking, speaking alienation effect'.[3] Not unlike this strange and wonderful play itself.

[1] Gerda Taranow, *The Bernhardt Hamlet* (New York: Peter Lang, 1996), xvii.
[2] Howard, *Women as Hamlet*, 108.   [3] *Ibid.*, 5.

NOTE ON THE TEXT

The basis of the modernised text given in this edition is fully discussed in the Textual Analysis, pp. 253–72. The section concludes with a summary of the argument and an explanation of some features and principles of the present text.

The collation confines itself almost entirely to recording the significant variations between Q2 and F, and to giving the source of all readings which do not derive from Q2 or F. In every case the reading of the present text is given first, followed by its source. Readings from the 'bad' Q1 are given when their agreement (or disagreement) with Q2 or F is of importance. The readings of seventeenth-century texts other than Q1, Q2, and F, and later editorial emendations not accepted in the present edition, are not normally recorded.

Hamlet
Prince of Denmark

LIST OF CHARACTERS

HAMLET, *Prince of Denmark*
CLAUDIUS, *King of Denmark, Hamlet's uncle*
GERTRUDE, *Queen of Demark, Hamlet's mother*
GHOST *of Hamlet's father, the former King of Denmark*
POLONIUS, *counsellor to the king*
LAERTES, *his son*
OPHELIA, *his daughter*
REYNALDO, *his servant*
HORATIO, *Hamlet's friend and fellow-student*
MARCELLUS
BARNARDO } *Officers of the watch*
FRANCISCO
VOLTEMAND } *ambassadors to Norway*
CORNELIUS
ROSENCRANTZ } *former schoolfellows of Hamlet*
GUILDENSTERN
FORTINBRAS, *Prince of Norway*
CAPTAIN *in the Norwegian army*
First PLAYER
Other PLAYERS
OSRIC
LORD } *courtiers*
GENTLEMAN
First CLOWN, *a gravedigger and sexton*
Second CLOWN, *his assistant*
SAILOR
MESSENGER
PRIEST
English AMBASSADOR
LORDS, ATTENDANTS, SAILORS, SOLDIERS, GUARDS

SCENE: *The Danish royal palace at Elsinore*

Notes

A list of 'The Persons Represented' (omitting the First Player) first appeared in the Players' Quarto of 1676.

GERTRUDE   So spelt in F. Normally Gertrard in Q2. See 'Names', 278.

POLONIUS   Concerning the change to Corambis or Corambus in stage performance, see 'Names', 270–1.

OFFICERS OF THE WATCH   Barnardo and Franciso are introduced as 'sentinels'(1.1.0 SD), and Francisco is called is called ' honest soldier' (1.1.16). But, although
Hamlet seems on friendlier terms with Marcellus than Barnardo (1.2.165–7), Horatio
calls them both 'gentlemen' (1.2.196).

PLAYERS   A minimum of four players in all is required, or three if 'Lucianus' also
speaks the prologue (3.2.130–2).

HAMLET
PRINCE OF DENMARK

[1.1] *Enter* BARNARDO *and* FRANCISCO, *two sentinels*

BARNARDO Who's there?
FRANCISCO Nay answer me. Stand and unfold yourself.
BARNARDO Long live the king!
FRANCISCO Barnardo?
BARNARDO He.   5
FRANCISCO You come most carefully upon your hour.
BARNARDO 'Tis now struck twelve, get thee to bed Francisco.
FRANCISCO For this relief much thanks, 'tis bitter cold
      And I am sick at heart.
BARNARDO Have you had quiet guard?
FRANCISCO   Not a mouse stirring.   10
BARNARDO Well, good night.
      If you do meet Horatio and Marcellus,
      The rivals of my watch, bid them make haste.
FRANCISCO I think I hear them.

            Enter HORATIO *and* MARCELLUS

                    Stand ho! Who is there?
HORATIO Friends to this ground.
MARCELLUS   And liegemen to the Dane.   15
FRANCISCO Give you good night.
MARCELLUS   Oh farewell honest soldier,
      Who hath relieved you?

Act 1, Scene 1   1.1] *Actus Primus. Scœna Prima.* F; *no indication in* Q2   1 Who's] F; Whose Q2   14 SD] *Adams; follows make haste in* Q2, F   14 Stand ho] Q2; Stand F   14 Who is] Q2; who's F   16 soldier] F; souldiers Q2

Act 1, Scene 1
  0 SD The sentinels enter from opposite sides of the stage. Barnardo is relieving Francisco. The action is to be seen taking place on the 'platform' (1.2.213; 1.2.251), a high terrace or battlement for mounting guns and keeping watch.
  2 Nay answer me Francisco, the sentinel on duty, should give the challenge, not the newcomer.
  2 unfold yourself reveal who you are.
  13 rivals partners.
  15 ground territory, country.
  15 liegemen sworn followers.
  15 the Dane the Danish king: compare 1.2.44 and 5.1.225.

FRANCISCO   Barnardo hath my place.
    Give you good night.   *Exit Francisco*
MARCELLUS   Holla, Barnardo!
BARNARDO   Say,
    What, is Horatio there?
HORATIO   A piece of him.
BARNARDO Welcome Horatio, welcome good Marcellus.   20
MARCELLUS What, has this thing appeared again tonight?
BARNARDO I have seen nothing.
MARCELLUS Horatio says 'tis but our fantasy,
    And will not let belief take hold of him
    Touching this dreaded sight, twice seen of us.   25
    Therefore I have entreated him along
    With us to watch the minutes of this night,
    That if again this apparition come
    He may approve our eyes, and speak to it.
HORATIO Tush, tush, 'twill not appear.
BARNARDO   Sit down awhile,   30
    And let us once again assail your ears,
    That are so fortified against our story,
    What we two nights have seen.
HORATIO   Well, sit we down,
    And let us hear Barnardo speak of this.
BARNARDO Last night of all,   35
    When yond same star that's westward from the pole

---

17 hath my] Q2; ha's my F 18–19 Say … there] *as one line* Q2, F 21 MARCELLUS] F, Q1; *Hora.* Q2 33 two nights have seen] F; haue two nights seene Q2, Q1

---

18 Give i.e. God give.
18 SD Exit Francisco The character has no further part in the play.
18–19 Say, / What, They are calling to each other in the supposed darkness, and these are excla-mation-words. They must not be taken to indicate Barnardo's surprise, since he is expecting Horatio.
19 A piece of him He is so cold he is not wholly himself.
21 What … tonight? Both F and Q1 give this line to Marcellus, strong indication that it was so spoken on the stage. Q2 assigns it to Horatio.

21 thing creature – without implying contempt.
23 fantasy imagination.
25 dreaded awful, fearsome.
26 along to come along.
27 watch … night keep watch for the period of this night.
29 approve our eyes confirm that we saw correctly.
33 What With what (following 'assail').
36 pole pole star.

Had made his course t'illume that part of heaven
Where now it burns, Marcellus and myself,
The bell then beating one –

Enter GHOST

MARCELLUS Peace, break thee off. Look where it comes again.   40
BARNARDO In the same figure, like the king that's dead.
MARCELLUS Thou art a scholar, speak to it Horatio.
BARNARDO Looks a not like the king? Mark it Horatio.
HORATIO Most like. It harrows me with fear and wonder.
BARNARDO It would be spoke to.
MARCELLUS   Question it Horatio.   45
HORATIO What art thou that usurp'st this time of night,
          Together with that fair and warlike form
          In which the majesty of buried Denmark
          Did sometimes march? By heaven I charge thee speak.
MARCELLUS It is offended.
BARNARDO   See, it stalks away.   50
HORATIO Stay! Speak, speak, I charge thee speak!

                                              Exit Ghost

MARCELLUS 'Tis gone and will not answer.
BARNARDO How now Horatio? you tremble and look pale.
          Is not this something more than fantasy?
          What think you on't?   55
HORATIO Before my God, I might not this believe
          Without the sensible and true avouch
          Of mine own eyes.

---

43 it] F, Q1; a Q2   44 harrows] F; horrowes Q2; horrors Q1   45 Question] F, Q1; Speake to Q2

---

37 illume illuminate. Shakespeare seems to have coined this word, and he does not use it elsewhere.

39 beating striking ('tolling' Q1).

41 figure shape, form.

42 scholar Horatio is learned enough to know how to address a spirit.

43 a he. This representation of an informal slurred pronunciation (ə) of the pronoun, presumed to derive from Shakespeare's MS, is retained in this text, in spite of occasional difficulties for the modern reader (see note to 3.3.73). F normally sophisticates 'a' to 'he', but here reads 'it' – with a gain in consistency, since everyone refers to the apparition as 'it'.

44 harrows deeply disturbs (breaks up with

a harrow).

46 usurp'st wrongfully takes over.

47 Together with The spirit is also appropriating the form of the old king.

48 buried Denmark the dead king of Denmark. This customary figure of speech (synecdoche) is very common in the play, emphasizing the interdependence of king and kingdom.

49 sometimes formerly.

50 stalks moves with a stately stride. Compare 66 below. *OED v*[1] c notes that 'stalk' is often used in connection with ghosts.

57 sensible sensory.

57 avouch warrant. The word as a noun is not recorded elsewhere.

MARCELLUS   Is it not like the king?

HORATIO As thou art to thyself.

          Such was the very armour he had on   60
          When he th'ambitious Norway combated;
          So frowned he once, when in an angry parle
          He smote the sledded Polacks on the ice.
          'Tis strange.

MARCELLUS Thus twice before, and jump at this dead hour,   65
          With martial stalk hath he gone by our watch.

HORATIO In what particular thought to work I know not,
          But in the gross and scope of mine opinion
          This bodes some strange eruption to our state.

MARCELLUS Good now sit down, and tell me he that knows,   70
          Why this same strict and most observant watch
          So nightly toils the subject of the land,
          And why such daily cast of brazen cannon,
          And foreign mart for implements of war,
          Why such impress of shipwrights, whose sore task   75
          Does not divide the Sunday from the week.
          What might be toward, that this sweaty haste
          Doth make the night joint-labourer with the day?
          Who is't that can inform me?

HORATIO   That can I –
          At least the whisper goes so. Our last king,   80
          Whose image even but now appeared to us,

---

61 he] Q2; *not in* F   61 th'] F; the Q2   63 sledded] F; sleaded Q2, Q1   63 Polacks] *Malone;* pollax Q2, Q1; Pollax F; Poleaxe F4   65 jump] Q2, Q1; iust F   68 mine] Q2; my F, Q1   73 why] F; with Q2   73 cast] F; cost Q2, Q1

61 **Norway** King of Norway.
62 **parle** parley. Properly a conference during a truce, but here seemingly used to mean an altercation leading to violence.
63 **sledded Polacks** Both Q1 and Q2 read 'sleaded pollax'; F reads 'sledded Pollax'. It is a celebrated question whether this refers to a poleaxe (often spelt 'pollax') or Polacks (= people of Poland, Poles). If the word is 'poleaxe', then the passage means that King Hamlet, during a heated exchange (with Norwegians?), struck his fighting axe on the ice. But it is then very dubious what 'sleaded' or 'sledded' can mean. It seems more likely that Horatio is talking of two encounters, one with Norwegians and one with Poles. In the second, in a confrontation, or after an angry exchange, he routed the Poles in their sledges. Julie Maxwell provides accounts and woodcuts of fighting on the ice in

'Counter-Reformation Versions of Saxo: A New Source for Hamlet?' *RQ* 57.2 (2004), 518–60.
65 **jump** precisely.
66 **martial stalk** See 50 above. The actor has to achieve a solemnity of movement that is both military and spectral.
67–8 **In what particular … opinion** i.e. I don't know in which particular area to concentrate my thoughts (in order to explain this) but, taking a wide view, so far as I can judge …
69 **eruption** disturbance, outbreak of war, or calamity.
70 **Good now** Please you.
72 **toils the subject** wearies the people with labour.
74 **foreign mart** bargaining abroad.
75 **impress** conscription.
77 **toward** in preparation, afoot.

Was as you know by Fortinbras of Norway,
Thereto pricked on by a most emulate pride,
Dared to the combat; in which our valiant Hamlet –
For so this side of our known world esteemed him –   85
Did slay this Fortinbras; who by a sealed compact,
Well ratified by law and heraldy,
Did forfeit (with his life) all those his lands
Which he stood seized of, to the conqueror;
Against the which a moiety competent   90
Was gagèd by our king, which had returned
To the inheritance of Fortinbras
Had he been vanquisher; as by the same comart
And carriage of the article design,
His fell to Hamlet. Now sir, young Fortinbras,   95
Of unimprovèd mettle hot and full,
Hath in the skirts of Norway here and there
Sharked up a list of landless resolutes
For food and diet to some enterprise
That hath a stomach in't; which is no other,   100

87 heraldy] Q2; Heraldrie F   88 those] F; these Q2   89 of] Q2; on F   91 returned] return'd F; returne Q2
93 comart] Q2; Cou'nant F   94 design] designe F; desseigne Q2; design'd F2   98 landless] Landlesse F; lawelesse
Q2; lawelsse Q1

83 **emulate pride** A sense of self-esteem which made him strive to equal and outdo others; 'emulate' as adjective is not recorded elsewhere.

86 **Did slay this Fortinbras** This was thirty years before. See 5.1.121, 138.

86 **sealed** i.e. agreed, confirmed.

87 **ratified by law and heraldy** sanctioned by law and the code of chivalry ('heraldy' is a less familiar form than 'heraldry').

89 **stood seized of** was the legal owner of (i.e. his personal estates were the forfeit, not his dominions as king).

90 **moiety competent** adequate portion.

91 **gagèd** pledged.

93–4 **as by … article design** as by the same compact and the intention of the agreement drawn up. The phrase is difficult. 'comart' (Q2) is a nonce-word having something to do with 'bargain' (compare 74), 'article' is probably an item in an agreement, hence 'stipulation' or 'condition', 'design' is usually

emended to 'designed'.

96 **unimprovèd mettle** undisciplined spirit. Shakespeare's only use of 'unimproved'.

98 **Sharked up** Gathered together indiscriminately, as the predatory shark swallows its prey.

98 **list** an assemblage or band of soldiers. (Compare 'the army list', or 'on the active list'; to enlist is to join such a band.)

98 **landless** So F, suggesting an army of disinherited gentry and younger sons who have nothing better to do. Q2 and Q1 read 'lawless', making Fortinbras's men a group of criminals.

99–100 **For food … stomach in't** The resolutes are prepared to enlist in return for their keep only, because they are attracted to an adventurous enterprise: 'diet' = 'diet-money', living expenses. The enterprise has 'stomach' in two senses: it provides the resolutes with their real nourishment, and it is bold and spirited.

As it doth well appear unto our state,
But to recover of us by strong hand
And terms compulsatory those foresaid lands
So by his father lost. And this, I take it,
Is the main motive of our preparations,   105
The source of this our watch, and the chief head
Of this post-haste and romage in the land.
[BARNARDO I think it be no other but e'en so.
Well may it sort that this portentous figure
Comes armèd through our watch so like the king   110
That was and is the question of these wars.
HORATIO A mote it is to trouble the mind's eye.
In the most high and palmy state of Rome,
A little ere the mightiest Julius fell,
The graves stood tenantless and the sheeted dead   115
Did squeak and gibber in the Roman streets;
As stars with trains of fire, and dews of blood,
Disasters in the sun; and the moist star,
Upon whose influence Neptune's empire stands,
Was sick almost to doomsday with eclipse.   120
And even the like precurse of feared events,
As harbingers preceding still the fates
And prologue to the omen coming on,
Have heaven and earth together demonstrated

---

101 As] Q2; And F   103 compulsatory] Q2; Compulsatiue F   107 romage] Romage F; Romeage Q2 *(uncorrected);* Romadge Q2 *(corrected)*   108–25] Q2; *not in* Q   115 tenantless] Q 1611; tennatlesse Q2   121 feared] *Ridley, conj.* Collier; feare Q2; fearce Q 1611

101 **our state** the Danish government.

103 **compulsatory** Pronounced 'compúlsat'ry': there is not much to choose between this reading (Q2) and F's 'compulsative'. Neither word is recorded in *OED* before this.

107 **romage** commotion and bustle, especially with relation to loading a ship's cargo (usually spelt 'rummage').

108–25 See Textual Analysis, 259.

109 **sort** be accordant with (Horatio's explanation).

111 **question** cause of dispute.

112 **A mote … eye** Like an irritant in the eye, it disturbs and perplexes the mind.

113–20 The portents preceding the assassination of Caesar had been extensively used by Shakespeare in the early acts of *Julius Caesar*.

113 **palmy** triumphant. No previous occurrence recorded in *OED*.

116 **gibber** utter inarticulate sounds. The word is another form of 'jabber'.

117–18 **As stars … sun** Either the beginning or the end of this is missing.

118 **Disasters** Portents of disaster. (Etymologically, the word implies evil astral influence.)

118 **the moist star** the moon.

120 **almost to doomsday** almost as if it were the day of judgement.

121 **precurse** advance warning (that which runs ahead). *OED* has no other example of this word.

122 **harbingers** Officials who went ahead of the king to announce his approach.

123 **omen** Used here for the calamity itself.

Unto our climatures and countrymen.]   125

Enter GHOST

But soft, behold, lo where it comes again!
I'll cross it though it blast me. Stay, illusion.

It spreads his arms

If thou hast any sound or use of voice,
Speak to me.
If there be any good thing to be done   130
That may to thee do ease, and grace to me,
Speak to me.
If thou art privy to thy country's fate,
Which happily foreknowing may avoid,
Oh speak.   135
Or if thou hast uphoarded in thy life
Extorted treasure in the womb of earth,
For which they say you spirits oft walk in death, *The cock crows*
Speak of it. Stay and speak! Stop it Marcellus.

MARCELLUS Shall I strike at it with my partisan?   140
HORATIO Do if it will not stand.

BARNARDO   'Tis here.

HORATIO   'Tis here.

MARCELLUS 'Tis gone.

Exit Ghost

We do it wrong being so majestical

---

127 SD] Q2; *not in* F; *He spreads his arms* Q 1676   138 you] F; *your* Q2   138 SD] Q2; *not in* F   140 strike at] F; strike Q2   142 SD] F; *not in* Q2

125 **climatures** regions (an unusual variant of 'climates').

126 **soft** enough! See note on 3.1.88.

127 **cross it** cross its path (or make the sign of the cross for protection).

127 SD *It spreads his arms* 'his' for 'its' is normal in Shakespeare (compare 5.2.90–1, 'put your bonnet to his right use'). A gesture by the Ghost, as prelude to the speech he never makes, could be extremely effective.

128–38 'Horatio shows a scholar's knowledge in his enumeration of the causes that send ghosts back to earth' (Kittredge).

134 **happily** haply, perhaps.

136 **uphoarded** hoarded up.

137 **Extorted** Obtained by unfair means.

140 **partisan** A long-handled weapon combining spear and axe.

143 **being so majestical** since it has such majesty. This is the accepted sense, and editors therefore normally put commas round the phrase. They thus make Marcellus give two separate reasons why they are wrong to offer violence: (1) the majesty of the Ghost; (2) its invulnerability. It may however be *they* who are being 'majestical' (= imperious) in offering violence: 'We do wrong to a ghost to be so overbearing as to offer it violence, because it is immaterial.'

To offer it the show of violence,
For it is as the air invulnerable,   145
And our vain blows malicious mockery.
BARNARDO It was about to speak when the cock crew.
HORATIO And then it started like a guilty thing
Upon a fearful summons. I have heard,
The cock, that is the trumpet to the morn,   150
Doth with his lofty and shrill-sounding throat
Awake the god of day; and at his warning,
Whether in sea or fire, in earth or air,
Th'extravagant and erring spirit hies
To his confine. And of the truth herein   155
This present object made probation.
MARCELLUS It faded on the crowing of the cock.
Some say that ever 'gainst that season comes
Wherein our Saviour's birth is celebrated,
This bird of dawning singeth all night long,   160
And then, they say, no spirit dare stir abroad,
The nights are wholesome, then no planets strike,
No fairy takes, nor witch hath power to charm,
So hallowed and so gracious is that time.
HORATIO So have I heard, and do in part believe it.   165
But look, the morn in russet mantle clad
Walks o'er the dew of yon high eastward hill.
Break we our watch up, and by my advice
Let us impart what we have seen tonight
Unto young Hamlet, for upon my life   170
This spirit, dumb to us, will speak to him.

150 morn] Q2; day F; morning Q1   158 say] Q2; sayes F   160 This] Q2; The F, Q1   161 dare stir] dare sturre Q2; can walke F; dare walke Q1   163 takes] Q2; talkes F   164 that] Q2; the F   167 eastward] Q2; Easterne F

146 **malicious mockery** a mockery or empty show of the malice we intend.
150 **trumpet** trumpeter.
152 **the god of day** In classical mythology, Phoebus Apollo.
154 **extravagant and erring** wandering beyond bounds (the original meanings of these words).
155 **confine** (1) one's own special territory, (2) a place of confinement. Both meanings are present here. See also 2.2.236.

156 **probation** proof.
158 **'gainst** just before.
161 **dare stir** See Textual Analysis, 275.
162 **strike** i.e. affect with their malign influence.
163 **takes** attacks, lays hold (*OED* v 7).
164 **gracious** full of grace.
166 **the morn** In a few minutes of acting time, we have moved from deepest midnight to the dawn.
166 **russet** The name of a coarse cloth worn by country people, and also its colour, a neutral reddish-brown.

Do you consent we shall acquaint him with it,
As needful in our loves, fitting our duty?
MARCELLUS Let's do't I pray, and I this morning know
Where we shall find him most conveniently.   *Exeunt*   175

1.2 *Flourish. Enter* CLAUDIUS *King of Denmark,* GERTRUDE *the Queen,*
HAMLET, POLONIUS, LAERTES, OPHELIA, [VOLTEMAND, CORNE-
LIUS,] LORDS *attendant*

CLAUDIUS Though yet of Hamlet our dear brother's death
          The memory be green, and that it us befitted
          To bear our hearts in grief, and our whole kingdom
          To be contracted in one brow of woe,
          Yet so far hath discretion fought with nature   5
          That we with wisest sorrow think on him,
          Together with remembrance of ourselves.
          Therefore our sometime sister, now our queen,
          Th'imperial jointress to this warlike state,
          Have we, as 'twere with a defeated joy,   10
          With one auspicious and one dropping eye,

---

175 conveniently] F, Q1; conuenient Q2   **Act 1, Scene 2**   **1.2**] *Scena Secunda* F   **0 SD**] *Florish. Enter Claudius, King of Denmarke, Gertrad the Queene, Counsaile: as Polonius, and his Sonne Laertes, Hamlet, Cum Alijs.* Q2; *Enter Claudius King of Denmarke, Gertrude the Queene, Hamlet, Polonius, Laertes, and his Sister Ophelia, Lords Attendant.* F   **8** sometime] Q2; sometimes F   **9** to] Q2; of F   **11** one ... one] F; an ... a Q2

Act 1, Scene 2

0 SD This SD combines elements from both Q2 and F. See Textual Analysis, 265–7, 277. F includes Ophelia, absent from Q2, although she has no speaking part. Q2's 'Counsaile: as' (? for 'Councillors') has by some been taken to indicate a formal meeting of the Danish council, which is highly implausible. A second omission in Q2 is the ambassadors, Voltemand and Cornelius. These are given a very awkward entry in F, half-way through Claudius's speech (25). Q2 puts Hamlet as the last in the train.

4 contracted ... woe drawn together in a single mourning visage.

7 Together ... ourselves Being also mindful of ourselves.

9 jointress A wife who shares certain property with her husband, and continues her rights in it

after his death. It is not clear whether Claudius is referring to Gertrude's share of the crown with her former husband or with himself. The word, in apposition to 'now our queen' and 'to rule this state with me', is used metaphorically, to convey their collaboration, and not in a proper legal sense. See Clarkson and Warren, *The Law of Property in Shakespeare* (Baltimore, MD: Johns Hopkins University Press, 1942), 81–4.

11 With one auspicious and one dropping eye 'auspicious': looking happily to the future; 'dropping': cast down with grief, or possibly dropping tears. Beatrice White found the genesis of this 'contradictory facial expression' in descriptions of the false and fickle goddess Fortune, and argued that the saying 'to cry with one eye and laugh with the other' became a standard phrase for hypocrisy

With mirth in funeral and with dirge in marriage,
In equal scale weighing delight and dole,
Taken to wife; nor have we herein barred
Your better wisdoms, which have freely gone   15
With this affair along – for all, our thanks.
Now follows that you know: young Fortinbras,
Holding a weak supposal of our worth,
Or thinking by our late dear brother's death
Our state to be disjoint and out of frame,   20
Colleaguèd with this dream of his advantage,
He hath not failed to pester us with message
Importing the surrender of those lands
Lost by his father, with all bands of law,
To our most valiant brother. So much for him.   25
Now for ourself and for this time of meeting
Thus much the business is: we have here writ
To Norway, uncle of young Fortinbras,
Who, impotent and bed-rid, scarcely hears
Of this his nephew's purpose, to suppress   30
His further gait herein, in that the levies,
The lists, and full proportions, are all made
Out of his subject; and we here dispatch
You, good Cornelius, and you, Voltemand,
For bearers of this greeting to old Norway,   35
Giving to you no further personal power
To business with the king, more than the scope

---

17 follows] Q2; followes, F   17 know:] *Dowden, conj. Walker;* know Q2; F   21 this] Q2; the F   24 bands] Q2; bonds F   35 bearers] Q2; bearing F

and inconstancy. 'To an Elizabethan … an indication of duplicity would have been at once apparent' (*Anglia* 77 (1959), 204–7). The reading of F, adopted here, is less likely to be a sophistication than Q's is to be a misreading.

13 dole grief.

14 Taken to wife See note to 1.2.157.

15 Your better wisdoms Your excellent wisdoms, or, perhaps, the best fruits of your wisdoms.

17 that you know what you already know.

18 supposal supposition, conjecture.

20 Our state to be disjoint and out of frame Claudius acknowledges, but dismisses, the possibility of political and social disorder.

21 Colleaguèd … advantage Having as an ally this illusion of a favourable opportunity.

24 bands agreements binding a person. F gives the alternative form 'bonds'.

29 impotent helpless, incapacitated.

31 gait i.e. proceedings.

32 lists See note to 1.1.98.

32 proportions given numbers of troops raised for specific purposes.

33 his subject those inhabitants who are subject to him. Compare the use of the collective singular in 1.1.72.

Of these dilated articles allow.
Farewell, and let your haste commend your duty.

CORNELIUS }
VOLTEMAND }   In that and all things will we show our duty.   40

CLAUDIUS We doubt it nothing, heartily farewell.
                              Exeunt Voltemand and Cornelius
And now Laertes, what's the news with you?
You told us of some suit, what is't Laertes?
You cannot speak of reason to the Dane
And lose your voice. What wouldst thou beg Laertes,   45
That shall not be my offer, not thy asking?
The head is not more native to the heart,
The hand more instrumental to the mouth,
Than is the throne of Denmark to thy father.
What wouldst thou have Laertes?   50

LAERTES   My dread lord,
Your leave and favour to return to France,
From whence though willingly I came to Denmark
To show my duty in your coronation,
Yet now I must confess, that duty done,
My thoughts and wishes bend again toward France,   55
And bow them to your gracious leave and pardon.

CLAUDIUS Have you your father's leave? What says Polonius?

POLONIUS He hath my lord wrung from me my slow leave
By laboursome petition, and at last
Upon his will I sealed my hard consent.   60
I do beseech you give him leave to go.

CLAUDIUS Take thy fair hour Laertes, time be thine,
And thy best graces spend it at thy will.
But now my cousin Hamlet, and my son —

---

38 dilated] F; delated Q2   40 CORNELIUS/VOLTEMAND] *Cor. Vo.* Q2; *Volt.* F   41 SD] F; *not in* Q2   50 My dread] Q2; Dread my F   55 toward] Q2; towards F   58 He hath] F; Hath Q2   58–60 wrung ... consent] Q2; *not in* F

38 **dilated** amply expressed. Q2's 'delated' is a spelling variant.
  44 **the Dane** the Danish king.
  45 **lose your voice** speak to no avail.
  46 **not thy asking** rather than thy asking.
  47 **native** naturally related.
  51 **Your leave and favour** The favour of your permission.
  56 **pardon** permission.

58–60 **wrung ... consent** Missing in F but recorded, with variations, in Q1.
  60 **Upon ... consent** I gave my reluctant agreement to his strong wish; 'sealed' suggests official or legal approval (compare 1.1.86).
  63 **thy best ... will** Claudius hopes that in enjoying himself Laertes will be exercising his best qualities.

HAMLET (*Aside*) A little more than kin, and less than kind.   65
CLAUDIUS How is it that the clouds still hang on you?
HAMLET Not so my lord, I am too much i'th'sun.
GERTRUDE Good Hamlet cast thy nighted colour off,
             And let thine eye look like a friend on Denmark.
             Do not forever with thy vailèd lids   70
             Seek for thy noble father in the dust.
             Thou know'st 'tis common, all that lives must die,
             Passing through nature to eternity.
HAMLET Ay madam, it is common.
GERTRUDE   If it be,
             Why seems it so particular with thee?   75
HAMLET Seems madam? nay it is, I know not seems.
             'Tis not alone my inky cloak, good mother,
             Nor customary suits of solemn black,
             Nor windy suspiration of forced breath,
             No, nor the fruitful river in the eye,   80
             Nor the dejected haviour of the visage,
             Together with all forms, moods, shapes of grief,
             That can denote me truly. These indeed seem,
             For they are actions that a man might play,
             But I have that within which passes show –   85
             These but the trappings and the suits of woe.
CLAUDIUS 'Tis sweet and commendable in your nature Hamlet,
             To give these mourning duties to your father;
             But you must know, your father lost a father,

---

65 *Aside*] *Theobald³; not in* Q2, F   67 Not so] F; Not so much Q2   67 i'th'sun] F; in the sonne Q2   68 nighted] Q2; nightly F   70 vailèd] Q2; veyled F   77 good] F; coold Q2   82 shapes] Q 1611; chapes Q2; shewes F   83 denote] F; deuote Q2   85 passes] Q2; passeth F

65 **A little ... kind** To call me 'son' is more than our actual kinship warrants; and there is less than the natural, favourable feelings of such a relationship between us. In this riddling aside, there is a play on the two meanings of 'kind': (1) belonging to nature, particularly to natural relationships; and (2) affectionate, benevolent.

67 **Not so ... sun** So F. Modern editors reject Q2's first 'much' but keep Q2's expanded form 'in the sun'. The Q2 compositors regularly expand contractions and syncopes which seem genuinely Shakespearean. In this case, the contraction is not only necessary for the metre, but also helps the quibble (i'th'sun; o'th'son).

68 **nighted colour** i.e. the darkness of both clothes and mood.

69 **Denmark** the king.

70 **vailèd lids** lowered eyes.

78 **customary** conventional.

79 **suspiration** sighing.

82 **moods** emotional states as outwardly displayed.

82 **shapes** external appearances. See note to 1.4.43.

85 **passes** So Q2. F reads 'passeth'; the presence of the older -th form in what is by and large a modernizing text is an argument for considering the F reading very carefully; 'passes show' is much easier to say. Either reading could be the original.

87 **commendable** The main accent falls on the first and not the second syllable.

That father lost, lost his, and the survivor bound   90
In filial obligation for some term
To do obsequious sorrow; but to persever
In obstinate condolement is a course
Of impious stubbornness, 'tis unmanly grief,
It shows a will most incorrect to heaven,   95
A heart unfortified, a mind impatient,
An understanding simple and unschooled.
For what we know must be, and is as common
As any the most vulgar thing to sense,
Why should we in our peevish opposition   100
Take it to heart? Fie, 'tis a fault to heaven,
A fault against the dead, a fault to nature,
To reason most absurd, whose common theme
Is death of fathers, and who still hath cried,
From the first corse till he that died today,   105
'This must be so.' We pray you throw to earth
This unprevailing woe, and think of us
As of a father, for let the world take note
You are the most immediate to our throne,
And with no less nobility of love   110
Than that which dearest father bears his son,
Do I impart toward you. For your intent
In going back to school in Wittenberg,
It is most retrograde to our desire,

---

96 a mind] F; or minde Q2   112 toward] Q2; towards F   114 retrograde] F; retrogard Q2

---

92 Scan 'Tŏ dŏ obséqŭious sórrŏw; bŭt
tŏ perséver'; 'obsequious' = relating to obsequies
(funeral rites or ceremonies) for the dead, thus
implying dutifulness.

93 **condolement** grief, mourning.

95 **incorrect to heaven** improperly directed as
regards heaven.

99 **As ... sense** As the most ordinary thing that
affects our senses.

101–2 **fault** wrongdoing, transgression (a stronger sense than in modern English).

105 **the first corse** A biblical allusion that
Claudius confuses. He tries to invoke the first dead
father, but the 'first corse' of Genesis is a murdered
brother, Abel, killed by his envious brother Cain.

107 **unprevailing** ineffective.

109 **the most immediate to our throne** i.e.
the next in succession. The monarchy being elective, not hereditary, Claudius, the most important
member of an electoral college, here gives his 'voice'
to Hamlet as his heir. Compare Hamlet's own
words at 5.2.335.

112 **impart toward you** convey to you.
The phrase is an unusual intransitive usage of
'impart', but the implied object is either the gift of
Claudius's vote or his love.

113 **to school** i.e. his studies.

113 **Wittenberg** The University of Wittenberg,
founded in 1502. Famous in Elizabethan England as
the university of Luther and thus the seat of
European Protestantism. The audience would also
have recognized it as the home of Dr Faustus.

114 **retrograde** contrary.

And we beseech you bend you to remain   115
Here in the cheer and comfort of our eye,
Our chiefest courtier, cousin, and our son.
GERTRUDE Let not thy mother lose her prayers Hamlet.
    I pray thee stay with us, go not to Wittenberg.
HAMLET I shall in all my best obey you madam.   120
CLAUDIUS Why, 'tis a loving and a fair reply.
    Be as ourself in Denmark. Madam, come.
    This gentle and unforced accord of Hamlet
    Sits smiling to my heart, in grace whereof,
    No jocund health that Denmark drinks today   125
    But the great cannon to the clouds shall tell,
    And the king's rouse the heaven shall bruit again,
    Re-speaking earthly thunder. Come away.

Flourish. Exeunt all but Hamlet

HAMLET O that this too too solid flesh would melt,
    Thaw and resolve itself into a dew,   130
    Or that the Everlasting had not fixed
    His canon 'gainst self-slaughter. O God, God,

---

119 pray thee] Q2; prythee F   127 heaven] Q2; Heauens F   128 SD] Q2; *Exeunt / Manet Hamlet.* F   129 solid] F;
sallied Q2, Q1   132 self] F; seale Q2   132 O God, God] Q2; O God, O God F

115 **bend you to** incline yourself to.
125 **Denmark** Once again, the king is meant.
127 **rouse** ceremonial drink, or toast. Compare
1.4.8–9.
127 **bruit** loudly proclaim (echoing the cannon).
129 **solid** So F. Q2 reads 'sallied'. Q1 has 'too
much griev'd and sallied flesh', which has been used
by editors to defend both F and Q2. 'sallied' is
usually emended to 'sullied', defiled. The evidence
is in 2.1.39, where Q2 has 'sallies' and F 'sulleyes',
and *Love's Labour's Lost* 5.2.352, 'unsallied'. Sallied
can also be understood as 'assailed' or 'advanced
upon'.

The case for 'sullied' emphasizes Hamlet's sense
of his body's contamination, while the case for
'solid' emphasizes Hamlet's sense of his body's
permanence or intractability.
132 **canon 'gainst self-slaughter** There seems
to be no biblical injunction specifically against suicide. But centuries of religious and legal commentary explained it as a type of murder (self-murder)
or as an expression of sinful despair, and thus contrary to divine, natural, and civil law. See
Introduction, 41–2.

How weary, stale, flat and unprofitable
Seem to me all the uses of this world!
Fie on't, ah fie, 'tis an unweeded garden   135
That grows to seed, things rank and gross in nature
Possess it merely. That it should come to this!
But two months dead – nay not so much, not two –
So excellent a king, that was to this
Hyperion to a satyr, so loving to my mother   140
That he might not beteem the winds of heaven
Visit her face too roughly – heaven and earth,
Must I remember? why, she would hang on him
As if increase of appetite had grown
By what it fed on, and yet within a month –   145
Let me not think on't; frailty, thy name is woman –
A little month, or ere those shoes were old
With which she followed my poor father's body
Like Niobe, all tears, why she, even she –
O God, a beast that wants discourse of reason   150
Would have mourned longer – married with my uncle,
My father's brother, but no more like my father
Than I to Hercules – within a month,
Ere yet the salt of most unrighteous tears
Had left the flushing in her gallèd eyes,   155
She married. Oh most wicked speed, to post
With such dexterity to incestuous sheets.

133 weary] F; wary Q2   134 Seem] Q2; Seemes F   135 ah fie] Q2; Oh fie, fie F   137 to this] F; thus Q2   143 would] F; should Q2   149 she, even she] F; she Q2   150 God] Q2; Heauen F   151 my] Q2; mine F   155 in] Q2, Q1; of F

133 **flat** lifeless, spiritless. Compare 4.7.31.

134 **uses** customs, practices.

137 **merely** absolutely.

140 **Hyperion** One of the Titans; frequently identified, as here, as the sun-god.

140 **satyr** Grotesque mythological creature, half-human half-goat, attendant on Dionysus, and associated with lechery and hedonism.

141 **beteem** allow. (The context insists on this meaning, but it is a strained usage of a rare word; see *OED*.)

147 **or ere** even before. Both words mean 'before', so the phrase 'or ere', 'or e'er', 'or ever' (see 1.2.183) is an intensification.

147 **those shoes were old** The new shoes Gertrude had worn for her husband's funeral were so little used as to be wearable for her marriage to Claudius.

149 **Niobe** In classical mythology, the mother of fourteen children who were slain by Apollo and Artemis after Niobe boasted about them. A well-

recognized symbol of maternal grief, she wept until she turned to stone, after which the stone continued weeping.

150 **discourse of reason** faculty of reasoning.

153 **Hercules** In classical mythology, the greatest of Greek heroes, best known for his completion of a cycle of seemingly impossible Labours.

155 **left ... eyes** (1) gone from the redness of her sore eyes, (2) ceased flowing in her sore eyes. The meaning of 'flushing' is uncertain here, and it is therefore difficult to choose between 'flushing in' (Q2, Q1) and 'flushing of' (F).

157 **incestuous** Marriage to a brother's wife – or, following Hamlet's logic here, marriage to a husband's brother – was explicitly forbidden by the Church. See the 'Table of Kindred and Affinity' in the Book of Common Prayer and its basis in Lev. 20.21. But Shakespeare's audience would have been familiar with a famous breach of this principle that was part of their own national history: Henry VIII had been given

It is not, nor it cannot come to good.
But break, my heart, for I must hold my tongue.

Enter HORATIO, MARCELLUS *and* BARNARDO

HORATIO Hail to your lordship.
HAMLET   I am glad to see you well.   160
Horatio – or I do forget myself.
HORATIO The same, my lord, and your poor servant ever.
HAMLET Sir, my good friend, I'll change that name with you.
And what make you from Wittenberg, Horatio?
Marcellus.   165
MARCELLUS My good lord.
HAMLET I am very glad to see you. (*To Barnardo*) Good even sir.
But what in faith make you from Wittenberg.
HORATIO A truant disposition, good my lord.
HAMLET I would not hear your enemy say so,   170
Nor shall you do my ear that violence
To make it truster of your own report
Against yourself. I know you are no truant.
But what is your affair in Elsinore?
We'll teach you to drink deep ere you depart.   175
HORATIO My lord, I came to see your father's funeral.
HAMLET I pray thee do not mock me fellow student,
I think it was to see my mother's wedding.
HORATIO Indeed my lord, it followed hard upon.

---

170 hear] Q2; haue F   171 my] Q2; mine F   175 to drink deep] F; for to drinke Q2   177 pray thee] F; prethee Q2
(corrected); pre thee Q2 *(uncorrected)*, Q1   178 see] F; *not in* Q2

---

special dispensation by the Pope to marry his brother's widow, Catherine of Aragon (see the biblical justification in Deut. 25.5–6). His later inability to obtain from the Pope a dissolution of his marriage precipitated England's break with Rome, advancing the English Reformation.

159 break, my heart i.e. with unuttered grief. The heart was thought to be kept in place by ligaments or tendons (the heart-strings) which might snap under the pressure of great emotion.

160 I ... well He has not yet recognized Horatio.

163 change exchange.

163 that name i.e. 'good friend'.

164–76 what make you ... funeral Hamlet's repeated queries to Horatio about being away from Wittenberg at Elsinore seem to defy probability:

how is it possible that Hamlet and Horatio have not encountered each other at court during the last few weeks? But Horatio's part is full of inconsistencies; he has already shown that he knows more about the state of Denmark than the Danish soldiers, while in 5.1.191 he has to be told who Laertes is. The badinage between the friends is another opportunity for Hamlet to emphasize the unseemly proximity of funeral and wedding.

177 pray thee Q2's 'pre thee' (corrected to 'prethee') is probably copied from Q1's 'pre thee'. F's form more probably derives from manuscript copy. The pronunciation of all forms is probably 'prithee'.

179 upon Used here adverbially, as elsewhere in Shakespeare, with another adverb, to denote a nearness in time.

HAMLET Thrift, thrift, Horatio. The funeral baked meats   180
        Did coldly furnish forth the marriage tables.
        Would I had met my dearest foe in heaven
        Or ever I had seen that day, Horatio.
        My father, methinks I see my father –
HORATIO Where my lord?
HAMLET   In my mind's eye, Horatio.   185
HORATIO I saw him once, a was a goodly king.
HAMLET A was a man, take him for all in all.
        I shall not look upon his like again.
HORATIO My lord, I think I saw him yesternight.
HAMLET Saw? Who?   190
HORATIO My lord, the king your father.
HAMLET   The king my father!
HORATIO Season your admiration for a while
        With an attent ear, till I may deliver
        Upon the witness of these gentlemen
        This marvel to you.
HAMLET   For God's love let me hear.   195
HORATIO Two nights together had these gentlemen,
        Marcellus and Barnardo, on their watch
        In the dead waste and middle of the night,
        Been thus encountered. A figure like your father,
        Armèd at point exactly, cap-a-pe,   200

---

183 Or ever I had] Q2; Ere I had euer F; Ere euer I had Q1   185 Where] Q2, Q1; Oh where F   186 a] Q2; he
F   187 A] Q2; He F   190 Saw? Who?] F; saw, who? Q2, Q1   195 God's] Q2; Heauens F   198 waste] wast Q2, F;
vast Q1; waist *Malone*   200 at point exactly,] at poynt, exactly Q2; at all points exactly, F; to poynt, exactly Q1

181 **coldly** The remains of the pies baked for the
funeral were economically served cold for the wedding feast.

182 **dearest** closest, most severe, most
esteemed.

182–3 **Would I … that day** Hamlet suggests
that the worst fate he can imagine is meeting his
greatest enemy in heaven. Kittredge suspected
a proverbial saying. It is nevertheless characteristic
of Hamlet to wish his opponents to go to hell (see
3.3.93–5 and 5.2.47).

183 **Or ever** See note to 147.

186 **I saw him once** Horatio has already
implied (1.1.59–64) that he has greater knowledge
of Hamlet Sr than this line suggests. (See also 211

below.)

190 **Saw? Who?** All three early texts give some
kind of a pause between 'saw' and 'who'.

192 **Season** Make more temperate, restrain.

192 **admiration** wonder.

193 **attent** attentive.

198 **waste** Q2 and F read 'wast'; Q1 has 'vast',
and in view of *The Tempest*'s 'vast of night' some
editors (e.g. Dowden, Kittredge, Cambridge) adopt
it. Malone reads 'waist'. The desolation of 'dead
waste' is surely what is required here, though the
latent pun 'waist' no doubt suggested 'middle' and
is echoed in 2.2.220–6.

200 **at point exactly, cap-a-pe** properly and
correctly, from head to foot.

Appears before them, and with solemn march
Goes slow and stately by them. Thrice he walked
By their oppressed and fear-surprisèd eyes
Within his truncheon's length, whilst they, distilled
Almost to jelly with the act of fear,   205
Stand dumb and speak not to him. This to me
In dreadful secrecy impart they did,
And I with them the third night kept the watch,
Where, as they had delivered, both in time,
Form of the thing, each word made true and good,   210
The apparition comes. I knew your father,
These hands are not more like.

HAMLET   But where was this?

MARCELLUS My lord, upon the platform where we watched.

HAMLET Did you not speak to it?

HORATIO   My lord, I did,
But answer made it none. Yet once methought   215
It lifted up it head and did address
Itself to motion like as it would speak;
But even then the morning cock crew loud,
And at the sound it shrunk in haste away
And vanished from our sight.

HAMLET   'Tis very strange.   220

HORATIO As I do live my honoured lord 'tis true,
And we did think it writ down in our duty
To let you know of it.

HAMLET Indeed, indeed sirs, but this troubles me.
Hold you the watch tonight?

MARCELLUS ⎫
BARNARDO ⎬   We do, my, lord.   225

204 distilled] distil'd Q2; bestil'd F   209 Where, as] Where as Q 1637; Whereas Q2, F   213 watched] watcht F; watch Q2   224 Indeed, indeed] F, Q1; Indeede Q2   225, 6, 7 MARCELLUS/BARNARDO] Capell; All. Q2, Q1; Both. F

204 **distilled** dissolved.

205 **act** action.

207 **dreadful** awe-struck, terrified (referring to the men's manner and emotional state). Thompson and Taylor identify it as an objective adjective, defining 'secrecy' rather than the men's subjective experience.

213 **platform** See note to 1.1.0 SD.

213 **watched** were on watch. Q2's 'watch' makes the meaning 'normally keep the watch'.

216 **it head** its head. The normal possessive

form of 'it' was 'his' (see note to 1.1.127 SD) but 'it' is occasionally used by Shakespeare, and less frequently 'its'.

216–17 **address … speak** started to move as though it were about to speak.

225 The speech heading in Q2 is '*All.*', and in F, '*Both.*' Capell's choice of '*Both*', meaning Marcellus and Barnardo, fits best, since Horatio is not a member of the watch. (All the same, it is notable that Barnardo never turns up for duty. See 1.4.0 SD.)

HAMLET Armed say you?

MARCELLUS ⎫
BARNARDO ⎭   Armed my lord.

HAMLET   From top to toe?

MARCELLUS ⎫
BARNARDO ⎭ My lord, from head to foot.

HAMLET Then saw you not his face?

HORATIO Oh yes my lord, he wore his beaver up.

HAMLET What, looked he frowningly?   230

HORATIO A countenance more in sorrow than in anger.

HAMLET Pale, or red?

HORATIO Nay very pale.

HAMLET   And fixed his eyes upon you?

HORATIO Most constantly.

HAMLET   I would I had been there.

HORATIO It would have much amazed you.   235

HAMLET Very like, very like. Stayed it long?

HORATIO While one with moderate haste might tell a hundred.

MARCELLUS ⎫
BARNARDO ⎭ Longer, longer.

HORATIO Not when I saw 't.

HAMLET   His beard was grizzled, no?

HORATIO It was as I have seen it in his life,   240
       A sable silvered.

HAMLET   I will watch tonight,
       Perchance 'twill walk again.

HORATIO   I warrant it will.

HAMLET If it assume my noble father's person,
       I'll speak to it though hell itself should gape
       And bid me hold my peace. I pray you all,   245

---

236 Very like, very like] F, Q1; Very like Q2   238 MARCELLUS/BARNARDO] *Capell; Both.* Q2; *All.* F; *Mar.* Q1   239 grizzled] grissl'd   Q2; grisly F; grisleld Q1   241 I will] Q2, Q1; Ile F   242 walk] walke Q2, Q1; wake F   242 warrant] Q1; warn't Q2; warrant you F

229 beaver the movable visor; worn up, his face would be visible.

235 amazed bewildered, thrown into confusion.

239 grizzled grey. F has 'grizzly', which means the same thing. Q2's 'grissl'd' looks as though it may derive from Q1 ('grisleld').

241 sable silvered black touched with white.

243 assume take on. Hamlet thinks of the apparition as a spirit appearing in the guise of his father, though a few lines later he speaks of 'my father's spirit' (254).

244 hell … gape the mouth of hell should open wide.

245 bid … peace As Thompson and Taylor point out, Hamlet is ready to risk damnation (the result of having commerce with a devil) in order to speak to the Ghost.

If you have hitherto concealed this sight,
Let it be tenable in your silence still,
And whatsomever else shall hap tonight,
Give it an understanding but no tongue.
I will requite your loves. So fare you well: 250
Upon the platform 'twixt eleven and twelve
I'll visit you.

ALL   Our duty to your honour.

HAMLET Your loves, as mine to you. Farewell.

                                              Exeunt all but Hamlet

My father's spirit, in arms! All is not well.
I doubt some foul play. Would the night were come.   255
Till then sit still my soul. Foul deeds will rise
Though all the earth o'erwhelm them to men's eyes.   *Exit*

1.3 *Enter* LAERTES *and* OPHELIA *his sister*

LAERTES My necessaries are embarked, farewell.
And sister, as the winds give benefit
And convoy is assistant, do not sleep
But let me hear from you.

OPHELIA   Do you doubt that?

LAERTES For Hamlet, and the trifling of his favour,   5
Hold it a fashion, and a toy in blood,
A violet in the youth of primy nature,
Forward, not permanent, sweet, not lasting,
The perfume and suppliance of a minute,
No more.

OPHELIA   No more but so?

---

247 tenable] Q2; treble F   248 whatsomever] what someuer Q2; whatsoeuer F, Q1   250 fare] F; farre Q2   250 you] Q2; ye F   251 eleven] F; a leauen Q2   253 loves] Q2, Q1; loue F   253 SD] *Cambridge; Exeunt. (252)* Q2, F; *Exeunt. Manet Hamlet.* Q 1676   254 spirit, in arms!] spirit (in armes) Q2; Spirit in Armes? F   256 Foul] foule F; fonde Q2   Act 1, Scene 3   1.3] *Scena Tertia* F   0 SD *his sister*] Q2; *not in* F   1 embarked] imbark't F; inbarckt Q2; in barkt Q1   3 convoy is] F; conuay, in Q2   5 favour] Q2; fauours F   8 Forward] Q2; Froward F   9 perfume and] Q2; *not in* F

247 **tenable** something that can be held.
248 **whatsomever** A quite regular form, eventually ousted by 'whatsoever'.
255 **doubt** suspect. This is the first time Hamlet voices explicit suspicions about the circumstances of his father's death.

Act 1, Scene 3
1 **necessaries are embarked** luggage is on board the ship

3 **convoy is assistant** conveyance is at hand.
6 **a fashion** just a way of behaving.
6 **a toy in blood** a whim of passion.
7 **the youth … nature** the spring-time of life ('primy' seems to be a Shakespearean coinage).
9 **suppliance** supply (i.e. the violet serves for a minute only).

LAERTES   Think it no more.   10
For nature crescent does not grow alone
In thews and bulk, but as this temple waxes
The inward service of the mind and soul
Grows wide withal. Perhaps he loves you now,
And now no soil nor cautel doth besmirch   15
The virtue of his will; but you must fear,
His greatness weighed, his will is not his own,
For he himself is subject to his birth.
He may not, as unvalued persons do,
Carve for himself, for on his choice depends   20
The sanctity and health of this whole state,
And therefore must his choice be circumscribed
Unto the voice and yielding of that body
Whereof he is the head. Then if he says he loves you,
It fits your wisdom so far to believe it   25
As he in his peculiar sect and force
May give his saying deed, which is no further
Than the main voice of Denmark goes withal.
Then weigh what loss your honour may sustain

---

12 bulk] F; bulkes Q2   12 this] Q2; his F   16 will] Q2; feare F   18 For … birth] F; *not in* Q2   21 sanctity] F; safty Q2; sanity *Hanmer, conj. Theobald*   21 this whole] Q2; the weole F   26 peculiar sect and force] F; particular act and place Q2

11–14 For nature … withal Growing up is not a matter of physical size only: while the body grows, the inner life of mind and soul develops also ('thews' = sinews.)

15 soil stain.

15 cautel deceitfulness.

17 His greatness weighed If you consider his greatness.

20 Carve for himself i.e. serve his own interests.

21 sanctity So F. Q2 reads 'safty' and most editions read 'safety'. Theobald conjectured 'sanity' (= soundness of condition), which Wilson and others accept. 'Safety' is less forceful as well as metrically awkward (though it could be pronounced as a tri-

syllable (NV)). 'Sanctity' fits the rather fervent and excessive way in which Laertes speaks of everything, and it underscores the play's broader concern with the spiritual health of the kingdom after the death of Hamlet Sr and the remarriage of Gertrude to Claudius.

23 voice and yielding will and consent.

24 The line has thirteen syllables.

26 his peculiar sect and force the special circumstances of his class position and the power it affords him. So F. Q2's more widely adopted 'particular act and place' shares the concern with social hierarchy and the specific acts and roles associated with class status.

28 main voice general assent.

If with too credent ear you list his songs,   30
Or lose your heart, or your chaste treasure open
To his unmastered importunity.
Fear it Ophelia, fear it my dear sister,
And keep you in the rear of your affection,
Out of the shot and danger of desire.   35
The chariest maid is prodigal enough
If she unmask her beauty to the moon.
Virtue itself scapes not calumnious strokes.
The canker galls the infants of the spring
Too oft before their buttons be disclosed,   40
And in the morn and liquid dew of youth
Contagious blastments are most imminent.
Be wary then, best safety lies in fear:
Youth to itself rebels, though none else near.

OPHELIA I shall th'effect of this good lesson keep   45
As watchman to my heart. But good my brother,
Do not as some ungracious pastors do,
Show me the steep and thorny way to heaven,
Whiles like a puffed and reckless libertine
Himself the primrose path of dalliance treads,   50
And recks not his own rede.

LAERTES   Oh fear me not.

---

34 you in] Q2; within F   45 th'effect] F; the effect Q2   46 watchman] Q2; watchmen F   48 steep] steepe Q2 *(corrected)*, F; step Q2 *(uncorrected)*   49 Whiles] Q2; Whilst F   49 like] F; *not in* Q2   51 recks] Q1, Pope; reakes Q2; reaks F

30 **credent** believing.
30 **list** listen to.
31 **your chaste treasure** the treasure of your chastity.
32 **importunity** persistent solicitation (*Shakespeare's Words*).
34 **keep ... affection** A military metaphor; Ophelia is not to go so far forward as her affection might lead her.
35 **shot** range, shooting distance.
36–7 **The chariest ... moon** The most cautious maid goes almost too far, even if she does no more than reveal her beauty to the moon (associated with chastity).
36, 38, 39 Q2 marks these lines with inverted commas to identify them as 'sentences', or improving moral generalities – the 'saws of books' which Hamlet later disavows. For a discussion of this punctuation in both Q1 and Q2 as a feature of printed plays meant to mark them as 'literary', see Zachary Lesser, Peter Stallybrass, and G. K.

Hunter, 'The First Literary Hamlet and the Commonplacing of Plays', *SQ* 59.4 (2008), 371–420.
39 **canker** insect pest feeding on plants. (For the more general, figurative use, see 5.2.69.)
40 **buttons be disclosed** i.e. buds open out.
42 **blastments** blightings. *OED* records no other usages of this word, except late ones deriving from this.
44 **to itself rebels** 'acts contrary to its better nature' (Kittredge).
48, 50 **thorny way / primrose path** The image of two contrasting roads was one of the commonest ways of distinguishing a life of virtuous labour from one of pleasurable vice and voluptuousness. It was frequently pictured as 'the choice of Hercules', showing the hero making up his mind which path to follow. See E. Panofsky, *Hercules am Scheidewege* (Leipzig: Teubener, 1930).
51 **recks ... rede** pays no attention to his own counsel.

Enter POLONIUS

I stay too long – But here my father comes.
A double blessing is a double grace;
Occasion smiles upon a second leave.

POLONIUS Yet here Laertes? Aboard, aboard for shame!   55
The wind sits in the shoulder of your sail,
And you are stayed for. There, my blessing with thee,
And these few precepts in thy memory
Look thou character. Give thy thoughts no tongue,
Nor any unproportioned thought his act.   60
Be thou familiar, but by no means vulgar.
Those friends thou hast, and their adoption tried,
Grapple them unto thy soul with hoops of steel,
But do not dull thy palm with entertainment
Of each new-hatched, unfledged courage. Beware   65
Of entrance to a quarrel, but being in,
Bear't that th'opposèd may beware of thee.
Give every man thy ear, but few thy voice;

---

57 with thee] Q2, Q1; with you F   59 Look] Q2; See F   62 Those] Q2, Q1; The F   63 unto] Q2; to F   65 new-hatched] new hatcht Q2; vnhatch't F   65 courage] Q2, Q1; Comrade F   68 thy ear] Q2; thine eare F

---

54 Occasion … leave A second leave-taking is a fortunate occurrence. As with Ophelia's two paths (above), this is an emblem or moral picture; Occasion or Opportunity is shown as a goddess. See H. Green, *Shakespeare and the Emblem Writers*, 1870, 261–5.

55 aboard for shame! 'for shame' attached to an imperative (or a word of injunction) creates an admonition. Compare 'Doff it for shame!' *King John* 3.1.128. Most editors put a comma after 'aboard' as though 'for shame' were a separate exclamation and reproof.

59 character inscribe. Accent on second syllable.

61 but … vulgar i.e. but don't be familiar with everybody.

62 and … tried whose worthiness to be adopted you have tested.

64 dull thy palm make your hand insensitive. The handshake is seen as a sensitive gauge of true friendship.

65 courage So Q2 and Q1. F reads 'comrade', a much easier reading. Kittredge suggested 'comrague', or fellow-rogue, and this, or 'comrogue' has won some support. *OED* (1b), giving the main meaning of 'courage' as heart, spirit, disposition, says it can be used of a person (as we use both 'heart' and 'spirit'). So the word means a man of spirit, and no doubt could be used in a derogatory way: a dashing but empty fellow. The accent must fall on the second syllable.

67 Bear't that Manage it so that, conduct it so that.

Take each man's censure, but reserve thy judgement.
Costly thy habit as thy purse can buy,   70
But not expressed in fancy: rich, not gaudy.
For the apparel oft proclaims the man,
And they in France of the best rank and station
Are of a most select and generous chief in that.
Neither a borrower nor a lender be,   75
For loan oft loses both itself and friend,
And borrowing dulls the edge of husbandry.
This above all, to thine own self be true,
And it must follow, as the night the day,
Thou canst not then be false to any man.   80
Farewell, my blessing season this in thee.

LAERTES Most humbly do I take my leave, my lord.

POLONIUS The time invites you. Go, your servants tend.

LAERTES Farewell Ophelia, and remember well
    What I have said to you.

OPHELIA   'Tis in my memory locked,   85
    And you yourself shall keep the key of it.

LAERTES Farewell.

                                    Exit Laertes

POLONIUS What is't Ophelia he hath said to you?

OPHELIA So please you, something touching the Lord Hamlet.

POLONIUS Marry, well bethought.   90
    'Tis told me he hath very oft of late
    Given private time to you, and you yourself

---

70 buy] Q2 *(corrected)*, F; by Q2 *(uncorrected)*   74 Are] F; Or Q2   74 generous] F; generous, Q2; generall Q1   74 chief]
chiefe Q2, Q1; cheff F   75 be] F; boy Q2   76 loan] lone F; loue Q2   77 dulls the] F; dulleth Q2   83 invites] F; inuests
Q2

69 **censure** judgement (not necessarily adverse).

70 **habit** apparel, clothes.

74 **Are ... that** i.e. have an exquisite and noble gift in choosing the right clothes. Of particular difficulty in this much-discussed line is 'chief', which appears in F as 'cheff'. With some strain, we can take it as a noun meaning 'excellence'. Furness in NV deletes 'of a' so that 'chief' can be read as an adverb, i.e. the French nobility are 'select and generous' chiefly in terms of apparel.

77 **husbandry** thrift.

81 **season** bring to due season, ripen.

83 **invites** A number of editors, from Theobald on, have felt that Q's 'invests' could be justified (= lays siege to). It is certainly an odd word to come up as a misreading, and it ought to be preferred on the principle of 'the more difficult reading', but F's 'invites' seems obviously correct.

83 **tend** attend.

90 **Marry** By the Virgin Mary.

90 **well bethought** he did well to think of that.

Have of your audience been most free and bounteous.
If it be so, as so 'tis put on me,
And that in way of caution, I must tell you   95
You do not understand yourself so clearly
As it behooves my daughter, and your honour.
What is between you? Give me up the truth.

OPHELIA He hath my lord of late made many tenders
Of his affection to me.   100

POLONIUS Affection? Puh! You speak like a green girl,
Unsifted in such perilous circumstance.
Do you believe his tenders as you call them?

OPHELIA I do not know my lord what I should think.

POLONIUS Marry I'll teach you. Think yourself a baby   105
That you have tane these tenders for true pay,
Which are not sterling. Tender yourself more dearly,
Or – not to crack the wind of the poor phrase,
Roaming it thus – you'll tender me a fool.

OPHELIA My lord, he hath importuned me with love   110
In honourable fashion.

POLONIUS Ay, fashion you may call it. Go to, go to.

OPHELIA And hath given countenance to his speech, my lord,
With almost all the holy vows of heaven.

POLONIUS Ay, springes to catch woodcocks. I do know,   115
When the blood burns, how prodigal the soul

97 behooves] Q2; behoues F   105 I'll] Ile F; I will Q2   106 these] Q2; his F   107 sterling] Q2; starling
F   109 Roaming] F; Wrong Q2; Running *Dyce, conj. Collier*   113–14 my lord / With] / My Lord, with Q2, F   114
almost] Q2; *not in* F   115 springes] F; springs Q2

94 **put on me** given to me.
97 **behooves** becomes, befits.
97 **honour** Several ideas are bound up in this
word as it relates to Ophelia: it implies nobility,
integrity, virtue, and reputation – all of which are
tied up with her honesty or chastity.
99 **tenders** offers of anything for acceptance, gifts.
101 **green girl** young, fresh, immature girl.
Gullible may be implied as well, though *OED* dates
its first use in this way to 1605. Shakespeare's audience would have heard resonances of 'green-sickness',
an anaemic illness ascribed to female longing in love.
102 **Unsifted** Inexperienced (literally, not
strained through a sieve).
106 **tane** taken: the common shortened form of
the past participle. Modern editions usually give the
awkward and unhistorical spelling 'ta'en', which
wrongly suggests a two-syllable pronunciation.
107 **Tender yourself** Look after yourself, value
or esteem yourself, with the implication of caring
for her chastity.
109 **Roaming it** So F. Polonius implies that he
doesn't want to overuse or improperly extend the
phrase. The use of 'it' as the indefinite object of

a more-or-less intransitive verb is fully exemplified
in Wilhelm Franz, *Die Sprache Shakespeares* (Halle:
Max Niemeyer, 1939), 272. Most examples are of
noun-verbs; e.g. 'I will queen it no inch farther'
(*Winter's Tale* 4.4.449). But compare 'I come to
wive it wealthily in Padua' (*Shrew* 1.2.73). See
further in *OED* It 9. Q2's 'Wrong', if emended to
'Wronging' (see NV), fits the sense suggested for F.
But it may be the result of a compositor mistaking
w and *r*, which are easily confused in Elizabethan
handwriting. Or Shakespeare's 'rom͡íg' might have
been read as 'rong' (compare, *MSH*, 315–16).
109 **tender me a fool** present me [to the court]
as a fool. (Other interpretations include 'present
yourself as a fool to me' and Dowden's ingenious
idea, 'present me with an illegitimate baby'.)
Polonius thus completes the wordplay on 'tender',
a series of puns that assumes Ophelia's role as an
object of potential sexual exchange.
110 **importuned** Accent on second syllable.
112 **fashion** See line 6 above.
115 **springes** snares.
116–17 **blood burns … Lends** i.e. When passion
flares, the soul is lavish ('prodigal') in lending.

Lends the tongue vows. These blazes daughter,
Giving more light than heat, extinct in both
Even in their promise as it is a-making,
You must not take for fire. From this time 120
Be something ter of your maiden presence.
Set your entreatments at a higher rate
Than a command to parley. For Lord Hamlet,
Believe so much in him, that he is young
And with a larger tedder may he walk 125
Than may be given you. In few Ophelia,
Do not believe his vows, for they are brokers,
Not of that dye which their investments show,
But mere implorators of unholy suits,
Breathing like sanctified and pious bonds, 130
The better to beguile. This is for all:
I would not in plain terms from this time forth
Have you so slander any moment leisure
As to give words or talk with the Lord Hamlet.
Look to't I charge you. Come your ways. 135
OPHELIA I shall obey, my lord.

                                        Exeunt

---

117 Lends] Q2, Q1; Giues F   120 From] Q2; For F   120 time] Q2; time Daughter F   121 something] Q2; somewhat
F   123 parley] F; parle Q2   125 tedder] Q 1676; tider Q2; tether F   128 that dye] that die Q2; the eye F   129
implorators] F; imploratotors Q2   130 bonds] Q2, F; bawds *Pope*[2], *conj. Theobald*   131 beguile] F; beguide Q2

122–3 Set … parley The military metaphor
revolves around 'entreatments' (= negotiations),
into which Ophelia should not enter at
Hamlet's mere command. 'When a besieger
appears before the castle of your heart and summons you to a parley, do not immediately enter
into negotiations (*entreatments*) for surrender'
(Kittredge).
125 tedder A widely used alternative form of
'tether'.
126 In few In few words.
127 brokers negotiators, esp. go-betweens,
pimps.

128 investments vestments, robes. The brokers
wear the garments of dignitaries.
129 mere no less than, out-and-out.
129 implorators solicitors. *OED* records no
other occurrence of the word.
130 bonds agreements, contracts. Theobald's
emendation, 'bawds', has been widely followed,
because of the difficulty of imagining anyone
breathing like a bond. But 'Breathing' here means
'speaking'.
133 slander disgrace, misuse.
135 your ways This is an adverbial form, 'on
your way'. See Franz, *Die Sprache Shakespeares*, 219.

[1.4] *Enter* HAMLET, HORATIO *and* MARCELLUS

HAMLET The air bites shrewdly, it is very cold.
HORATIO It is a nipping and an eager air.
HAMLET What hour now?
HORATIO   I think it lacks of twelve.
MARCELLUS No, it is struck.
HORATIO Indeed? I heard it not. It then draws near the season   5
         Wherein the spirit held his wont to walk.
                  A flourish of trumpets and two pieces goes off
         What does this mean, my lord?
HAMLET The king doth wake tonight and takes his rouse,
         Keeps wassail, and the swaggering up-spring reels,
         And as he drains his draughts of Rhenish down,   10
         The kettle-drum and trumpet thus bray out
         The triumph of his pledge.
HORATIO   Is it a custom?
HAMLET Ay marry is't,
         But to my mind, though I am native here
         And to the manner born, it is a custom   15
         More honoured in the breach than the observance.
         [This heavy-headed revel east and west

Act 1, Scene 4   1.4] Scene IV *Capell; no indication in* Q2, F   1 shrewdly] F; shroudly Q2   1 it is] Q2; is it F   2 is a] F; is Q2   5 Indeed?] *Capell;* Indeede; Q2; Indeed F, Q1   5 It then] Q2; then it F   6 SD] Q2; *not in* F   9 wassail] wassell Q2; wassels F   14 But] Q2; And F, Q1   17–38 This heavy-headed ... scandal] Q2; *not in* F

Act 1, Scene 4

0 SD In this and the next scene, we return to the 'platform' of the first scene.

1 shrewdly keenly, injuriously. (The original meaning of 'shrewd' is 'malicious', 'ill-disposed'.)

2 eager sharp, biting. Compare 1.5.69.

3 lacks of i.e. is just short of.

6 held his wont had its custom.

6 SD *two pieces goes off* i.e. a salvo from two cannons is fired.

8 wake make a night-time celebration.

8–9 takes his rouse, / Keeps wassail More or less synonymous phrases for ceremonious carousal and wine-drinking.

9 swaggering up-spring reels The meaning is uncertain, 'up-spring' may be a German dance.

Jenkins argues that 'reel' means to dance riotously, and that the subject of the verb is Claudius, who dances the up-spring.

10 Rhenish Rhine wine.

10–12 And as ... pledge As the king had promised. See 1.2.124–8.

12 triumph Properly, a public celebration of an important event. Used ironically here.

12 pledge toast.

15 to the manner born i.e. accustomed to this behaviour since birth (with a likely play on manor).

16 More honoured ... observance i.e. The custom is best followed by not being practised.

17–38 For this passage's syntactical difficulties as well as its absence from F, see Textual Analysis, 259.

17 east and west everywhere (i.e. by other nations everywhere).

Makes us traduced and taxed of other nations.
They clepe us drunkards, and with swinish phrase
Soil our addition; and indeed it takes   20
From our achievements, though performed at height,
The pith and marrow of our attribute.
So, oft it chances in particular men,
That for some vicious mole of nature in them,
As in their birth, wherein they are not guilty,   25
Since nature cannot choose his origin,
By their o'ergrowth of some complexion,
Oft breaking down the pales and forts of reason,
Or by some habit that too much o'erleavens
The form of plausive manners – that these men,   30
Carrying I say the stamp of one defect,
Being nature's livery or fortune's star,
His virtues else be they as pure as grace,
As infinite as man may undergo,
Shall in the general censure take corruption   35
From that particular fault. The dram of eale
Doth all the noble substance of a doubt
To his own scandal.]

Enter GHOST

HORATIO   Look my lord, it comes!

19 clepe] Q 1637; clip Q2   23 So, oft] *Theobald*² ; So oft Q2   27 their] Q2; the *Pope*

18 traduced and taxed of slandered and cen-
sured by.
19 clepe call.
19–20 with swinish … addition pollute our
proper title or description ('addition') by calling us
pigs.
20–2 it takes … attribute our fondness for
drink robs the best of our achievements of the
very essence of the reputation due to us.
24 mole of nature natural mark, but with
a censorious slant: a natural blemish, fault.
26 his its.
27 their o'ergrowth of some complexion the
excessive development of a particular disposition.
The figure depends upon the doctrine of the four
humours, the bio-psychological theory of
Shakespeare's time that associated the body's fluids
(blood, phlegm, choler (yellow bile), and melancholy
(black bile)) with specific emotional states and tem-
peraments (sanguine, phlegmatic, choleric, and melancholic). Proper balance was necessary for health; an
'o'ergrowth' would imply mental and physical illness.

28 pales palisades, enclosures.
29 habit (here) a bad habit.
**29–30 too much o'erleavens … plausive
manners** As too much leaven in the dough will
ruin the bread, so too great an admixture of 'some
habit' will ruin the form of pleasing behaviour.
32 nature's livery nature's badge or token; nature's costume or uniform (*Shakespeare's Words*).
32 fortune's star a destiny falling to one by
chance. For 'star' in this transferred sense (cause
for effect), see *OED sv sb*¹ 3c which cites *Hamlet*
2.2.139, 'a prince out of thy star'.
34 undergo support.
36–8 dram of eale … scandal There is a long
history of efforts to solve the puzzle of these lines, the
'most famous [crux] of its kind in the whole
Shakespearian canon' (Wilson, 25). 'eale' is almost
certainly a misreading; 'of a doubt' can also be challenged as a printing error. But the underlying significance is clear, as it recapitulates the idea that has been
building throughout the passage: even a 'single blemish' (Theobald) ruins an otherwise virtuous character.

HAMLET Angels and ministers of grace defend us!
    Be thou a spirit of health, or goblin damned,   40
    Bring with thee airs from heaven or blasts from hell,
    Be thy intents wicked or charitable,
    Thou com'st in such a questionable shape
    That I will speak to thee. I'll call thee Hamlet,
    King, father, royal Dane. Oh answer me.   45
    Let me not burst in ignorance, but tell
    Why thy canonised bones, hearsèd in death,
    Have burst their cerements; why the sepulchre,
    Wherein we saw thee quietly enurned,
    Hath oped his ponderous and marble jaws   50
    To cast thee up again. What may this mean,
    That thou, dead corse, again in complete steel
    Revisits thus the glimpses of the moon,
    Making night hideous, and we fools of nature
    So horridly to shake our disposition   55
    With thoughts beyond the reaches of our souls?
    Say, why is this? wherefore? What should we do?
             Ghost beckons Hamlet
HORATIO It beckons you to go away with it,
    As if it some impartment did desire
    To you alone.
MARCELLUS   Look with what courteous action   60

---

42 intents] Q2; euents F   45 Oh] ô Q2, Q1; Oh, oh, F   49 enurned] F; interr'd Q2, Q1   56 the reaches] Q2; thee; reaches F   57 SD] F; *Beckins* Q2

40 spirit of health an uncorrupted spirit, bringing 'airs from heaven' (41) and 'charitable' intents (42).

40 goblin damned a demon, bringing 'blasts from hell' (41) and 'wicked' intents (42).

43 questionable shape The Ghost's 'shape' – its visible form or appearance – can be interrogated. But the adjective 'questionable' can also refer to the response the Ghost elicits from Hamlet, who has many questions for it (see Jonathan Hope, *Shakespeare's Grammar* (London: Thomson, 2003), 45, 1.2.2).

47 canonised consecrated. Accent on second syllable.

47 hearsèd coffined. Accent on first syllable. The line as a whole gets a strong rhythmic effect from disputing the underlying iambic structure; i.e. 'Why thy canónis'd bónes, heársèd iñ deáth.'

48 cerements grave-clothes. Pronounced seerments.

49 enurned So F ('enurn'd'). Some modern editions prefer Q2's 'interr'd', which also appears in Q1. '[U]rn' was often used loosely by Shakespeare and others to mean a grave, but the word is here not literal but metaphorical: the sepulchre envelops and encloses the body as though it were a funerary urn.

52 complete steel full armour ('cómplete').

53 glimpses pale gleams.

54 fools of nature natural creatures, limited in our understanding.

55 horridly … disposition to upset ourselves so violently.

59 impartment communication.

It wafts you to a more removèd ground.
But do not go with it.

HORATIO   No, by no means.

HAMLET It will not speak. Then I will follow it.

HORATIO Do not my lord.

HAMLET   Why, what should be the fear?
I do not set my life at a pin's fee,   65
And for my soul, what can it do to that,
Being a thing immortal as itself?
It waves me forth again. I'll follow it.

HORATIO What if it tempt you toward the flood my lord,
Or to the dreadful summit of the cliff   70
That beetles o'er his base into the sea,
And there assume some other horrible form
Which might deprive your sovereignty of reason,
And draw you into madness? Think of it.
[The very place puts toys of desperation,   75
Without more motive, into every brain
That looks so many fathoms to the sea
And hears it roar beneath.]

HAMLET It wafts me still. Go on, I'll follow thee.

MARCELLUS You shall not go my lord.

HAMLET   Hold off your hands.   80

HORATIO Be ruled, you shall not go.

HAMLET   My fate cries out,
And makes each petty arture in this body

---

61 wafts] F; waues Q2, Q1   63 I will] Q2; will I F, Q1   70 summit] *Rowe;* somnet Q2; Sonnet F   70 cliff] F; cleefe Q2   71 beetles] F; bettles Q2   72 assume] Q2, Q1; assumes F   75–8 The very ... beneath] Q2; *not in* F   79 wafts] F; waues Q2   80 off] F; of Q2   80 hands] Q2; hand F   82 arture] Q2; Artire F

61 **wafts** so F; it means the same as Q2's 'waves', which is probably derived from Q1. Compare *Timon* 1.1.70, '[W]afts Fortune with her ivory hand wafts to her'. '[W]afts' for Q2's 'waves' occurs again at 79, but both texts agree on 'waves' at 68.

65 **fee** payment; hence 'worth'.

69 **flood** sea.

71 **beetles o'er** overhangs like bushy eyebrows. As *OED* notes, Shakespeare coined the verb 'beetle' from a recollection of a passage in Sidney's *Arcadia*, Book 1, ch. 10, 'they past in a pleasant valley, (of either side of which high hils lifted up their beetle-

brows, as if they would over looke the pleasantness of their under-prospect)'.

73 **deprive ... reason** take away the sovereignty (supremacy) of your reason.

75–8 For a discussion of these four lines, found only in Q2, see Textual Analysis, 258–9.

75 **toys of desperation** whims of desperate behaviour (i.e. suicidal impulse).

81 **My fate cries out** My destiny is calling. That is, his future lies in what the Ghost has to tell him.

82 **arture** artery, thought to convey the vital spirits.

As hardy as the Nemean lion's nerve.
Still am I called. Unhand me gentlemen!
By heaven I'll make a ghost of him that lets me.   85
I say away! – Go on, I'll follow thee.

Exit Ghost and Hamlet

HORATIO He waxes desperate with imagination.
MARCELLUS Let's follow, 'tis not fit thus to obey him.
HORATIO Have after. To what issue will this come?
MARCELLUS Something is rotten in the state of Denmark.   90
HORATIO Heaven will direct it.
MARCELLUS   Nay let's follow him.

Exeunt

[**1.5**] *Enter* GHOST *and* HAMLET

HAMLET Whither wilt thou lead me? Speak, I'll go no further.
GHOST Mark me.
HAMLET   I will.
GHOST   My hour is almost come
        When I to sulph'rous and tormenting flames
        Must render up myself.
HAMLET   Alas poor ghost!
GHOST Pity me not, but lend thy serious hearing   5
        To what I shall unfold.
HAMLET   Speak, I am bound to hear.
GHOST So art thou to revenge, when thou shalt hear.
HAMLET What?
GHOST I am thy father's spirit,
        Doomed for a certain term to walk the night,   10

---

87 imagination] F; imagion Q2   **Act 1, Scene 5**   1.5] Scene V *Capell; no indication in* Q2, F   1 Whither] Whether Q2;
Where F; whither Q1

83 **Nemean lion** Hercules's first Labour was to
kill the terrible Nemean lion. Pronounced Né-me-
an.
   83 **nerve** sinew.
   85 **lets** hinders.
   87 **waxes … imagination** has become totally
reckless with agitated thought.
   89 **Have after** Let us go after him.
Act 1, Scene 5
   6 **bound** all prepared. The word came to be

used for proceeding in a certain direction, as in
'homeward bound'. The Ghost in his reply puns
on the word's other meaning of 'obliged' or
'compelled'.
   10–20 The Ghost makes clear in these lines that
he is an inhabitant of Purgatory, the third realm of
the afterlife where souls are punished for, and
purged of, sins for which they did not atone satis-
factorily on earth. Protestants rejected its
existence.

And for the day confined to fast in fires,
Till the foul crimes done in my days of nature
Are burnt and purged away. But that I am forbid
To tell the secrets of my prison house,
I could a tale unfold whose lightest word   15
Would harrow up thy soul, freeze thy young blood,
Make thy two eyes like stars start from their spheres,
Thy knotted and combinèd locks to part
And each particular hair to stand an end
Like quills upon the fretful porpentine.   20
But this eternal blazon must not be
To ears of flesh and blood. List, list, oh list!
If thou didst ever thy dear father love –

HAMLET O God!

GHOST Revenge his foul and most unnatural murder.   25

HAMLET Murder?

GHOST Murder most foul, as in the best it is,
But this most foul, strange, and unnatural.

HAMLET Haste me to know't, that I with wings as swift
As meditation or the thoughts of love   30
May sweep to my revenge.

GHOST   I find thee apt,
And duller shouldst thou be than the fat weed
That rots itself in ease on Lethe wharf,

---

18 knotted Q2, Q1; knotty F   20 fretful] F, Q1; fearefull Q2   22 List, list] Q2; list *Hamlet* F   24 God] Q2; Heauen
F   29 Haste me] Q2, Q1; Hast, hast me F   29 know't] Q2; know it F, Q2   29 that I with] Q2; That with F   33 rots]
F; rootes Q2, Q1

11 **fast in fires** A form of Purgatorial punish-ment necessary for the Ghost's purification (see 1.5.13).

12 **foul crimes** The Ghost acknowledges the fact of his earthly transgressions. Hamlet will repeat the language in the prayer scene (3.3.81). In both places, the language is strong with revulsion against the poisoner who did not allow King Hamlet the absolution he would have sought at the time of death. (However, absolution, or remission of the guilt of sin, does not necessarily imply the remission of temporal punishment for sin, for which the spirit must suffer in Purgatory.) For crimes = faults, see 2.1.43.

16 **harrow up** See note to 1.1.44.

17 **Make ...... spheres** i.e. make your eyes start from your head as though they were stars jerked out of their appointed spheres (so indicating a dislocation in nature).

19 **an end** Obsolete form of 'on end'.

20 **fretful** angry, irritated. So F. Q2's 'fearefull' is a weaker reading which does not accord with the contemporary animal-lore. Compare Joseph Hall, 'The Satire should be like the Porcupine, / That shoots sharp quills out in each angry line' (*Virgidemiarum*, 1599, V, 3, 1–2).

20 **porpentine** porcupine. The name was spelled in many different ways: this is the normal Shakespearean form.

21 **eternal blazon** description or revelation of what belongs to the eternal world.

22 **List, list, oh list!** So Q2. F's rendering ('list *Hamlet*') is the first time the Ghost speaks the name.

31 **apt** quick in response.

32 **fat** heavy, torpid, sluggish.

33 **rots** So F. Both Q2 and Q1 read 'rootes', which is widely accepted by editors (Kittredge and Hoy being notable exceptions).

Wouldst thou not stir in this. Now Hamlet, hear.
'Tis given out that, sleeping in my orchard,   35
A serpent stung me. So the whole ear of Denmark
Is by a forgèd process of my death
Rankly abused; but know, thou noble youth,
The serpent that did sting thy father's life
Now wears his crown.

HAMLET   O my prophetic soul!   40
My uncle?

GHOST Ay, that incestuous, that adulterate beast,
With witchcraft of his wits, with traitorous gifts –
O wicked wit and gifts that have the power
So to seduce – won to his shameful lust   45
The will of my most seeming virtuous queen.
O Hamlet, what a falling off was there,
From me whose love was of that dignity
That it went hand in hand even with the vow
I made to her in marriage, and to decline   50
Upon a wretch whose natural gifts were poor
To those of mine.
But virtue as it never will be moved,
Though lewdness court it in a shape of heaven,

---

35 'Tis] Q2, Q1; It's F   35 my] Q2, Q1; mine F   40–1 O ... uncle] *as one line* Q2, F   41 My] Q2, Q1; mine F   43 wits]
Q2, F; wit *Pope*   43 with] Q2; hath F   45 to his] Q2; to to this F   47 what a] F; what Q2   52–3 To ... moved] *as one
line* Q2, F

33 **Lethe** a river in Hades. The spirits of the
dead, waiting to cross, drank its waters and so
became oblivious of their previous existence.

35 **given out** reported publicly.

35 **orchard** garden.

37 **process** narrative.

40 **my prophetic soul** Implying not that
Hamlet had already guessed the truth, but that the
Ghost's revelation confirms Hamlet's general suspicions about Claudius and about the circumstances
of his father's death (1.2.255).

42 **adulterate** Active meanings include both
impurity and debasement (*OED* 1.1) as well as par-
ticipating in adultery (*OED* 1.2). It remains an issue
of debate whether the Ghost is accusing Claudius –
and by extension Gertrude – of enjoying a sexual
liaison while Hamlet Sr was still alive.

43 **wits** Pope and many succeeding editors read
'wit', to balance the singular in the next line, and
with the idea that 'wit' (= intellectual activity) is
more appropriate. Shakespeare frequently uses
'wits' in the sense of 'activities of the mind'; e.g.
Shrew 1.1.170, 'Bend thoughts and wits to achieve

her.' The singular 'wit' in the following line is the
assemblage of the activities of the mind into 'mind'
itself.

43 **gifts** talents (see 'natural gifts', 51 below).

46 **The will** This is more than inclination or
assent, since the word has strong sexual undertones.
Gertrude was sexually responsive to Claudius's
advances. This passage again raises the question of
adultery, this time explicitly in terms of Gertrude.
In Belleforest's narrative, Gertrude does betray
Hamlet Sr with Fengon (Claudius) before his death,
and the Ghost's indignation about his 'most seeming-
virtuous queen' suggests that this could be the case in
the play. But the language may reflect a husband's
emotional experience of a wife's remarriage rather
than a literal fact. Hamlet's recreation of the scenario,
the dumb-show of 3.2, presents a loving Queen who
resists the poisoner's wooing after the King's death
before she 'in the end accepts his love'.

49 **even with the vow** with the very vow (*not*
even as far as the vow).

53 **virtue as it** as virtue.

54 **shape** See note to 1.4.43.

So lust, though to a radiant angel linked,   55
Will sate itself in a celestial bed,
And prey on garbage.
But soft, methinks I scent the morning air;
Brief let me be. Sleeping within my orchard,
My custom always of the afternoon,   60
Upon my secure hour thy uncle stole,
With juice of cursèd hebenon in a vial,
And in the porches of my ears did pour
The leperous distilment, whose effect
Holds such an enmity with blood of man   65
That swift as quicksilver it courses through
The natural gates and alleys of the body,
And with a sudden vigour it doth posset
And curd, like eager droppings into milk,
The thin and wholesome blood. So did it mine,   70
And a most instant tetter barked about,
Most lazar-like, with vile and loathsome crust,
All my smooth body.
Thus was I, sleeping, by a brother's hand,
Of life, of crown, of queen, at once dispatched;   75
Cut off even in the blossoms of my sin,
Unhouseled, disappointed, unaneled;

55 lust] F; but Q2   55 angel] F; Angle Q2   56 sate] F; sort Q2   58 morning] Q2; Mornings F   59 my] Q2, Q1; mine
F   60 of] Q2; in F, Q1   62 hebenon] Hebenon F; Hebona Q2, Q1   63 my] Q2, Q1; mine F   68 posset] F; possesse
Q2   69 eager] Q2, Q1; Aygre F   71 barked] barckt Q2; bak'd F   75 of queen] Q2; and Queene F

56 **sate itself** feed itself, glut itself.

61 **Upon my secure hour** (sécure) At a time
when I felt free from all danger ('secure' implied an
absence of precaution, almost the opposite of its
modern meaning.)

62 **hebenon** Both the true reading and the
meaning are uncertain. Q2's 'Hebona' seems to
derive from Q1. Marlowe has 'the juice of hebon'
as a poison in *The Jew of Malta* 3.4.101. *Hebenus* is
Latin for ebony, but was applied to other trees, and
the resin of the guaiacum tree has been suggested as
the drug in question. Possibly there is confusion
with henbane, which *is* a poison. See R. R. Simpson
in *The Listener*, 17 April 1947.

63 **the porches of my ears** i.e. the ears as
porches of, or entryways into, the body. It was
widely believed that drugs, therapeutic or toxic,
could be administered via the ear; the Ghost's
description calls 'attention [to] the
vulnerability . . . . . . of the ear' (Tanya Pollard,

Drugs and Theater in Early Modern England
(Oxford University Press, 2005), 123).

64 **leperous** causing leprosy.

64 **distilment** distillation (in a general sense;
a liquid preparation).

68 **posset** curdle.

69 **eager** sour, acid. French *aigre*.

71 **tetter** skin disease.

71 **barked about** surrounded like bark.

72 **lazar-like** like a leper (from Lazarus, in
Luke 16.20).

75 **dispatched** bereft by being put to death.

76 **in the blossoms of my sin** i.e. in a state of
sinfulness. Compare the similar image in 3.3.81,
'his crimes broad blown, as flush as May'.

77 **Unhouseled . . . . . . unaneled** Without the
sacrament of the Eucharist; without the sacrament
of penance; without the sacrament of extreme unction. The latter two were not accepted as sacraments in Protestantism.

No reckoning made, but sent to my account
With all my imperfections on my head –
Oh horrible, oh horrible, most horrible!   80
If thou hast nature in thee bear it not;
Let not the royal bed of Denmark be
A couch for luxury and damnèd incest.
But howsomever thou pursues this act
Taint not thy mind, nor let thy soul contrive   85
Against thy mother aught. Leave her to heaven
And to those thorns that in her bosom lodge
To prick and sting her. Fare thee well at once.
The glow-worm shows the matin to be near,
And gins to pale his uneffectual fire.   90
Adieu, adieu, adieu. Remember me.   *Exit*
HAMLET O all you host of heaven! O earth! what else?
And shall I couple hell? Oh fie! Hold, hold, my heart,
And you my sinews grow not instant old
But bear me stiffly up. Remember thee?   95
Ay thou poor ghost, whiles memory holds a seat
In this distracted globe. Remember thee?

---

84 howsomever] Q2; howsoeuer F   84 pursues] Q2; pursuest F   85 Taint] F; Tain't Q2   91 Adieu, adieu, adieu] Q2; Adue, adue, *Hamlet* F   91 SD] F; *not in* Q2   93 Hold, hold] Q2; hold F   95 stiffly] F; swiftly Q2   96 whiles] Q2; while F

---

78 reckoning settling of spiritual debts.

78 account appearance and evaluation at the judgment seat of God.

80 Dr Johnson accepted a suggestion that this ought to be Hamlet's line, giving emphasis to the great injunction of the Ghost, which immediately follows.

81 nature natural feelings. Here, filial affection especially. Compare 3.2.354.

83 luxury lust.

84 howsomever The older form of 'howsoever'.

84 thou pursues this -es rather than -est before a following th- (see Franz, *Die Sprache Shakespeares*, §152, 154).

85 Taint not thy mind Do not let your mind become corrupted. The Ghost foreshadows the moral and psychological harm that might follow the demand for revenge: Hamlet may become spiritually tarnished as well as psychically overtaxed.

89 matin morning.

91 Remember The Ghost thus leaves Hamlet with two injunctions: to revenge and to remember.

93 And shall I couple hell? The enormity of what he has heard makes Hamlet appeal first to heaven to witness, then turn to earth as the scene of these crimes, and finally to hell as their source.

95 bear me stiffly up keep me from collapsing.

97 this distracted globe It is tempting to see this as a triple pun on three possible meanings: the troubled world of Denmark, Hamlet's troubled head or mind, and the Globe Theatre.

Yea, from the table of my memory
I'll wipe away all trivial fond records,
All saws of books, all forms, all pressures past,   100
That youth and observation copied there,
And thy commandment all alone shall live
Within the book and volume of my brain,
Unmixed with baser matter: yes, by heaven!
O most pernicious woman!   105
O villain, villain, smiling damnèd villain!
My tables – meet it is I set it down
That one may smile, and smile, and be a villain;
At least I'm sure it may be so in Denmark. [*Writing*]
So uncle, there you are. Now to my word: 110
It is 'Adieu, adieu, remember me.'
I have sworn't.
HORATIO (*Within*) My lord, my lord!
MARCELLUS (*Within*)   Lord Hamlet!

Enter HORATIO *and* MARCELLUS

HORATIO   Heavens secure him!
HAMLET So be it.
MARCELLUS Illo, ho, ho, my lord!   115

---

104 yes] Q2; yes, yes F, Q1   **107** My tables] Q2; My Tables, my Tables F   **109** I'm] F; I am Q2   **109** SD] *Rowe; not in*
Q2, F   **113** SH HORATIO] *Hora.* Q2; *Hor. & Mar.* F   **113** SD *Within*] F; *not in* Q2   **113** SD *Enter ...* MARCELLUS]
Capell; after sworn't Q2; *after* my lord! F   **113** Heavens] Q2, Q1; *Heauen* F   **114** SH HAMLET] *Ham.* Q2; *Mar.* F   **115**
SH MARCELLUS] *Mar.* Q2; *Hor.* F

98 table tablet, slate. The metaphor may be
literalized in 107 and SD 109 if Hamlet takes out
and uses writing materials. See Peter Stallybrass,
Roger Chartier, T. Franklin Mowery, and Heather
Wolfe, 'Hamlet's Tables and the Technologies of
Writing in Renaissance England', *SQ* 55.4 (2004),
379–419.
99 fond foolish.
99 records Things written down worthy to be
remembered. Accent on second syllable.
100 saws common sayings or maxims.
100 forms set phrases, formulistic thoughts.
100 pressures imprints or impressions (continues the image of clichés and stereotyped
thoughts).

101 observation dutiful attention or study.
Hamlet is not talking of what he had noted from
a personal and independent viewpoint: 'observation' more often than not meant in Shakespeare's
time a deferential, even obsequious, attention to
one's superiors, and imitation of them or obedience
to them.
107 tables memorandum book (see 98 above)
108–9 smile ... Denmark The general maxim
applies to Hamlet's personal experience.
110 Now to my word Hamlet has not yet
vowed to obey the Ghost's command. He now
gives his word – very solemnly, perhaps kneeling
as Wilson suggests, and rising with 'I have sworn't'
(112) or 'So be it' (114).

HAMLET Hillo, ho, ho, boy! Come bird, come.

MARCELLUS How is't, my noble lord?

HORATIO   What news my lord?

HAMLET Oh, wonderful!

HORATIO Good my lord, tell it.

HAMLET   No, you will reveal it.

HORATIO Not I my lord, by heaven.

MARCELLUS   Nor I my lord.   120

HAMLET How say you then, would heart of man once think it –
        But you'll be secret?

HORATIO   ⎫
                    Ay, by heaven, my lord.
MARCELLUS ⎭

HAMLET There's ne'er a villain dwelling in all Denmark
        But he's an arrant knave.

HORATIO There needs no ghost, my lord, come from the grave,   125
        To tell us this.

HAMLET   Why right, you are i'th'right,
        And so without more circumstance at all
        I hold it fit that we shake hands and part –
        You as your business and desire shall point you,
        For every man hath business and desire,   130
        Such as it is, and for my own poor part,
        Look you, I'll go pray.

HORATIO These are but wild and whirling words, my lord.

HAMLET I'm sorry they offend you, heartily,
        Yes faith, heartily.

HORATIO   There's no offence my lord.   135

HAMLET Yes by Saint Patrick but there is Horatio,
        And much offence too. Touching this vision here,

---

116 Come bird,] F; come, and Q2   119 you will] Q2; you'l F, QI   122 my lord] F; *not in* Q2   123 ne'er] nere F; neuer Q2, QI   126 i'th'right] F; in the right Q2, QI   129 desire] Q2; desires F, QI   130 hath] Q2; ha's F   131 my] Q2, QI; mine F   132 Look you, I'll] F; I will Q2   133 whirling] whurling Q2; hurling F   134 I'm] F; I am Q2, QI   136 Horatio] Q2, QI; my Lord F

116 Come bird Hamlet mocks the hallooing by pretending they are out hawking.

127 circumstance roundabout talk and formality.

132 Look you So F; not in Q2. It is a characteristic turn of Hamlet's speech; e.g. 3.2.326, 329.

132 I'll go pray Hamlet has no 'business and desire' because his proper office has been taken from him by the usurper Claudius, and because his continued life as a student at Wittenberg has been refused him. So, he jokes, he'll have to say his prayers. But the audience knows that he has urgent 'business and desire', and, for that, prayer might well be needful. Nowhere else in the play does Hamlet talk of praying.

136 Saint Patrick Fifth-century Apostle of Ireland who had the power to intercede on behalf of souls in Purgatory. His place of retreat on the island of Lough Derg was known from the early Middle Ages as St Patrick's Purgatory.

It is an honest ghost, that let me tell you.
For your desire to know what is between us,
O'ermaster't as you may. And now good friends,   140
As you are friends, scholars, and soldiers,
Give me one poor request.

HORATIO What is't my lord? we will.

HAMLET Never make known what you have seen tonight.

HORATIO ⎫
MARCELLUS ⎭ My lord we will not.

HAMLET   Nay but swear't.

HORATIO   In faith   145
My lord not I.

MARCELLUS   Nor I my lord in faith.

HAMLET Upon my sword.

MARCELLUS   We have sworn my lord already.

HAMLET Indeed, upon my sword, indeed.

GHOST Swear.   *Ghost cries under the stage*

HAMLET Ha, ha, boy, sayst thou so? art thou there truepenny?   150
Come on, you hear this fellow in the cellarage,
Consent to swear.

HORATIO   Propose the oath my lord.

HAMLET Never to speak of this that you have seen,
Swear by my sword.

GHOST Swear.   155

HAMLET *Hic et ubique?* then we'll shift our ground.
Come hither gentlemen,
And lay your hands again upon my sword.
Never to speak of this that you have heard,
Swear by my sword.   160

GHOST Swear.

HAMLET Well said old mole, canst work i'th'earth so fast?

145–6 In faith ... not I] *as one line* Q2, F   150 Ha, ha,] Q2; Ah ha F   151 Come on, you hear] Q2; Come on you here
F   156 our] Q2; for F   159–60] F; *lines transposed, in* Q2   161 Swear.] F; *Sweare by his sword.* Q2   162 earth] Q2, Q1;
ground F

138 **honest** honourable, genuine.
  146 **not I .... Nor I** They here promise not to
divulge what they have seen – they are not refusing
to swear: 'We have sworn already', they say next
(referring to 120).
  147 **Upon my sword** The hilt forms a cross.
  149 SD The area under the stage was associated
with hell and devils.
  150 **truepenny** trusty fellow.
  151 **in the cellarage** down below, in the cellars.
  156 *Hic et ubique* Here and everywhere.
  159–61 So F. Lines 159 and 160 are

transposed in Q2, and the Ghost in 161 is
made to say 'Swear by his sword.' Q1 resembles
F, with variations.
  162 **mole** Small burrowing mammal known for
its poor vision. *OED* gives its use here as one of the
first examples of its meaning of a 'person who works
underground; a person who works in darkness or in
secrecy' (II.3.a). De Grazia explains the image's function in Hamlet's 'many put-downs' of the Ghost,
which 'reduc[e] the king who ruled over the land to
a subterranean creature synonymous with base earth'
('*Hamlet' without Hamlet*, 43).

A worthy pioneer. Once more remove, good friends.
HORATIO O day and night, but this is wondrous strange.
HAMLET And therefore as a stranger give it welcome.   165
There are more things in heaven and earth, Horatio,
Than are dreamt of in your philosophy.
But come –
Here as before, never so help you mercy,
How strange or odd some'er I bear myself,   170
As I perchance hereafter shall think meet
To put an antic disposition on –
That you at such times seeing me never shall,
With arms encumbered thus, or this head-shake,
Or by pronouncing of some doubtful phrase,   175
As 'Well, well, we know,' or 'We could and if we would,'
Or 'If we list to speak,' or 'There be and if they might,'
Or such ambiguous giving out, to note
That you know aught of me: this not to do,
So grace and mercy at your most need help you,   180
Swear.
GHOST Swear.
HAMLET Rest, rest, perturbèd spirit. So gentlemen,
With all my love I do commend me to you,

---

167 your] Q2, Q1; our F   167–8 Than … come] *as one line* Q2, F   170 some'er] so mere Q2; so ere F   173 times] Q2, Q1; time F   174 this] Q2; thus, F   176 Well, well] Q2, Q1; well F   177 they] Q2; there F   179 this not to do] F, Q1; this doe sweare Q2   181 Swear] F, Q1; *not in* Q2

---

163 **pioneer** soldier responsible for excavations and tunnelling.

165 **as a stranger … welcome** i.e. it has a special call on your hospitality.

167 **your philosophy** So Q2 and Q1. F's 'our' may be a compositor's error. The pronoun does not blame Horatio for his scepticism; rather it indicates slight contempt for philosophy itself (meaning intellectual investigation, science). Compare 5.1.145, 'a sore decayer of your whoreson dead body'.

170 **How strange … myself** Hamlet introduces the kind of behaviour that will characterize his 'antic disposition' (172).

172 **an antic disposition** fantastic, grotesque manner or physical condition.

174 **encumbered** entangled. An unusual word

in this context, but see Johnson's *Dictionary*.

176, 177 **and if** if.

177 **list** wished.

179–81 **this not to do … Swear** So F and Q1. Q2 puts it differently. Shakespeare had got Hamlet into a difficult grammatical tangle, but the sense is clear: the men should not reveal that they know Hamlet's 'antic' behaviour is a performance.

183 Perhaps at this point Horatio and Marcellus silently swear on the hilt of Hamlet's sword. Wilson, Spencer, and Jenkins think they swear silently three separate times. There is no indication in the text of when, if ever, the formal oath is taken.

184 **I do commend me to you** I entrust myself to you. This routine way of expressing devotion has here something of the force of the phrase's proper meaning.

And what so poor a man as Hamlet is   185
May do t'express his love and friending to you,
God willing shall not lack. Let us go in together,
And still your fingers on your lips I pray. –
The time is out of joint: O cursèd spite,
That ever I was born to set it right. –   190
Nay come, let's go together.

                                                        Exeunt

[2.1] *Enter* POLONIUS *and* REYNALDO

POLONIUS Give him this money, and these notes, Reynaldo.
REYNALDO I will my lord.
POLONIUS You shall do marvellous wisely, good Reynaldo,
          Before you visit him, to make inquire
          Of his behaviour.
REYNALDO   My lord, I did intend it.   5
POLONIUS Marry well said, very well said. Look you sir,
          Inquire me first what Danskers are in Paris,
          And how, and who, what means, and where they keep,
          What company, at what expense; and finding
          By this encompassment and drift of question   10
          That they do know my son, come you more nearer
          Than your particular demands will touch it.
          Take you as 'twere some distant knowledge of him,
          As thus, 'I know his father and his friends,

Act 2, Scene 1   2.1] *Actus Secundus* F; *no indication in* Q2   0 SD] F; *Enter old Polonius, with his man or two* Q2   1 this]
Q2; his F   3 marvellous] Q 1611; meruiles Q2; maruels F   4 to make] Q2; you make F   4 inquire] Q2; inquiry
F   14 As] Q2; And F

188 **still** always.
189 **The time … joint** The present state of the
world is disordered, injured like a dislocated bone
that needs resetting.
189 **cursèd spite** the accursèd malice of life!

Act 2, Scene 1
1 Shakespeare gives several indications of a lapse
of time between Acts 1 and 2. Laertes is settled in
Paris, Ophelia has refused to see Hamlet or receive
his letters (Scene 1). The king and queen have been
alarmed by the transformation in Hamlet's behaviour and have sent for Rosencrantz and
Guildenstern, who have reached Elsinore.

The ambassadors have been to Norway and have
returned (Scene 2).
    0 SD *Enter* … REYNALDO So F. See collation for
Q2's striking authorial direction.
    3 **marvellous** marvellously, extremely. Two
syllables.
    7 **Danskers** Danes.
    8 **what means** what means they have.
    8 **keep** lodge, stay.
    10 **encompassment** action of surrounding, i.e.
talking round the topic.
    10 **drift** driving, directing.
    11 **come you** you will come.
    11 **nearer** i.e. to an understanding of Laertes's
behaviour.

And in part him' – do you mark this Reynaldo?   15
REYNALDO Ay, very well, my lord.
POLONIUS 'And in part him, but' – you may say – 'not well,
         But if't be he I mean, he's very wild,
         Addicted so and so' – and there put on him
         What forgeries you please; marry, none so rank   20
         As may dishonour him, take heed of that,
         But sir, such wanton, wild, and usual slips
         As are companions noted and most known
         To youth and liberty.
REYNALDO   As gaming my lord?
POLONIUS Ay, or drinking, fencing, swearing,   25
         Quarrelling, drabbing – you may go so far.
REYNALDO My lord, that would dishonour him.
POLONIUS Faith no, as you may season it in the charge.
         You must not put another scandal on him,
         That he is open to incontinency,   30
         That's not my meaning. But breathe his faults so quaintly
         That they may seem the taints of liberty,
         The flash and outbreak of a fiery mind,
         A savageness in unreclaimèd blood,
         Of general assault.
REYNALDO   But my good lord –   35
POLONIUS Wherefore should you do this?
REYNALDO   Ay my lord,
         I would know that.
POLONIUS   Marry sir, here's my drift,
         And I believe it is a fetch of warrant.
         You laying these slight sullies on my son,

---

24 lord?] *Adams;* lord. Q2, F   28 Faith no] F; Fayth Q2   34–5 A savageness . . . assault] Q2; *as one line* F   36–7 Ay . . . that] *as one line* Q2, F   38 warrant] F; wit Q2   39 sullies] sulleyes F; sallies Q2

20 **forgeries** invented matters.
20 **rank** gross.
24 **gaming** playing games such as cards, dice, often associated with gambling.
25 **fencing** i.e. spending time in fencing-schools.
26 **drabbing** going round with drabs, or prostitutes.
28 **season** modify.
30 **incontinency** sexual excess. Polonius may be making a distinction between the occasional visit to a prostitute ('drabbing'), which he would permit, and notorious profligacy ('incontinency'),

which he would not. Or this may be a joke at his expense: although Polonius prides himself on a knowledge of the world, he supposes that young men like his son might associate with undesirable females without actual fornication, and so believes that 'drabbing' is not necessarily 'incontinency'.
31 **quaintly** artfully.
32 **taints of liberty** faults of free-living.
34 **savageness … blood** wildness of unreformed impulse.
35 **Of general assault** Which assails everyone.
38 **fetch of warrant** approved stratagem.
39 **sullies** See collation and note to 1.2.129.

As 'twere a thing a little soiled i'th'working,   40
Mark you,
Your party in converse, him you would sound,
Having ever seen in the prenominate crimes
The youth you breathe of guilty, be assured
He closes with you in this consequence,   45
'Good sir', or so, or 'friend', or 'gentleman',
According to the phrase and the addition
Of man and country.

REYNALDO   Very good my lord.

POLONIUS And then sir does a this – a does – what was I about to say?
By the mass I was about to say something. Where did I leave?   50

REYNALDO At 'closes in the consequence', at 'friend, or so', and
'gentleman'.

POLONIUS At 'closes in the consequence' – ay marry,
He closes with you thus: 'I know the gentleman,
I saw him yesterday, or th'other day,   55
Or then, or then, with such or such, and as you say,
There was a gaming, there o'ertook in's rouse,
There falling out at tennis', or perchance,
'I saw him enter such a house of sale' –
Videlicet, a brothel – or so forth. See you now,   60
Your bait of falsehood takes this carp of truth,
And thus do we of wisdom and of reach,
With windlasses and with assays of bias,

---

40 i'th'] F; with Q2; wi'th' *P. Alexander*   41–2 Mark … sound] *as one line* Q2, F   47 and] F; or Q2   49–50 And
then … leave] *as prose Malone*; say? / By … something, / Where Q2; this? / He does … say? / I was F   49 a] Q2; he F
[*twice*]   50 By the mass] Q2; *not in* F   51–2 at 'friend … 'gentleman'] F; *not in* Q2   54 with you] F; *not in* Q2   55
th'other] Q2; t other F   56 such or such] Q2; such and such F   57 a] Q2; he F   57 there o'ertook] there o'retooke F;
there, or tooke Q2   61 takes] F; take Q2   61 carp] carpe Q2; Cape F

40 **As 'twere a thing** Laertes is the slightly
dirtied 'thing' in this comparison.

40 **i'th'working** in the process of making it.

43 **prenominate** already named.

43 **crimes** faults. See note to 1.5.12.

44 **breathe of** speak about.

45 **closes with you** will fall into conversation
with you.

45 **in this consequence** in the following way.

47–8 **the phrase … country** The mode of
address varies with the country's conventions *and*
the status of the speaker. So F. In Polonius's chias-
mus, 'phrase' (= conventional expression) goes with
'country', and 'addition' (= title) goes with 'man'.
Q2's 'or' ('the phrase or the addition') is less precise.

51–2 **at 'friend' … 'gentleman'** So F; not in
Q2.

57 **a** he.

57 **o'ertook in's rouse** overtaken (by drink)
while carousing. That is, he got drunk.

60 **Videlicet** 'viz.', that is to say.

62 **we of wisdom and of reach** we who are
wise and far-seeing.

63 **windlasses** circuitous movement (in hunt-
ing), from which develops the figurative meaning of
a round-about process or crafty device.

63 **assays of bias** indirect attempts.
The metaphor is from the game of bowls: the
'bias' is the weighting which makes the bowl take
a curved course towards the jack.

By indirections find directions out.
So, by my former lecture and advice,   65
Shall you my son. You have me, have you not?
REYNALDO My lord, I have.
POLONIUS   God buy ye, fare ye well.
REYNALDO Good my lord.
POLONIUS Observe his inclination in yourself.
REYNALDO I shall my lord.   70
POLONIUS And let him ply his music.
REYNALDO   Well my lord.
POLONIUS Farewell.

                                        Exit Reynaldo

                Enter OPHELIA

            How now Ophelia, what's the matter?
OPHELIA Oh my lord, my lord, I have been so affrighted.
POLONIUS With what, i'th'name of God?
OPHELIA My lord, as I was sewing in my closet,   75
            Lord Hamlet with his doublet all unbraced,
            No hat upon his head, his stockings fouled,
            Ungartered, and down-gyvèd to his ankle,
            Pale as his shirt, his knees knocking each other,
            And with a look so piteous in purport   80
            As if he had been loosèd out of hell
            To speak of horrors – he comes before me.
POLONIUS Mad for thy love?
OPHELIA   My lord I do not know,
            But truly I do fear it.
POLONIUS   What said he?
OPHELIA He took me by the wrist, and held me hard;   85
            Then goes he to the length of all his arm,

---

67 ye] Q2; you F *[twice]*   67 fare] F; far Q2   72 SD] Q2 *at 71; Exit. F at 71*   73 Oh my lord, my lord] Q2; Alas my Lord F   74 i'th'] Q2; in the F   74 God] Q2; Heauen F   75 closet] Q2; Chamber F

64 directions the way things are going.
67 God buy ye One of the many ways of writing the shortened 'God be with ye' = goodbye.
69 in yourself personally.
75 closet private room.
76 doublet the Elizabethan jacket.
76 unbraced unfastened.

78 down-gyvèd fallen down and resembling fetters.
80 in purport in what it expressed.
83 Mad for thy love? Totally beside himself, for love of thee? The blending of eros, woe, and madness in the 'the ecstasy of love' (100 below), was part of Elizabethan theories of melancholy.

And with his other hand thus o'er his brow
He falls to such perusal of my face
As a would draw it. Long stayed he so;
At last, a little shaking of mine arm,   90
And thrice his head thus waving up and down,
He raised a sigh so piteous and profound
As it did seem to shatter all his bulk,
And end his being. That done, he lets me go,
And with his head over his shoulder turned   95
He seemed to find his way without his eyes,
For out-a-doors he went without their helps
And to the last bended their light on me.
POLONIUS Come, go with me, I will go seek the king.
    This is the very ecstasy of love,   100
    Whose violent property fordoes itself,
    And leads the will to desperate undertakings
    As oft as any passion under heaven
    That does afflict our natures. I am sorry.
    What, have you given him any hard words of late?   105
OPHELIA No my good lord; but as you did command,
    I did repel his letters, and denied
    His access to me.
POLONIUS   That hath made him mad.
    I am sorry that with better heed and judgement
    I had not quoted him. I feared he did but trifle,   110
    And meant to wrack thee, but beshrew my jealousy.
    By heaven, it is as proper to our age
    To cast beyond ourselves in our opinions
    As it is common for the younger sort

---

89 a] Q2; he F   93 As] Q2; That F   95 shoulder] Q2, Q1; shoulders F   97 helps] Q2; helpe F, Q1   99 Come, go] Q2; Goe F   103 passion] F; passions Q2   109 heed] Q2; speed F   110 quoted] F; coted Q2   110 feared] fear'd Q2; feare F   112 By heaven] Q2; It seemes F

92 **piteous** full of pity (for himself), arousing pity.

98 **bended their light** fixed his gaze.

99, 115 **Come, go with me ... Come, go we to the king** But Polonius goes alone to the king (2.2.40). In Q1, however, Ophelia does accompany him. See Textual Analysis, 271–2.

100 **ecstasy** madness, with the sense of being beside oneself, transported.

101 **Whose ... itself** Whose characteristic force or violence results in self-destruction.

110 **quoted** noted, observed. Q2's 'coted', a frequent Shakespearean spelling, indicates the contemporary pronunciation.

111 **wrack** ruin, by seducing.

111 **beshrew my jealousy** shame upon my suspiciousness.

112 **as proper to** as characteristic of.

113 **cast** calculate, reckon. The old read too much into things, while the young are too heedless of possible implications.

To lack discretion. Come, go we to the king.   115
This must be known, which being kept close, might move
More grief to hide than hate to utter love.
Come.

Exeunt

[2.2] *Flourish. Enter* KING *and* QUEEN, ROSENCRANTZ *and* GUILDEN-
STERN, *with others*

CLAUDIUS Welcome dear Rosencrantz and Guildenstern!
Moreover that we much did long to see you,
The need we have to use you did provoke
Our hasty sending. Something have you heard
Of Hamlet's transformation – so call it,   5
Sith nor th'exterior nor the inward man
Resembles that it was. What it should be,
More than his father's death, that thus hath put him
So much from th'understanding of himself,
I cannot dream of. I entreat you both,   10
That being of so young days brought up with him,
And sith so neighboured to his youth and haviour,
That you vouchsafe your rest here in our court
Some little time, so by your companies
To draw him on to pleasures, and to gather   15
So much as from occasion you may glean,
Whether aught to us unknown afflicts him thus,

---

118 Come] Q2; *not in* F   **Act 2, Scene 2**   2.2] *Scena Secunda* F   0.1 SD *Flourish*] Q2; *not in* F   0.2 SD *with others*] *Cum
alijs* F; *not in* Q2   5 so call] Q2; *so I call* F   6 Sith] Q2; *Since* F   6 nor ... nor] Q2; *not ... nor* F   10 dream] Q2;
deeme F   12 sith] Q2; *since* F   12 haviour] Q2; *humour* F   16 occasion] Q2; *Occasions* F   17 Whether ... thus] Q2;
not in F

116 close secret.
116–17 might move ... love i.e. might cause
more sorrow by concealment than unpleasantness
by making the love known.

Act 2, Scene 2
2.2 After this, there are no further indications of
act or scene division in either quarto or Folio.
   0 SD *with others* This is F's addition ('*Cum alijs*')
to Q2, showing the theatre's usual concern that
royalty should be attended.
   1 Rosencrantz and Guildenstern For the

forms of these names in F and Q2, see Appendix 2,
'Names', 278–9.
   2 Moreover that In addition to the fact that.
   6 Sith Since.
   11 of from.
   12 sith This probably has the causative sense
used in 6 above. It is *because* they are 'so neighboured' to him that they have been invited. Some
editors give an adverbial sense, = 'afterward'.
F gives 'since' here and at 6.
   12 youth and haviour youthful way of
behaving.
   16 occasion opportunity.

That opened lies within our remedy.

GERTRUDE Good gentlemen, he hath much talked of you,
    And sure I am, two men there is not living   20
    To whom he more adheres. If it will please you
    To show us so much gentry and good will
    As to expend your time with us a while,
    For the supply and profit of our hope,
    Your visitation shall receive such thanks   25
    As fits a king's remembrance.

ROSENCRANTZ   Both your majesties
    Might by the sovereign power you have of us
    Put your dread pleasures more into command
    Than to entreaty.

GUILDENSTERN   But we both obey,
    And here give up ourselves in the full bent   30
    To lay our service freely at your feet
    To be commanded.

CLAUDIUS Thanks Rosencrantz, and gentle Guildenstern.

GERTRUDE Thanks Guildenstern, and gentle Rosencrantz.
    And I beseech you instantly to visit   35
    My too much changèd son. Go some of you
    And bring these gentlemen where Hamlet is.

GUILDENSTERN Heavens make our presence and our practices
    Pleasant and helpful to him.

GERTRUDE   Ay, amen.

        Exeunt Rosencrantz and Guildenstern [and some Attendants]

              Enter POLONIUS

POLONIUS Th'ambassadors from Norway, my good lord,   40
    Are joyfully returned.

---

20 is] Q2; are F   29 But we] Q2; We F   31 service] Q2; Seruices F   36 you] Q2; ye F   37 these] Q2; the F   39 Ay]
I Q2; *not in* F   39 SD *Exeunt ... Guildenstern*] Q2; *Exit* F *(after* to him*)*   39 SD *and some Attendants*] Malone, *following*
Capell; *not in* Q2, F

18 **opened** being revealed.
   20 **there is** So Q2. Corrected in F to 'there are',
but the use of 'there is' and 'here is' with a plural
subject is frequent in Shakespeare. See Franz, *Die
Sprache Shakespeares*, § 672 565–6.
   22 **gentry** courtesy.
   24 **supply** aid.
   24 **profit** advancement.
   24 **our hope** what we hope for.
   26 **remembrance** notice or recognition of ser-
vices rendered. Compare 3.1.93.

27 **of** over.
   28 **dread pleasures** This extension of the very
common 'my dread lord', etc., is not found elsewhere in Shakespeare, and illustrates the comic
obsequiousness of the speakers.
   30 **bent** extent. From bending a bow. Compare
'to the top of my bent', 3.2.346.
   38 **practices** doings, activities. But as the word
was very frequently used to mean a stratagem, or
underhand scheme (e.g. 4.7.66), it has ironic overtones here.

CLAUDIUS Thou still hast been the father of good news.
POLONIUS Have I my lord? Assure you, my good liege,
          I hold my duty, as I hold my soul,
          Both to my God and to my gracious king;   45
          And I do think, or else this brain of mine
          Hunts not the trail of policy so sure
          As it hath used to do, that I have found
          The very cause of Hamlet's lunacy.
CLAUDIUS Oh speak of that, that do I long to hear.   50
POLONIUS Give first admittance to th'ambassadors;
          My news shall be the fruit to that great feast.
CLAUDIUS Thyself do grace to them and bring them in.
                                                          [*Exit Polonius*]
          He tells me, my dear Gertrude, he hath found
          The head and source of all your son's distemper.   55
GERTRUDE I doubt it is no other but the main:
          His father's death, and our o'erhasty marriage.
CLAUDIUS Well, we shall sift him.

          Enter POLONIUS, VOLTEMAND *and* CORNELIUS

                              Welcome my good friends.
          Say Voltemand, what from our brother Norway?
VOLTEMAND Most fair return of greetings and desires.   60
          Upon our first, he sent out to suppress
          His nephew's levies, which to him appeared
          To be a preparation 'gainst the Polack;
          But better looked into, he truly found
          It was against your highness; whereat grieved   65
          That so his sickness, age and impotence

---

43 Assure you] F; I assure Q2, Q1   45 and] Q2; one F   48 it hath] Q2; I haue F; it had Q1   52 fruit] Q2; Newes F   53
SD] *Rowe; not in* Q2, F   54 my dear Gertrude] my deere *Gertrard* Q2; my sweet Queene, that F   57 o'erhasty] F; hastie
Q2   58 SD] F; *Enter Embassadors* Q2

44 **hold** maintain. He means he maintains his
duty to his God and king as firmly as he guards his
soul.
  47 **policy** statecraft.
  49 **lunacy** Claudius more delicately called it
a 'transformation' (5 above).
  54 **my dear Gertrude** F reads 'my sweet
Queene, that', maintaining the decorum of royalty

on stage at the cost of Q's intimacy.
  56 **doubt** suspect.
  56 **the main** the main matter.
  58 **sift him** examine carefully what he
(Polonius) has to say.
  61 **Upon our first** As soon as we relayed our
messages to him.
  66 **impotence** helplessness.

Was falsely borne in hand, sends out arrests
On Fortinbras, which he in brief obeys,
Receives rebuke from Norway, and in fine
Makes vow before his uncle never more   70
To give th'assay of arms against your majesty.
Whereon old Norway, overcome with joy,
Gives him three thousand crowns in annual fee,
And his commission to employ those soldiers,
So levied as before, against the Polack;   75
With an entreaty, herein further shown,
That it might please you to give quiet pass
Through your dominions for this enterprise,
On such regards of safety and allowance
As therein are set down.
                    [*Gives a document*]
CLAUDIUS   It likes us well,   80
And at our more considered time we'll read,
Answer, and think upon this business.
Meantime, we thank you for your well-took labour.
Go to your rest; at night we'll feast together.
Most welcome home.
                              Exeunt Ambassadors
POLONIUS   This business is well ended.   85
My liege, and madam, to expostulate
What majesty should be, what duty is,
Why day is day, night night, and time is time,
Were nothing but to waste night, day, and time.
Therefore, since brevity is the soul of wit   90
And tediousness the limbs and outward flourishes,
I will be brief. Your noble son is mad.

---

73 three thousand] F, Q1; threescore thousand Q2   76 shown] shewne F; shone Q2   78 this] Q2; his F   80 SD] *gives a paper / Malone (76); not in Q2, F*   85 well] Q2; very well F   90 since] F; *not in Q2*

67 **borne in hand** imposed on, abused with false pretences.
69 **in fine** in conclusion.
71 **give th'assay** make the trial.
73 **three thousand** So F and Q1. Q2 reads 'threescore thousand', which bedevils the metre.
73 **fee** payment.
79 **regards** considerations.
79 **allowance** permission.
80 **likes** pleases.

81 **more considered time** time more suitable for consideration.
82 **Answer, and think** Either this is the wrong way round, or Claudius means by 'think' that he will reflect upon what this affair implies for the future.
86 **expostulate** argue about, discuss.
90 **wit** intellectual keenness.
91 **tediousness** prolixity, long-windedness.
91 **flourishes** embellishments.

Mad call I it, for to define true madness,
What is't but to be nothing else but mad?
But let that go.
GERTRUDE   More matter with less art.   95
POLONIUS Madam, I swear I use no art at all.
That he is mad, 'tis true; 'tis true 'tis pity,
And pity 'tis 'tis true – a foolish figure,
But farewell it, for I will use no art.
Mad let us grant him then, and now remains   100
That we find out the cause of this effect,
Or rather say, the cause of this defect,
For this effect defective comes by cause.
Thus it remains, and the remainder thus.
Perpend.   105
I have a daughter – have while she is mine –
Who in her duty and obedience, mark,
Hath given me this. Now gather and surmise.

Reads the letter

'To the celestial, and my soul's idol, the most beautified Ophelia,' –
That's an ill phrase, a vile phrase, 'beautified' is a vile phrase – but   110
you shall hear. Thus:
'In her excellent white bosom, these, *et cetera.*'
GERTRUDE Came this from Hamlet to her?
POLONIUS Good madam stay awhile, I will be faithful.
'Doubt thou the stars are fire,   115
Doubt that the sun doth move,

---

97 he is] F; hee's Q2   98 'tis 'tis] Q2; it is F   106 while] Q2, Q1; whil'st F   108 SD] Kittredge; The Letter F; Letter Q2 (115)   111 Thus] Q2; these F   112 et cetera.] &c. Q2; not in F

93–4 for to define … but mad? In joking that it would be madness to try to define madness, Polonius finds himself giving a circular definition of madness as being mad. He dismisses his rhetoric – 'But let that go.'

98 figure rhetorical device (as in figure of speech).

103 For this … cause For this manifestation, which is a defect (madness), does have a cause.

105 Perpend Ponder, consider.

108 gather and surmise make your deductions.

109–22 Scholars as well as Hamlet himself ('I am ill at these numbers') are disappointed by the letter. (Harold Goddard went as far as suggesting that the letter was a forgery by Polonius ('Hamlet to Ophelia', *College English* 16.7 (1955), 403–15.) Its

lack of poetic grace has also been attributed to the antic disposition. But the letter in question would have been written before Hamlet assumed this guise, as Ophelia has refused to receive his letters since then (2.1.107; 2.2.144). The urge to 'doubt', however unpoetic, is consistent with Hamlet's other expressions of scepticism.

109 beautified The word was quite widely used; by Shakespeare himself in *Two Gentlemen of Verona* 4.1.53. Greene's contemptuous use of it in his attack on Shakespeare in 1592 may have rankled ('an upstart crow, beautified with our feathers').

112 In … et cetera This is a continuation of the florid address of the letter. It is directed to her heart. '[T]hese, *et cetera*' is a formal abbreviation (for 'these present greetings' or whatever).

Doubt truth to be a liar,
But never doubt I love.
'O dear Ophelia, I am ill at these numbers, I have not art to reckon
my groans; but that I love thee best, O most best, believe it. Adieu.   120
    'Thine evermore, most dear lady, whilst this machine is
        to him, Hamlet.'
    This in obedience hath my daughter shown me,
    And, more above, hath his solicitings,
    As they fell out, by time, by means, and place,   125
    All given to mine ear.
CLAUDIUS   But how hath she
    Received his love?
POLONIUS   What do you think of me?
CLAUDIUS As of a man faithful and honourable.
POLONIUS I would fain prove so. But what might you think,
    When I had seen this hot love on the wing –   130
    As I perceived it, I must tell you that,
    Before my daughter told me – what might you,
    Or my dear majesty your queen here, think,
    If I had played the desk, or table-book,
    Or given my heart a winking, mute and dumb,   135
    Or looked upon this love with idle sight –
    What might you think? No, I went round to work,
    And my young mistress thus I did bespeak:
    'Lord Hamlet is a prince out of thy star.
    This must not be'. And then I prescripts gave her,   140
    That she should lock herself from his resort,

---

123 This] F; *Pol.* This Q2   123 shown] Q2; shew'd F   124 above] F; about Q2   124 solicitings] Q2; soliciting
F   126–7 But ... love] *as one line* Q2, F   135 winking] F; working Q2   140 prescripts] Q2; Precepts F   141 his] F;
her Q2

117 **Doubt truth** 'Doubt' changes meaning
here from the two previous lines' sense of 'question'
to 'suspect', but taken together all of the lines support Hamlet's appeal to Ophelia to believe in his
love for her.
119 **ill at these numbers** no good at making
verses.
119 **reckon** enumerate in metrical form, or
'numbers'.
121 **this machine** his body.
124 **more above** furthermore, moreover.
124–6 **hath his ... mine ear** She has given
Polonius information about all his overtures to
her, in their order of occurrence, with details of
the time, the means of communication, and the

place.
129 **fain** gladly. Always used by Shakespeare in
the construction 'would fain'.
134 **played ... or table-book** i.e. taken note
and said nothing.
135 **given ... winking** closed the eyes of his
heart; i.e. connived at the affair.
137 **round** (= roundly) thoroughly, without
qualification.
138 **bespeak** speak to.
139 **out of thy star** outside your destiny (with
an additional sense of 'beyond your social status').
See note to 1.4.32.
140 **prescripts** orders.
141 **his resort** his visiting.

Admit no messengers, receive no tokens.
Which done, she took the fruits of my advice,
And he, repulsed – a short tale to make –
Fell into a sadness, then into a fast,   145
Thence to a watch, thence into a weakness,
Thence to a lightness, and by this declension
Into the madness wherein now he raves,
And all we mourn for.

CLAUDIUS   Do you think 'tis this?
GERTRUDE It may be, very like.   150
POLONIUS Hath there been such a time, I'd fain know that,
        That I have positively said, 'tis so,
        When it proved otherwise?
CLAUDIUS   Not that I know.
POLONIUS Take this from this, if this be otherwise.
        If circumstances lead me, I will find   155
        Where truth is hid, though it were hid indeed
        Within the centre.
CLAUDIUS   How may we try it further?
POLONIUS You know sometimes he walks four hours together
        Here in the lobby.
GERTRUDE   So he does indeed.
POLONIUS At such a time I'll loose my daughter to him.   160

---

144 repulsed] F; repell'd Q2   146 watch] F; wath Q2   147 a] F; *not in* Q2   148 wherein] Q2; whereon F   149 mourn] Q2; waile F   149 'tis] F; *not in* Q2   150 like] Q2; likely F   151 I'ld] I'de F; I would Q2   159 does] Q2; ha's F

143 took the fruits received the benefit; reaped the harvest.
144 repulsed So F. Q2 reads 'repell'd'. F is the stronger and rarer reading. Ophelia 'repels' Hamlet's letters (2.1.107), but Hamlet himself is 'repulsed'.
146 watch wakefulness.
147 lightness lightheadedness. The word is not otherwise recorded in this sense, but editors point to *Othello* 4.1.269, 'Is he not light of brain?'
147 declension decline, deterioration.
149 mourn So Q2. F reads 'wail', which did not have its present exclusive meaning of loud crying, but signified 'lament' in any form.
154 Take this from this Polonius may make a gesture here that reinforces his certainty. Theobald thought he pointed to his head and shoulders; Dowden suggested he might have offered the wand of office from his hand.
157 centre (of the earth).

157 try test.
159 lobby ante-room, vestibule. It is on an upper floor of the palace (4.3.33–4). Dover Wilson believed that Hamlet began to enter at this point and overheard the plot (*What Happens in 'Hamlet'* (New York: Macmillan, 1935), 106). Beerbohm Tree had already tried this out on the stage (Arthur Colby Sprague, *Shakespeare and the Actors: The Stage Business in His Plays (1660–1905)* (Cambridge, MA: Harvard University Press, 1944), 146–7). Hamlet's foreknowledge of the eavesdropping would put a totally different complexion on his behaviour in the nunnery scene; but there is no authority whatever for the early entry. See also note to 3.1.126.
160 loose release, let go. Thompson and Taylor note sexual overtones; it is certainly consistent with Polonius's treatment of Ophelia as an object of his control.

Be you and I behind an arras then.
Mark the encounter: if he love her not,
And be not from his reason fallen thereon,
Let me be no assistant for a state,
But keep a farm and carters.

CLAUDIUS   We will try it.   165

Enter HAMLET *reading on a book*

GERTRUDE But look where sadly the poor wretch comes reading.
POLONIUS Away, I do beseech you both, away.
I'll board him presently.

Exeunt Claudius and Gertrude [and Attendants]
Oh give me leave.

How does my good Lord Hamlet?
HAMLET Well, God-a-mercy.   170
POLONIUS Do you know me, my lord?
HAMLET Excellent well, y'are a fishmonger.
POLONIUS Not I my lord.
HAMLET Then I would you were so honest a man.
POLONIUS Honest my lord?   175
HAMLET Ay sir. To be honest, as this world goes, is to be one man
picked out of ten thousand.
POLONIUS That's very true my lord.
HAMLET For if the sun breed maggots in a dead dog, being a good
kissing carrion – Have you a daughter?   180

---

165 But] Q2; And F   165 SD *reading on a book*] F; *not in* Q2   168 SD *Exeunt ... Gertrude*] *Exit King & Queen* F; *at 167 in*
Q2   168 SD *and Attendants*] Malone; *and Train* / Capell; *not in* Q2, F   172 Excellent well] Q2; Excellent, excellent well
F   172 y'are] F, Q1; you are Q2   177 ten] tenne Q2, Q1; two F   179 good] Q2, F; god Warburton

161 **arras** tapestry or hangings covering a wall,
often with enough space between the two to conceal
people (*OED* 1.2).
165 **carters** cart drivers.
165 At this point in Q1, the plan to use Ophelia
as decoy is put into immediate effect (Ophelia has
entered with Polonius). Gertrude exits, Claudius
and Polonius withdraw, Hamlet enters with
'To be or not to be'. After the confrontation,
Polonius remains on stage, and the fishmonger
scene follows. See Textual Analysis, 271–3.
168 **board** approach, address.
170–210 The conversation between Polonius

and Hamlet is informed by the antic disposition,
which licenses Hamlet's derogatory, absurd-yet-
accurate comments.
172 **fishmonger** seller of fish. Editorial tradition suggests a play on fleshmonger (bawd or pan-
der) as well as fisher or baiter of secrets.
179–80 **the sun ... a good kissing carrion ...**
daughter The sun breeds maggots by kissing
a dead dog, whose flesh is good for that purpose.
Hamlet moves from this talk of kissing and breeding to ask about Ophelia, 'Have you a daughter?'
Here and in 182 Hamlet has in mind the sun/son
pun of 1.2.

POLONIUS I have my lord.

HAMLET Let her not walk i'th'sun. Conception is a blessing, but as your
daughter may conceive – Friend, look to't.

POLONIUS (*Aside*) How say you by that? Still harping on my daughter.
Yet he knew me not at first, a said I was a fishmonger – a is far   185
gone, far gone. And truly, in my youth I suffered much extremity
for love, very near this. I'll speak to him again. – What do you read
my lord?

HAMLET Words, words, words.

POLONIUS What is the matter, my lord?   190

HAMLET Between who?

POLONIUS I mean the matter that you read, my lord.

HAMLET Slanders sir, for the satirical rogue says here that old men have
grey beards, that their faces are wrinkled, their eyes purging thick
amber and plumtree gum, and that they have a plentiful lack of wit,   195
together with most weak hams. All which sir, though I most
powerfully and potently believe, yet I hold it not honesty to have
it thus set down. For yourself sir shall grow old as I am, if like a
crab you could go backward.

POLONIUS (*Aside*) Though this be madness, yet there is method   200
in't. – Will you walk out of the air, my lord?

HAMLET Into my grave?

POLONIUS Indeed that's out of the air. (*Aside*) How pregnant sometimes
his replies are! a happiness that often madness hits on, which reason
and sanity could not so prosperously be delivered of. I will leave   205

---

182 but as] Q2; but not as F   184 SD *Aside*] Malone; not in Q2, F   185 a said] Q2; he said F   185 a is] Q2; he is
F   185–6 far gone, far gone] F; farre gone Q2   192 matter that you] Q2; matter you F, Q1   192 read] Q2; meane
F   193 rogue] Q2; slaue F   195 amber and] Amber, & Q2; Amber, or F   195 lack] Q2; locke F   196 most weak] Q2;
weake F   198 yourself] Q2, Q1; you yourselfe F   198 shall grow] Q2; should be F; shalbe Q1   202 grave?] F; graue.
Q2   203 that's out of the] Q2; that is out o' th' F   205 sanity] F; sanctity Q2

184 **harping on** To harp on one string was
a proverbial phrase for sticking to a single subject.

185 **a is** Represents the slurred pronunciation of
'he is' (something like 'uz'?). Compare 3.3.73.

190 **matter** subject-matter (but Hamlet pretends to understand it as the subject of contention
or dispute).

194 **purging** discharging.

195 **amber and plumtree gum** Whereas the
latter is a very familiar resin, 'amber' was used very
vaguely and could mean half-a-dozen substances,
from the Baltic fossil-resin to ambergris. Here it
presumably means liquidambar, a tree resin. See
OED Amber *sb*[1] 7.

195 **wit** understanding.

197 **honesty** i.e. honourable.

201 **out of the air** The open air, presumably; but
this scene is supposed to be taking place indoors, in
the lobby. Compare 2.2.159, 3.2.339, and note.

203 **pregnant** quick-witted (*OED sv a*[2] 3).

204 **happiness** successful aptness (*OED* 3).

205–8 Q2 omits twelve words, reading 'I will
leave him and my daughter. My Lord, I will take
my leave of you.' This omission occurs in what
seems to have been a vexed area of the plot – the
organization of, and spying on, the meeting between
Hamlet and Ophelia. See Textual Analysis, 271–2.
The typography of the passage in F is discussed by
Jenkins. It seems highly likely that the imperfections of both Q2 and F at this point are related.

him, and suddenly contrive the means of meeting between him and my daughter. – My honourable lord, I will most humbly take my leave of you.

HAMLET You cannot sir take from me anything that I will more willingly part withal; except my life, except my life, except my life. 210

POLONIUS Fare you well my lord.

HAMLET These tedious old fools!

Enter GUILDENSTERN *and* ROSENCRANTZ

POLONIUS You go to seek the Lord Hamlet, there he is.

ROSENCRANTZ God save you sir.

[Exit Polonius]

GUILDENSTERN My honoured lord! 215

ROSENCRANTZ My most dear lord!

HAMLET My excellent good friends! How dost thou Guildenstern? Ah, Rosencrantz. Good lads, how do you both?

ROSENCRANTZ As the indifferent children of the earth.

GUILDENSTERN Happy in that we are not over-happy; on Fortune's 220 cap we are not the very button.

HAMLET Nor the soles of her shoe?

ROSENCRANTZ Neither, my lord.

HAMLET Then you live about her waist, or in the middle of her favours?

GUILDENSTERN Faith, her privates we. 225

HAMLET In the secret parts of Fortune? Oh most true, she is a strumpet. What news?

ROSENCRANTZ None my lord, but that the world's grown honest.

HAMLET Then is doomsday near – but your news is not true. Let me

---

206 and suddenly ... between him] F; *not in* Q2   207 honourable lord] F; Lord Q2   207 most humbly] F; *not in* Q2   209 sir] F; *not in* Q2   209 will] F; will not Q2   210 except my life, except my life, except my life] Q2; except my life, my life F   212 SD] Q2 *at 210*, F *at 213 with names interchanged*   213 the] Q2; my F   214 SD] Capell; *not in* Q2, F   215 My] Q2; Mine F   217 excellent] F; extent Q2   217 Ah,] A Q2; Oh, F   218 you] Q2; ye F   220 over] F; euer Q2   221 cap] F; lap Q2   227 What news] Q2; What's the newes F   228 but that the] F; but the Q2   229–56 Let me ... attended] F; *not in* Q2

---

206 **suddenly** immediately.

219 **indifferent** i.e. in-between, at neither extreme.

220 **Fortune's** The men's series of jokes depends upon the Roman figure of goddess Fortuna, goddess of fate and known for her fickleness.

221–2 **very button ... her shoe** i.e. neither on the top nor trodden down.

224 **favours** Fortune's favours are compared with the sexual favours of a woman. (The word is not much used in this sense now, but was important in less free-spoken ages. See *OED* favour *sb* 2d.)

225 **her privates we** 'we are *very* intimate with her', since privates = genitals. (*OED* gives this as the first use (C.I.4).) 'Private' was not yet a term of military rank.

229–56 This whole passage is not found in Q2. It is much more likely that this is a cut than that F provides a later addition. By the time Q2 was printed in 1604, the position of Anne of Denmark as King James's consort might have made the printer cautious about setting up material naming Denmark as one of the worst prisons in the world. This qualm, however, does not seem to have affected the printing in Q2 of 'Something is rotten ...' (1.4.90).

question more in particular. What have you, my good friends,   230
deserved at the hands of Fortune, that she sends you to prison
hither?

GUILDENSTERN Prison, my lord?

HAMLET Denmark's a prison.

ROSENCRANTZ Then is the world one.   235

HAMLET A goodly one, in which there are many confines, wards, and
dungeons; Denmark being one o'th'worst.

ROSENCRANTZ We think not so my lord.

HAMLET Why then 'tis none to you, for there is nothing either good
or bad but thinking makes it so. To me it is a prison.   240

ROSENCRANTZ Why then your ambition makes it one; 'tis too narrow
for your mind.

HAMLET O God, I could be bounded in a nutshell, and count myself
a king of infinite space, were it not that I have bad dreams.

GUILDENSTERN Which dreams indeed are ambition, for the very   245
substance of the ambitious is merely the shadow of a dream.

HAMLET A dream itself is but a shadow.

ROSENCRANTZ Truly, and I hold ambition of so airy and light a quality
that it is but a shadow's shadow.

HAMLET Then are our beggars bodies, and our monarchs and out-   250
stretched heroes the beggars' shadows. Shall we to th'court? for by
my fay I cannot reason.

BOTH We'll wait upon you.

HAMLET No such matter. I will not sort you with the rest of my
servants; for to speak to you like an honest man, I am most   255

---

236 confines, wards Terms for places of confinement.

239–40 nothing ... makes it so Hamlet's relativism – his sceptical uncertainty about absolutes which reverberates throughout the play – here applies to happiness: whether a place is good or bad to be in depends on one's mental attitude.

245, 248 Rosencrantz and Guildenstern make strenuous attempts to keep the conversation on the subject of ambition.

245–6 the very substance ... dream Ambitious people live or feed on their aspirations, making of themselves merely shadows of such dreams.

250–1 Hamlet seems to mean that if the substance of the ambitious is a shadow, only the lowest in society will have real bodies. Real bodies cast shadows, and this is the status of monarchs and great men. ('outstretched' indicates those who have aspired or reached out, also applicable to a long shadow.)

252 fay faith.

252 I cannot reason Hamlet hints, lightly but explicitly, at his antic disposition.

254 sort you class you.

255–6 I am ... attended I have such an inferior lot of servants. But the phrase has private meanings for Hamlet, including the pressure of his own thoughts or his awareness of Claudius's surveillance. Derick R. C. Marsh suggests that the phrase must bring the Ghost to mind (*SQ* 33.2 (1982), 181–2).

dreadfully attended. But in the beaten way of friendship, what make

you at Elsinore?

ROSENCRANTZ To visit you my lord, no other occasion.

HAMLET Beggar that I am, I am even poor in thanks, but I thank you – and sure, dear friends, my thanks are too dear a halfpenny. 260
Were you not sent for? Is it your own inclining? Is it a free visitation? Come, deal justly with me. Come, come. Nay, speak.

GUILDENSTERN What should we say my lord?

HAMLET Why, anything but to the purpose. You were sent for – and there is a kind of confession in your looks which your modesties 265
have not craft enough to colour. I know the good king and queen have sent for you.

ROSENCRANTZ To what end my lord?

HAMLET That you must teach me. But let me conjure you, by the rights of our fellowship, by the consonancy of our youth, by the obligation 270
of our ever-preserved love, and by what more dear a better proposer can charge you withal, be even and direct with me, whether you were sent for or no.

ROSENCRANTZ (*To Guildenstern*) What say you?

HAMLET (*Aside*) Nay then I have an eye of you. – If you love me, hold 275
not off.

GUILDENSTERN My lord, we were sent for.

HAMLET I will tell you why. So shall my anticipation prevent your discovery, and your secrecy to the king and queen moult no feather. I have of late, but wherefore I know not, lost all my mirth, forgone 280

---

259 even] F; euer Q2   262 Come, deal] F; come, come, deale Q2   264 Why] F; *not in* Q2   265 kind *of*] Q2, kinde
F   272 can] Q2; could F   274 SD *To Guildenstern*] Theobald²; *not in* Q2, F   275 SD *Aside*] Steevens³; *not in* Q2,
F   279 and your] Q2; of your F

256 beaten ... friendship He means he has neglected the ordinary politeness of greeting and now offers one.

259 Beggar that I am A beggar, in the terms of the preceding conversation, as he is not ambitious; but a beggar in his own eyes as a dispossessed prince in prison.

260 too dear a halfpenny (i.e. at a halfpenny) not worth anything; certainly not like a king's remembrance (see 26 above).

265 modesties sense of shame.

269 conjure solemnly entreat.

270 consonancy accord, agreement. He means the harmony between them in their younger days

(see 11 above).

272 even straightforward, 'on the level'.

275 of you on you.

278-9 my anticipation ... discovery my proactive explanation will save you from having to disclose your commission.

279 your secrecy ... feather You won't have to lose or shed any aspect of your pact with the king and queen.

280-90 The compelling expressions of world-weariness in this famous speech are also part of Hamlet's campaign to mislead Rosencrantz and Guildenstern, whom he has just learned are working in the service of the king and queen.

all custom of exercises; and indeed it goes so heavily with my
disposition that this goodly frame, the earth, seems to me a sterile
promontory; this most excellent canopy the air, look you, this brave
o'erhanging firmament, this majestical roof fretted with golden
fire – why, it appeareth no other thing to me but a foul and pestilent   285
congregation of vapours. What a piece of work is a man! How noble
in reason, how infinite in faculties, in form and moving how express
and admirable, in action how like an angel, in apprehension how
like a god! The beauty of the world, the paragon of animals – and
yet to me, what is this quintessence of dust? Man delights not   290
me – no, nor woman neither, though by your smiling you seem to
say so.

ROSENCRANTZ My lord, there was no such stuff in my thoughts.

HAMLET Why did ye laugh then, when I said man delights not me?

ROSENCRANTZ To think, my lord, if you delight not in man, what   295
lenten entertainment the players shall receive from you. We coted
them on the way, and hither are they coming to offer you service.

HAMLET He that plays the king shall be welcome, his majesty shall have
tribute of me; the adventurous knight shall use his foil and target,
the lover shall not sigh gratis, the humorous man shall end his part   300
in peace, the clown shall make those laugh whose lungs are tickle

---

281 exercises] Q2; exercise F   281 heavily] Q2; heauenly F   284 firmament] Q2; *not in* F   285 appeareth] Q2; appeares
F   285 no other thing] F; nothing Q2   285 but] Q2; than   F   286 What a] F; What Q2   287 faculties] Q2; faculty
F   287 moving how] F; moouing, how Q2   288 admirable, in] admirable? in F; admirable in Q2   288 angel, in] Angel?
in F; Angell in Q2   291 no, nor] F; nor Q2   291 woman] F; women Q2   294 ye] Q2; you F   294 then] Q2, Q1; *not in*
F   299 of] F; on Q2   301–2 the clown ... sere] F; *not in* Q2   301 tickle] *Clark and Wright, conj. Staunton;*
tickled F

---

281 **custom of exercises** i.e. pursuing the
activities of a gentleman, such as fencing, riding,
hawking, dancing. F reads 'custom of exercise',
a very different matter, meaning 'exercise' as we
would use it – what you do to keep your body fit.
Thompson and Taylor point out that Hamlet contradicts such lethargy in 5.2.184–5.

282–3 **sterile promontory** A promontory is
a point of high land which juts out over a body of
water. Kittredge paraphrases the image of the earth
as 'a barren rocky point jutting out into the sea of
eternity'.

284 **fretted** interlaced, patterned (as in
a decorated ceiling).

287 **faculties** abilities or capacities

287–9 **in form ... god** Punctuation follows F;
the punctuation in Q2 gives a quite different
meaning.

287 **express** well-formed or well-designed, but

perhaps also expressive.

289 **paragon** pattern of excellence.

296 **lenten entertainment** austere reception.

296–7 **coted them** passed them by.

298–9 **his majesty ... tribute of me**
As we pay money and offer adulation to real
kings, so the Player King will get payment and
praise. There is an intentional confusion of actor
and role here, which continues through the
sentence.

299 **foil and target** sword and shield.

300 **gratis** for nothing.

300 **humorous man** eccentric character, one
who displays an exaggerated temperament or disposition. See note to 1.4.27.

301–2 **tickle o'th'sere** easily triggered (the
'sere' is a catch affecting the trigger-mechanism of
a gun; 'tickle' means lightly set – and, of course,
'ticklish').

o'th'sere, and the lady shall say her mind freely – or the blank verse
shall halt for't. What players are they?

ROSENCRANTZ Even those you were wont to take such delight in, the
tragedians of the city.   305

HAMLET How chances it they travel? their residence, both in reputation
and profit, was better both ways.

ROSENCRANTZ I think their inhibition comes by the means of the late
innovation.

HAMLET Do they hold the same estimation they did when I was in the   310
city? Are they so followed?

ROSENCRANTZ No indeed are they not.

HAMLET How comes it? Do they grow rusty?

ROSENCRANTZ Nay, their endeavour keeps in the wonted pace, but
there is sir an eyrie of children, little eyases, that cry out on the   315
top of question and are most tyrannically clapped for't. These are

---

302 blank] F; black Q2   304 such delight] Q2; delight F, Q1   306 travel] trauaile Q2, F   311 are they] Q2; they are
F   313–33 HAMLET How … load too] F; *not in* Q2

302–3 the lady … halt for't If the lady can't
say all she has to say – which will be the part that is
written down for her – then clearly there will be
some holes in the blank verse.

303 halt limp.

305 tragedians Properly, tragic actors; here,
actors generally.

306–7 their residence … ways they did better
in reputation and profit when they stayed at home
(i.e. in the city).

308–9 their inhibition … innovation i.e. they
are forbidden to play in the city because of
a disturbance or change in their environment.
That change could have several possible referents.
It may gesture to events within the world of the play
itself – that is, to the recent political upheaval at
Elsinore and the impending war with Fortinbras.
But it may be a topical allusion to English rather
than Danish issues. It may refer to theatrical conditions in London at the time of the play's performance, when the fashion for the children's
companies seemed to threaten the livelihood of the
adult actors, or to non-theatrical events or restraints
(such as Essex's rebellion of February 1601). See
Introduction, 8–9.

313–33 This whole passage, a bravura on contemporary theatre problems unique in Shakespeare, is
missing from Q2 and condensed in Q1 ('Yfaith my
Lord, noueltie carries it away, / For the principall
publike audience that / Came to them, are turned to
priuate playes, / And to the humour of children').
Based on the news that the players are touring, Hamlet
asks Rosencrantz about the status of the troupe and
learns that their reputation has fallen, not because they
do not perform or perform poorly but because of
competition from a company of child actors, whom
audiences prefer and whose satire frightens the audience away from the adults at the public theatres ('common stages'). Hamlet then asks questions about who is
responsible for these performances. This is a reference
to the 'Poetomachia', or 'War of the Theatres',
a contest waged between individual playwrights as
well as between adult and children's troupes.
The revival around 1600 of the two boy companies,
Paul's Boys and the Children of the Chapel, prompted
the sparring, as the boy players' success was perceived
as a threat to the adults' secure place with audiences in
London. As James P. Bednarz points out, this passage
records concern about only one of the children's companies, the Children of the Chapel, who played at
Blackfriars; at the time it was composed,
Shakespeare's company, the Chamberlain's Men,
was 'allied with' the children of Paul's (*Shakespeare
and the Poets' War*, 229).

The date of the passage has been debated by scholars. According to Bednarz, the passage was written
and inserted into the play in 1601, after it premiered.
Its absence from Q2 is thus likely the result of
a deliberate cut; it may also have been overlooked by
or not available to the Q2 compositors. If the passage
was developed in 1608, as maintained by Roslyn
Knutson, the reason for its absence from Q2 is clear.
See the Introduction, 8–9.

315 eyrie … eyases nest of little unfledged hawks
(as a metaphor for one company of child actors).

315–16 cry … question 'question' frequently
means 'dispute' or 'controversy'. Perhaps this
means that the boys enthusiastically carry on the
theatre war in their treble voices.

316 tyrannically inordinately, outrageously.

now the fashion, and so be-rattle the common stages (so they call them) that many wearing rapiers are afraid of goose-quills, and dare scarce come thither.

HAMLET What, are they children? Who maintains 'em? How are they
escoted? Will they pursue the quality no longer than they can sing?
Will they not say afterwards, if they should grow themselves to
common players – as it is most like if their means are no better, their
writers do them wrong to make them exclaim against their own
succession?

ROSENCRANTZ Faith, there has been much to do on both sides, and
the nation holds it no sin to tar them to controversy. There was
for a while no money bid for argument unless the poet and the
player went to cuffs in the question.

HAMLET Is't possible?

GUILDENSTERN Oh there has been much throwing about of brains.

HAMLET Do the boys carry it away?

ROSENCRANTZ Ay that they do my lord, Hercules and his load too.

HAMLET It is not very strange, for my uncle is king of Denmark, and
those that would make mouths at him while my father lived give
twenty, forty, fifty, a hundred ducats apiece for his picture in little.
'Sblood, there is something in this more than natural, if philosophy
could find it out.

Flourish for the Players

GUILDENSTERN There are the players.

320

325

330

335

---

317 be-rattle] F2; be-ratled F   323 most like] *Pope;* like most F   334 very strange] Q2; strange F   334 my] Q2, Q1;
mine F   335 mouths] Q2; mows F   336 fifty] Q2; *not in* F   336 a] Q2; an F   337 'Sblood] Q2; *not in* F   338
SD *Flourish for the Players*] F; *A flourish* Q2

317 **be-rattle** rattle, shake.
317 **common stages** The usual term for the amphitheatres in the suburbs of London where the adult companies played (in contrast to the smaller indoor theatres, within the city walls, where the children performed). The distinction is often made in terms of public (outdoor) and private (indoor).
318 **many ... rapiers** the men-about-town, the gallants allowed to carry weapons.
318 **afraid of goose-quills** The satire of the children's dramatists has so discredited the public theatres that fashionable gallants don't like being seen there (Dowden's suggestion).
321 **escoted** maintained financially. (From the French *escotter*; very rare in English.)
321 **quality** profession.
323 **common players** professional actors.
323 **if their means ... better** if they do not acquire a better means of supporting themselves.
325 **succession** their future profession (that to which they will succeed).
327 **nation** Not the country or state but a group

of individuals associated with the theatre, including the audience.
327 **tar** incite, provoke. (Editors often preserve the old spelling 'tarre'.)
328 **no money ... argument** i.e. no company was willing to pay for a new play.

332 **Do the boys carry it away?** Does the boy company have the advantage, do they win?
333 **Hercules and his load** The emblem of the Globe Theatre is supposed to have been Hercules carrying the celestial globe on his shoulders.
335 **make mouths** grimace. So Q2. F reads 'mows', which means the same thing.
336 **ducats** coins of gold or silver, used in many European countries. The value might be two or three to the English pound at the time. (A pound in Elizabethan England would be worth roughly £140 in the early twenty-first century.)
337–8 **more than natural ... find it out** i.e. there is something abnormal about it as scientific investigation would show.

HAMLET Gentlemen, you are welcome to Elsinore. Your hands, come   340
  then. Th'appurtenance of welcome is fashion and ceremony. Let
  me comply with you in this garb, lest my extent to the players, which
  I tell you must show fairly outwards, should more appear like
  entertainment than yours. You are welcome – but my uncle-father
  and aunt-mother are deceived.   345
GUILDENSTERN In what my dear lord?
HAMLET I am but mad north-north-west. When the wind is southerly,
  I know a hawk from a handsaw.

Enter POLONIUS

POLONIUS Well be with you gentlemen.
HAMLET Hark you Guildenstern, and you too – at each ear a hearer.   350
  That great baby you see there is not yet out of his swaddling clouts.
ROSENCRANTZ Happily he's the second time come to them, for they
  say an old man is twice a child.
HAMLET I will prophesy: he comes to tell me of the players, mark
  it. – You say right sir, a Monday morning, 'twas then indeed.   355
POLONIUS My lord, I have news to tell you.
HAMLET My lord, I have news to tell you. When Roscius was an actor
  in Rome –
POLONIUS The actors are come hither my lord.
HAMLET Buzz, buzz!   360
POLONIUS Upon my honour.
HAMLET Then came each actor on his ass –
POLONIUS The best actors in the world, either for tragedy, comedy,
  history, pastoral, pastoral-comical, historical-pastoral, tragical-

---

340–1 come then. Th'] come then, th' Q2; come: The F   342 this garb] Q2; the Garbe F   342 lest my] F; let me Q2   343
outwards] Q2; outward F   351 swaddling] swadling Q2, Q1; swathing F   352 he's] F; he is Q2   355 a] Q2; for
a F   357 was] Q2; *not in* F   361 my] Q2; mine F   362 came] Q2; can F   364–5 tragical- . . . pastoral] F; *not in* Q2

341 Th'appurtenance The usual accompani-
ment.

342 comply with you pay you the usual cour-
tesies (compare 5.2.165, 'comply with his dug').
Hamlet is concerned from 342–4 that his welcome
to the players might seem more generous than that
which he gave to Rosencrantz and Guildenstern..

342 garb manner of doing things.

342 my extent what I extend, how I behave.

344 entertainment welcome.

347 but mad north-north-west He means (1)
that he is only a little away from the true north of
sanity, and (2) that he is not mad at all points of the
compass, i.e. at all times.

**347–8 When the wind … a hawk from
a handsaw** Hamlet maintains that he is only mad
in particular circumstances. But he undermines his
claim, since the difference he notes (between a hawk

and a handsaw) is the distinction of a madman.
Thus, even as he pretends to impart the secret
that he is not mad, he confirms that he is raving.
Some editors have argued for the relation between
the two, suggesting that the 'handsaw' is
a 'hernshaw', a kind of heron (and thus comparable
to a hawk), and that the 'hawk' is the plasterer's tool
so named (and thus comparable a saw).

352 Happily Perhaps.

357 Roscius A great Roman comic actor (d.
62 BC).

360 Buzz, buzz! A 'buzz' is a rumour. Hamlet is
making a stock response, imitating the 'rude noise'
of an 'anal emission of wind' (Eric Partridge,
Shakespeare's Bawdy (Abingdon, Oxon: Routledge,
2001; first published 1947, Routledge & Kegan
Paul)) to a report which he doesn't trust or already
knows.

historical, tragical-comical-historical-pastoral, scene individable or   365
poem unlimited. Seneca cannot be too heavy, nor Plautus too light.
For the law of writ and the liberty, these are the only men.

HAMLET O Jephtha judge of Israel, what a treasure hadst
thou!

POLONIUS What a treasure had he my lord?

HAMLET Why –   370
'One fair daughter and no more,
The which he lovèd passing well.'

POLONIUS Still on my daughter.

HAMLET Am I not i'th'right, old Jephtha?

POLONIUS If you call me Jephtha my lord, I have a daughter that I   375
love passing well.

HAMLET Nay, that follows not.

POLONIUS What follows then my lord?

HAMLET Why –
'As by lot God wot,'   380
And then you know –
'It came to pass, as most like it was,' –
the first row of the pious chanson will show you more, for look where
my abridgement comes.

---

365 individable] indeuidible Q2; indiuible F   371–2 more, / The] F; *not divided in* Q2   383 pious chanson] Q2; *Pons Chanson* F   384 abridgement comes] Q2, Q1; Abridgements come F

365 **tragical-comical-historical-pastoral**
Shakespeare mocks efforts to categorize compre-
hensively the drama of his day.

365–6 **scene … unlimited** The traditional
interpretation is that this contrasts plays which
observe the unities of time, place, and action with
those that don't. But Jenkins interestingly suggests
that 'individable' and 'unlimited' are the terms to
use when there can be no further refinement or
subdivision   in   this   absurd   progress   of
categorization.

366 **Seneca … Plautus** These Roman dramatists, one tragic and one comic, were the classical
playwrights best known to the Elizabethans, and
who most influenced their work.

367 **the law of writ and the liberty** Obscure:
possibly Polonius means plays which obey pre-
scribed rules ('writ' = authoritative guidance), and
those which are free from such rules.

368–72 **Jephtha … passing well** The reference is to the biblical Jephtha (Judges 11–12).
Before going to war against the Ammonites,
Jephtha vowed that if he was victorious, he would
sacrifice the first living thing that came out of his
house upon his return. That person was his own
daughter, and he sacrificed her after she had gone
into the mountains to 'bewail her virginity' – so she

died and 'knew no man' (Judges 11.30–40).
The ballad Hamlet quotes is known in an early-
seventeenth-century version: 'Had one faire
daughter and no moe, / Whom he beloved passing
well, / And as by lot God wot, / It came to passe,
most like it was'. (The single surviving copy of this
print, in the Manchester Central Library, differs
in its readings from the reprints quoted by Jenkins
and others.)

377 **that follows not** A play on words, according to which Hamlet means that Polonius's statement is neither the logical next step nor the next line
of the ballad.

383 **first row … chanson** A 'row' is properly
a line, but, as this does not make much sense, some
editors suggest, without much authority, 'stanza' –
i.e. 'you'll have to read the first stanza of this pious
ballad if you want more'. Q1 says 'the first verse of
the godly Ballet'.

384 **abridgement** that which shortens my
recitation. It is frequently suggested, because of
the use of the word in *A Midsummer Night's
Dream* 5.1.39, in a context suggesting the meaning 'entertainment', that Hamlet is here punning
on two senses, 'abbreviation', and 'entertainment'. But this secondary meaning is not well
attested.

Enter the PLAYERS

Y'are welcome masters, welcome all. I am glad to see thee well.   385
Welcome good friends. Oh, my old friend! why, thy face is valanced
since I saw thee last; com'st thou to beard me in Denmark? What,
my young lady and mistress – byrlady, your ladyship is nearer to
heaven than when I saw you last by the altitude of a chopine. Pray
God your voice like a piece of uncurrent gold be not cracked within   390
the ring. Masters, you are all welcome. We'll e'en to't like French
falconers, fly at anything we see: we'll have a speech straight. Come
give us a taste of your quality: come, a passionate speech.

I PLAYER What speech, my good lord?

HAMLET I heard thee speak me a speech once, but it was never acted,   395
or if it was, not above once, for the play I remember pleased not
the million: 'twas caviary to the general. But it was, as I received
it, and others whose judgementsin such matters cried in the top
of mine, an excellent play, well digested in the scenes, set down
with as much modesty as cunning. I remember one said there were   400
no sallets in the lines to make the matter savoury, nor no matter in
the phrase that might indict the author of affectation, but called it

---

384 SD] Q2; *Enter foure or fine Players* F   385 Y'are] F; You are Q2   386 my old] F, Q1; old Q2   386 why] Q2;
not in F   386 valanced] valanct Q2; valiant F   388 byrlady] Byrlady F; by lady Q2   388 nearer to] Q2; neerer
F   391–2 French falconers] F; friendly Fankners Q2   394 my good lord] Q2; my Lord F   398 judgements] Q2;
iudgement F   400 were] Q2; was F   402 affectation] F; affection Q2

---

384 SD So Q2. F's 'four or five players' is
a characteristic example of the scribe's preliminary
efforts to put limits on the permissiveness of
Shakespeare's MS. See Textual Analysis, 266–8.

386 valanced fringed, curtained round – figurative for bearded.

387 beard challenge, defy; following 386, he
sports a beard.

388 my young lady A boy actor who takes
female roles; presumably the Player Queen of 3.2.

388 byrlady by our Lady. Pronounced berlády.
See note to 3.2.118.

389 chopine Additional base to a lady's shoe to
increase height.

390–1 your voice ... cracked ... ring A joke
on the boy player getting older so that his voice
might crack like a bad coin and be 'rendered unfit
for currency' (Douce, in NV). But there is also
a bawdy quibble on losing virginity; see Partridge,
Shakespeare's Bawdy, under 'crack/crackt'.

Hamlet means 'I hope you haven't lost your virginity as a player of female parts, and ceased to be
acceptable (current), by the breaking of your
voice.'

393 quality professional skill.

395 me Ethical dative (to or for me)

397 caviary A common early form of 'caviar'.
Pronounced caviáry.

397 the general people in general, the
multitude.

398–9 cried ... mine An unusual phrase.
It must mean 'counted more than mine'.

399 digested arranged, disposed.

400 modesty moderation, restraint (*OED* 1).

400 cunning skill.

401 sallets salads. Generally thought to mean
'spicy bits' – indecencies.

402 affectation So F. Q2 reads 'affection',
which some claim means 'affectation', but the argument is not strong.

an honest method, as wholesome as sweet and by very much more
handsome than fine. One speech in't I chiefly loved, 'twas Aeneas'
tale to Dido, and thereabout of it especially where he speaks of   405
Priam's slaughter. If it live in your memory, begin at this line, let
me see, let me see –
            'The rugged Pyrrhus, like th'Hyrcanian beast' –
'Tis not so, it begins with Pyrrhus –
            'The rugged Pyrrhus, he whose sable arms,   410
            Black as his purpose, did the night resemble
            When he lay couchèd in the ominous horse,
            Hath now this dread and black complexion smeared
            With heraldy more dismal. Head to foot
            Now is he total gules, horridly tricked   415
            With blood of fathers, mothers, daughters, sons,
            Baked and impasted with the parching streets,
            That lend a tyrannous and a damnèd light
            To their lord's murder. Roasted in wrath and fire,
            And thus o'er-sizèd with coagulate gore,   420
            With eyes like carbuncles, the hellish Pyrrhus
            Old grandsire Priam seeks –'
So, proceed you.
POLONIUS 'Fore God my lord, well spoken, with good accent and good
        discretion.   425

403–4 as wholesome … fine] Q2; *not in* F   404 speech] Q2; cheefe Speech F   404 in't] Q2; in it F   405 tale] F; talke
Q2   405 where] F; when Q2   408 th'Hyrcanean] F; Th'ircanian Q2   409 'Tis] Q2; It is F   412 the] F; th' Q2   414
heraldy] Q2; Heraldry F   415 total] Q2; to take F   418 a damnèd] Q2; damned F   419 lord's murder] Lords murther
Q2; vilde Murthers F   420 o'er-sized] o're-sized F; ore-cised Q2   423 So, proceed you] Q2; *not in* F

403 method The arrangement of material in
a literary work.
    404 fine showy, over-elaborate.
    404–6 Aeneas' tale … slaughter See Virgil's
Aeneid II, 506–58. Shakespeare had an intense
interest in this epic (see Introduction, 39–40).
Priam's death is the subject of an extended passage
in *Dido, Queen of Carthage* by Marlowe and Nashe,
and it is certain that Shakespeare had this earlier
treatment in mind when creating the speech which
now follows.
    408 rugged rough and fierce. Applied to an
animal, it could mean shaggy, which is perhaps
why Hamlet makes a false start on the Hyrcanian
beast.
    408 Pyrrhus Pyrrhus, or Neoptolemus, the son
of Achilles, was summoned to the Trojan War to
avenge his father. With Hamlet, Fortinbras, and

Laertes, he makes a fourth son avenging a father.
He was renowned for his savagery and barbarity.
    408 Hyrcanian beast Tiger from Hyrcania,
near the Caspian sea. Virgil spoke of them in
Aeneid IV, 368.
    412 couchèd concealed.
    414 heraldy See note to 1.1.87.
    414 dismal sinister.
    415 gules The heraldic name for red.
    415 tricked decorated.
    417 Baked … streets The blood is dried into
a paste on Pyrrhus by the heat of the burning street.
    418 tyrannous ferocious.
    420 o'er-sized To oversize is to cover over with
size, the sticky wash used as a preparative by
painters.
    421 carbuncles large and supposedly luminous
precious stones of a red colour.

I PLAYER   'Anon he finds him,
Striking too short at Greeks; his antique sword,
Rebellious to his arm, lies where it falls,
Repugnant to command. Unequal matched,
Pyrrhus at Priam drives, in rage strikes wide,   430
But with the whiff and wind of his fell sword
Th'unnervèd father falls. Then senseless Ilium,
Seeming to feel this blow, with flaming top
Stoops to his base, and with a hideous crash
Takes prisoner Pyrrhus' ear; for lo, his sword,   435
Which was declining on the milky head
Of reverend Priam, seemed i'th'air to stick.
So, as a painted tyrant, Pyrrhus stood,
And like a neutral to his will and matter,
Did nothing.   440
But as we often see against some storm,
A silence in the heavens, the rack stand still,
The bold winds speechless, and the orb below
As hush as death, anon the dreadful thunder
Doth rend the region; so after Pyrrhus' pause,   445
A rousèd vengeance sets him new a-work,
And never did the Cyclops' hammers fall
On Mars's armour, forged for proof eterne,
With less remorse than Pyrrhus' bleeding sword
Now falls on Priam.   450
Out, out, thou strumpet Fortune! All you gods,
In general synod take away her power,
Break all the spokes and fellies from her wheel,

---

427 antique] *Pope;* anticke Q2, F   429 matched] matcht Q2; match F   432 Then . . . Ilium] F; *not in* Q2   433 this] Q2; his F   439 And] F; *not in* Q2   439–40 matter, / Did] Q2; *not divided in* F   448 Mars's] *Marses* Q2; Mars his F   448 armour] Q2; *Armours* F   453 fellies] F4; follies Q2; *Fallies* F

426 **Anon** Presently.
429 **Repugnant to** Resisting.
432 **senseless** insensible.
432 **Ilium** Troy. Used here, Kittredge points out, for the citadel and not the whole city.
436 **milky** i.e. white-haired.
438 **painted tyrant** tyrant in a painting.
439 **like a neutral … matter** 'As a neutral stands idle between two parties, so Pyrrhus paused midway between his purpose and its fulfilment' (Kittredge).
441 **against** before.
442 **rack** cloud-formation.

443 **orb** globe, hence earth.
445 **region** sky.
447 **Cyclops** The one-eyed giants worked in Vulcan's smithy.
448 **proof eterne** everlasting resistance.
449 **remorse** pity.
452 **synod** assembly, council
453 **fellies** wooden pieces forming the rim of a wheel.
453 **wheel** Fortuna was traditionally pictured with a wheel, whose constant turning was an emblem of the fickleness of fate.

And bowl the round nave down the hill of heaven
As low as to the fiends.'   455
POLONIUS This is too long.
HAMLET It shall to th' barber's with your beard. Prithee say on.
  He's for a jig or a tale of bawdry, or he sleeps. Say on, come to
  Hecuba.
1 PLAYER 'But who – ah woe! – had seen the mobled queen –'   460
HAMLET The mobled queen?
POLONIUS That's good, 'mobled queen' is good.
1 PLAYER 'Run barefoot up and down, threat'ning the flames
              With bisson rheum, a clout upon that head
              Where late the diadem stood, and, for a robe,   465
              About her lank and all o'er-teemèd loins
              A blanket, in th'alarm of fear caught up –
              Who this had seen, with tongue in venom steeped
              'Gainst Fortune's state would treason have pronounced.
              But if the gods themselves did see her then,   470
              When she saw Pyrrhus make malicious sport
              In mincing with his sword her husband's limbs,
              The instant burst of clamour that she made,
              Unless things mortal move them not at all,
              Would have made milch the burning eyes of heaven,   475
              And passion in the gods.
POLONIUS Look where he has not turned his colour, and has tears in's
  eyes. Prithee no more.
HAMLET 'Tis well, I'll have thee speak out the rest of this soon. – Good
  my lord, will you see the players well bestowed? Do you hear, let   480

---

457 to th'] to'th F; to the Q2 460 ah woe] a woe Q2; O who F, Q1 460, 461 mobled] Q2, Q1; inobled
F 462 'mobled … good] F (Inobled); not in Q2 463 flames] Q2; flame F 464 bisson rheum] Bisson Rheume F;
Bison rehume Q2 464 upon] Q2; about F 467 th'alarm] th'Alarum F; the alarme Q2 472 husband's] F; husband
Q2 478 Prithee] Q2; Pray you F 479 of this] Q2; not in F 480 you hear] Q2; ye heare F

454 nave hub of the wheel.

458 He's for a jig Polonius wants to see a jig, the afterpiece, with song and dance, which often concluded theatre performances.

460 mobled muffled. It is made clear that this is a rare word. It appears as 'mobble' in 1655, indicating the pronunciation.

464 bisson Means blind, or near-blind. Her tears ('rheum') are blinding her.

464 clout cloth.

466 all o'er-teemèd loins loins which had borne too many children. The count of Hecuba's children varied greatly – seventeen, nineteen or

more. In *Dido, Queen of Carthage* (2.1.234), Priam says he is 'father of fifty sons' – but they were not supposed to be all Hecuba's. See *Aeneid* II, 501–5.

469 state government.

475 milch Properly, exuding milk. The stars would weep milky tears (because of the Milky Way?).

476 passion violent sorrow.

477 Look where See if. '[W]here' is a common contracted form of 'whether'. The forms given by editors ('whe'r', 'whe'er', etc.) are orthographic inventions (compare 'ta'en'; see 1.3.106).

 ı be well used, for they are the abstract and brief chronicles
ıe time. After your death you were better have a bad epitaph
n their ill report while you live.

ıus My lord, I will use them according to their desert.

HAMLET God's bodkin man, much better. Use every man after his 485
desert, and who shall scape whipping? Use them after your own
honour and dignity; the less they deserve, the more merit is in your
bounty. Take them in.

POLONIUS Come sirs. *Exit Polonius*

HAMLET Follow him friends, we'll hear a play tomorrow. – Dost thou 490
hear me old friend, can you play *The Murder of Gonzago?*

I PLAYER Ay my lord.

HAMLET We'll ha't tomorrow night. You could for a need study a
speech of some dozen or sixteen lines, which I would set down and
insert in't, could you not? 495

I PLAYER Ay my lord.

HAMLET Very well. Follow that lord, and look you mock him not.
Exeunt Players
My good friends, I'll leave you till night. You are welcome to
Elsinore.

ROSENCRANTZ Good my lord. 500
Exeunt Rosencrantz and Guildenstern

HAMLET Ay so, God bye to you. Now I am alone.
—— O what a rogue and peasant slave am I!
Is it not monstrous that this player here,
But in a fiction, in a dream of passion,
Could force his soul so to his own conceit 505

---

481 abstract] Q2; Abstracts F   483 live] Q2; liued F   485 bodkin] Q2; bodykins F   485 much better] Q2; better
F   486 shall] Q2; should F   489 SD] F; *not in* Q2; *Exit Polonius with all the Players except the First / Dyce (490)*
493 a need] F; neede Q2   494 dozen . . . lines] F; dosen lines, or sixteene lines Q2   495 you] Q2; ye F   497 SD] *This
edn; Exeunt Pol. and Players.* Q2(*after* Elsinore, *499*); *not in* F   498 till] F; tell Q2   500 SD] *Capell; Exeunt.* Q2;
Exeunt. / Manet Hamlet. F   501 God bye to you] Q2 *(buy);* God buy 'ye F   505 own] Q2; whole F

481 **abstract** epitome, summary, distillation.
485 **God's bodkin** Euphemism for the sacrile-
gious 'God's bodykins' (= God's dear body), which
is the reading of F – a surprising survivor of the
post-1606 removal of profanities. See Textual
Analysis, 275.
489 SD *Exit Polonius* So F. Q2 gives a general

exeunt for Polonius and the players at 535, which is
awkward. See Textual Analysis, 267.
494 **dozen or sixteen lines** The identification
of these in the play as acted is a famous but insoluble
problem. For Shakespeare's hesitation over this
phrase, see Textual Analysis, 255.
505 **conceit** imaginings.

That from her working all his visage wanned,
Tears in his eyes, distraction in's aspect,
A broken voice, and his whole function suiting
With forms to his conceit? And all for nothing?
For Hecuba!   510
What's Hecuba to him, or he to Hecuba,
That he should weep for her? What would he do,
Had he the motive and the cue for passion
That I have? He would drown the stage with tears,
And cleave the general ear with horrid speech,   515
Make mad the guilty and appal the free,
Confound the ignorant, and amaze indeed
The very faculties of eyes and ears. Yet I,
A dull and muddy-mettled rascal, peak
Like John-a-dreams, unpregnant of my cause,   520
And can say nothing – no, not for a king,
Upon whose property and most dear life
A damned defeat was made. Am I a coward?
Who calls me villain, breaks my pate across,
Plucks off my beard and blows it in my face,   525
Tweaks me by th'nose, gives me the lie i'th'throat
As deep as to the lungs? Who does me this?

---

506 his] F; the Q2   506 wanned] wand Q2; warm'd F   507 in's] F; in his Q2   511 he to Hecuba] F; he to her
Q2   513 the cue] F; that Q2   516 appal] *Rowe;* appale Q2; apale F   518 faculties] Q2; faculty F   526 th'nose] F;
the nose Q2

506 from her working by reason of her (the soul's) activity.

506 wanned grew pale.

508–9 his whole function … conceit all his bodily powers producing the expressions proper to his imaginings. The player, by imagining himself in the situation, in 'a dream of passion', becomes so affected that he weeps.

516 free those who are free of crime. Compare 3.2.219.

517 Confound Astonish and confuse.

517 amaze A much stronger word then than now; 'paralyse'. See 1.2.235.

518 Yet I Hypermetrical; some editors give it a separate line.

519 muddy-mettled dull-spirited.

519 peak A word of uncertain meaning. Because of Shakespeare's own 'dwindle, peak, and pine' in *Macbeth*, it is usually taken to mean 'go into a decline', 'droop', or 'mope'. But the dominant meaning seems to be 'slink' or 'creep' (*OED v*[1] 1).

520 John-a-dreams Apparently a nickname for a dreamy person.

520 unpregnant of my cause 'Pregnant' means quick, prompt, ready, apt – so to be 'unpregnant' of something means *not* reacting quickly to it. '[P]regnant' is not used by Shakespeare to mean 'with child'.

522 property i.e. the kingdom (rather than his material possessions).

523 defeat destruction.

524 pate crown of the head.

526 gives me the lie accuses me of lying.

526–7 i'th'throat … lungs i.e. deep-rooted and not superficial or casual lies.

Ha, 'swounds, I should take it, for it cannot be
But I am pigeon-livered, and lack gall
To make oppression bitter, or ere this   530
I should ha' fatted all the region kites
With this slave's offal. Bloody, bawdy villain!
Remorseless, treacherous, lecherous, kindless villain!
Oh, vengeance!
Why, what an ass am I! This is most brave,   535
That I, the son of the dear murderèd,
Prompted to my revenge by heaven and hell,
Must like a whore unpack my heart with words,
And fall a-cursing like a very drab,
A scullion!   540
Fie upon't, foh! About, my brains. Hum, I have heard
That guilty creatures sitting at a play
Have by the very cunning of the scene
Been struck so to the soul, that presently
They have proclaimed their malefactions;   545

---

528 'swounds] Q2; Why F   531 ha'] a Q2; haue F   532 Bloody, bawdy villain] Q2; bloody: a Bawdy villaine
F   534 Oh, vengeance!] F; *not in* Q2   535 Why] Q2; Who F   535 This] Q2; I sure, this F   536 the dear murderèd]
the Deere murthered F; a deere murthered Q2; my deare father Q1; a deere father murthered Q 1611   540 scullion] F;
stallyon Q2   541 brains] braines Q2 *(corrected)*; braues Q2 *(uncorrected)*; Braine F   541 Hum] Q2; *not in* F

528 'swounds God's wounds.

529 pigeon-livered cowardly. The liver is seen
as the seat of courage, while the pigeon was believed
to be fearful. The pigeon was believed to have no
gall, the secretion associated with anger.

530 To make oppression bitter i.e. to make
Claudius's domination distasteful to Claudius himself. But Hamlet may also be indicting himself: he
does not experience his uncle's rule as bitter enough
to induce action.

531 region kites hawks, or birds of prey, circling in the sky.

533 Remorseless Pitiless.

533 kindless without natural feeling.

534 Oh, vengeance! So F. Q2 omits the phrase
altogether. Many editors follow, although the short
line, which could be directed against Claudius or
against Hamlet himself, is an important marker in
this soliloquy.

536 the son … murderèd the son of the loved
victim. So F. Q2 reads 'a dear murdered'. Most

editors revise to 'the son of a dear father murdered',
which stems from the Q1 reading, 'the son of my
dear father', but is not necessary.

537 by heaven and hell Hamlet probably
means that the whole supernatural world of good
and evil lies behind his revenge, which is instigated
by heaven in its war against the workings of hell,
visible in Claudius's achievements. The alternative,
that he is urged by both heaven and hell, making
him one of hell's victims, is explored in 551–8.

538 unpack unload, relieve.

540 A scullion! 'a domestic servant of the lowest
rank … a person of the lowest order, esp. as an
abusive epithet' (*OED*). So F. Q2 reads 'stallyon',
and a number of editions give 'stallion', supposing
that Hamlet means it in the sense, available at the
time, of either a male whore or a courtesan (*OED* 2.
b, 3.a).

541 About Go to it!

543 cunning skill.

543 scene dramatic presentation.

For murder, though it have no tongue, will speak
With most miraculous organ. I'll have these players
Play something like the murder of my father
Before mine uncle. I'll observe his looks,
I'll tent him to the quick. If a do blench,   550
I know my course. The spirit that I have seen
May be a devil – and the devil hath power
T'assume a pleasing shape. Yea, and perhaps,
Out of my weakness and my melancholy,
As he is very potent with such spirits,   555
Abuses me to damn me. I'll have grounds
More relative than this. The play's the thing   *action*
Wherein I'll catch the conscience of the king.

Exit

thru the play

[3.1] *Enter* KING, QUEEN, POLONIUS, OPHELIA, ROSENCRANTZ,
GUILDENSTERN, LORDS

CLAUDIUS And can you by no drift of circumstance
         Get from him why he puts on this confusion,
         Grating so harshly all his days of quiet
         With turbulent and dangerous lunacy?
ROSENCRANTZ He does confess he feels himself distracted,   5
         But from what cause a will by no means speak.
GUILDENSTERN Nor do we find him forward to be sounded,

---

550 a do] Q2; he but F   552 a devil] Q 1611; a deale Q2; the Diuell F   Act 3, Scene 1   3.1] Act III. Scene I.
Q 1676   1 And] F; An Q2   1 circumstance] F; conference Q2   6 a] Q2; he F

550 **tent** probe.
550 **to the quick** i.e. to where it hurts.
550 **blench** flinch and turn aside.
553 **assume** Compare 1.2.243 and 1.4.72.
555 **very potent with such spirits** It was
a commonplace of ghost-lore that melancholics
were specially prone to visitation by demons. See
Prosser, *Hamlet and Revenge*, 110
556–7 **grounds … relative** reasons for acting
which are nearer at hand, more tangible.

Act 3, Scene 1
1 **drift of circumstance** steering of round-
about enquiry. Compare Polonius's 'encompass-
ment and drift of question', 2.1.10. For
'circumstance' (which means circuitous talk, as in
1.5.127), Q2 reads 'conference'.
2 **puts on** Claudius may intuit that Hamlet is
assuming a guise of madness.
3 **Grating** The physical action of roughening by
scraping and rasping.
7 **forward** disposed, inclined.

But with a crafty madness keeps aloof
When we would bring him on to some confession
Of his true state.

GERTRUDE   Did he receive you well?   10
ROSENCRANTZ Most like a gentleman.
GUILDENSTERN But with much forcing of his disposition.
ROSENCRANTZ Niggard of question, but of our demands
Most free in his reply.
GERTRUDE   Did you assay him
To any pastime?   15
ROSENCRANTZ Madam, it so fell out that certain players
We o'er-raught on the way; of these we told him,
And there did seem in him a kind of joy
To hear of it. They are about the court,
And as I think, they have already order   20
This night to play before him.
POLONIUS   'Tis most true,
And he beseeched me to entreat your majesties
To hear and see the matter.
CLAUDIUS With all my heart, and it doth much content me
To hear him so inclined.   25
Good gentlemen, give him a further edge,
And drive his purpose on to these delights.
ROSENCRANTZ We shall my lord.
                                   Exeunt Rosencrantz and Guildenstern
CLAUDIUS   Sweet Gertrude, leave us too,
For we have closely sent for Hamlet hither,

14–15 Did … pastime] *as one line* Q2, F   19 are about] F; are heere about Q2   24 heart, and] F; hart, / And Q2   27 on
to] F; into Q2   28 SD] Q2; *Exeunt* F   28 too] F; two Q2

8 **crafty madness** an affected madness (see
'mad in craft' at 3.4.189). This affected madness is
also cunning, in that it protects Hamlet from revealing more than he wishes.

13–14 **Niggard … reply** Rosencrantz is
anxious to cover up the cross-examination which
led to the disclosure that they were being employed
by Claudius. Unfortunately, this leads him into
contradicting Guildenstern about Hamlet's readiness to answer questions.

14–15 **assay … To** i.e. try him with the suggestion of.

17 **o'er-raught** (over-reached) came up to

and passed, overhauled.

21 **This night** This conversation is taking place
on the day after the events of the previous scene.
See 2.2.493.

26 **edge** keenness (of appetite).

27 **on to** So F. Q2 reads 'into', but the sense of
'drive … on' is 'urge on', as contrasted with 'drive
me into a toil' at 3.2.314–15, where the image is of
penning in a hunted animal.

29 **closely** secretly, applying to Claudius's purpose. But when Hamlet arrives he shows no knowledge of having been 'sent for'.

That he, as 'twere by accident, may here   30
Affront Ophelia. Her father and myself,
Lawful espials,
Will so bestow ourselves, that seeing unseen,
We may of their encounter frankly judge,
And gather by him, as he is behaved,   35
If't be th'affliction of his love or no
That thus he suffers for.
GERTRUDE   I shall obey you.
And for your part Ophelia, I do wish
That your good beauties be the happy cause
Of Hamlet's wildness. So shall I hope your virtues   40
Will bring him to his wonted way again,
To both your honours.
OPHELIA   Madam, I wish it may.
                              [*Exit* GERTRUDE *with* LORDS]
POLONIUS Ophelia walk you here. – Gracious, so please you,
We will bestow ourselves. – Read on this book,
That show of such an exercise may colour   45
Your loneliness. – We are oft to blame in this:
'Tis too much proved, that with devotion's visage,
And pious action, we do sugar o'er
The devil himself.
CLAUDIUS (*Aside*)   Oh, 'tis too true.
How smart a lash that speech doth give my conscience!   50

---

30 here] Q2; *there* F   32 Lawful espials] F; *not in* Q2   33 Will] F; Wee'le Q2   42 SD] *Exit Queen* / *Theobald²; not in* Q2, F   43 please you] Q2; *please ye* F   46 loneliness] F; lowlines Q2   48 sugar] Q2; *surge* F   49 too] Q2; *not in* F

31 **Affront** come face-to-face with.
32 **Lawful espials** This extra-metrical phrase occurs only in F, where it appears in a parenthesis at the end of 31. An 'espial' is a spy.
33, 44 **bestow ourselves** station or position ourselves.
34 **frankly** freely, without obstacle.
43 **Gracious** i.e. your grace (to the king) – not a usual form of address.

44 **this book** a prayer-book (see 47, 89).
45 **colour** provide a pretext for.
46 **loneliness** being alone.
47 **devotion's visage** a face expressing devoutness.
50 **How smart ... conscience** Claudius confirms for the audience that he is guilty and, for the moment, conscience-stricken. He does not, however, identify his crime or sin.

The harlot's cheek, beautied with plastering art,
Is not more ugly to the thing that helps it
Than is my deed to my most painted word.
O heavy burden!
POLONIUS I hear him coming. Let's withdraw, my lord.   55
                        Exeunt Claudius and Polonius

                        Enter HAMLET

HAMLET To be, or not to be, that is the question –
Whether 'tis nobler in the mind to suffer
The slings and arrows of outrageous fortune,
Or to take arms against a sea of troubles,
And by opposing end them. To die, to sleep –   60
No more; and by a sleep to say we end
The heart-ache and the thousand natural shocks
That flesh is heir to – 'tis a consummation
Devoutly to be wished. To die, to sleep –
To sleep, perchance to dream. Ay, there's the rub,   65
For in that sleep of death what dreams may come,
When we have shuffled off this mortal coil,
Must give us pause. There's the respect
That makes calamity of so long life,
For who would bear the whips and scorns of time,   70
Th'oppressor's wrong, the proud man's contumely,

---

55 Let's] F; *not in* Q2   55 SD *Exeunt ... Polonius*] Capell; *not in* Q2; *Exeunt.* F   55 SD *Enter* HAMLET] F; *after 54 in*
Q2   71 proud] Q2; poore F

52 **to the thing that helps it** as compared with
the cosmetic adornment.
56 **To be, or not to be** Concerning the placing of
this soliloquy and the nunnery scene which follows,
see the Textual Analysis, 270. For a discussion of the
soliloquy itself, see Introduction, 41–2.
56 **that is the question** There are many opinions on the precise question posed by 'to be ...'
They tend to fall into two categories: (1) Hamlet is
debating whether or not to take his own life; and (2)
Hamlet is considering the value or advantages of
human existence.
57 **in the mind to suffer** 'to endure mentally'.
The phrasing sets pain suffered in the mind against
bodily action.
58 **slings** missiles (by metonymy: that-which-
throws standing for that-which-is-thrown; Latin
funda could similarly mean either sling or

slingshot). A sling may be a hand-sling, a ballista,
or even a cannon.
59–60 **take arms ... by opposing end them**
The alternative to patient endurance of earthly woes
is to fight against them and to be destroyed in the
process. The result is 'self-slaughter', whether
direct or indirect.
63 **consummation** completion, fitting end, or
conclusion.
65 **rub** impediment (from the game of bowls).
67 **shuffled ... coil** got rid of the turmoil of
living. There is a sense of malpractice or fraudu-
lence here, as there is in the use of 'shuffled' at
3.3.61 and 4.7.136, where it implies 'manipulat[ion]'
with intent to deceive'.
68 **respect** consideration.
69 **of so long life** so long-lived.
70 **time** the times; compare 1.5.189.

The pangs of disprized love, the law's delay,
The insolence of office, and the spurns
That patient merit of th'unworthy takes,
When he himself might his quietus make   75
With a bare bodkin? Who would fardels bear,
To grunt and sweat under a weary life,
But that the dread of something after death,
The undiscovered country from whose bourn
No traveller returns, puzzles the will,   80
And makes us rather bear those ills we have
Than fly to others that we know not of?
Thus conscience does make cowards of us all,
And thus the native hue of resolution
Is sicklied o'er with the pale cast of thought,   85
And enterprises of great pitch and moment
With this regard their currents turn awry

---

72 disprized] dispriz'd F; despiz'd Q2   76 fardels] Q2; these Fardles F   83 of us all] F; *not in* Q2   85 sicklied] F;
sickled Q2   86 pitch] Q2; pith F   87 awry] Q2; away F

72 **disprized** unvalued. So F; Q2 is 'despiz'd'.

74 **of th'unworthy takes** receives from unworthy people.

75 **quietus** discharge or acquittance of accounts (from the law phrase *quietus est*); frequently used in connection with death, probably because of the original Latin sense of repose and peace.

76 **a bare bodkin** a mere dagger. ('bodkin' was the name for sharp pointed instruments with various different uses; probably Hamlet is not being very specific.)

76 **fardels** burdens.

79 **bourn** boundary, frontier.

80 **No traveller returns** For many commentators, the Ghost's appearance in Elsinore contradicts this portrayal of the afterlife. But, as Jenkins points out, the Ghost's confinement to 'fast in fires' hardly counts as a return. Hamlet's phrasing echoes biblical, classical, and humanist treatments of the after-life.

80 **puzzles the will** i.e. brings it to a halt in confusion; 'puzzle' was a stronger word than it is now.

83 **conscience** the inner knowledge of right and wrong (though many commentators claim it means 'introspection' or fear of punishment).

83–8 It is in these lines that, for the first time in the soliloquy, Hamlet turns, if indirectly, to the question of killing Claudius, and, as in the second soliloquy, he upbraids himself for being tardy. Thinking too much about the rights and wrongs of suicide stultifies the impulse to do away with oneself: thinking too much about rights and wrongs stultifies *all* action, including the one he's supposed to be engaged in.

84 **native hue** natural colour or complexion.

85 **sicklied o'er** unhealthily covered.

85 **cast** tinge, tint. Though Hamlet has in mind the pallor of a sick man, the nearness of 'o'er' and 'cast' suggests also the pallor of clouds staining the face of the sun, as in Sonnet 33.

85 **thought** contemplation. Thinking causes the sickness of inaction.

86 **pitch** height, scope.

87 **With this regard** On this account.

And lose the name of action. Soft you now,
The fair Ophelia. – Nymph, in thy orisons
Be all my sins remembered.

OPHELIA   Good my lord,   90
How does your honour for this many a day?

HAMLET I humbly thank you, well, well, well.

OPHELIA My lord, I have remembrances of yours
That I have longèd long to re-deliver.
I pray you now receive them.

HAMLET   No, not I,   95
I never gave you aught.

OPHELIA My honoured lord, you know right well you did,
And with them words of so sweet breath composed
As made the things more rich. Their perfume lost,
Take these again, for to the noble mind   100
Rich gifts wax poor when givers prove unkind.
There my lord.

HAMLET Ha, ha, are you honest?

OPHELIA My lord?

HAMLET Are you fair?   105

OPHELIA What means your lordship?

HAMLET That if you be honest and fair, your honesty should admit no
discourse to your beauty.

OPHELIA Could beauty, my lord, have better commerce than with
honesty?   110

---

92 well, well, well] F; well Q2   95 No, not I] Q2; No, no F   97 you know] Q2; I know F   99 the] F; these
Q2   99 Their] Q2; then F   99 lost] Q2; left F   107 your honesty] F; you Q2   109 with] Q2; your F

88 soft you As usual, 'soft' as a verb in the imperative means 'restrain yourself, leave off, be cautious'. Compare 1.1.126, 1.5.58, 3.2.353, 4.2.3, 4.4.8, 4.7.153, 5.1.184.

89 Nymph Perhaps a sarcastic, perhaps a tender, way to address Ophelia.

91 for this many a day It is often pointed out that Ophelia had met Hamlet yesterday as she reported in 2.1. But that was an unsettling interview, and the line registers Ophelia's nervousness about being placed in front of Hamlet on behalf of Claudius and Polonius.

93 remembrances keepsakes, gifts.

98 of so sweet breath composed 'breath' can here mean 'utterance' or 'language'; Ophelia may refer to words either spoken or written.

99 Their perfume lost The sweetness of both the words and the gifts has disappeared, because of the unkindness of the giver.

103 honest chaste. Hamlet's sudden, violent change of topic and tone may indicate that he suspects her in a more general sense, perhaps for not mentioning her own part in the breach between them. Some editors suggest that Hamlet recognizes that she has become Claudius and Polonius's 'decoy' (Wilson).

107–8 your honesty … your beauty your virtue should not allow your beauty to converse with it. (An alternative gloss is 'your virtue ought to keep away those who want to chat with your beauty'; if that is correct, then Ophelia misunderstands him.)

HAMLET Ay truly, for the power of beauty will sooner transform
    honesty from what it is to a bawd, than the force of honesty can
    translate beauty into his likeness. This was sometime a paradox, but
    now the time gives it proof. I did love you once.

OPHELIA Indeed my lord you made me believe so.   115

HAMLET You should not have believed me, for virtue cannot so
    inoculate our old stock but we shall relish of it. I loved you not.

OPHELIA I was the more deceived.

HAMLET Get thee to a nunnery – why wouldst thou be a breeder of
    sinners? I am myself indifferent honest, but yet I could accuse me   120
    of such things, that it were better my mother had not borne me.
    I am very proud, revengeful, ambitious, with more offences at my
    beck than I have thoughts to put them in, imagination to give them
    shape, or time to act them in. What should such fellows as I do
    crawling between earth and heaven? We are arrant knaves all,   125
    believe none of us. Go thy ways to a nunnery. Where's your father?

OPHELIA At home my lord.

HAMLET Let the doors be shut upon him, that he may play the fool
    nowhere but in's own house. Farewell.

OPHELIA Oh help him you sweet heavens!   130

HAMLET If thou dost marry, I'll give thee this plague for thy dowry:

---

117 inoculate] innocculate F; euocutat Q2   119 thee to a] F; thee a Q2   125 earth and heaven] Q2; Heauen and Earth
F   125 all] F; *not in* Q2   129 nowhere] Q2; no way F

117 **inoculate our old stock** The image is from
grafting fruit trees or bushes. We cannot so engraft
a new stem of virtue onto the old sinful trunk as to
eradicate all trace of our previous nature.

117 **relish** have a touch or tinge.

119 **Get thee to a nunnery** Some commentators hear the 'fairly common Elizabethan slang
sense "brothel"' (*Shakespeare's Bawdy*). This sense
does not erase from the passage the word's standard
meaning (convent). It gives focus to Hamlet's attack
on both men and women, including himself and
Ophelia, for the kinds of moral frailty exemplified

in sex and reproduction. Only in a convent will
Ophelia be able to resist the inclinations of her
own nature – or be protected from the desires of
men such as Hamlet.

120 **indifferent honest** moderately virtuous.

122 **proud, revengeful, ambitious** Hamlet's
depiction of his own sinfulness may be part of his
antic display, but it contains a nugget of truth.

126 **Where's your father?** Some commentators
think that Hamlet knew all the time he was being
watched; some think he guessed it early in the interview; some think he learns it here.

be thou as chaste as ice, as pure as snow, thou shalt not escape
calumny. Get thee to a nunnery, go. Farewell. Or if thou wilt needs
marry, marry a fool, for wise men know well enough what monsters
you make of them. To a nunnery go, and quickly too. Farewell.   135
OPHELIA O heavenly powers, restore him!
HAMLET I have heard of your paintings too, well enough. God hath
given you one face and you make yourselves another. You jig, you
amble, and you lisp, you nickname God's creatures, and make your
wantonness your ignorance. Go to, I'll no more on't, it hath made   140
me mad. I say we will have no mo marriages. Those that are married
already, all but one shall live, the rest shall keep as they are. To
a nunnery, go.   *Exit*
OPHELIA Oh what a noble mind is here o'erthrown!
    The courtier's, soldier's, scholar's, eye, tongue, sword,   145
    Th'expectancy and rose of the fair state,
    The glass of fashion and the mould of form,
    Th'observed of all observers, quite, quite down,

---

133 go] F; *not in* Q2   136 O] F; *not in* Q2   137 paintings] Q2, Q1; pratlings F   137 too] F; *not in* Q2   137 hath] Q2;
has F   138 face] Q2; pace F   138 yourselves] your selfes Q2; your selfe F   138–9 you amble] F; & amble
Q2   139 lisp] F; list Q2   139 you nickname] Q2; and nickname F   140 your ignorance] F; ignorance Q2   141 mo]
Q2; more F   141 marriages] F; marriage Q2   143 SD] Q2; *Exit Hamlet* F   146 expectancy] expectansie F; expectation
Q2

132–3 **be thou … thou shalt not escape
calumny** Regardless of her actual behaviour,
Ophelia will be slandered for unchasteness.

134 **monsters** i.e. horned cuckolds, husbands
with cheating wives.

138 **jig** This may refer more to singing than
dancing. Compare *Love's Labour's Lost* 3.1.11–12,
'to jig off a tune at the tongue's end'.

138–9 **you amble, and you lisp** you walk and
talk affectedly.

139–40 **make your wantonness your ignorance** pretend your licence is just simplicity and
innocence.

140–1 **it hath made me mad** Hamlet calls
attention to his emotional extremity.

141 **mo** more.

141–2 **Those … all but one shall live** All

married couples, except one, may remain married,
but all single people are to stay single ('the rest shall
keep as they are'). The exception is the marriage of
Gertrude and Claudius, which Hamlet will end
with the king's death.

146 **Th'expectancy** The hope.

147 **glass … form** the ideal image of self-con-
struction (self-fashioning) and the model of behaviour by which others shape themselves and their
actions.

148 **Th'observed of all observers** Looked up
to respectfully by all who turn to others for guidance. 'Observe' is a difficult word: see note to
1.5.101. Although it is possible that this could
mean 'one who is watched attentively by all who
note men carefully', the context of the previous line
suggests the older meaning of 'observe'.

And I of ladies most deject and wretched,
That sucked the honey of his music vows,   150
Now see that noble and most sovereign reason,
Like sweet bells jangled, out of time and harsh;
That unmatched form and feature of blown youth
Blasted with ecstasy. Oh woe is me
T'have seen what I have seen, see what I see.   155

Enter KING *and* POLONIUS

CLAUDIUS Love? His affections do not that way tend;
          Nor what he spake, though it lacked form a little,
          Was not like madness. There's something in his soul
          O'er which his melancholy sits on brood,
          And I do doubt the hatch and the disclose   160
          Will be some danger; which for to prevent,
          I have in quick determination
          Thus set it down: he shall with speed to England
          For the demand of our neglected tribute.
          Haply the seas, and countries different,   165
          With variable objects, shall expel
          This something-settled matter in his heart,
          Whereon his brains still beating puts him thus
          From fashion of himself. What think you on't?
POLONIUS It shall do well. But yet do I believe   170
          The origin and commencement of his grief
          Sprung from neglected love. How now Ophelia?
          You need not tell us what Lord Hamlet said,
          We heard it all. My lord, do as you please,
          But if you hold it fit, after the play,   175

---

149 And] Q2; Haue F   150 music] Musicke F; musickt Q2   151 that] F; what Q2   152 time] Q2; tune F   153 fea-
ture] F; stature Q2   161 for to] Q2; to F   168–71 ... thus / ... on't? / ... believe / ... grief] F; ... beating / ...
himselfe. / ... on't? / ... well. / ... greefe, Q2   171 his] Q2; this F

153 blown youth youth in full bloom.
154 Blasted with ecstasy Destroyed by
madness.
155 At the end of this line some copies of Q2
print *'Exit'*. Q1 also has Ophelia leave at this point.
156 affections emotions.
159 sits on brood Like a bird sitting on eggs –

see 'hatch' in the next line.
164 tribute A historically imperfect reference to
payment supplied by the English to save land from
Viking attacks.
169 fashion of himself his own proper way of
behaving.

> Let his queen mother all alone entreat him
> To show his grief. Let her be round with him,
> And I'll be placed, so please you, in the ear
> Of all their conference. If she find him not,
> To England send him; or confine him where   180
> Your wisdom best shall think.
> CLAUDIUS   It shall be so.
> Madness in great ones must not unwatched go.
>
>   *Exeunt*

3.2 *Enter* HAMLET *and two or three of the* PLAYERS

HAMLET Speak the speech I pray you as I pronounced it to you,
trippingly on the tongue; but if you mouth it as many of our players
do, I had as lief the town-crier spoke my lines. Nor do not saw the
air too much with your hand thus, but use all gently; for in the
very torrent, tempest, and, as I may say, whirlwind of your passion,   5
you must acquire and beget a temperance that may give it
smoothness. Oh, it offends me to the soul to hear a robustious
periwig-pated fellow tear a passion to totters, to very rags, to split
the ears of the groundlings, who for the most part are capable of

---

177 grief] Q2; Greefes F   182 unwatched] F; vnmatcht Q2   Act 3, Scene 2 3.2] Scene II *Capell*   0 SD *two or three*] F;
three Q2   1 pronounced] pronounc'd F; pronoun'd Q2   2 our] Q2; your F   3 lief] liue Q2, F   3 spoke] Q2; had spoke
F   4 with] Q2; *not in* F   5 whirlwind] Q2; the Whirle-winde F   5 your passion] Q2; Passion F   7 hear] Q2; see
F   8 periwig] Pery-wig F; perwig Q2   8 totters] Q2, Q1; tatters F   8 split] F; spleet Q2

177 **round** direct and outspoken.
179 **find him not** fails to discover his secret.
182 **Madness** … Though Claudius has just
doubted the sincerity of Hamlet's madness (158).

Act 3, Scene 2
0 SD **two or three** So F. Q2 gives 'three'; for
Shakespeare's MS to be so specific against an MS
with theatre influence is remarkable, especially as
there is no need for three players. Probably
a compositor's omission.
1 The time is the evening of the same day.
Hamlet now appears sane and utterly intent on the
acting of his play.
3 **I had as lief** It would be as agreeable to me
that.

4 **thus** Hamlet makes the exaggerated gestures
he criticizes.
4–6 **in the very torrent … acquire and
beget a temperance** Hamlet describes an acting
process by which the actors should obtain, even as
they generate intense emotion, a balance and control that they should then convey in their
performance.
7 **robustious** rough and rude.
8 **periwig-pated** wearing a wig.
8 **totters** So Q2 (and Q1); an alternative form of
'tatters', which F gives.
9 **groundlings** Audience members who stood in
the open yard of the amphitheatre, admission to
which was the least expensive option.
9 **are capable of** have a capacity for, can
understand.

nothing but inexplicable dumb-shows and noise. I would have such   10
a fellow whipped for o'erdoing Termagant – it out-Herods Herod.
Pray you avoid it.

I PLAYER I warrant your honour.

HAMLET Be not too tame neither, but let your own discretion be your
    tutor. Suit the action to the word, the word to the action, with this   15
    special observance, that you o'erstep not the modesty of nature. For
    anything so o'erdone is from the purpose of playing, whose end both
    at the first and now, was and is, to hold as 'twere the mirror up
    to nature; to show virtue her own feature, scorn her own image,
    and the very age and body of the time his form and pressure. Now   20
    this overdone, or come tardy off, though it makes the unskilful
    laugh, cannot but make the judicious grieve, the censure of the
    which one must in your allowance o'erweigh a whole theatre of
    others. Oh, there be players that I have seen play, and heard others
    praise and that highly, not to speak it profanely, that neither having   25

---

10 would] Q2; could F   16 o'erstep] ore-steppe Q2; ore-stop F   17 o'erdone] ore-doone Q2; ouer-done F   19 own
feature] F; feature Q2   21 makes] Q2; make F   22–3 the which] F; which Q2   25 praise] F; praysd Q2

---

10 **inexplicable dumb-shows** Shakespeare
does not use 'inexplicable' elsewhere. The context
of dumb-shows, by which Hamlet invokes old-fash-
ioned spectacles, suggests 'meaningless'.

11 **Termagant** A deity supposed to be wor-
shipped by Muslims, invoked to signify a user of
excessive or senseless terms.

11 **Herod** Ruler of Judaea from 37 BCE to 4
BCE; familiar as a ranting tyrant in the medieval
biblical cycles who ordered the slaughter of children
in an attempt to kill Jesus Christ.

15 **Suit … action** 'action' is used here in two
different senses, both belonging to the theatre.
First, it means acting – in its fullest sense of an
actor's management of himself on the stage, and not
just gesture (*OED* 6). In the second phrase, it means
the action of the play. '[W]ord' also has two meanings; first, the language of the play, and, in
the second phrase, the actor's speech. Hamlet
instructs the Player to let his acting be governed
by what he is given to speak, and to let his speech be

governed by what he is given to act.

16 **modesty** restraints, limitations, measure.
Compare 2.2.400.

17 **from** away from.

18 **mirror** Reveals things not as they seem, but
as they really are.

19 **scorn** i.e. that which is to be scorned.

20 **the very … pressure** i.e. gives an impression of the shape of our times in the clearest detail.
Many commentators think that 'very age' and 'body
of the time' are separate and parallel phrases, but
the run of the sentence clearly puts 'age and body'
together.

21 **come tardy off** done inadequately or
imperfectly.

21 **unskilful** ignorant and undiscerning.

22 **censure** judgement.

22–3 **of the which one** of one of whom.

23 **your allowance** i.e. what you will permit or
sanction, hence 'your scale of values'.

th'accent of Christians, nor the gait of Christian, pagan, nor man,
have so strutted and bellowed that I have thought some of nature's
journeymen had made men, and not made them well, they imitated
humanity so abominably.

I PLAYER I hope we have reformed that indifferently with us, sir.   30

HAMLET Oh reform it altogether. And let those that play your clowns
speak no more than is set down for them, for there be of them that
will themselves laugh, to set on some quantity of barren spectators
to laugh too, though in the meantime some necessary question of
the play be then to be considered. That's villainous, and shows   35
a most pitiful ambition in the fool that uses it. Go make you ready.

Exeunt Players

Enter POLONIUS, ROSENCRANTZ *and* GUILDENSTERN

How now my lord, will the king hear this piece of work?

POLONIUS And the queen too, and that presently.

HAMLET Bid the players make haste.

Exit Polonius

Will you two help to hasten them?   40

ROSENCRANTZ Ay my lord.

Exeunt Rosencrantz and Guildenstern

HAMLET What ho, Horatio!

Enter HORATIO

HORATIO Here sweet lord, at your service.

HAMLET Horatio, thou art e'en as just a man
As e'er my conversation coped withal.   45

HORATIO Oh my dear lord.

HAMLET   Nay, do not think I flatter,
For what advancement may I hope from thee,
That no revenue hast but thy good spirits

26 th'accent] Q2; the accent F   26 nor man] Q2; or Norman F   30 sir] F; *not in* Q2   36 SD *Exeunt Players*] F2; *Exit Players* F; *not in* Q2   36.1 SD] F; *after 37 in* Q2   39 SD] F; *not in* Q2   41 ROSENCRANTZ Ay] Ros. I Q2; Both. We will F   41 SD] *Exeunt they two* Q2; *Exeunt* F   42 ho] hoa F; howe Q2   44 SH HAMLET] *Ham.* F; *not in* Q2

27–8 **nature's journeymen** These bad actors must have been made not by God (hence Hamlet's 'not to speak it profanely'), but by some of Nature's hired men, little better than apprentices.

29 **abominably** Spelt in Q2 and F 'abhominably', indicating what, from a false etymology, they thought the word meant: 'away from the nature of man'.

30 **indifferently** reasonably well.

34 **necessary question** i.e. essential part of the plot.

38 **presently** immediately.

44 **e'en** Emphatic, like modern 'absolutely'.

44 **just** Not 'judicious' but 'honourable', 'upright'.

45 **my conversation coped withal** my encounters with people have brought me in touch with.

48 Scan 'That nó revénue hást but thý good spirits'.

48 **spirits** inner qualities.

To feed and clothe thee? Why should the poor be flattered?
No, let the candied tongue lick absurd pomp   50
And crook the pregnant hinges of the knee
Where thrift may follow fawning. Dost thou hear?
Since my dear soul was mistress of her choice,
And could of men distinguish her election,
Sh'ath sealed thee for herself, for thou hast been   55
As one in suffering all that suffers nothing,
A man that Fortune's buffets and rewards
Hast tane with equal thanks. And blest are those
Whose blood and judgement are so well commeddled
That they are not a pipe for Fortune's finger   60
To sound what stop she please. Give me that man
That is not passion's slave, and I will wear him
In my heart's core, ay in my heart of heart,
As I do thee. Something too much of this.
There is a play tonight before the king: 65
One scene of it comes near the circumstance
Which I have told thee of my father's death.
I prithee when thou seest that act afoot,
Even with the very comment of thy soul
Observe my uncle. If his occulted guilt   70
Do not itself unkennel in one speech,

---

50 lick] Q2; like F   52 fawning] fauning Q2; faining F   53 her] Q2; my F   54 distinguish her election,] Q2; distinguish, her election F   55 Sh'ath] S'hath Q2; Hath F   58 Hast] Q2; Hath F   59 commeddled] comedled Q2; co-mingled F   69 thy] Q2; my F   70 my] Q2; mine F

50–1 The courtier kissing his patron's hands and bowing is pictured, in beast-fable fashion, as a fawning dog licking and crouching – though the dog is nowhere specifically mentioned.

50 candied sugared.

50 absurd ridiculous in its vanity and self-love. Accent on first syllable.

51 pregnant 'quick, ready, prompt' (Johnson).

52 thrift ('thriving') profit, prosperity.

54–5 And could … herself From the time Hamlet's soul could be discriminating in her choice amongst men, she has marked you out. So Q2. F's meaning is different: 'and could discriminate amongst men, her choice hath marked you out'.

55 sealed … herself In the legal sense, put a lawful seal on you as her property; hence, 'solemnly attested that you are hers'. There are biblical resonances as well with Ephesians 4.30, 2 Cor. 1.22, and Rom 11.5, 28 (see Naseeb Shaheen, *Biblical References in Shakespeare's Plays* (Newark:

University of Delaware Press, 1999), 549).

59 blood and judgement passion and reason.

59 commeddled mixed together; 'meddle' is common, but 'commeddle' is rare, and F gives 'commingled'.

61 stop Note produced by closing a finger-hole in a wind instrument (*Shakespeare's Words*).

66 circumstance circumstances, details.

69–70 Even with … uncle i.e. use your most intense powers of observation in watching my uncle; 'comment' stands for the power to comment.

70 occulted hidden.

71 unkennel come into the open. The word was used of dislodging or driving a fox from his hole or lair.

71 in one speech Thompson and Taylor point out that this could refer either to Hamlet's inserted lines (2.2.493–4) or to the anticipated admission of guilt by Claudius (2.2.542–5).

It is a damnèd ghost that we have seen,
And my imaginations are as foul
As Vulcan's stithy. Give him heedful note,
For I mine eyes will rivet to his face,   75
And after we will both our judgements join
In censure of his seeming.
HORATIO   Well my lord.
If a steal aught the whilst this play is playing
And scape detecting, I will pay the theft.
                    Sound a flourish
HAMLET They are coming to the play. I must be idle.   80
Get you a place.

Danish march (trumpets and kettle-drums). Enter KING, QUEEN,
POLONIUS, OPHELIA, ROSENCRANTZ, GUILDENSTERN *and Other*
LORDS *attendant, with his* GUARD *carrying torches*

CLAUDIUS How fares our cousin Hamlet?
HAMLET Excellent i'faith, of the chameleon's dish: I eat the air,
    promise-crammed. You cannot feed capons so.

---

74 stithy] Q2; Stythe F   74 heedful] Q2; needfull F   77 In] Q2; To F   78 a] Q2; he F   79 detecting] F; detected
Q2   79 SD *Sound a flourish*] F*(concludes SD which follows); not in* Q2   81 SD] *This edn; Enter Trumpets and Kettle
Drummes, King, Queene, Polonius, Ophelia.* Q2; *Enter King, Queene, Polonius, Ophelia, Rosincrance, Guildensterne, and other
Lords attendant, with his Guard carrying Torches. Danish March. Sound a Flourish.* F

72 a damnèd ghost ... seen the ghost which
we have seen came from hell (and was an impostor
and a liar).
73 my imaginations what Hamlet's mind has
suggested to him in the wake of the conversation
with the Ghost. To have given credence to the
Ghost, and built on its tale, shows a disease of his
mind.
74 Vulcan's stithy In classical mythology,
Vulcan is the god of fire, and thus his stithy (=
forge) was regarded as hellish.
77 In censure of his seeming in weighing up
his appearance. They will have to infer from his
outward expression what he is actually feeling.
77 Well my lord Expresses Horatio's concurrence and approval.
78 If a steal aught i.e. if he conceals anything.
80 idle Not 'unoccupied', but 'idle-headed' =
crazy.
81 SD F's rich version of this grand entry shows

how the theatre worked on the bare essentials given
by Shakespeare (as recorded in Q2). The two versions have been conflated by suggesting that F's
'Danish March' was, in fact, played by Q2's
'Trumpets and Kettle Drummes'. F's 'Sound
a flourish' has also been separated from the main
body of the SD, since it is the warning flourish that
alerts Hamlet to the entry.
82 fares Hamlet chooses to understand this in
its alternative sense of being fed.
82 cousin Any close relation. *OED* notes that
the term was often used by a sovereign to another
sovereign, or to one of his nobles. Compare 1.2.117,
'our cousin and our son'. Hamlet and Claudius now
come together for the first time since the second
scene of the play.
83 the chameleon's dish The chameleon was
supposed to live on air.
84 capons castrated cocks, fattened for the
table.

CLAUDIUS I have nothing with this answer Hamlet, these words are not   85
    mine.

HAMLET No, nor mine now. – My lord, you played once i'th'university,
    you say.

POLONIUS That did I my lord, and was accounted a good actor.

HAMLET And what did you enact?   90

POLONIUS I did enact Julius Caesar. I was killed i'th'Capitol. Brutus
    killed me.

HAMLET It was a brute part of him to kill so capital a calf there. – Be
    the players ready?

ROSENCRANTZ Ay my lord, they stay upon your patience.   95

GERTRUDE Come hither my dear Hamlet, sit by me.

HAMLET No good mother, here's metal more attractive.

POLONIUS Oh ho, do you mark that?

HAMLET Lady, shall I lie in your lap?

OPHELIA No my lord.   100

HAMLET I mean, my head upon your lap?

OPHELIA Ay my lord.

HAMLET Do you think I meant country matters?

OPHELIA I think nothing my lord.

HAMLET That's a fair thought to lie between maids' legs.   105

OPHELIA What is, my lord?

HAMLET Nothing.

OPHELIA You are merry my lord.

HAMLET Who, I?

OPHELIA Ay my lord.   110

HAMLET O God, your only jig-maker. What should a man do but be
    merry? for look you how cheerfully my mother looks, and my father
    died within's two hours.

---

87 mine now. – My lord,] *Johnson (substantially); mine now my Lord.* Q2; *mine. Now my Lord,* F   89 did I] Q2; I did
F   90 And what] F; *What* Q2   96 dear] Q2; *good* F   101–2 HAMLET I mean . . . lord] F; *not in* Q2

85 **have nothing with** gain nothing from.

85–6 **are not mine** do not belong to my
question.

91–2 **I did enact … killed me** For this as an
allusion to Shakespeare's own *Julius Caesar*, see
Introduction, 7–8.

93 **part** action (compare *2 Henry IV* 4.5.63) –
but also, continuing the theatre-language, 'part to
play', role.

93 **calf** Commonly used for a dolt or stupid
person.

97 **metal more attractive** literally, a substance
more magnetic; figuratively, a person more

appealing. But 'mettle' (the spelling in both Q2
and F) means also 'disposition', 'spirit'.

103 **country matters** the sort of thing that goes
on among rustics in the country; coarse or indecent
things; sex (with a pun on the first syllable of
country).

107 **Nothing** 'Thing' was commonly used to
refer to the sexual organ of either men or women;
'nothing' was also used to refer to the female
genitals.

111 **your only jig-maker** i.e. 'there's no one
like me for providing farcical entertainments'.

OPHELIA Nay, 'tis twice two months my lord.

HAMLET So long? Nay then let the devil wear black, for I'll have a suit   115
of sables. O heavens! die two months ago, and not forgotten yet?
Then there's hope a great man's memory may outlive his life half
a year, but byrlady a must build churches then, or else shall a suffer
not thinking on, with the hobby-horse, whose epitaph is, 'For O,
for O, the hobby-horse is forgot.'   120

Hoboys play. The dumb-show enters

Enter a KING *and a* QUEEN, *very lovingly, the Queen embracing him. She*
kneels and makes show of protestation unto him. He takes her up, and   declines

---

115 devil] Diuel F; deule Q2   118 byrlady] F; ber lady Q2   118 a must] Q2; he must F   118 shall a] Q2; shall
he F   120.1 SD *Hoboys ... enters*] F; *The Trumpets sounds. Dumbe show followes* Q2   120.2 SD a QUEEN] Q2; *Queene*
F   120.2 SD *very lovingly*] F; *not in* Q2   120.2 *embracing him.*] F; *embracing him, and he her,* Q2   120.2–3 SD *She ... him*]
F; *not in* Q2

---

114 twice two months Compare 1.2.138 – it
was then less than two months since the former
king's death: a further indication of the gap in
time between Acts 1 and 2.

115–16 let the devil ... sables 'sables' means
the fur of a northern animal, the sable, which is
brown. But 'sable' is also the heraldic word for
'black'. So this is a typical riddling remark of
Hamlet's. Since his father has been dead so long,
the devil can have his mourning garments and he
will start wearing rich furs – but, by the pun, he will
actually continue mourning.

118 byrlady Compare 2.2.388. This is F's spelling. Q2's 'ber lady' may represent Shakespeare's
spelling and pronunciation.

119 not thinking on being forgotten.

119–20 hobby-horse ... forgot The hobby-
horse was one of the additional characters in the
Morris dance in the traditional English summer
festivities. A man wore a huge hooped skirt in the
likeness of a horse. The phrase 'the hobby horse is
forgot' is very common (see *OED*) and nearly
always had a sexual connotation (see *Othello*
4.1.154; *Winter's Tale* 1.2.276). A. Brissenden
(*RES* xxx (1979), 1–11) describes how the horse
used to sink to the ground as though dead, then
come to energetic life again. So the hobby-horse
does not die to be forgotten, but comes back with
a vengeance, like Hamlet's father.

120 SD The versions of the dumb-show in Q2
and F differ in three ways: (1) Q2 accidentally
omits what is almost certainly part of the original
SD (chiefly 'She kneels...unto him', 2–3); (2)
F firms up for stage presentation, altering the
music, identifying characters ('Fellow', 'King',
'Mutes'), and inserting exits; (3) F substitutes
more familiar and descriptive words like 'loath and
unwilling' for 'harsh'. What is printed here is an
eclectic version, accepting some changes from F,
but preserving Q2's language. There are three problems about the dumb-show. (1) It is most unusual
for a dumb-show to mime the action of the entire
play to follow; (2) Did Hamlet know the dumb-
show was going to be presented? (3) Why does
Claudius not react? As regards (1), the show clearly
puzzles Ophelia, and is therefore probably meant to
seem rather peculiar. As regards (2), although
Hamlet's ensuing remarks *can* be interpreted as
showing anger towards the players, they do not in
the least demand that interpretation, and it is safer
to assume that the sponsor of the play knew what
was going to take place. (3) There are many ways of
explaining Claudius's silence, but an impassive, or
nearly impassive, Claudius is theatrically very effective, providing an enigma for Hamlet and Horatio,
as well as the audience.

120.1 *Hoboys* Oboes.

120.3 *protestation* solemn vow.

his head upon her neck. He lies him down upon a bank of flowers. She, seeing
him asleep, leaves him. Anon comes in another man, takes off his crown, kisses
it, pours poison in the sleeper's ears, and leaves him. The Queen returns,
finds the King dead, and makes passionate action. The poisoner, with some
two or three mutes, comes in again, seeming to condole with her. The dead
body is carried away. The poisoner woos the Queen with gifts. She seems
harsh awhile, but in the end accepts his love.   *Exeunt*

OPHELIA What means this my lord?
HAMLET Marry this is miching mallecho, it means mischief.
OPHELIA Belike this show imports the argument of the play?

Enter PROLOGUE

HAMLET We shall know by this fellow; the players cannot keep counsel,
      they'll tell all.   125
OPHELIA Will a tell us what this show meant?
HAMLET Ay, or any show that you'll show him. Be not you ashamed
      to show, he'll not shame to tell you what it means.
OPHELIA You are naught, you are naught. I'll mark the play.

PROLOGUE For us and for our tragedy,   130
         Here stooping to your clemency,
         We beg your hearing patiently.

HAMLET Is this a prologue, or the posy of a ring?
OPHELIA 'Tis brief my lord.
HAMLET As woman's love.   135

Enter the PLAYER KING *and* QUEEN

120.4 SD *He lies*] Q2; *Layes* F   120.5 SD *comes*] F; *come* Q2   120.5 SD *another man*] Q2; *a Fellow* F   120.6 SD *pours*] Q2;
and powres F   120.6 SD *the sleeper's*] Q2; *the Kings* F   120.6 SD *leaves him*] Q2; *Exits* F   120.7 SD *and makes*] F; *makes*
Q2   120.8 SD *two or three mutes*] F; *three or foure* Q2   120.8 SD *comes*] F; *come* Q2   120.8 SD *seeming*] F; *seeme*
Q2   120.8 SD *condole*] Q2; *lament* F   120.10 SD *harsh*] Q2; *loath and unwilling* F   120.10 SD *his love*] F;
loue Q2   120.10 SD *Exeunt*] F; *not in* Q2   122 is] F; *not in* Q2   122 miching] Miching F; munching Q2; myching
Q1   122 mallecho] Malone; *Mallico; Mallico* F; Mallico Q1   122 it] Q2; that F   123 play?] F; play. Q2   123 SD]
Q2; *after 129 in* F   124 this fellow] Q2; these Fellowes F   124 counsel] F; *not in* Q2   126 a] Q2; they F   127 you'll]
F; you will Q2   133 posy] posie Q2; Poesie F   135 SD] P. Alexander; Enter King and Queene Q2; Enter King and his
Queene F

120.10 **harsh** i.e. she is disdainful, cross.
122 **miching mallecho** Another insoluble problem. '[M]iching' is F's word; Q2 has 'munching'.
'[M]iching' is a good English word meaning 'skulk-
ing'; 'mallecho' (Q2, *Mallico*; F, *Malicho*) may be for
Spanish *malhecho*, a misdeed.
123 **Belike ... play?** 'Perhaps this dumb-show
explains what the play is about?'
125 **they'll tell all** It would seem unnecessary
to point out that this is a joke, but some have taken it
as a sign of Hamlet's anxiety lest his scheme should

be sabotaged.
127 **any show ...** Hamlet continues his bawdy
innuendos.
129 **naught** wicked.
133 **posy** inscribed motto or rhyme; a shortened
version of 'poesie', which is how the word is spelt in
F and Q1.
135 SD **KING ... QUEEN** According to Hamlet in
216–18, it is a Duke called Gonzago and his wife
Baptista. F makes an effort to call the Queen-
Duchess '*Bap.*' or '*Bapt*' in speech headings – no
doubt to distinguish her from Gertrude – but does

PLAYER KING Full thirty times hath Phoebus' cart gone round
　　　　　Neptune's salt wash and Tellus' orbèd ground,
　　　　　And thirty dozen moons with borrowed sheen
　　　　　About the world have times twelve thirties been,
　　　　　Since love our hearts, and Hymen did our hands,　　　140
　　　　　Unite commutual in most sacred bands.
PLAYER QUEEN So many journeys may the sun and moon
　　　　　Make us again count o'er ere love be done.
　　　　　But woe is me, you are so sick of late,
　　　　　So far from cheer and from your former state,　　　145
　　　　　That I distrust you. Yet though I distrust,
　　　　　Discomfort you my lord it nothing must.
　　　　　For women's fear and love hold quantity,
　　　　　In neither aught, or in extremity.
　　　　　Now what my love is, proof hath made you know;　　　150
　　　　　And as my love is sized, my fear is so.
　　　　　[Where love is great, the littlest doubts are fear;
　　　　　Where little fears grow great, great love grows there.]
PLAYER KING Faith, I must leave thee love, and shortly too:
　　　　　My operant powers their functions leave to do;　　　155
　　　　　And thou shalt live in this fair world behind,
　　　　　Honoured, beloved; and haply one as kind
　　　　　For husband shalt thou –
PLAYER QUEEN　　　　　　　　　Oh confound the rest!
　　　　　Such love must needs be treason in my breast.
　　　　　In second husband let me be accurst:　　　160
　　　　　None wed the second but who killed the first.

---

137 orbèd ground] F; orb'd the ground Q2 142, 158, 197 SH PLAYER QUEEN] *Steevens²; Quee.* Q2; *Bap.* F 145 your] F; our Q2 145 former] Q2; forme F 147 *Following this line* Q2 *inserts* For women feare too much, euen as they loue, 148 For] F; And Q2 148 hold] Q2; holds F 149 In] F; Eyther none, in Q2 150 love] F; Lord Q2 152–3] Q2; *not in* F 155 their] Q2; my F

nothing to alter 'King'. Interestingly, Q1 calls them Duke and Duchess throughout.

136 Phoebus' cart The chariot of the classical god of the sun, i.e. the sun.

136–9 The emphasis on thirty years of marriage has been compared with the emphasis on Hamlet's age as 30 at 5.1.122–38.

137 Neptune's … Tellus' orbèd ground The ocean and the sphere of the earth, the globe.

138 borrowed sheen reflected light.

140 Hymen God of marriage.

146 distrust you worry about your health.

148 Fear and love go together in a woman. Either they are both non-existent, or they are both present in full. For Shakespeare's hesitations here, see Textual Analysis, 255–6.

150 proof experience, trial.

151 sized in size.

152–3 These two lines are omitted in F. See Textual Analysis, 255–6.

155 leave to do cease to perform.

161 None wed … first No explicit accusation or

HAMLET That's wormwood, wormwood.

PLAYER QUEEN The instances that second marriage move
          Are base respects of thrift, but none of love.
          A second time I kill my husband dead   165
          When second husband kisses me in bed.

PLAYER KING I do believe you think what now you speak,
          But what we do determine oft we break.
          Purpose is but the slave to memory,
          Of violent birth but poor validity,   170
          Which now like fruit unripe sticks on the tree,
          But fall unshaken when they mellow be.
          Most necessary 'tis that we forget
          To pay ourselves what to ourselves is debt.
          What to ourselves in passion we propose,   175
          The passion ending, doth the purpose lose.
          The violence of either grief or joy
          Their own enactures with themselves destroy.
          Where joy most revels, grief doth most lament;
          Grief joys, joy grieves, on slender accident.   180
          This world is not for aye, nor 'tis not strange
          That even our loves should with our fortunes change,
          For 'tis a question left us yet to prove,
          Whether love lead fortune, or else fortune love.
          The great man down, you mark his favourite flies;   185
          The poor advanced makes friends of enemies,

162 That's wormwood, wormwood] *Wilson;* That's wormwood Q2 *(margin);* Wormwood, Wormwood F   163 SH PLAYER QUEEN] *Steevens²; not in* Q2; *Bapt.* F   167 you think] Q2; you. Think F   171 like] F; the Q2   177 either] Q2; other F   180 joys] F; ioy Q2   180 grieves] F; griefes Q2   185 favourite] Q2; fauourites F

indictment of Gertrude for the murder of Hamlet Sr has been made so far in the play. (Hamlet accuses her at 3.4.30.)

162 wormwood *Artemisia absinthium,* a bitter herb.

163 instances motives.

164 thrift profit, advancement.

167–78 The whole of this speech makes gnomic comments on Hamlet's own predicament.

169 Purpose is … memory The fulfilment of plans depends on memory.

170 Of violent birth Very strong at the beginning.

170 validity health and strength.

175–6 in passion … purpose lose Extends the sentiment of 169, only now the fulfilment of a plan depends upon the maintenance of emotional fervour.

177–8 The violence … destroy Repeats the preceding couplet. Violent grief and joy, when they cease, destroy the 'enactures' or actions which are associated with them.

179–80 Where joy … accident Those who have most capacity for joy have most capacity for grief, and the one changes into the other on the slightest occasion.

181 for aye for ever.

And hitherto doth love on fortune tend;
For who not needs shall never lack a friend,
And who in want a hollow friend doth try
Directly seasons him his enemy.   190
But orderly to end where I begun,
Our wills and fates do so contrary run
That our devices still are overthrown;
Our thoughts are ours, their ends none of our own.
So think thou wilt no second husband wed,   195
But die thy thoughts when thy first lord is dead.

PLAYER QUEEN Nor earth to me give food, nor heaven light,
Sport and repose lock from me day and night,
[To desperation turn my trust and hope,
An anchor's cheer in prison be my scope,]   200
Each opposite that blanks the face of joy
Meet what I would have well, and it destroy;
Both here and hence pursue me lasting strife,
If once a widow, ever I be wife.

HAMLET If she should break it now!   205

PLAYER KING 'Tis deeply sworn. Sweet, leave me here awhile;
My spirits grow dull, and fain I would beguile
The tedious day with sleep.
                                        Sleeps
PLAYER QUEEN   Sleep rock thy brain,
And never come mischance between us twain.   *Exit*
HAMLET Madam, how like you this play?   210
GERTRUDE The lady doth protest too much methinks.
HAMLET Oh but she'll keep her word.

---

197 to me give] Q2; to giue me F   199–200] Q2; *not in* F   200 An] *Theobald;* And Q2   204 once a] F; once I be
a Q2   204 wife] F; a wife Q2   208 SD] F*(after* brain*); not in* Q2   209 SD] F; *Exeunt* Q2   211 doth protest] Q2;
protests F

187 **hitherto** to this extent.
187 **tend** attend, wait.
189 **try** make trial of.
190 **seasons** As in 1.3.81, 'to season' means 'to cause change by the passage of time', usually 'to ripen', but here simply 'changes (him into)'.
193 **devices** schemes, plans.
200 **anchor's cheer** the fare of an anchorite or

religious hermit.
200 **scope** limit.
201 **opposite** opposing force.
201 **blanks** blanches, makes pale. Not used elsewhere by Shakespeare.
207 **spirits** vital spirits.
211 **doth protest** makes protestation or promises.

CLAUDIUS Have you heard the argument? Is there no offence in't?

HAMLET No, no, they do but jest, poison in jest, no offence i'th'world.

CLAUDIUS What do you call the play?   215

HAMLET The Mousetrap. Marry how? Tropically. This play is the
image of a murder done in Vienna. Gonzago is the duke's name,
his wife Baptista. You shall see anon. 'Tis a knavish piece of work,
but what o' that? Your majesty, and we that have free souls, it
touches us not. Let the galled jade winch, our withers are unwrung. 220

Enter LUCIANUS

This is one Lucianus, nephew to the king.

OPHELIA You are as good as a chorus my lord.

HAMLET I could interpret between you and your love if I could see the
puppets dallying.

OPHELIA You are keen my lord, you are keen.   225

HAMLET It would cost you a groaning to take off mine edge.

OPHELIA Still better and worse.

HAMLET So you mistake your husbands. Begin, murderer. Pox, leave
thy damnable faces and begin. Come, the croaking raven doth
bellow for revenge.   230

---

219 o' that] F; of that Q2   220 SD] F; *after 221 in* Q2   222 as good as a] Q2, Q1; a good F   226 mine] Q2; my
F   228 your] Q2; *not in* F   228 Pox] F; *not in* Q2

213–14 Is there … no offence i'th'world
Claudius is probably asking whether there is anything censorable in the play, but Hamlet chooses to
interpret it as a question about whether there is
something criminal in it. Hamlet's assurance that
it is only a mock-crime includes the first verbal
mention of poison in the inset play.

216 Tropically As a trope, a figure of speech.

219 free innocent. See 2.2.516.

220 Let … winch 'galled jade' is a poor horse
with saddle-sores, 'winch' = 'wince'. It was
a common saying that it was the galled horse that
would soonest wince (Tilley H700).

220 withers The high part of a horse's back,
between the shoulder-blades.

220 unwrung not pressed tight, pinched or
chafed. See *OED* wring v 4.

221 nephew to the king In identifying
Lucianus thus, Hamlet brings together past and
future: Claudius's killing of his brother, and his
own projected killing of his uncle.

223–4 I could … dallying I could act as
a chorus in explaining what goes on between you
and your lover if I could see the dalliance or flirting
in the form of a puppet show. Many commentators
suspect some indecent secondary meaning in 'puppets', which is fully in keeping with Hamlet's

treatment of Ophelia. The explanation may well
lie in Q1's 'poopies'. It has been shown by
H. Hulme that 'poop' meant the female genitals
(Hilda M. Hulme, *Explorations in Shakespeare's
Language: Some Problems of Lexical Meaning in the
Dramatic Text* (New York: Barnes & Noble, 1963),
114). That the word could mean 'rump' is clear
from *OED*, and the obscene use is probably only
an extension of that meaning, probably to the geni-
tal organs of either sex.

225 keen sharp and bitter.

226 groaning of childbirth or loss of maiden-
head. '[E]dge' = sexual appetite.

227 Still better and worse Ophelia refers to
Hamlet's continual 'bettering' of her meaning, i.e.
'Always a "better" meaning with a more offensive
slant'.

228 mistake i.e. mis-take, trick: 'with such
vows (for better or for worse) you falsely take your
husbands'.

229–30 the croaking … revenge Simpson
noted (NV) in 1874 that this was a 'satirical con-
densation' of two lines from *The True Tragedy of
Richard III* (printed 1594): 'The screeking raven
sits croaking for revenge, / Whole herds of beasts
come bellowing for revenge' (Malone Society
Reprint, 1892–3).

LUCIANUS Thoughts black, hands apt, drugs fit, and time agreeing,
  Confederate season, else no creature seeing.
  Thou mixture rank, of midnight weeds collected,
  With Hecat's ban thrice blasted, thrice infected,
  Thy natural magic and dire property   235
  On wholesome life usurp immediately.
                Pours the poison in his ears
HAMLET A poisons him i'th'garden for's estate. His name's Gonzago.
  The story is extant, and written in very choice Italian. You shall
  see anon how the murderer gets the love of Gonzago's wife.
OPHELIA The king rises.   240
HAMLET What, frighted with false fire?
GERTRUDE How fares my lord?
POLONIUS Give o'er the play.
CLAUDIUS Give me some light. Away!
LORDS Lights, lights, lights!   245
                Exeunt all but Hamlet and Horatio
HAMLET Why, let the strucken deer go weep,
  The hart ungallèd play,
  For some must watch while some must sleep,
  Thus runs the world away.

---

232 Confederate] F; Considerat Q2   234 infected] F; inuected Q2   236 usurp] F; vsurps Q2   236 SD] F; *not in* Q2   237 A] Q2; He F   237 for's] F; for his Q2   238 written] Q2; writ F   238 very choice] Q2; choyce F   241 HAMLET ... fire] F; *not in* Q2   245 SH LORDS] *This edn; Pol.* Q2; *All* F   245 SD] Q2; *Exeunt / Manet Hamlet & Horatio* F   249 Thus] Q2, Q1; So F

231 **apt** ready.
232 **Confederate season** i.e. this moment of time is his ally, and his only witness.
233 **of midnight weeds collected** put together from weeds gathered at midnight; '[C]ollected' refers to the mixing of the weeds, the concoction, and not the picking. Compare 4.7.143.
234 **Hecat** Hecate, goddess of witchcraft.
234 **ban** curse.
235 **dire property** baleful quality.
236 **usurp** So F. Q2 reads 'usurps', but it is quite clear from the syntax that Lucianus is invoking the

poison to work.
237 **estate** position (as king). Compare 3.3.5.
241 **false fire** gunfire with blank charge.
245 LORDS Q2 gives this to Polonius; F to '*All*.' The royal guard came in bearing torches (81 SD above); Claudius orders these torchbearers to light him to his own quarters.
246–9 **Why, let …world away** This song or ballad has not been identified.
247 **ungalled** uninjured.
248 **watch** keep awake.

Would not this, sir, and a forest of feathers, if the rest of my fortunes   250
turn Turk with me, with two provincial roses on my razed shoes,
get me a fellowship in a cry of players, sir?
HORATIO Half a share.
HAMLET A whole one I.
       For thou dost know, O Damon dear,   255
          This realm dismantled was
       Of Jove himself, and now reigns here
          A very, very – pajock.
HORATIO You might have rhymed.
HAMLET O good Horatio, I'll take the ghost's word for a thousand   260
pound. Didst perceive?
HORATIO Very well my lord.
HAMLET Upon the talk of the poisoning?
HORATIO I did very well note him.

    Enter ROSENCRANTZ *and* GUILDENSTERN

HAMLET Ah ha! – Come, some music! Come, the recorders!   265
    For if the king like not the comedy,

---

251 two] F; *not in* Q2   251 razed] raz'd Q2; rac'd F   252 sir] F; *not in* Q2   264 SD] F; *after 268 in* Q2   265 Ah ha!] Ah ha, Q2; Oh, ha? F

250 **this** The success of the performance?

250 **forest of feathers** The plumes which were a derided feature of the gallant's outfit were a notable feature of theatre costume.

251 **turn Turk with me** To 'turn Turk' is to renounce one's religion, apostasize or become a renegade; 'with' has here the sense of 'against' (as we still use it in 'fight' or 'compete' *with* someone). So the phrase means 'renege on me', or 'renounce and desert me'.

251 **provincial roses** Roses originating either from Provins in northern France or from Provence. (Jenkins in a long note strongly defends the latter origin.) Hamlet is speaking of rosettes and not the real flowers.

251 **razed shoes** Shoes which were 'razed', 'rased' or 'raced' were ornamented by cuts or slits in the leather.

252 **fellowship** partnership; the technical term was a 'share'.

252 **cry** pack (of hounds).

255 **Damon** Known from classical literature as a paragon (with Pythias) of friendship.

256 **dismantled** stripped, divested; i.e. the realm lost Jove himself (sovereign god of the Romans) as king.

258 **pajock** T. McGrath, in 1871 (cited in NV), cleverly suggested that 'pajock' is the 'patchock' used by Edmund Spenser in *A View of the Present State of Ireland* (ed. W. L. Renwick (London: Scholartis Press, 1934), 64) in a context suggesting a despicable person: 'as very patchocks as the wild Irish'. This is supported by *OED* sv Patchock. In the following line, Horatio suggests that he expected Hamlet to finish with a rhyme, likely 'ass'.

263 **Upon the talk of the poisoning** May refer either to Lucianus's words (231–6) or to Hamlet's outburst (237–9).

264 SD So placed by F. Q2 places it later, after 268. F shows Hamlet pointedly ignoring Rosencrantz and Guildenstern by calling for music and singing a little song.

266–7 **if … perdy** It has been suggested that this is an echo of the lines in *The Spanish Tragedy* (4.1.197–8), also referring to a revenger's playlet, 'And if the world like not this tragedy, / Hard is the hap of old Hieronimo'. ('Perdy' = by God.)

Why then – belike he likes it not, perdy.
Come, some music!

GUILDENSTERN Good my lord, vouchsafe me a word with you.

HAMLET Sir, a whole history.   270

GUILDENSTERN The king, sir –

HAMLET Ay sir, what of him?

GUILDENSTERN Is in his retirement marvellous distempered.

HAMLET With drink sir?

GUILDENSTERN No my lord, rather with choler.   275

HAMLET Your wisdom should show itself more richer to signify this
     to his doctor, for, for me to put him to his purgation would perhaps
     plunge him into far more choler.

GUILDENSTERN Good my lord, put your discourse into some frame,
     and start not so wildly from my affair.   280

HAMLET I am tame sir, pronounce.

GUILDENSTERN The queen your mother, in most great affliction of
     spirit, hath sent me to you.

HAMLET You are welcome.

GUILDENSTERN Nay good my lord, this courtesy is not of the right   285
     breed. If it shall please you to make me a wholesome answer, I will
     do your mother's commandment. If not, your pardon and my return
     shall be the end of my business.

HAMLET Sir, I cannot.

ROSENCRANTZ What, my lord?   290

HAMLET Make you a wholesome answer; my wit's diseased. But, sir,
     such answer as I can make, you shall command, or rather, as you
     say, my mother. Therefore no more, but to the matter. My mother,
     you say.

ROSENCRANTZ Then thus she says. Your behaviour hath struck her   295
     into amazement and admiration.

---

275 rather with] F; with Q2   **277** his doctor] F; the Doctor Q2   **278** far more] F; more Q2   **280** start] F; stare Q2   **288** my business] F; busines Q2   **290** SH ROSENCRANTZ] *Ros.* Q2; *Guild,* F   **291** answer] Q2; answers F   **292–3** as you say] Q2; you say F

273 distempered out of humoral balance. But the word was also used as a euphemism for being drunk, as Hamlet's bland enquiry indicates.

275 choler anger.

277 purgation The practice, based on humoral theory, of getting rid of the excess yellow bile that has distempered Claudius. See 1.4.27.

277 signify announce.

277–8 for me … more choler the way in which I would cure him of his distemper would make him much angrier.

279 frame ordered structure.

280 start make a sudden movement, like a startled horse.

281 tame subdued; i.e. a manageable horse that will not 'start'.

286 wholesome healthy, i.e. sane.

287 pardon permission (to leave).

292 command have at your service.

296 amazement See notes to 1.2.235, 2.2.517.

296 admiration wonder.

HAMLET O wonderful son that can so stonish a mother! But is there
no sequel at the heels of this mother's admiration? Impart.

ROSENCRANTZ She desires to speak with you in her closet ere you go
to bed.   300

HAMLET We shall obey, were she ten times our mother. Have you any
further trade with us?

ROSENCRANTZ My lord, you once did love me.

HAMLET And do still, by these pickers and stealers.

ROSENCRANTZ Good my lord, what is your cause of distemper? You   305
do surely bar the door upon your own liberty if you deny your griefs
to your friend.

HAMLET Sir, I lack advancement.

ROSENCRANTZ How can that be, when you have the voice of the king
himself for your succession in Denmark?   310

HAMLET Ay sir, but while the grass grows – the proverb is something
musty.

Enter the PLAYERS *with recorders*

Oh, the recorders. Let me see one. To withdraw with you – Why
do you go about to recover the wind of me, as if you would drive
me into a toil?   315

GUILDENSTERN O my lord, if my duty be too bold, my love is too
unmannerly.

HAMLET I do not well understand that. Will you play upon this pipe?

297 stonish] Q2; astonish F   298 Impart] Q2; *not in* F   304 And] Q2; So I F   306 surely] Q2; freely F   306 upon]
Q2; of F   311 sir] Q2; *not in* F   312 SD] Q2 *(after 310);* Enter one with a Recorder F   313 recorders] Q2; Recorder
F   313 Let me see one] Q2; Let me see F

301 **were she … mother** In sane conversation,
this would go with a *refusal* to obey.

304 **pickers and stealers** hands. From the
Catechism in the Book of Common Prayer:
'To keep my hands from picking and stealing'.

306 **bar … liberty** Rosencrantz means Hamlet
would be more free in his mind, less burdened, if he
would communicate his problems.

308 **I lack advancement** Hamlet brazenly
offers the explanation which Rosencrantz and
Guildenstern had previously suggested and which
he had denied (2.2.241–4).

311 **while the grass grows** – While waiting for
the grass to grow, the horse starves. As Hamlet

indicates, this is an old proverb (Tilley G423).

312 SD **So** Q2. F's modification of this direction
and the subsequent dialogue cut down the number of
characters necessary. See Textual Analysis, 266–8.

313 **To withdraw with you** Hamlet moves
Rosencrantz and Guildenstern aside with him.

314 **recover** gain. The huntsman will try to
move to the windward of his prey, and so get the
animal, scenting him, to run away from him and
towards the trap.

316–17 **if my duty … unmannerly** 'If my
respectful attention seems to you too bold, you
accuse love of being ill-mannered'.

GUILDENSTERN My lord, I cannot.

HAMLET I pray you. 320

GUILDENSTERN Believe me I cannot.

HAMLET I do beseech you.

GUILDENSTERN I know no touch of it my lord.

HAMLET 'Tis as easy as lying. Govern these ventages with your fingers
and thumb, give it breath with your mouth, and it will discourse 325
most eloquent music. Look you, these are the stops.

GUILDENSTERN But these cannot I command to any utterance of
harmony. I have not the skill.

HAMLET Why look you now how unworthy a thing you make of me.
You would play upon me, you would seem to know my stops, you 330
would pluck out the heart of my mystery, you would sound me from
my lowest note to the top of my compass – and there is much music,
excellent voice, in this little organ, yet cannot you make it speak.
'Sblood, do you think I am easier to be played on than a pipe? Call
me what instrument you will, though you can fret me, you cannot 335
play upon me.

Enter POLONIUS

God bless you sir.

POLONIUS My lord, the queen would speak with you, and presently.

HAMLET Do you see yonder cloud that's almost in shape of a camel?

POLONIUS By th'mass, and 'tis like a camel indeed. 340

HAMLET Methinks it is like a weasel.

---

324 'Tis] F; It is Q2   324 fingers] Q2; finger F   325 thumb] thumbe F; the vmber Q2   326 eloquent] Q2; excellent
F   332 the top of] F; *not in* Q2   333 speak] Q2; *not in* F   334 'Sblood] Q2; Why F   334 think I] Q2, Q1; thinke, that
I F   335 can fret me] F; fret me not Q2   339 yonder] Q2, Q1; that F   339 in shape of] Q2; in shape like F   340 mass]
masse Q2; Misse F   340 'tis] Q2; it's F

324 ventages vents, i.e. finger holes of the
recorder.

331 mystery the skills of a particular craft. I.e.
you would learn the innermost secret of my working, as a musician would learn the secret of playing
the recorder.

333 this little organ the recorder.

335 fret 'frets' are the raised bars for fingering

on a lute, providing a pun with 'irritate'.

338 presently immediately.

339 see yonder cloud This scene is supposed to
be taking place indoors at night. But Shakespeare
has already puzzled the difference between inside
and outside in scenes between Hamlet and Polonius
(see 2.2.201).

POLONIUS It is backed like a weasel.

HAMLET Or like a whale?

POLONIUS Very like a whale.

HAMLET Then I will come to my mother by and by. – They fool me   345
    to the top of my bent. – I will come by and by.

POLONIUS I will say so.   *Exit*

HAMLET By and by is easily said. – Leave me, friends.

                                   Exeunt all but Hamlet

    'Tis now the very witching time of night,
    When churchyards yawn, and hell itself breathes out   350
    Contagion to this world. Now could I drink hot blood,
    And do such bitter business as the day
    Would quake to look on. Soft, now to my mother.
    O heart, lose not thy nature; let not ever
    The soul of Nero enter this firm bosom.   355
    Let me be cruel, not unnatural:
    O will speak daggers to her but use none.
    My tongue and soul in this be hypocrites,
    How in my words somever she be shent,
    To give them seals never my soul consent. *Exit*   360

---

343 whale?] F; Whale. Q2   345 SH HAMLET] F; *as catchword only in* Q2   345 I will] Q2; will I F   347–8 POLONIUS...
friends.] F; Leaue me friends. / I will, say so. By and by is easily said, Q2   350 breathes] breaths F; breakes Q2   352
bitter business as the day] F; busines as the bitter day Q2   357 daggers] F; dagger Q2   360 SD] Q2; *not in* F

345 by and by presently, quite soon.

345–6 They fool me ... bent They tax to the
uttermost my capacity to play the madman.

349 witching time bewitching time, time of
sorcery and enchantment. The reference is to the
witches' sabbath, when their ceremonies conjured
up the devil in physical form.

351 Now could I drink hot blood Witches
were supposed to open the graves of newly buried
children whom their charms had killed, boil the
bodies, and drink the liquid. Drinking of blood
was one of the most frequent charges against
witches. See Reginald Scot, *Discovery of Witchcraft*
(London, 1584), E1.

353 Soft That's enough! (see 3.1.88 note).

354 nature natural feelings (as regards his
mother). Compare 1.5.81.

355 Nero Tyrannical Roman emperor who contrived the murder of his mother.

358 My tongue ... hypocrites Hamlet estab-
lishes the disjunction between what he will say and
what he feels or wishes.

359 shent castigated, punished (by rebuke or
reproach).

360 give them seals i.e. by deeds.

[3.3] *Enter* CLAUDIUS, ROSENCRANTZ *and* GUILDENSTERN

CLAUDIUS I like him not, nor stands it safe with us
      To let his madness range. Therefore prepare you:
      I your commission will forthwith dispatch,
      And he to England shall along with you.
      The terms of our estate may not endure   5
      Hazard so near us as doth hourly grow
      Out of his brows.
GUILDENSTERN   We will ourselves provide.
      Most holy and religious fear it is
      To keep those many many bodies safe
      That live and feed upon your majesty.   10
ROSENCRANTZ The single and peculiar life is bound
      With all the strength and armour of the mind
      To keep itself from noyance; but much more
      That spirit upon whose weal depends and rests
      The lives of many. The cess of majesty   15
      Dies not alone, but like a gulf doth draw
      What's near it with it. It is a massy wheel
      Fixed on the summit of the highest mount,
      To whose huge spokes ten thousand lesser things
      Are mortised and adjoined, which when it falls,   20
      Each small annexment, petty consequence,
      Attends the boisterous ruin. Never alone
      Did the king sigh, but with a general groan.

Act 3, Scene 3   3.3] *Capell*   6 near us] Q 1676; neer's Q2; dangerous F   7 brows] browes Q2; Lunacies F   14 weal]
Q2; spirit F   15 cess] cesse Q2; cease F   17 It is] F; or it is Q2   18 summit] *Rowe*; somnet Q2; Somnet F   19 huge]
F; hough Q2   22 ruin] F; raine Q2   23 but with] F; but Q2

Act 3, Scene 3
   1 **I like him not** i.e. I do not like the way he is
behaving.
   1 **us** i.e. the person of the king.
   3 **dispatch** make ready.
   4 **along** go along. Compare 1.1.26.
   5 **The terms of our estate** The conditions of
my position as king.
   7 **Out of his brows** So Q2. '[B]rows' means
'effrontery' (which derives from Latin *frons* =
brow). Though 'effrontery' is not recorded in the
language of Shakespeare's day in *OED*, 'effronted'
(= barefaced, shameless) does exist.
   7 **ourselves provide** make provision for

ourselves (to travel to England).
   11 **The single and peculiar life** The life that
belongs to the individual only.
   13 **noyance** harm.
   14 **weal** well-being.
   15 **cess** cessation. So Q2. F gives the now more
familiar 'cease'.
   16 **gulf** whirlpool (*OED* 3).
   17 **massy** massive.
   21 **annexment** adjunct, supplement. A rare
word – Shakespeare's is the first example, and one
of only two, in *OED*.
   21 **consequence** attachment. Again a curious
usage.

CLAUDIUS Arm you I pray you to this speedy voyage,
　　　　　For we will fetters put about this fear   25
　　　　　Which now goes too free-footed.
ROSENCRANTZ　　　　　　　　　　　　We will haste us.
　　　　　　　　　Exeunt Rosencrantz and Guildenstern

　　　　　　　　　Enter POLONIUS

POLONIUS My lord, he's going to his mother's closet.
　　　　　Behind the arras I'll convey myself
　　　　　To hear the process. I'll warrant she'll tax him home,
　　　　　And as you said, and wisely was it said,   30
　　　　　'Tis meet that some more audience than a mother,
　　　　　Since nature makes them partial, should o'erhear
　　　　　The speech of vantage. Fare you well my liege,
　　　　　I'll call upon you ere you go to bed
　　　　　And tell you what I know.
CLAUDIUS　　　　　　　　　　　　Thanks, dear my lord.   35
　　　　　　　　　　　　　　　Exit Polonius
　　　　　Oh my offence is rank, it smells to heaven;
　　　　　It hath the primal eldest curse upon't,
　　　　　A brother's murder. Pray can I not,
　　　　　Though inclination be as sharp as will.
　　　　　My stronger guilt defeats my strong intent,   40
　　　　　And like a man to double business bound,
　　　　　I stand in pause where I shall first begin,
　　　　　And both neglect. What if this cursèd hand
　　　　　Were thicker than itself with brother's blood,
　　　　　Is there not rain enough in the sweet heavens   45
　　　　　To wash it white as snow? Whereto serves mercy

24 voyage] F; viage Q2   25 about] Q2; vpon F   26 SH ROSENCRANTZ] *Ros.* Q2; *Both.* F   26 SD *Exeunt ...*
Guildenstern] *Hanmer; Exeunt Gent.* Q2, F   33 Fare] F; farre Q2   35 SD] *Capell; Exit.* Q2; *not in* F

24 **Arm you** Prepare yourselves.
28 **convey myself** secretly move myself.
29 **the process** what goes on.
29 **tax him home** censure him severely.
30 **as you said** Polonius's transfer of responsibility for the scheme is a matter of prudence as well as deference (see 3.1.175–9).
31 **meet** suitable.
33 **of vantage** from a good position.
37 **primal eldest curse** Cain's murder of his brother Abel in Genesis 4.10–11.
39 **Though inclination ... will** Claudius

cannot pray although his desire to do so is as great as his determination. Thompson and Taylor point out that he may mean that he cannot pray because his desire to do so is matched by his will to sin, as indicated in the next line.
41 **double   business**   two   incompatible purposes.
41 **bound** Probably this means 'directed towards' (as in 'bound for England', 4.6.9), rather than 'obliged' or 'sworn'.
46–7 **Whereto ... offence?** What is mercy for, except to meet crime face to face?

But to confront the visage of offence?
And what's in prayer but this two-fold force,
To be forestallèd ere we come to fall,
Or pardoned being down? Then I'll look up,   50
My fault is past. But oh, what form of prayer
Can serve my turn? 'Forgive me my foul murder'?
That cannot be, since I am still possessed
Of those effects for which I did the murder,
My crown, mine own ambition, and my queen.   55
May one be pardoned and retain th'offence?
In the corrupted currents of this world
Offence's gilded hand may shove by justice,
And oft 'tis seen the wicked prize itself
Buys out the law. But 'tis not so above;   60
There is no shuffling, there the action lies
In his true nature, and we ourselves compelled
Even to the teeth and forehead of our faults
To give in evidence. What then? What rests?
Try what repentance can. What can it not?   65
Yet what can it when one cannot repent?
Oh wretched state! Oh bosom black as death!
Oh limèd soul that struggling to be free
Art more engaged! Help, angels! – Make assay:
Bow stubborn knees, and heart with strings of steel   70
Be soft as sinews of the new-born babe.
All may be well.

                    [*He kneels*]

---

50 pardoned] pardon'd F; pardon Q2   **58** shove] F; showe Q2   **72** SD *He kneels*] Q1; *not in* Q2, F

54 effects things acquired or achieved.

55 mine own ambition i.e. those things I was ambitious for.

56 th'offence i.e. the fruits of the offence.

58 shove by thrust aside.

59 wicked prize reward achieved by wicked means.

61 shuffling trickery, sharp practice, deception. See 3.1.67 note.

61 the action lies A legal phrase, meaning that a case is admitted to exist. But it also means that every deed lies exposed to God's scrutiny.

63–4 Even to … evidence to give evidence even about the worst of our sins. We are witnesses for the prosecution of ourselves; 'teeth' is for savagery and 'forehead' for effrontery (compare 'brows' above, 7).

64 rests remains.

68 limèd The image is of a bird caught by the smearing of a very sticky substance, called birdlime, on twigs and branches.

69 Make assay Claudius is probably addressing himself rather than the angels, since he knows that it is he who must make the effort.

Enter HAMLET

HAMLET Now might I do it pat, now a is a-praying,
And now I'll do't – and so a goes to heaven,
And so am I revenged. That would be scanned.   75
A villain kills my father, and for that,
I his sole son do this same villain send
To heaven.
Why, this is hire and salary, not revenge.
A took my father grossly, full of bread,   80
With all his crimes broad blown, as flush as May,
And how his audit stands who knows save heaven?
But in our circumstance and course of thought
'Tis heavy with him. And am I then revenged
To take him in the purging of his soul,   85
When he is fit and seasoned for his passage?
No.
Up sword, and know thou a more horrid hent,
When he is drunk asleep, or in his rage,
Or in th'incestuous pleasure of his bed,   90
At game a-swearing, or about some act
That has no relish of salvation in't –
Then trip him that his heels may kick at heaven,

---

73 do it pat] F; do it, but Q2   73 a is a-praying] Q2; he is praying F   74 a] Q2; he F   75 revenged] reueng'd F; reuendge Q2   76 A] Q2; He F   77 sole] Q2; foule F   79 Why] Q2; Oh F   79 hire and salary] F; base and silly Q2   81 flush] Q2; fresh F   89 drunk asleep] F; drunke, a sleep Q2   91 At game a-swearing] At game a swearing Q2; at game swaring Q1; at gaming, swearing F

73 **pat** neatly, aptly.

73 **a is** Represents a slurred pronunciation of 'he is'; compare 2.2.185. We would write 'he's', but perhaps the pronunciation was nearer 'uz'.

75 **would be scanned** needs to be examined.

79 **hire and salary** So F. Q2's 'base and silly' is suspect, though it too emphasizes that killing Claudius at this moment would be beneath Hamlet and the demands of revenge.

80 **grossly** i.e. without consideration or decency.

80 **full of bread** Malone noted that this was a biblical echo, quoting Ezekiel 16.49: 'the iniquity of thy sister Sodom, pride, fulness of bread, and abundance of idleness'.

81 **broad blown** in full blossom.

81 **flush** vigorous.

83 **circumstance ... thought** 'circumstance', as at 1.5.127 and 3.1.1, has the sense of circuitous or circling discourse. The construction here is the familiar Shakespearean use of two nouns for an adjective and a noun, i.e. 'circumstantial course of thought' = our course of thought which is necessarily indirect.

88 **hent** grasp (a rare word). He puts his sword up in its scabbard, promising to lay hold of it at a 'more horrid' opportunity.

89 **drunk asleep** i.e. in a drunken sleep.

91 **At game a-swearing** Gambling, and cursing the dice or cards as he plays. Although 'at game' is not elsewhere used by Shakespeare, there can be little doubt about the correctness of Q2 (followed here) which is supported by Q1, as against F's paraphrase, 'At gaming, swearing'.

92 **relish** touch, trace.

93–5 **trip him ... it goes** This ambition to bring Claudius to eternal damnation – a speech, said Dr Johnson, 'too terrible to be read or to be uttered' – is discussed in the Introduction, 19.

And that his soul may be as damned and black
As hell whereto it goes. My mother stays.   95
This physic but prolongs thy sickly day.   *Exit*
CLAUDIUS My words fly up, my thoughts remain below.
Words without thoughts never to heaven go.   *Exit*

[3.4] *Enter* GERTRUDE *and* POLONIUS

POLONIUS A will come straight. Look you lay home to him.
Tell him his pranks have been too broad to bear with,
And that your grace hath screened and stood between
Much heat and him. I'll silence me e'en here.
Pray you be round with him.   5
HAMLET (*Within*) Mother, mother, mother!
GERTRUDE I'll warrant you, fear me not. Withdraw, I hear him coming.
              [*Polonius hides himself behind the arras*]

              Enter HAMLET

HAMLET Now mother, what's the matter?
GERTRUDE Hamlet, thou hast thy father much offended.
HAMLET Mother, you have my father much offended.   10
GERTRUDE Come, come, you answer with an idle tongue.

Act 3, Scene 4   3.4] Capell   1 A] Q2; He F   4 e'en] e'ene F; euen Q2   5 with him] F; *not in* Q2   6 HAMLET …
mother!] F; *not in* Q2; Mother, mother Q1   7 warrant] F; wait Q2   7 SD *Polonius … arras*] *Rowe; not in* Q2, F

96 This physic Hamlet sees his decision as
a medicine temporarily preserving Claudius's life.
Some commentators think the physic is Claudius's
prayer.

Act 3, Scene 4
3.4 This is generally known as the 'closet scene'
(see 3.2.299), a closet being a private apartment.
See Introduction, 45.
  1 lay home to him charge him to the full.

3 screened acted as a fire-screen – as the sentence goes on to illustrate.
  4 I'll silence me Dowden thought this ironical,
since it is Polonius's shout (24) that causes his
death. Q1's reading is gruesomely apt, 'I'le shrowd
myself behind the arras.'
  5 round See 3.1.177.
  6 Mother, mother, mother! Not in Q2, though
in keeping with Hamlet's behaviour.

HAMLET Go, go, you question with a wicked tongue.
GERTRUDE Why, how now Hamlet?
HAMLET   What's the matter now?
GERTRUDE Have you forgot me?
HAMLET   No by the rood, not so.
    You are the queen, your husband's brother's wife,   15
    And, would it were not so, you are my mother.
GERTRUDE Nay, then I'll set those to you that can speak.
HAMLET Come, come and sit you down, you shall not budge.
    You go not till I set you up a glass
    Where you may see the inmost part of you.   20
GERTRUDE What wilt thou do? thou wilt not murder me?
    Help, help, ho!
POLONIUS (*Behind*) What ho! Help, help, help!
HAMLET (*Draws*) How now, a rat? Dead for a ducat, dead.
                Kills Polonius
POLONIUS (*Behind*) Oh, I am slain!
GERTRUDE   Oh me, what hast thou done?   25
HAMLET Nay I know not, is it the king?
GERTRUDE Oh what a rash and bloody deed is this!
HAMLET A bloody deed? Almost as bad, good mother,
    As kill a king and marry with his brother.
GERTRUDE As kill a king?
HAMLET   Ay lady, 'twas my word.   30
    [*Lifts up the arras and reveals the body of Polonius*]
    Thou wretched, rash, intruding fool, farewell.
    I took thee for thy better. Take thy fortune.
    Thou find'st to be too busy is some danger. –

---

12 a wicked] Q2; an idle F   16 And, would it] And would it Q2; But would you F   20 inmost] F; most Q2   22 Help, help, ho!] F; Helpe how. Q2   23, 25 SD *Behind*] *Capell; not in* Q2, F   23 Help, help, help!] F; helpe. Q2   24 SD *Draws*] *Malone (after* rat); *not in* Q2, F   24 SD *Kills Polonius*] F; *not in* Q2   30 'twas] F; it was Q2   30 SD] *following Capell (26) and Cambridge; not in* Q2, F   32 better] Q2; Betters F

14 **forgot me** forgotten who I am.
14 **the rood** the cross of Christ.
17 **can speak** Is this the understatement 'will have something to say to you'?
18 **Come, come** This is much more than the 'now then!' of Gertrude's 'Come, come' (12), as it prompts Gertrude to think she is under threat (21).
18 **budge** move away (to fetch the others).
19 **glass** a mirror, this time one which reveals actions in their sinful nature. See notes to 3.2.18 and 3.1.147.
24 **rat** proverbially associated with spying or chicanery (Tilley).

24 **Dead for a ducat** Possibly, as Kittredge suggests, a wager, i.e. 'I'll bet a ducat I kill it.'
30 **As kill a king? ... word** It is extraordinary that neither of them takes up this all-important matter again. Gertrude does not press for an explanation; Hamlet does not question further the queen's involvement. In Q1, Hamlet reiterates the fact that his father was murdered ('damnably murdred'), and the queen says 'I never knew of this most horride murder.'
32 **I ... thy better** Hamlet thought he was striking at Claudius.

Leave wringing of your hands. Peace! Sit you down
And let me wring your heart, for so I shall   35
If it be made of penetrable stuff,
If damnèd custom have not brazed it so,
That it be proof and bulwark against sense.
GERTRUDE What have I done, that thou dar'st wag thy tongue
In noise so rude against me?
HAMLET   Such an act   40
That blurs the grace and blush of modesty,
Calls virtue hypocrite, takes off the rose
From the fair forehead of an innocent love
And sets a blister there, makes marriage vows
As false as dicers' oaths. Oh such a deed   45
As from the body of contraction plucks
The very soul, and sweet religion makes
A rhapsody of words. Heaven's face doth glow;
Yea, this solidity and compound mass,
With tristful visage as against the doom,   50
Is thought-sick at the act.
GERTRUDE   Ay me, what act,
That roars so loud and thunders in the index?

---

38 be] Q2; is F   44 sets] Q2; makes F   48 doth] F; dooes Q2   49 Yea] F; Ore Q2   50 tristful] F; heated
Q2   52 That] F; *Ham.* That Q2

---

37 **brazed** made brazen, hardened like brass.
38 **proof** armour.
38 **sense** feeling.
40 **Such an act** In the speech which follows,
Hamlet quite certainly implies the breaking of marriage vows (see note to 1.5.46). But when Gertrude
directly asks him 'what act?' (51), he does not
directly answer 'adultery', but charges her with
inconstancy, immoderate sexual desire, and a lack
of any sense of value, in exchanging King Hamlet
for Claudius. He does not pursue the charge of
adultery, but nothing he says shows him forgetting
it.
42 **rose** A figurative rose, symbol of true love.
44 **sets a blister there** Assumed to mean the
burn-mark from the branding of a harlot on the
forehead, with the backing of Laertes's speech at
4.5.119–20, 'brands the harlot / Even here, between
the chaste unsmirchèd brow'. But Shakespeare is
probably speaking figuratively, thinking of the

forehead as the place which declares innocence or
boldness (compare 3.3.7). The 'blister' then would
indicate disease or taint. It was not the custom in
Elizabethan times to brand prostitutes in the face,
though this dire punishment was threatened by
Henry VIII in 1513 and by the Commonwealth in
1650.
46 **contraction** pledging, making vows or
contracts.
48 **rhapsody** a medley, a miscellaneous or confused collection.
48–51 **Heaven's face … at the act** i.e. the skies
blush with shame, and the huge earth itself, with
a countenance as sad as if it were doomsday, is
distressed in mind by your act.
49 **Yea** So F. Q2, substituting 'O'er' ('Ore') for
'Yea', treats the visage as belonging to the glowing
sun and supplies 'heated' for 'tristful'.
52 **index** table of contents (prefixed to a book).

HAMLET Look here upon this picture, and on this,
The counterfeit presentment of two brothers.
See what a grace was seated on this brow;   55
Hyperion's curls, the front of Jove himself,
An eye like Mars, to threaten and command;
A station like the herald Mercury,
New-lighted on a heaven-kissing hill;
A combination and a form indeed,   60
Where every god did seem to set his seal
To give the world assurance of a man.
This was your husband. Look you now what follows.
Here is your husband, like a mildewed ear
Blasting his wholesome brother. Have you eyes?   65
Could you on this fair mountain leave to feed
And batten on this moor? Ha! have you eyes?
You cannot call it love, for at your age
The heyday in the blood is tame, it's humble,
And waits upon the judgement; and what judgement   70
Would step from this to this? [Sense sure you have,
Else could you not have motion, but sure that sense
Is apoplexed, for madness would not err,
Nor sense to ecstasy was ne'er so thralled,
But it reserved some quantity of choice   75

---

53 SH HAMLET] *Ham.* F; *not in* Q2   57 and] Q2; *or* F   59 heaven-kissing] F; heaue, a kissing Q2   65 brother] Q2;
breath F   71–6 Sense ... difference] Q2; *not in* F

53 **this picture, and ... this** Hamlet displays
images of Hamlet Sr and Claudius to Gertrude – he
may point to two different portraits or tapestries
hung on the wall or he may show her miniatures or
lockets.
54 **counterfeit presentment** i.e. portraits,
representations in art.
56 **Hyperion** See 1.2.140.
56 **front** forehead.
57 **Mars** in classical mythology, Roman god of
war.
58 **station** stance, way of standing.
59 **New-lighted** Newly alighted.
60 **combination** i.e. of divine qualities.
61 **set his seal** place his confirming mark.
64 **ear** of corn.
65 **Blasting** Blighting.

67 **batten** feed and grow fat. (Not an easy thing
to do on moorland. The 'fair mountain' is faintly
biblical: Wilson suggests an undertone of 'black-
amoor' in 'moor'.)
69 **heyday** excitement.
69 **blood** passions, sexual desire.
71–6, 78–81 F makes two major excisions in the
remainder of this speech. See Textual Analysis,
257–8.
71–6 **Sense ... difference** Hamlet allows that
Gertrude has ability to reason, but says that this
ability was so severely impaired that she was unable
to distinguish between Claudius and her former
husband.
73 **apoplexed** paralysed.
74 **thralled** in thrall, enslaved.

To serve in such a difference.] What devil was't
That thus hath cozened you at hoodman-blind?
[Eyes without feeling, feeling without sight,
Ears without hands or eyes, smelling sans all,
Or but a sickly part of one true sense   80
Could not so mope.]
O shame, where is thy blush? Rebellious hell,
If thou canst mutine in a matron's bones,
To flaming youth let virtue be as wax
And melt in her own fire. Proclaim no shame   85
When the compulsive ardour gives the charge,
Since frost itself as actively doth burn,
And reason panders will.

GERTRUDE   O Hamlet, speak no more.
Thou turn'st my eyes into my very soul,
And there I see such black and grainèd spots   90
As will not leave their tinct.

HAMLET   Nay, but to live
In the rank sweat of an enseamèd bed,
Stewed in corruption, honeying and making love
Over the nasty sty.

---

77 hoodman] F; hodman Q2   78–81 Eyes ... mope] Q2; *not in* F   86 ardour] ardure Q2, F   88 And] Q2; As F   88 panders] F; pardons Q2   89 turn'st my] Q2; turn'st mine F   89 eyes ... soul] F; very eyes into my soule Q2   90 grainèd] F; greeued Q2   91 will not] F; will Q2   91 their] F; there their Q2   92 enseamèd] F; inseemed Q2

76 serve ... difference i.e. to assist in differentiating between the two men.

77 cozened ... hoodman-blind deceived you in a game of blindman's buff. (The devil substituted Claudius for King Hamlet when the blindfold Gertrude chose him.)

81 mope move around aimlessly, in a daze or trance.

82 Rebellious hell Hamlet's way of conflating sexual desire with the defiant as well as punitive force of hell, or his suggestion that the powers of hell encourage lower urges to rebel against judgement and reason.

83 mutine incite mutiny (*OED v* 2).

84–5 To flaming youth ... fire The argument runs that it is no good insisting on virtue as a rigid and unbending guide of conduct in the young, when age gives such a bad example. Virtue, in these circumstances, becomes a soft wax melting in the fire of youthful ardour.

86 gives the charge signals the attack.

88 reason panders will reason assists the

passions to obtain their ends.

90 grainèd engrained, deep-dyed.

91 leave their tinct surrender their colour.

92 enseamèd The word has to do with 'grease'. Its commonest context in Shakespeare's time was scouring or purging animals, especially hawks and horses, of (it was thought) superfluous internal grease or fat. But 'enseam' could also mean not to *remove* but to *apply* grease, especially to cloth. The least disgusting meaning here would therefore be 'greasy'. It is more than likely, however, that what is uppermost in Hamlet's mind is the idea of evacuated foulness. The echo 'semen' is surely present. The bed is greasy with offensive semen.

93 Stewed cooked. Shakespeare combines the heat, sweat, and greasiness with the odium of the brothels, widely known as 'the stews'.

93 honeying ... sty i.e. covering over foulness with sweet words and endearments; 'making love' has its usual pre-1950 sense of courtship, love-talk; sty is an area for swine (*OED* 3.1) but is also understood as a place of moral pollution generally (*OED* 3.3).

GERTRUDE   Oh speak to me no more.
    These words like daggers enter in my ears.   95
    No more sweet Hamlet.
HAMLET   A murderer and a villain,
    A slave that is not twentieth part the tithe
    Of your precedent lord, a vice of kings,
    A cutpurse of the empire and the rule,
    That from a shelf the precious diadem stole   100
    And put it in his pocket.
GERTRUDE   No more!

Enter GHOST

HAMLET A king of shreds and patches –
    Save me and hover o'er me with your wings,
    You heavenly guards! – What would your gracious figure?
GERTRUDE Alas he's mad!   105
HAMLET Do you not come your tardy son to chide,
    That lapsed in time and passion lets go by
    Th'important acting of your dread command? Oh say!
GHOST Do not forget. This visitation
    Is but to whet thy almost blunted purpose.   110
    But look, amazement on thy mother sits.
    Oh step between her and her fighting soul:
    Conceit in weakest bodies strongest works.
    Speak to her, Hamlet.
HAMLET   How is it with you lady?
GERTRUDE Alas, how is't with you,   115
    That you do bend your eye on vacancy,

---

95 my] Q2; mine F   97 tithe] tythe F; kyth Q2   104 your] Q2; you F   116 do] Q2; *not in* F

97 tithe tenth part.

98 vice clown or trickster of the old drama.

99 cutpurse pickpocket, thief.

101 SD Q1 gives '*Enter the ghost in his night gowne.*'

102 shreds and patches i.e. the patchwork costume of the stage-clown.

107 lapsed … lets go by failed or neglectful in the timely and passionate pursuit of revenge. If 'lapsed' = apprehended or arrested, then Hamlet is saying that he is taken or surprised by the Ghost.

108 important Neither 'momentous' nor 'urgent'; compare *All's Well* 3.7.21, 'his important blood will not deny'. We have no adjective which has the same sense of demanding or insisting: 'The acting – so urged on me and required of me – of your dread command'.

110 blunted purpose Hamlet is misusing his energies or is being distracted from the central goal of revenge. Compare Sonnet 95: 'the hardest knife, ill-used, doth lose his edge'.

111 amazement utter bewilderment. Compare 3.2.296.

113 Conceit Imagination.

And with th'incorporal air do hold discourse?
Forth at your eyes your spirits wildly peep,
And, as the sleeping soldiers in th'alarm,
Your bedded hair, like life in excrements,   120
Start up and stand an end. O gentle son,
Upon the heat and flame of thy distemper
Sprinkle cool patience. Whereon do you look?

HAMLET On him, on him! Look you how pale he glares.
His form and cause conjoined, preaching to stones,   125
Would make them capable. – Do not look upon me,
Lest with this piteous action you convert
My stern effects. Then what I have to do
Will want true colour: tears perchance for blood.

GERTRUDE To whom do you speak this?   130

HAMLET Do you see nothing there?

GERTRUDE Nothing at all, yet all that is I see.

HAMLET Nor did you nothing hear?

GERTRUDE No, nothing but ourselves.

HAMLET Why, look you there – look how it steals away –   135
My father in his habit as he lived –
Look where he goes, even now out at the portal.

Exit Ghost

GERTRUDE This is the very coinage of your brain.
This bodiless creation ecstasy
Is very cunning in.

---

117 th'incorporal] Q2; their corporall F   130 whom] Q2; who F   137 SD] Q2; *Exit* F   139–40 This … in] *as one line*
Q2, F

118 **spirits wildly peep** 'In moments of excitement the *spirits* or "vital forces" were thought to come, as it were, to the surface, and to cause various symptoms of agitation' (Kittredge).

119 **as the sleeping … alarm** like soldiers startled out of sleep by a call to arms.

120 **hair** (considered plural).

120 **like life in excrements** 'excrement' can be either what is voided from, or what, like hair and nails, grows out of, the body. Probably 'as though there were independent life in such outgrowths'.

121 **an end** A common form of 'on end'.

124 **how pale he glares** He is gazing fixedly with a ghastly expression; 'glares' is not necessarily an angry stare, 'pale' is several times used by Shakespeare in connection with a dying or lacklustre look of the eyes. Schmidt compares *Troilus* 5.3.81, 'Look how thou diest, look how thy eye

turns pale.'

126 **capable** receptive, sensitive.

127 **piteous action** behaviour which excites pity.

128 **effects** intended deeds (seen as issuing from anger and indignation). At their first meeting, the Ghost warned Hamlet not to pity him (1.5.5), presumably taking the same view that pity is not a state of mind likely to generate violent action.

129 **true colour** The 'effects' of pity would be colourless tears instead of blood. (The Ghost's reappearance seems to be weakening Hamlet's resolve instead of strengthening it.)

136 **in his habit as he lived** in the clothes he wore when alive.

138 **very** mere.

139 **ecstasy** madness.

140 **cunning** skilful.

HAMLET   Ecstasy?   140
    My pulse as yours doth temperately keep time,
    And makes as healthful music. It is not madness
    That I have uttered. Bring me to the test,
    And I the matter will reword, which madness
    Would gambol from. Mother, for love of grace,   145
    Lay not that flattering unction to your soul,
    That not your trespass but my madness speaks;
    It will but skin and film the ulcerous place,
    Whiles rank corruption, mining all within,
    Infects unseen. Confess yourself to heaven,   150
    Repent what's past, avoid what is to come,
    And do not spread the compost on the weeds
    To make them ranker. Forgive me this my virtue,
    For in the fatness of these pursy times
    Virtue itself of vice must pardon beg,   155
    Yea, curb and woo for leave to do him good.
GERTRUDE Oh Hamlet, thou hast cleft my heart in twain.
HAMLET Oh throw away the worser part of it
    And live the purer with the other half.
    Good night – but go not to my uncle's bed;   160
    Assume a virtue if you have it not.
    [That monster custom, who all sense doth eat,

---

140 Ecstasy?] F; *not in* Q2   144 And I] F; And Q2   146 that] Q2; a F   149 Whiles] Q2; Whil'st F   152 on] Q2; or
F   153 ranker] Q2; ranke F   154 these] Q2; this F   156 woo] wooe Q2; woe F   159 live] F; leaue Q2   160 my] Q2;
mine F   162–6 That monster ... put on] Q2; *not in* F

145 **gambol from** spring away from.
146 **unction** healing oil or ointment.
148 **skin and film** serve as a skin and film over.
149 **mining** undermining.
152 **spread ... weeds** She is not to use the good words of Hamlet as an encouragement to her vice, by supposing them to proceed only from his madness.
153–6 **Forgive me ... good** Hamlet is self-justifying in his apology, saying, in effect, 'I am sorry I have to apologize for speaking like this: virtue ought not to cringe before vice, but it is necessary because vice is so dominant these days.'
154 **fatness** grossness, ill condition (see note to 1.5.32 and 5.2.264).
154 **pursy** This is the same word as 'pursive' and it meant both short of breath and flatulent; it

could be conveniently applied to a person who was grossly out of condition, panting, belching, and breaking wind. Compare *Timon of Athens* 5.4.12, 'pursy insolence shall break his wind'. As *OED* indicates, the word had connotations of corpulence. The words 'fatness' and 'pursy' move towards each other in meaning, suggesting in sum an overweight, pampered person in poor physical condition.
156 **curb** bow, make obeisance (Fr. *courber*).
162–6 This passage is not present in the Folio. See Textual Analysis, 259.
162–6 **That monster ... put on** Custom is a monster who destroys sensitivity or reason, and thus leads to devilish habits; but also an angel, in that he can make us accustomed to good actions; 'aptly' = readily.

Of habits devil, is angel yet in this,
That to the use of actions fair and good
He likewise gives a frock or livery   165
That aptly is put on.] Refrain tonight,
And that shall lend a kind of easiness
To the next abstinence, [the next more easy,
For use almost can change the stamp of nature,
And either ... the devil, or throw him out,   170
With wondrous potency.] Once more good night,
And when you are desirous to be blessed,
I'll blessing beg of you. For this same lord,
I do repent; but heaven hath pleased it so,
To punish me with this, and this with me,   175
That I must be their scourge and minister.
I will bestow him, and will answer well
The death I gave him. So again, good night.
I must be cruel only to be kind;
Thus bad begins, and worse remains behind.   180
One word more good lady.
GERTRUDE   What shall I do?
HAMLET Not this by no means that I bid you do:
Let the bloat king tempt you again to bed,
Pinch wanton on your cheek, call you his mouse,
And let him for a pair of reechy kisses,   185
Or paddling in your neck with his damned fingers,
Make you to ravel all this matter out,

---

166 Refrain tonight] F; to refraine night Q2   168–71 the next ... potency] Q2; *not in* F   180 Thus] F; This Q2   181 One ... lady] Q2; *not in* F   183 bloat] blowt Q2; blunt F   187 ravel] F; rouell Q2

168–71 This passage is not present in the Folio. See Textual Analysis, 259.

170 either ... the devil A verb is missing. Many editions supply 'master' from the 1611 quarto.

172–3 when you are ... beg of you When you are contrite enough to ask God's blessing (or perhaps Hamlet's), I'll seek your blessing (as is appropriate for a son).

174–6 heaven ... minister It is the will of heaven, in making me the agent of their chastisement, that I myself should be punished by being the cause of Polonius's death, and that Polonius should be punished in his death at my hands.

177 answer well i.e. give good reasons for.

Jenkins also gives 'atone for'.

179–80 I must be cruel ... behind The remarkable change of tone in this couplet led one editor to suggest they were spoken aside. They do indeed have a meditative quality, and, in this recognition of the heaviness of his task, they resemble the couplet at the end of Act 2 – 'The time is out of joint ...'. His own cruelty repels him; he sees the death of Polonius as the bad beginning of a vengeance that will yet be 'worse'.

183 bloat bloated, swollen (with drink).

184 wanton wantonly, lasciviously.

185 reechy soiled, emitting smoke or other foul smells (*OED*).

187 ravel ... out unravel, disentangle.

That I essentially am not in madness,
But mad in craft. 'Twere good you let him know,
For who that's but a queen, fair, sober, wise,   190
Would from a paddock, from a bat, a gib,
Such dear concernings hide? Who would do so?
No, in despite of sense and secrecy,
Unpeg the basket on the house's top,
Let the birds fly, and like the famous ape,   195
To try conclusions, in the basket creep
And break your own neck down.
GERTRUDE Be thou assured, if words be made of breath,
And breath of life, I have no life to breathe
What thou hast said to me.   200
HAMLET I must to England, you know that?
GERTRUDE   Alack,
I had forgot. 'Tis so concluded on.
HAMLET [There's letters sealed, and my two schoolfellows,
Whom I will trust as I will adders fanged,
They bear the mandate. They must sweep my way   205
And marshal me to knavery. Let it work,
For 'tis the sport to have the engineer
Hoist with his own petar, an't shall go hard
But I will delve one yard below their mines

---

189 mad] Q2; made F   201–2 Alack / I ... on.] *Capell;* Alack ... forgot. / Tis ... on. Q2; Alacke ... on. F   203–11 There's letters ... meet] Q2; *not in* F

189 **in craft** by design.
189–92 **'Twere good ... concernings hide** Sarcastic. A respectable queen, as you consider yourself to be, has of course no reason to keep a secret from her loathsome husband.
191 **paddock** frog or toad.
191 **gib** tom-cat (an abbreviation of 'Gilbert'; the 'g' is hard).
193 **secrecy** discretion.
194–7 **Unpeg ... neck down** Oddly enough, there is no record of this fable. It more or less explains itself, however. An ape takes a birdcage onto a roof; he opens the door and the birds fly out. In order to imitate them, he gets into the basket, jumps out and, instead of flying, falls to the ground.
196 **To try conclusions** To test results.
197 **down** Either an intensifier – 'utterly' or

'completely' – or adverbial – 'falling down'.
198–200 In Q1, the queen promises also to assist Hamlet in his revenge.
201 **I must to England** Though Hamlet has not yet been told explicitly of Claudius's plan to send him away (see 3.1.163, 3.3.4).
203–11 **There's letters ... meet** These nine lines are not found in F. See Textual Analysis, 260–1.
205 **sweep my way** clear a path for me.
207 **engineer** one who constructs or designs military machines or contrivances, especially for use in sieges. Q2 gives it the normal spelling for the time, 'enginer'.
208 **Hoist** i.e. blown up.
208 **petar** bomb. Also 'petard'.
208 **an't** and it.

And blow them at the moon. Oh 'tis most sweet   210
When in one line two crafts directly meet.]
This man shall set me packing.
I'll lug the guts into the neighbour room.
Mother, good night. Indeed, this counsellor
Is now most still, most secret, and most grave,   215
Who was in life a foolish prating knave.
Come sir, to draw toward an end with you.
Good night mother.
            Exit Hamlet tugging in Polonius; [Gertrude remains]

[4.1] *Enter* CLAUDIUS *with* ROSENCRANTZ *and* GUILDENSTERN

CLAUDIUS There's matter in these sighs, these profound heaves.
         You must translate, 'tis fit we understand them.
         Where is your son?
GERTRUDE [Bestow this place on us a little while.]
                              [*Exeunt Rosencrantz and Guildenstern*]
         Ah mine own lord, what have I seen tonight!   5
CLAUDIUS What, Gertrude? How does Hamlet?
GERTRUDE Mad as the sea and wind, when both contend
         Which is the mightier. In his lawless fit,
         Behind the arras hearing something stir,
         Whips out his rapier, cries 'A rat, a rat!',   10
         And in this brainish apprehension kills
         The unseen good old man.
CLAUDIUS   Oh heavy deed!

---

216 foolish] F; most foolish Q2   218 SD *Exit ... Polonius*] F; *Exit* Q2   218 SD *Gertrude remains*] *following Wilson; not in*
Q2, F   **Act 4, Scene 1**   4.1] Q 1676   0 SD] *Wilson (substantially); Eenter King, and Queene, with Roscraus and*
Guyldensterne Q2; *Enter King* F   1 Matter] Q2; matters F   4 Bestow ... while] Q2; *not in* F   4 SD] Q 1676; *not in* Q2,
F   5 mine own] Q2; my good F   7 sea] Q2; Seas F   10 Whips ... cries] Q2; He whips his Rapier out, and
cries F   11 this] Q2; his F

211 **in one line** The image is of the mine and the
countermine.
212 **This man ... packing** The murder of
Polonius will make the king send me off
immediately.
217 **draw ... with you** conclude our discourse.
Act 4, Scene 1
0 SD Since the 1676 quarto, most editors begin
a new act at this point. Everyone agrees with

Johnson that the division is 'not very happy'
because the action continues from the closet scene:
Gertrude remains on stage, and Claudius enters to
her. (Q2 gives a re-entry for the queen though no
previous exit for her.) The Folio makes clear the
continuity of the action, F also cuts out the awkward
entry of Rosencrantz and Guildenstern and their
immediate dismissal by the queen.
11 **brainish** headstrong, rash.

It had been so with us had we been there.
His liberty is full of threats to all,
To you yourself, to us, to everyone.   15
Alas, how shall this bloody deed be answered?
It will be laid to us, whose providence
Should have kept short, restrained, and out of haunt,
This mad young man. But so much was our love,
We would not understand what was most fit,   20
But like the owner of a foul disease,
To keep it from divulging, let it feed
Even on the pith of life. Where is he gone?
GERTRUDE To draw apart the body he hath killed,
O'er whom his very madness, like some ore   25
Among a mineral of metals base,
Shows itself pure; a weeps for what is done.
CLAUDIUS Oh Gertrude, come away!
The sun no sooner shall the mountains touch
But we will ship him hence, and this vile deed   30
We must with all our majesty and skill
Both countenance and excuse. Ho, Guildenstern!

Enter Rosencrantz and Guildenstern

Friends both, go join you with some further aid.
Hamlet in madness hath Polonius slain,
And from his mother's closet hath he dragged him.   35
Go seek him out, speak fair, and bring the body
Into the chapel. I pray you haste in this.
                    Exeunt Rosencrantz and Guildenstern
Come Gertrude, we'll call up our wisest friends
And let them know both what we mean to do
And what's untimely done.   40
[Whose whisper o'er the world's diameter,

22 let] Q2; let's F   27 a] Q2; He F   35 mother's closet] Q2; Mother Clossets F   35 dragged] drag'd F; dreg'd Q2
37 SD] *Rowe; Exit Gent,* F; *not in* Q2   39 And] Q2; To F   41–4 Whose whisper ... air] Q2; *not in* F

16 **answered** accounted for.
17 **providence** forethought and provision.
18 **kept short** restricted.
18 **out of haunt** away from public resort.
22 **divulging** being generally known.
25–7 **his very madness ... pure** even in
Hamlet's madness, there was a streak of pure feeling
('ore').

26 **a mineral** the contents of a mine.
32 **countenance** accept; 'majesty' will 'countenance' and 'skill' will 'excuse'.
40 The last half of the line is lost. See next note.
Capell's ingenious suggestion 'so haply slander' is
supplied in most editions.
41–4 This passage is not found in F. See Textual
Analysis, 256–7.

As level as the cannon to his blank,
Transports his poisoned shot, may miss our name
And hit the woundless air.] Oh come away,
My soul is full of discord and dismay.   45

Exeunt

[4.2] *Enter* HAMLET

HAMLET Safely stowed.
GENTLEMEN (*Within*) Hamlet! Lord Hamlet!
HAMLET But soft, what noise? Who calls on Hamlet? Oh here they
   come.

Enter ROSENCRANTZ *and* GUILDENSTERN

ROSENCRANTZ What have you done my lord with the dead body?   5
HAMLET Compounded it with dust whereto 'tis kin.
ROSENCRANTZ Tell us where 'tis, that we may take it thence and bear
   it to the chapel.
HAMLET Do not believe it.
ROSENCRANTZ Believe what?   10
HAMLET That I can keep your counsel and not mine own. Besides, to
   be demanded of a sponge, what replication should be made by the
   son of a king?
ROSENCRANTZ Take you me for a sponge my lord?
HAMLET Ay sir, that soaks up the king's countenance, his rewards, his   15
   authorities. But such officers do the king best service in the end:
   he keeps them like an ape in the corner of his jaw, first mouthed

---

Act 4, Scene 2   4.2] *Pope*   0 SD] F; *Enter Hamlet, Rosencraus, and others* Q2   2 GENTLEMEN … Lord Hamlet] F; *not in*
Q2   3 But soft] Q2; *not in* F   6 Compounded] F; Compound Q2   17 ape] F; apple Q2

42 **level** directly aimed.
42 **blank** target.
44 **woundless** invulnerable.

Act 4, Scene 2
3 **soft** be cautious. See 3.1.88.
6 **Compounded** Mixed. Compare Sonnet 71,
'When I … compounded am with clay'. Hamlet
has put the body in a dusty place.
11 **keep … mine own** To keep counsel is to
maintain silence about one's judgements and

intentions. Hamlet's riddling remark hints that he
knows the secrets of Rosencrantz and Guildenstern
but is not revealing his own.
11–12 **to be demanded of** if one is interrogated
by.
12 **replication** formal response.
15 **countenance** favour.
17 **like an ape** as an ape does. Q1 reads 'as an
Ape doth nuttes'. Q2's 'apple' has been adopted by
some as 'like an ape an apple'.

to be last swallowed. When he needs what you have gleaned, it is
but squeezing you, and, sponge, you shall be dry again.

ROSENCRANTZ I understand you not my lord.   20

HAMLET I am glad of it, a knavish speech sleeps in a foolish ear.

ROSENCRANTZ My lord, you must tell us where the body is, and go
with us to the king.

HAMLET The body is with the king, but the king is not with the body.   25
The king is a thing –

GUILDENSTERN A thing my lord?

HAMLET Of nothing. Bring me to him. Hide fox, and all after!

Exeunt

[4.3] *Enter* CLAUDIUS, *and two or three*

CLAUDIUS I have sent to seek him, and to find the body.
How dangerous is it that this man goes loose,
Yet must not we put the strong law on him;
He's loved of the distracted multitude,
Who like not in their judgement, but their eyes;   5
And where 'tis so, th'offender's scourge is weighed,
But never the offence. To bear all smooth and even,
This sudden sending him away must seem
Deliberate pause. Diseases desperate grown

---

27 Hide ... after] F; *not in* Q2   Act 4, Scene 3   4.3] *Pope*   0 SD] *Enter King, and two or three* Q2; *Enter King* F
7 never] Q2; *neerer* F

21 **a knavish ... ear** You are too much of a fool
to understand my insults.

24 **The body ... with the body** As Nigel
Alexander has argued (see *Poison, Play and Duel:
A Study in Hamlet*, 177), this is a riddling reference
to the much-debated theory of the king's two bodies,
natural and politic, made famous in Ernst
Kantorowicz's book (*The King's Two Bodies:
A Study in Mediaeval Political Theology* (Princeton
University Press, 1957). Claudius has a body, but
the kingship of Denmark is not inherent in *that*
body. Hamlet does not believe in kingship as an
abstraction, as did those who stressed the importance
of the Body Politic. He believes fiercely in kings as
rightful kings, true royal persons. This king is 'a thing
of nothing'.

27 **Hide fox ... after** Q2 omits. Hamlet runs out
followed by the others. The reference is presumably
to a children's game of chase or hide-and-seek.

Act 4, Scene 3

0 SD *two or three* So Q2; F makes Claudius enter
alone, which changes Claudius's considered and
calculated remarks to his councillors into a self-
communing. This speech is part of the 'countenance and excuse' mentioned in 4.1.32.

4 **distracted** disordered, irrational.

5 **their eyes** i.e. by appearances.

6–7 **th'offender's scourge ... offence** more
attention is paid to the criminal's sufferings than
to his crime.

9 **Deliberate pause** Carefully considered
reflection.

9–10 **Diseases ... relieved** Proverbial; Tilley
D357.

By desperate appliance are relieved,   10
Or not at all.

Enter ROSENCRANTZ

How now, what hath befallen?

ROSENCRANTZ Where the dead body is bestowed, my lord,
We cannot get from him.

CLAUDIUS   But where is he?

ROSENCRANTZ Without, my lord, guarded, to know your pleasure.

CLAUDIUS Bring him before us.

ROSENCRANTZ   Ho! bring in my lord.   15

Enter HAMLET *and* GUILDENSTERN

CLAUDIUS Now Hamlet, where's Polonius?

HAMLET At supper.

CLAUDIUS At supper? Where?

HAMLET Not where he eats, but where a is eaten. A certain convocation   20
of politic worms are e'en at him. Your worm is your only emperor
for diet: we fat all creatures else to fat us, and we fat ourselves for
maggots. Your fat king and your lean beggar is but variable service,
two dishes, but to one table; that's the end.

CLAUDIUS Alas, alas.

HAMLET A man may fish with the worm that hath eat of a king, and   25
eat of the fish that hath fed of that worm.

CLAUDIUS What dost thou mean by this?

HAMLET Nothing but to show you how a king may go a progress
through the guts of a beggar.

CLAUDIUS Where is Polonius?   30

HAMLET In heaven, send thither to see. If your messenger find him not

---

11 SD] F; *Enter Rosencraus and all the rest* Q2   15 Ho! bring] How, bring Q2; Hoa, *Guildensterne?* Bring F   15 my] F; the
Q2   15 SD] F; *They enter* Q2   19 a is] Q2; he is F   20 politic] Q2; *not in* F   21 ourselves] Q2; our selfe F   23 two]
Q2; to F   24–6 CLAUDIUS *Alas … that worm*] Q2; *not in* F   27 SH CLAUDIUS] *King.* F; *King. King.* Q2

11 SD **Enter** ROSENCRANTZ Q2's addition 'and
all the rest' contradicts '*They enter*' at 15, where
F has Rosencrantz call for Guildenstern, who has
been guarding Hamlet.
  19 where a is eaten Compare 3.3.73.
Presumably Shakespeare intended the syncope
which nowadays we would write as 'he's'.
  19–21 convocation … diet Hamlet offers
a particularly topical pun on the Diet (or assembly)
of Worms (the city on the Rhine). The most famous
meeting of the Diet was that called by the emperor,

Charles V, in 1521, before which Luther appeared
to justify his doctrines. The use of the worm to
signify the transience of human life and the levelling
power of death is also biblical (Is. 51.8, Job 21.26,
24.20; see Shaheen, *Biblical References*, 556–7).
  20 politic worms 'such worms as might breed in
a politician's corpse' (Dowden); '[P]olitic' = shrewd.
  22 variable interchangeable, i.e. they may be different dishes, but they are both served to the one table.
  28 progress elaborate journey by the sovereign
through his or her dominions.

there, seek him i'th'other place yourself. But if indeed you find him
not within this month, you shall nose him as you go up the stairs
into the lobby.

CLAUDIUS Go seek him there.   35

HAMLET A will stay till you come.

[*Exeunt Attendants*]

CLAUDIUS Hamlet, this deed, for thine especial safety,
       Which we do tender, as we dearly grieve
       For that which thou hast done, must send thee hence
       With fiery quickness. Therefore prepare thyself.   40
       The bark is ready and the wind at help,
       Th'associates tend, and everything is bent
       For England.

HAMLET   For England?

CLAUDIUS   Ay Hamlet.

HAMLET   Good.

CLAUDIUS So is it if thou knew'st our purposes.

HAMLET I see a cherub that sees them. But come, for England!   45
       Farewell dear mother.

CLAUDIUS Thy loving father, Hamlet.

HAMLET My mother. Father and mother is man and wife, man and
       wife is one flesh, and so, my mother. Come, for England.   *Exit*

CLAUDIUS Follow him at foot, tempt him with speed aboard.   50
       Delay it not, I'll have him hence tonight.
       Away, for everything is sealed and done
       That else leans on th'affair. Pray you make haste.

[*Exeunt Rosencrantz and Guildenstern*]

       And England, if my love thou hold'st at aught,
       As my great power thereof may give thee sense,   55
       Since yet thy cicatrice looks raw and red

---

32 if indeed] Q2; indeed, if F   **33** within this month] Q2; this moneth F   **36** A will] Q2; He will F   **36** you] Q2; ye
F   **36** SD] *Capell; not in* Q2, F   **37** for thine] Q2; of thine, for thine F   **40** With … quickness] F; *not in* Q2   **42** is] Q2; at
F   **45** them] Q2; him F   **49** and so] F; so Q2   **50** foot, tempt] *Rowe;* foote, / Tempt Q2, F   **53** SD] *Theobald²; not in*
Q2, F

32 ith'other place hell

34 the lobby A main corridor or ante-room.
Compare 'here in the lobby' in 2.2.159.

38 tender have regard for.

42 tend attend.

42 bent in a state of readiness.

45 I see a cherub … them Hamlet both hints at
his own knowledge and warns Claudius that heaven
is watching him.

48–9 Hamlet's application of the biblical formulation from Gen. 2.4, Eph. 5.31, Matt. 19.5, Mark
20.7, also represented in the Elizabethan Marriage
Service. See Shaheen, *Biblical References*, 558.

50 at foot close at heel.

53 leans on appertains to.

54 England the king of England. Thompson
and Taylor point out that this might have been an
opportunity to involve the audience at the Globe.

54 at aught at any value.

55 thereof … sense may give you a feeling of
the importance of valuing my love.

56–7 cicatrice … sword A cicatrice is a scar;
the lines, which suggest a Danish victory over the
English, reinforce the earlier plan to collect a tribute
(3.1.164).

After the Danish sword, and thy free awe
Pays homage to us – thou mayst not coldly set
Our sovereign process, which imports at full,
By letters congruing to that effect, 60
The present death of Hamlet. Do it England,
For like the hectic in my blood he rages,
And thou must cure me. Till I know 'tis done,
Howe'er my haps, my joys were ne'er begun. *Exit*

[4.4] *Enter* FORTINBRAS *with his army over the stage*

FORTINBRAS Go captain, from me greet the Danish king.
　　　　　Tell him that by his licence, Fortinbras
　　　　　Craves the conveyance of a promised march
　　　　　Over his kingdom. You know the rendezvous.
　　　　　If that his majesty would aught with us, 5
　　　　　We shall express our duty in his eye,
　　　　　And let him know so.
CAPTAIN　　　　　　　　　　I will do't, my lord.
FORTINBRAS Go softly on.

　　　　　　　　　[*Exit Fortinbras, with the army*]

　　　　　[*Enter* HAMLET, ROSENCRANTZ, *etc.*

HAMLET Good sir, whose powers are these?
CAPTAIN They are of Norway sir.
HAMLET How purposed sir I pray you? 10
CAPTAIN Against some part of Poland.

---

60 congruing] Q2; coniuring F 64 were ne'er begun] F; will nere begin Q2 Act 4, Scene 4 4.4] *Pope* 0 SD] Q2; *Enter Fortinbras with an Armie* F 3 Craves] Q2, Q1; Claimes F 8 softly] Q2; safely F 8 SD] *Theobald²; not in* Q2; *Exit* F 8.1 SD– 66 *Enter* HAMLET ... *Worth. Exit*] Q2; *not in* F

57 **free** uncompelled.
58 **coldly set** regard with indifference.
59 **process** writ.
60 **congruing** agreeing. So Q2. '[C]ongrue' is a word unique to Shakespeare, occurring only here and in the bad quarto of *Henry V*.
61 **present** immediate.
62 **hectic** chronic fever.
64 **haps** fortunes.

Act 4, Scene 4
3 **conveyance** grant. See 2.2.76–80. Fortinbras

asks for the formal execution of a previous promise. Many editors think he is asking for an escort.
6 **duty** humble respect.
6 **in his eye** in his presence.
8 **softly** circumspectly (being careful not to give offence).
8.2 SD – 66 *Enter* Hamlet ... The whole of the remainder of this scene is omitted in the Folio. See Textual Analysis, 260–3.
9 **powers** forces, troops.

HAMLET Who commands them sir?
CAPTAIN The nephew to old Norway, Fortinbras.
HAMLET Goes it against the main of Poland sir,   15
    Or for some frontier?
CAPTAIN Truly to speak, and with no addition,
    We go to gain a little patch of ground
    That hath in it no profit but the name.
    To pay five ducats, five, I would not farm it,   20
    Nor will it yield to Norway or the Pole
    A ranker rate, should it be sold in fee.
HAMLET Why then the Polack never will defend it.
CAPTAIN Yes, it is already garrisoned.
HAMLET Two thousand souls and twenty thousand ducats   25
    Will not debate the question of this straw.
    This is th'impostume of much wealth and peace,
    That inward breaks, and shows no cause without
    Why the man dies. I humbly thank you sir.
CAPTAIN God buy you sir.   *[Exit]*
ROSENCRANTZ   Will't please you go my lord?   30
HAMLET I'll be with you straight; go a little before.
                            [Exeunt all but Hamlet]
    How all occasions do inform against me,
    And spur my dull revenge! What is a man
    If his chief good and market of his time
    Be but to sleep and feed? A beast, no more.   35
    Sure he that made us with such large discourse,
    Looking before and after, gave us not
    That capability and god-like reason
    To fust in us unused. Now whether it be
    Bestial oblivion, or some craven scruple   40
    Of thinking too precisely on th'event –
    A thought which quartered hath but one part wisdom
    And ever three parts coward – I do not know
    Why yet I live to say this thing's to do,

---

30 SD *Exit*] *Dyce; Exit Captain / Capell; not in* Q2   31 SD] *Dyce, following Rowe; not in* Q2

15 **main** whole.
17 **addition** exaggeration.
22 **ranker** more abundant.
22 **in fee** i.e. outright, without restrictions.
26 **Will not debate the question** Are not
enough to fight out the dispute.
27 **impostume** abscess.
32 **occasions** occurrences, facts, considerations.

34 **market** profit.
36 **discourse** faculty of reasoning.
39 **fust** grow mouldy.
40 **oblivion** forgetfulness.
40 **craven** cowardly.
41 **precisely** scrupulously, pedantically.
41 **event** result, consequence.

Sith I have cause, and will, and strength, and means   45
To do't. Examples gross as earth exhort me.
Witness this army of such mass and charge,
Led by a delicate and tender prince,
Whose spirit with divine ambition puffed
Makes mouths at the invisible event,   50
Exposing what is mortal and unsure
To all that fortune, death and danger dare,
Even for an egg-shell. Rightly to be great
Is not to stir without great argument,
But greatly to find quarrel in a straw   55
When honour's at the stake. How stand I then,
That have a father killed, a mother stained,
Excitements of my reason and my blood,
And let all sleep, while to my shame I see
The imminent death of twenty thousand men,   60
That for a fantasy and trick of fame
Go to their graves like beds, fight for a plot
Whereon the numbers cannot try the cause,
Which is not tomb enough and continent
To hide the slain. Oh from this time forth,   65
My thoughts be bloody or be nothing worth.   *Exit*]

45 **Sith** Since.
46 **gross** palpable, obvious.
47 **mass and charge** size and expense.
49 **puffed** inflated.
50 **Makes mouths at** Makes faces at, despises (compare 2.2.335).
52 **dare** Means little more here than 'can do'.
54 **not to stir** This should be understood as a double negative – 'not not to stir', that is, 'not a matter of refusing to stir'. Many commentators think that Hamlet is saying that one is *not* great if one stirs without great argument. But the force of Hamlet's argument is that true greatness has

nothing to do with the size of the dispute, but everything to do with a willingness to act when honour is involved.
56 **at the stake** in hazard, as a wager.
60 **twenty thousand men** In 25 above it was 20,000 ducats and only 2,000 men.
61 **trick** illusion, deceit (see 4.5.5 below).
62 **graves like beds** The soldiers go to their graves as if going to bed.
63–5 **Whereon ... slain** i.e. the plot of ground is not big enough to hold those who are to fight for it, or to bury those who are killed.

[4.5] *Enter* HORATIO, GERTRUDE *and a* GENTLEMAN

GERTRUDE I will not speak with her.
GENTLEMAN She is importunate, indeed distract;
　　　　Her mood will needs be pitied.
GERTRUDE   What would she have?
GENTLEMAN She speaks much of her father, says she hears
　　　　There's tricks i'th'world, and hems, and beats her heart,　　5
　　　　Spurns enviously at straws, speaks things in doubt
　　　　That carry but half sense. Her speech is nothing,
　　　　Yet the unshapèd use of it doth move
　　　　The hearers to collection. They yawn at it,
　　　　And botch the words up fit to their own thoughts,　　10
　　　　Which, as her winks and nods and gestures yield them,
　　　　Indeed would make one think there might be thought,
　　　　Though nothing sure, yet much unhappily.
HORATIO 'Twere good she were spoken with, for she may strew
　　　　Dangerous conjectures in ill-breeding minds.　　15
GERTRUDE Let her come in.
　　　　　　　　　　　　　[Exit Gentleman]
　　　　(*Aside*) To my sick soul, as sin's true nature is,
　　　　Each toy seems prologue to some great amiss.
　　　　So full of artless jealousy is guilt,
　　　　It spills itself in fearing to be spilt.　　20

　　　　　　Enter OPHELIA *distracted*

Act 4, Scene 5 4.5] *Pope* o SD] Q2; *Enter Queene and Horatio* F 2, 4 SH GENTLEMAN] *Gent.* Q2; *Hor.* F 9 yawn] Q2; ayme F 12 might] Q2; would F 14 SH HORATIO] *Hora.* Q2; *Qu.* F 16 GERTRUDE Let her come in.] *Hanmer (substantially)*: Q2 *prints* Let her come in. *as the conclusion of Horatio's speech.* F *conflates the speeches of Horatio and Gertrude* 16 SD] *Hanmer; not in* Q2, F 17 SD *Aside*] *Capell; not in* Q2, F 20 SD] F; *Enter Ophelia* Q2 *(at 16)*

Act 4, Scene 5

　1–15 F gives the Gentleman's speeches to Horatio, and Horatio's to Gertrude.
　3 Her mood … pitied Her state of mind must necessarily cause pity.
　5 hems makes the noise 'H'm'.
　6 Spurns … straws 'takes offence angrily at trifles' (Kittredge).
　6 in doubt of uncertain meaning.
　8 unshapèd uncontrolled, lacking form (*Shakespeare's Words*).
　9 to collection to infer a meaning.
　9 yawn gape with surprise.
　10 botch … thoughts patch the words up into patterns conforming to their own ideas. Compare the 'dangerous conjectures' feared by Horatio in 15 below.
　13 unhappily clumsily.
　15 ill-breeding intent on making mischief.
　18 toy trifle.
　19 artless unskilled, hence blundering, foolish.
　19 jealousy suspicion.
　20 It spills … spilt i.e. fear of detection leads to the very exposure one is trying to avert; 'spill' means 'destroy', but here has an obvious double sense with 'reveal'.
　20 SD Q1 gives the famous direction: '*Enter Ofelia playing on a Lute, and her haire downe singing.*'

OPHELIA Where is the beauteous majesty of Denmark?

GERTRUDE How now Ophelia?

OPHELIA   *She sings*
    How should I your true love know
     From another one?
    By his cockle hat and staff   25
     And his sandal shoon.

GERTRUDE Alas sweet lady, what imports this song?

OPHELIA Say you? Nay, pray you mark.
    He is dead and gone lady,   *Song*
     He is dead and gone;   30
    At his head a grass-green turf,
     At his heels a stone.

  Oho!

GERTRUDE Nay but Ophelia –

OPHELIA Pray you mark.   35
    White his shroud as the mountain snow –   *Song*

    Enter CLAUDIUS

GERTRUDE Alas, look here my lord.

OPHELIA   Larded all with sweet flowers,
    Which bewept to the grave did not go
     With true-love showers.   40

CLAUDIUS How do you, pretty lady?

OPHELIA Well good dild you. They say the owl was a baker's daughter.

---

23 SD *She sings*] Q2; *not in* F 23–4 How ... one] *as one line* Q2, F 25–6 By ... shoon] *as one line* Q2, F 26 sandal] F; Sendall Q2 29 SD *Song*] Q2; *not in* F 29–30 He ... gone] *as one line* Q2, F 31–2 At ... stone] *as one line* Q2, F 33 Oho!] O ho. Q2; *not in* F 36 SD *Song*] Q2 *(at 38); not in* F 38 Larded all] Q2; *Larded* F, Q1 39 grave] F; ground Q2 41 you] Q2; ye F 42 good dild] Q2; God dil'd F

23–6 A recollection of the famous Walsingham ballad, which brings together a lonely pilgrim and a deserted lover. See the version attributed to Sir Walter Ralegh in *The Poems of Sir Walter Ralegh*, ed. Agnes M. C. Latham (London: Constable & Co. Ltd, 1929), 100–1. For the music, see Sternfeld, 59–62.

25 **cockle hat** a hat with a 'cockle' or scallop-shell on it (the pilgrim's emblem was a scallop shell, originally a sign that he had been to the shrine of St James of Compostella in Spain).

26 **shoon** shoes.

28 **Say you? ... mark** i.e. 'Is that your question? Just pay attention.' Then she proceeds with the ballad.

38 **Larded all** Strewn, decorated. F omits the extra-metrical 'all'.

39 **did not go** It seems very likely that Ophelia

inserts the 'not' into the original song, to suit the fate of Polonius.

42 **good dild you** God yield, or reward, you. The phrase means 'thank you'.

42 **owl ... baker's daughter** This was recognized in the eighteenth century as a reference to a folktale in which a baker's daughter was parsimonious with the dough when a beggar asked her for bread. The beggar was Jesus, and he turned her into an owl. K. M. Briggs gives two English versions (*A Dictionary of British Folk-tales in the English Language* (London: Routledge & Kegan Paul, 1970–1), I: 124, 443). It is indexed as A 1958.0.1 in Stith Thompson, *Motif Index of Folk Literature*, rev. edn (Bloomington: Indiana University Press, 1955), I: 258. The tale is in Ophelia's mind as a story of transformation.

Lord, we know what we are, but know not what we may be. God
be at your table.

CLAUDIUS Conceit upon her father.   45

OPHELIA Pray let's have no words of this, but when they ask you what
it means, say you this –

> Tomorrow is Saint Valentine's day,   *Song*
> All in the morning betime,
> And I a maid at your window,   50
> To be your Valentine.
> Then up he rose and donned his clothes
> And dupped the chamber door;
> Let in the maid that out a maid
> Never departed more.   55

CLAUDIUS Pretty Ophelia!

OPHELIA Indeed la! Without an oath I'll make an end on't.

> By Gis and by Saint Charity,
> Alack and fie for shame,
> Young men will do't if they come to't –   60
> By Cock, they are to blame.
> Quoth she, 'Before you tumbled me,
> You promised me to wed.'

46 Pray] Q2; Pray you F   48 SD *Song*] Q2; *not in* F   48–9 Tomorrow ... betime] Q2; *as one line* F   50–1 And ...
Valentine] Q2; *as one line* F   52 clothes] F; close Q2   52–3 Then ... door] *as one line* Q2, F   54–5 Let ... more] *as one
line* Q2, F   57 Indeed la!] Indeed la? F; Indeede Q2   62–3 Quoth ... wed] F; *as one line* Q2   64 He answers] Q2; *not in*
F   65 ha'] F; a Q2

43–4 **God be at your table** – and bless you in
your transformation.

45 **Conceit upon her father** Thoughts connected with her father.

46–7 **ask you ... say you this** There is constant
reference to a hidden meaning in Ophelia's utter-
ances, introduced first by the Gentleman's speech,
4–13. Ophelia's 'explanations' go from one of her
sadnesses to the other – from Hamlet to Polonius
and back again.

48 **Tomorrow is Saint Valentine's day**
The words of this are not known elsewhere. For
Chappell's rendering of the tune traditionally given
in the theatre, see the NV, and Sternfeld, 62–4.

53 **dupped** 'dup' = do up = open.

54–5 **Let in ... departed more** These lines
have invited various interpretations about whether

or not Hamlet and Ophelia have had sexual
relations.

57 **Indeed la!** Scornful assent to Claudius's
'Pretty Ophelia!' '[L]a' intensifies an asseveration,
as in *Coriolanus* 1.3.67. Q2 omits 'la', F's punctuation, 'la?', indicates either a question or an
exclamation.

57 **Without an oath** N. Alexander points to
Ophelia's substitution of 'Gis' and 'Cock' for Jesus
and God.

61 **Cock** A common 'mincing' of God. Used
here with an obvious double meaning.

62 **tumbled** had sexual intercourse with.
Compare 'lie tumbling in the hay' (*Winter's Tale*
4.3.12) and 'to tumble on the bed of Ptolemy'
(*Antony and Cleopatra* 1.4.17).

He answers –

So would I ha' done, by yonder sun,   65
And thou hadst not come to my bed.

CLAUDIUS How long hath she been thus?

OPHELIA I hope all will be well. We must be patient, but I cannot
choose but weep to think they would lay him i'th' cold ground. My
brother shall know of it, and so I thank you for your good counsel   70
Come, my coach. Good night ladies, good night sweet ladies, good
night, good night.   *Exit*

CLAUDIUS Follow her close, give her good watch I pray you.

                                                  [*Exit Horatio*]

Oh this is the poison of deep grief, it springs
All from her father's death, [and now behold –]   75
Oh Gertrude, Gertrude,
When sorrows come, they come not single spies,
But in battalions. First, her father slain;
Next, your son gone, and he most violent author
Of his own just remove; the people muddied,   80
Thick and unwholesome in their thoughts and whispers
For good Polonius' death – and we have done but greenly
In hugger-mugger to inter him; poor Ophelia
Divided from herself and her fair judgement,
Without the which we are pictures, or mere beasts;   85
Last, and as much containing as all these,
Her brother is in secret come from France,
Feeds on his wonder, keeps himself in clouds,

---

64 He answers] Q2; *not in* F   65 ha'] F; a Q2   67 thus] Q2; this F   69 would] Q2; should F   71–2 Good … good …
good … good] God … god … god … god Q2   72 SD] F; *not in* Q2   73 SD] *Theobald²; not in* Q2, F   74–6 springs /
All … behold – / Oh … Gertrude,] *Steevens³; two lines of prose* Q2; springs / All … *Gertrude*, F   75 and now behold] Q2;
not in F   78 battalions] battalians Q2; Battaliaes F   81 their] F; *not in* Q2   88 Feeds on] Q2; Keepes on F   88 his] F;
this Q2

66 **And** If.
74–6 **Oh this … Gertrude, Gertrude** Q2
prints all of this as two lines of prose. F omits 'and
now behold', creating two lines of regular verse.
80 **muddied** stirred up like muddy water,
disturbed.
82 **greenly** foolishly, as though from
inexperience.
83 **In hugger-mugger** With secrecy.
Shakespeare does not use this phrase elsewhere.
It is used in North's translation of Plutarch's Life

of Brutus (the source of *Julius Caesar*) which had
become associated with Polonius because of
3.2.91–2. Plutarch said that Antony, fearing that
people might be further incensed, was anxious
that Caesar's body 'should be honourably buried,
and not in hugger-mugger'.
86 **as much containing … these** i.e. as serious
as all the others together.
88 **Feeds … clouds** i.e. instead of finding out
what has actually happened, he keeps himself in the

And wants not buzzers to infect his ear
With pestilent speeches of his father's death,   90
Wherein necessity, of matter beggared,
Will nothing stick our person to arraign
In ear and ear. O my dear Gertrude, this,
Like to a murdering piece, in many places
Gives me superfluous death.   95

A noise within

GERTRUDE Alack, what noise is this?
CLAUDIUS Attend! Where are my Swissers? Let them guard the door.

Enter a MESSENGER

What is the matter?
MESSENGER   Save yourself my lord.
The ocean, overpeering of his list,
Eats not the flats with more impitious haste   100
Than young Laertes in a riotous head
O'erbears your officers. The rabble call him lord,
And, as the world were now but to begin,
Antiquity forgot, custom not known,
The ratifiers and props of every word,   105
They cry 'Choose we! Laertes shall be king.'
Caps, hands and tongues applaud it to the clouds,
'Laertes shall be king, Laertes king!'
GERTRUDE How cheerfully on the false trail they cry!

---

92 person] Q2; persons F   96 GERTRUDE … this?] F; *not in* Q2   97 Attend] Q2; *not in* F   97 are] F; is
Q2   97 Swissers] Q2; *Switzers* F   97 SD] *after 95 in* Q2, F   106 They] F; The Q2

clouds of suspicion, and finds food for anger in his
own uncertainty, or in what he guesses ('wonder').
This use of the noun 'wonder' is unusual in
Shakespeare, though the verb is used to indicate
doubt, as well as surprise and admiration.
89 **buzzers** rumour-mongers.
91–2 **necessity … nothing stick** i.e. having no
evidence, they are obliged to invent and have no
scruples in doing so.
93 **ear and ear** i.e. whispering to person after
person.
94 **murdering piece** The name of a small cannon which was used to fire charges of small shot
against infantry.
95 **superfluous death** i.e. kills him over and
over again.
97 **Swissers** Swiss guards. F calls them

'Switzers'.
99 **overpeering of his list** rising above (literally, looking over) its boundary.
100 **impitious** Some think this a form of
'impetuous' but it is more likely a Shakespearean
coinage = 'pitiless'.
105 **ratifiers and props … word** The line
modifies 'Antiquity' and 'custom', i.e. 'Tradition,
which should support everything we say, is
neglected.'
106 **'Choose we! …'** The emphasis is on 'we'.
The 'distracted multitude', who were supposed to
'love' Hamlet (4.3.4), have given their allegiance to
Laertes, and are demanding to take over the pre-
rogative of the electoral body which made Claudius
king.

Oh this is counter, you false Danish dogs!   110
                    A noise within
CLAUDIUS The doors are broke.

                Enter LAERTES *with others*

LAERTES Where is this king? – Sirs, stand you all without.
ALL No, let's come in.
LAERTES I pray you give me leave.
ALL We will, we will.   115
LAERTES I thank you. Keep the door.
                                        [*Exeunt followers*]
                        O thou vile king,
        Give me my father.
GERTRUDE   Calmly, good Laertes.
LAERTES That drop of blood that's calm proclaims me bastard,
        Cries cuckold to my father, brands the harlot
        Even here, between the chaste unsmirchèd brow   120
        Of my true mother.
CLAUDIUS   What is the cause, Laertes,
        That thy rebellion looks so giant-like? –
        Let him go, Gertrude, do not fear our person.
        There's such divinity doth hedge a king
        That treason can but peep to what it would,   125
        Acts little of his will. – Tell me Laertes,
        Why thou art thus incensed. – Let him go Gertrude. –
        Speak man.
LAERTES   Where is my father?
CLAUDIUS   Dead.
GERTRUDE   But not by him.

---

110 SD *A noise within*] Q2 (*after* cry *109*); *Noise within* F   111 SD   *Enter ... others*] *placed by Capell; after* dogs (*110*) *in* Q2; *Enter Laertes* F (*after* 'Noise within')   112 this king? – Sirs] this King? sirs Q2; the King, sirs? F   116 SD] *Kittredge* (*substantially*); *not in* Q2, F; *Exeunt / Theobald*[2]   118 that's calm] Q2; that calmes F   128 Where is] Q2; Where's F

110 counter ... dogs 'Hounds run *counter*, when they trace the trail backwards' (Johnson).

111 SD F omits '*with others*' in conformity with its consistent policy in reducing the number of extras who would need to be costumed, etc. Laertes's followers are kept firmly outside the door.

119–20 brands the harlot ... brow See note to 3.4.44. Laertes, like Hamlet previously, does not imply that harlots were so branded. The forehead is the symbolic showplace of chastity and unchastity. See *Comedy of Errors* 2.2.136, 'tear the stained skin

off my harlot brow'.

120 between in the middle of.

120 unsmirchèd clean, unstained.

123 Let him go Laertes must be moving threateningly towards Claudius, with Gertrude stepping in to protect him.

124 hedge surround with a defensive hedge or fence.

125 peep ... would Continues the image of the hedge. Treason can only peer through, and cannot carry out its plans.

CLAUDIUS Let him demand his fill.

LAERTES How came he dead? I'll not be juggled with.   130
　　　　To hell allegiance, vows to the blackest devil,
　　　　Conscience and grace to the profoundest pit!
　　　　I dare damnation. To this point I stand,
　　　　That both the worlds I give to negligence,
　　　　Let come what comes, only I'll be revenged   135
　　　　Most throughly for my father.

CLAUDIUS   Who shall stay you?

LAERTES My will, not all the world.
　　　　And for my means, I'll husband them so well,
　　　　They shall go far with little.

CLAUDIUS   Good Laertes,
　　　　If you desire to know the certainty   140
　　　　Of your dear father, is't writ in your revenge
　　　　That, soopstake, you will draw both friend and foe,
　　　　Winner and loser?

LAERTES   None but his enemies.

CLAUDIUS Will you know them then?

LAERTES To his good friends thus wide I'll ope my arms,   145
　　　　And like the kind life-rendering pelican,
　　　　Repast them with my blood.

CLAUDIUS   Why now you speak
　　　　Like a good child and a true gentleman.
　　　　That I am guiltless of your father's death,
　　　　And am most sensibly in grief for it,   150
　　　　It shall as level to your judgement pierce

---

137 world] F; worlds Q2   139–40 Good . . . certainty] F; *as one line* Q2   141 father] Q2; Fathers death F   141 is't] Q2;
if F   146 pelican] Q2; Politician F   150 sensibly] Q2; sensible F

130 juggled with cheated or deceived as by a juggler or trickster.

132 grace holy disposition.

134 give to negligence i.e. disregard, despise.

137 My will, … world '[B]y my will' is an expression of determination. It is, however, just possible that Laertes is abbreviating the oath 'God's my will'; compare *As You Like It* 4.3.17, 'Od's my will.'

138–9 And for my means … little Laertes will be careful and economical in equipping himself for revenge.

142 soopstake This form, found in both Q2 and

F, is short for 'swoopstake', an alternative form of 'sweepstake', the act of a gambler in taking all stakes at one go.

142 draw draw in.

146 kind … pelican The pelican was supposed to pierce its breast with its bill, and allow its young to feed on the blood.

147 repast feed.

151 level See 4.1.42.

151 pierce So F. Q2 reads 'peare', which Dr Johnson and many later editors have supposed to be an aphetic form of 'appear'; 'pierce' is a stronger and more Shakespearean word, often used for a

As day does to your eye.

A noise within: 'Let her come in'

LAERTES How now, what noise is that?

Enter OPHELIA

O heat dry up my brains, tears seven times salt
Burn out the sense and virtue of mine eye!   155
By heaven, thy madness shall be paid with weight
Till our scale turn the beam. O rose of May,
Dear maid, kind sister, sweet Ophelia –
O heavens, is't possible a young maid's wits
Should be as mortal as an old man's life?   160
Nature is fine in love, and where 'tis fine,
It sends some precious instance of itself
After the thing it loves.

OPHELIA   They bore him bare-faced on the bier   *Song*
                 Hey non nonny, nonny, hey nonny,   165
                 And in his grave rained many a tear –
Fare you well my dove.

LAERTES Hadst thou thy wits, and didst persuade revenge,
It could not move thus.

OPHELIA You must sing a-down a-down, and you call him a-down-a. 170
Oh how the wheel becomes it. It is the false steward that stole his
master's daughter.

---

152 SD] *A noise within. Let her come in* F; *A noyse within* Q2 *(giving* let her come in *to Laertes)* 153 SD *Enter* OPHELIA]
Q2, F *(after* 152 SD*)* 156 with weight] Q2; by waight F 157 Till] F; Tell Q2 157 turn] Q2; turnes F 160 an old] F;
a poore Q2 161–3 Nature ... loves] F; *not in* Q2 164 SD *Song*] Q2; *not in* F 165 Hey ... nonny] F; *not in*
Q2 166 in] Q2; on F 166 rained] rain'd Q2; raines F 168–9 Hadst ... thus] Q2; *as prose* F 170 a-down a-down]
a downe a downe Q2; downe a-downe F

communication to the senses, as in the Epilogue to
The Tempest ('prayer, / Which pierces so …….').
Claudius's meaning is 'My innocence will come as
sharply home to your judgement as daylight strikes
the eye.'

155 sense and virtue sensitivity and efficacy.

161–3 Nature … loves Love refines our nature,
and this refined nature sends part of itself after the
loved one. That is, Ophelia has parted with some of
her wits to send to Polonius. So F, not in Q2.

164–5 They bore him … hey nonny Ophelia
sings a lament, but gives as burden (the refrain) the
'hey nonny no' of a love ditty. Perhaps that is why
she then says 'You must sing a-down a-down.'

170 a-down a-down A popular refrain. Two
songs, printed in 1600, which use it, have associations
suitable for Ophelia's plight. The song at the end of
Dekker's *Shoemakers' Holiday* begins 'cold's the wind,
and wet's the rain': 'Let's sing a dirge for St Hugh's
soul, / And down it merrily. / Down a down, hey
down a down …' In *England's Helicon* (Q2r) is a song
about the miseries of love, which maidens are better to
avoid; it begins 'Hey down a down did Dian sing.'

171 wheel Unexplained; 'refrain', 'spinning-
wheel' and 'the wheel of Fortune' have been
suggested.

171–2 It is the false steward … daughter
A puzzling line which can be taken as Ophelia's

LAERTES This nothing's more than matter.

OPHELIA There's rosemary, that's for remembrance – pray you, love,
remember – and there is pansies, that's for thoughts.   175

LAERTES A document in madness, thoughts and remembrance fitted.

OPHELIA There's fennel for you, and columbines. There's rue for you,
and here's some for me; we may call it herb of grace a Sundays.
Oh you must wear your rue with a difference. There's a daisy. I
would give you some violets, but they withered all when my father   180
died. They say a made a good end.

[Sings]
For bonny sweet Robin is all my joy.

LAERTES Thought and affliction, passion, hell itself,
She turns to favour and to prettiness.

OPHELIA   And will a not come again?   *Song* 185
And will a not come again?
No, no, he is dead,
Go to thy death-bed,
He never will come again.

---

174 pray you] Q2; Pray F   175 pansies] Pancies Q2; Paconcies F   178 herb of grace] Q2; Herbe-Grace F   179 Oh you
must] F; you may Q2   181 a made] Q2; he made F   182 SD Sings] Capell; not in Q2, F   183 affliction] F; afflictions
Q2   185, 186 will a not] Q2; will he not F   185 SD Song] Q2; not in F   187–8 No ... death-bed] as one line Q2, F

approximation, in her madness, of her 'theft' by
Hamlet. Mark Thornton Burnett proposes biblical
and literary references ('Olivia's "False Steward"
Contextualized', *RES* 46.181 (1995), 48–56).

174–5 pray … remember Ophelia gives the
rosemary and pansies to Laertes, though Laertes
merges in her mind with Hamlet. To whom,
Claudius or Gertrude, she gives the fennel and
columbines and to whom the rue is much debated.
See the long discussion in Jenkins, 536–42.

175 pansies … thoughts The name comes
from the French, *pensées*. As elsewhere in this
scene, 'thoughts' has the special meaning of *sad*
thoughts, melancholy.

176 A document … fitted '[D]ocument', not
used elsewhere by Shakespeare, means 'instruction'. Ophelia finds a lesson in flowers, and in her
interpretation of them Laertes finds a lesson in
madness, for a mad person's 'thoughts' are conti-
nually 'fitted' (connected) with the 'remembrance'
of dark happenings.

177 fennel Widely associated with flattery (see
Robert Nares's *A Glossary* (London, 1822)). But
E. Le Comte points out (*TLS*, 22 Oct. 1982) that,
as a gift to Claudius, fennel is appropriate because it
was a food much liked by serpents (see *Paradise*

Lost, IX, 581).

177 columbines For ingratitude and infidelity
(see Nares, *Glossary*, and Jenkins, 539).

177 rue For sorrow and repentance.

178 herb of grace Another name for rue (also
herb-grace, herby-grass).

179 with a difference A term in heraldry;
a mark to distinguish a coat of arms from that of
another member or branch of the family.

179 daisy No special symbolism, but, as
N. Alexander says, daisies and violets are flowers
of springtime and love.

182 bonny sweet Robin Sternfeld gives the
music (68–78) and says 'Bonny Robin songs deal
with lovers, unfaithfulness and extra-marital affairs'
(58); 'the popularity of this simple ditty excelled by
far that of "Greensleeves"'. Harry Morris (*PMLA*
73 (1958), 601–3) believes Robin to be a name for
the male sex-organ.

183 Thought Melancholy.

184 favour beauty.

185 And will a not come again? The words of
this song are not otherwise known. The tune traditional in the theatre is given in NV and in Sternfeld,
67–9.

His beard was as white as snow,   190
All flaxen was his poll,
    He is gone, he is gone,
    And we cast away moan,
God-a-mercy on his soul.
And of all Christian souls, I pray God. God buy you.   *Exit*   195
LAERTES Do you see this, O God?
CLAUDIUS Laertes, I must commune with your grief,
    Or you deny me right. Go but apart,
    Make choice of whom your wisest friends you will,
    And they shall hear and judge 'twixt you and me.   200
    If by direct or by collateral hand
    They find us touched, we will our kingdom give,
    Our crown, our life, and all that we call ours,
    To you in satisfaction. But if not,
    Be you content to lend your patience to us,   205
    And we shall jointly labour with your soul
    To give it due content.
LAERTES   Let this be so.
    His means of death, his obscure funeral,
    No trophy, sword, nor hatchment o'er his bones,
    No noble rite, nor formal ostentation,   210
    Cry to be heard, as 'twere from heaven to earth,
    That I must call't in question.
CLAUDIUS   So you shall.
    And where th'offence is, let the great axe fall.
    I pray you go with me.
                                Exeunt

---

190 was as] Q2; as F   191 All flaxen] F; Flaxen Q2   191 poll] *Hanmer*; pole Q2, F   192–3 He … moan] *as one line* Q2,
F   194 God-a-mercy] God a mercy Q2; Gramercy F   194–5 God-a-mercy … souls] F; *as one line* Q2   195 Christian]
F; Christians Q2   195 I pray God] F; *not in* Q2   195 buy you] Q2; buy ye F   195 SD *Exit*] *Exeunt Ophelia* F; *not in*
Q2   196 you see this] F; you this Q2   196 O God] Q2; you Gods F   197 commune] Q2; common F   208 funeral]
Q2; buriall F   210 rite] F; right Q2   212 call't] Q2; call F

191 **flaxen … poll** i.e. white-haired ('poll' =
head).
193 **cast away moan** i.e. lamenting is useless.
195 SD *Exit*. J. P. Kemble here provided an exit
for Gertrude too; a sensible innovation, which
became customary.
197 **commune** Accent on first syllable. I think
the meaning here is 'converse', as usually in
Shakespeare, not 'share' or 'participate' as Boswell
and others suggest. Claudius is insisting on 'getting
through' to Laertes's grief, and informing him of

the true state of affairs.
199 **whom** whichever of.
201 **collateral** indirect.
202 **touched** concerned, implicated.
208 **His means of death** The way he died.
208 **obscure** Accent on first syllable.
209 **trophy** memorial (such as the insignia of his
rank and office).
209 **hatchment** Coat of arms placed over the
dead; usually a diamond-shaped tablet.
212 **call't in question** demand an examination.

[4.6] *Enter* HORATIO *with an* ATTENDANT

HORATIO What are they that would speak with me?
ATTENDANT Seafaring men sir, they say they have letters for you.
HORATIO Let them come in.

                                                     [Exit Attendant]

      I do not know from what part of the world
      I should be greeted, if not from Lord Hamlet.   5

                Enter SAILORS

1 SAILOR God bless you sir.
HORATIO Let him bless thee too.
1 SAILOR A shall sir, and please him. There's a letter for you sir, it came
    from th'ambassador that was bound for England, if your name be
    Horatio, as I am let to know it is.   10
HORATIO (*Reads the letter*) 'Horatio, when thou shalt have overlooked
    this, give these fellows some means to the king; they have letters
    for him. Ere we were two days old at sea, a pirate of very warlike
    appointment gave us chase. Finding ourselves too slow of sail, we
    put on a compelled valour, and in the grapple I boarded them. On   15
    the instant they got clear of our ship, so I alone became their
    prisoner. They have dealt with me like thieves of mercy, but they
    knew what they did: I am to do a good turn for them. Let the king
    have the letters I have sent, and repair thou to me with as much
    speed as thou wouldest fly death. I have words to speak in thine   20
    ear will make thee dumb, yet are they much too light for the bore
    of the matter. These good fellows will bring thee where I am.
    Rosencrantz and Guildenstern hold their course for England. Of
    them I have much to tell thee. Farewell.

                  He that thou knowest thine,   25
                       Hamlet.'

Act 4, Scene 6   4.6] *Capell*   **0** SD *an* ATTENDANT] F; *others* Q2   **2** SH ATTENDANT] *P. Alexander; Gent* Q2; *Ser.*
F   **2** Seafaring men] Q2; *Saylors* F   **3** SD] *P. Alexander; Exit Ser. / Hanmer; not in* Q2, F   **5** SD SAILORS] *Saylers* Q2;
Saylor F   **8** A shall] Q2; *Hee shall* F   **8** and] Q2; *and't* F   **8** came] Q2; *comes* F   **9** ambassador] *Ambassadours*
F   **11** SD *Reads the letter*] F(*as separate line*); *not in* Q2   **15** valour, and in] Q2; *Valour. In* F   **18** good turn] F; *turne*
Q2   **20** speed] Q2; *hast* F   **20** thine] Q2; *your* F   **21** bore] F; *bord* Q2

Act 4, Scene 6
  4 what part of the world i.e. what distant part
of the world (involving communication by sea).
  8 and please if it please.
  17 thieves of mercy thieves with merciful
hearts.

17–18 they knew what they did i.e. their
mercy was calculated.
  21–2 for the bore of the matter for the gravity
of the substance they speak of. The image is from
artillery – the words are too small for the bore of the
cannon.

Come, I will give you way for these your letters,
And do't the speedier that you may direct me
To him from whom you brought them.

Exeunt

[4.7] *Enter* CLAUDIUS *and* LAERTES

CLAUDIUS Now must your conscience my acquittance seal,
    And you must put me in your heart for friend,
    Sith you have heard, and with a knowing ear,
    That he which hath your noble father slain
    Pursued my life.

LAERTES   It well appears. But tell me   5
    Why you proceeded not against these feats,
    So crimeful and so capital in nature,
    As by your safety, wisdom, all things else,
    You mainly were stirred up.

CLAUDIUS   Oh for two special reasons,
    Which may to you perhaps seem much unsinewed,   10
    But yet to me they're strong. The queen his mother
    Lives almost by his looks, and for myself,
    My virtue or my plague, be it either which,
    She's so conjunctive to my life and soul,
    That as the star moves not but in his sphere,   15
    I could not but by her. The other motive,

---

27 Come] F; *Hor.* Come Q2 27 give] F; *not in* Q2 29 SD *Exeunt*] Q2; *Exit* F **Act 4, Scene 7** 4.7] Capell 6 proceeded] F; proceede Q2 7 crimeful] F; criminall Q2 8 safety, wisdom] F; safetie, greatnes, wisdome Q2 10 unsinewed] vnsinnow'd Q2; vnsinnowed F 11 But yet] Q2; And yet F 11 they're] tha'r Q2; they are F 14 She's] F; She is Q2 14 conjunctive] F; concliue Q2

Act 4, Scene 7
   1 **my acquittance seal** confirm my discharge; i.e. acknowledge my innocence.
   3 **knowing** understanding, intelligent.
   6 **feats** exploits. For this pejorative meaning, Schmidt cites also *Macbeth* 1.7.80 and *Henry V* 3.3.17.
   8 **safety, wisdom** So F. Q2 inserts 'greatnes'

between these words, making the line too long. It is likely that Q2 preserves a Shakespearean false start. Claudius is 'stirred up' to take action on account of his safety and by persuasion of his wisdom, 'greatness' seems irrelevant.
   14 **conjunctive** closely joined.
   15 **sphere** One of the series of hollow, transparent globes supposed to encircle the earth and carry the heavenly bodies.

Why to a public count I might not go,
Is the great love the general gender bear him,
Who, dipping all his faults in their affection,
Work like the spring that turneth wood to stone,   20
Convert his gyves to graces, so that my arrows,
Too slightly timbered for so loud a wind,
Would have reverted to my bow again,
And not where I had aimed them.
LAERTES And so have I a noble father lost,   25
A sister driven into desperate terms,
Whose worth, if praises may go back again,
Stood challenger on mount of all the age
For her perfections. But my revenge will come.
CLAUDIUS Break not your sleeps for that. You must not think   30
That we are made of stuff so flat and dull
That we can let our beard be shook with danger
And think it pastime. You shortly shall hear more.
I loved your father, and we love ourself,
And that I hope will teach you to imagine –   35

Enter a MESSENGER *with letters*

How now? What news?
MMESSENGER   Letters my lord from Hamlet.
This to your majesty, this to the queen.
CLAUDIUS From Hamlet? Who brought them?
MESSENGER Sailors my lord they say, I saw them not;
They were given me by Claudio – he received them   40
Of him that brought them.

20 Work] Q2; Would F   22 loud a wind] F; loued Arm'd Q2   24 And] F; But Q2   24 had] F; haue Q2   24 aimed]
aym'd Q2; arm'd F   27 Whose worth] Q2; Who was F   35 SD] Q2; *Enter a Messenger* F   36 How … Hamlet] F; *not in*
Q2   37 This] F; These Q2   41 Of … them] Q2; *not in* F

17 **count** indictment (*OED sb*¹ 8).
18 **general gender** common people.
20 **Work** Act, operate.
20 **spring … stone** Dowden notes that in
William Harrison's *Description of England* it is stated
that the baths at King's Newnham in Warwickshire
turn wood to stone. Scot's *Discovery of Witchcraft*
says 'wood is by the quality of divers waters here in
England transubstantiated into a stone. (Of late
experience near Coventry, etc.)' (Aa2v).
21 **gyves** fetters.

22 **Too slightly timbered** i.e. too light.
23 **reverted** returned.
26 **desperate terms** an extreme or hopeless
state.
27 **back again** i.e. to what she was.
28 **on mount of** Probably 'mounted above' (=
'placed on high above').
31 **flat** inert, spiritless. Compare 1.2.133.
32 **with danger** with dangerous intent,
threateningly.
40 **Claudio** The name or character has not been
mentioned before this and will not be after.

CLAUDIUS   Laertes, you shall hear them. –
          Leave us.

                                                           Exit Messenger
[Reads] 'High and mighty, you shall know I am set naked on your
kingdom. Tomorrow shall I beg leave to see your kingly eyes, when
I shall, first asking your pardon thereunto, recount th'occasion of   45
my sudden and more strange return.
                                               Hamlet.'
          What should this mean? Are all the rest come back?
          Or is it some abuse, and no such thing?
LAERTES Know you the hand?
CLAUDIUS   'Tis Hamlet's character. Naked?   50
          And in a postscript here he says alone.
          Can you devise me?
LAERTES I'm lost in it my lord. But let him come –
          It warms the very sickness in my heart
          That I shall live and tell him to his teeth   55
          'Thus didest thou!'
CLAUDIUS   If it be so, Laertes –
          As how should it be so? – how otherwise? –
          Will you be ruled by me?
LAERTES   Ay my lord,
          So you will not o'errule me to a peace.
CLAUDIUS To thine own peace. If he be now returned,   60
          As checking at his voyage, and that he means
          No more to undertake it, I will work him
          To an exploit, now ripe in my device,

---

42 SD] F; *not in* Q2   43 SD *Reads*] *Capell; not in* Q2, F   45 th'] F; the Q2   45 occasion] Q2; *Occasions* F   47 Hamlet]
not in Q2   49 and] Q2; Or F   52 devise] Q2; aduise F   53 I'm] F; I am Q2   55 shall live] F; live Q2   56 didest]
diddest F; didst Q2   58 Ay my lord] I my Lord Q2; If F   59 you will] Q2; you'l F   61 checking] F; the King Q2

43 naked destitute, with a secondary meaning of unarmed.
49 abuse imposition, deception.
49 no such thing i.e. no such thing has happened.
50 character handwriting.
52 devise So Q2. F reads 'advise'. Since Dover Wilson's defence, editors have generally accepted Q2's variant. *OED* 10 gives a meaning of 'conjecture, guess', so Claudius may mean 'Can you guess (the meaning of this) for me?' The more regular sense of 'devise' occurs below at 68.

54 warms does good to.
54 very real.
56 Thus Laertes mimes or imagines a sword-thrust. The ferocious retaliation which he relishes in anticipation is completely lost in the unnecessary emendation accepted by Wilson and Jenkins, 'Thus diest thou.'
61 checking at turned from. A phrase from falconry, used when a hawk is diverted in his pursuit by some new object.
63 ripe in my device i.e. a scheme of mine come to maturity.

Under the which he shall not choose but fall,
And for his death no wind of blame shall breathe,   65
But even his mother shall uncharge the practice
And call it accident.
[LAERTES   My lord, I will be ruled,
The rather if you could devise it so
That I might be the organ.
CLAUDIUS   It falls right.
You have been talked of since your travel much,   70
And that in Hamlet's hearing, for a quality
Wherein they say you shine. Your sum of parts
Did not together pluck such envy from him
As did that one, and that in my regard
Of the unworthiest siege.
LAERTES   What part is that my lord?   75
CLAUDIUS A very riband in the cap of youth,
Yet needful too, for youth no less becomes
The light and careless livery that it wears
Than settled age his sables and his weeds
Importing health and graveness.] Two months since   80
Here was a gentleman of Normandy.
I've seen myself, and served against, the French,
And they can well on horseback, but this gallant
Had witchcraft in't. He grew unto his seat,
And to such wondrous doing brought his horse   85
As had he been incorpsed and demi-natured

67–80 LAERTES My lord ... graveness] Q2; *not in* F   76 riband] Q 1611; ribaud Q2   80 Two months] Q2; Some two
Monthes F   80 since] Q2; hence F   82 I've] F; I haue Q2   84 unto] Q2; into F

66 uncharge the practice i.e. not press the accusation that it was a criminal contrivance.

67–80 F omits this, and resumes with 'Some two Monthes hence', to make an exact metrical join with 'And call it accident' (67).

68 devise contrive.

69 organ instrument.

75 Of the unworthiest siege Of the least account. Claudius flatters Laertes by saying that the great skill in arms which Hamlet so envied is the least of his virtues.

76 very riband mere ribbon.

77 becomes is in accord with, suits.

80 Importing ... graveness Which indicates a concern for health and dignity.

83 can well are very skilful.

86 incorpsed of one body. Seemingly a Shakespearean coinage.

86 demi-natured i.e. he, as man, was half of the total nature of a united man–horse creature.

With the brave beast. So far he topped my thought,
That I in forgery of shapes and tricks
Come short of what he did.

LAERTES   A Norman was't?

CLAUDIUS A Norman.   90

LAERTES Upon my life Lamord.

CLAUDIUS   The very same.

LAERTES I know him well, he is the brooch indeed
And gem of all the nation.

CLAUDIUS He made confession of you,
And gave you such a masterly report   95
For art and exercise in your defence,
And for your rapier most especial,
That he cried out 'twould be a sight indeed
If one could match you. [Th'escrimers of their nation
He swore had neither motion, guard, nor eye,   100
If you opposed them.] Sir, this report of his
Did Hamlet so envenom with his envy
That he could nothing do but wish and beg
Your sudden coming o'er to play with you.
Now out of this –

LAERTES   What out of this, my lord?   105

CLAUDIUS Laertes, was your father dear to you?
Or are you like the painting of a sorrow,
A face without a heart?

LAERTES   Why ask you this?

CLAUDIUS Not that I think you did not love your father,

---

87 topped] topt Q2; past F   87 my] F; me Q2   91 Lamord] Q2; *Lamound* F   93 the] Q2; our F   94 made] Q2; mad
F   97 especial] Q2; especially F   99–101 Th'escrimers ... opposed them] Q2; *not in* F   99 Th'escrimers] th'escri-
meurs *White;* the Scrimures Q2   104 you] Q2; him F   105 What] Q2; Why F

---

87 **topped my thought** surpassed what I could
imagine.

88 **in forgery ... tricks** in imagining displays of
horsemanship.

92 **brooch** jewel.

94 **made confession of you** acknowledged
you.

96 **art and exercise** skilful accomplishments.
(A hendiadys.)

99–101 F cuts these two lines.

99 **Th'escrimers** fencers (*OED*). Q2, our only
authority here, gives 'the Scrimures', and, since the
quarto of 1611, editions have given 'the scrimers',
though there is no such word. The French *escrimeur*
(master of fencing), is found in sixteenth-century
English (see *OED*).

100 **motion** the skilled movements of the
trained fencer.

102 **envenom** embitter (literally, poison).
Hamlet was poisoned by others' praise of Laertes.

But that I know love is begun by time,   110
And that I see, in passages of proof,
Time qualifies the spark and fire of it.
[There lives within the very flame of love
A kind of wick or snuff that will abate it,
And nothing is at a like goodness still,   115
For goodness, growing to a plurisy,
Dies in his own too much. That we would do,
We should do when we would, for this 'would' changes,
And hath abatements and delays as many
As there are tongues, are hands, are accidents;   120
And then this 'should' is like a spendthrift sigh,
That hurts by easing. But to the quick of th'ulcer –]
Hamlet comes back; what would you undertake
To show yourself in deed your father's son
More than in words?

LAERTES   To cut his throat i'th'church.   125

CLAUDIUS No place indeed should murder sanctuarize;
           Revenge should have no bounds. But, good Laertes,
           Will you do this, keep close within your chamber;
           Hamlet, returned, shall know you are come home;
           We'll put on those shall praise your excellence,   130

113–22 There lives … th'ulcer –] Q2; *not in* F   114 wick] *Rowe;* weeke Q2   121 spendthrift] Q 1676; spend thrifts
Q2   124 in deed … son] *Steevens²;* indeede your fathers sonne Q2; your Fathers sonne indeede F

110 by time by suitable time, by the proper
occasion. Love is a creature of time and belongs to
time, in that a suitable moment brings it to birth,
and the succession of moments, less auspicious, will
dull it.
  111 passages of proof things that have happened which bear me out.
  112 qualifies reduces, weakens.
  113–22 F omits the whole passage. Compare
a similar effort to shorten at 5.2.100.
  114 snuff the burnt part of the wick.
  115 still all the time.
  116 plurisy (1) excess; (2) the inflammation of
the chest (pleurisy) thought to be caused by 'excess'
of humours.
  121 spendthrift sigh The Q2 reading (i.e.
'spendthrift's') may possibly be right, but it is really
the sigh itself that is a spendthrift – it does harm in
the pleasure of indulging itself. Painful breathing is

the main feature of pleurisy. Claudius says that if we
don't act in due time, our duty becomes painful and
difficult.
  122 to the quick of th'ulcer to the heart of the
matter. Claudius moves from one disease-image to
another.
  126 should murder sanctuarize should offer
refuge for a murderer. This is the first instance of
such usage (*OED*). Claudius's remark runs in two
directions at once. (1) No church should offer sanctuary and protection to a man who, like Hamlet, has
committed murder; (2) no church should be
regarded as a sanctuary where the throat-cutting
you mention cannot be carried out.
  128 Will you do this If you are to do this.
  128 keep close remain confined.
  130 put on those shall praise arrange for some
to praise.

And set a double varnish on the fame
The Frenchman gave you; bring you in fine together,
And wager on your heads. He being remiss,
Most generous, and free from all contriving,
Will not peruse the foils, so that with ease,   135
Or with a little shuffling, you may choose
A sword unbated, and in a pass of practice
Requite him for your father.
LAERTES   I will do't,
And for that purpose I'll anoint my sword.
I bought an unction of a mountebank,   140
So mortal that but dip a knife in it,
Where it draws blood no cataplasm so rare,
Collected from all simples that have virtue
Under the moon, can save the thing from death
That is but scratched withal. I'll touch my point   145
With this contagion, that if I gall him slightly,
It may be death.
CLAUDIUS   Let's further think of this,
Weigh what convenience both of time and means
May fit us to our shape. If this should fail,
And that our drift look through our bad performance,   150
'Twere better not assayed. Therefore this project
Should have a back or second, that might hold
If this did blast in proof. Soft, let me see.
We'll make a solemn wager on your cunnings –
I ha't!   155

---

133 on] F; ore Q2   137 pass] passe F; pace Q2   139 that] F; *not in* Q2   141 that but dip] Q2; I but dipt F   149 shape.
If] *Rowe;* shape if Q2; shape, if F   153 did] Q2; should F   154 cunnings] Q2; commings F   155 ha't] F; hate Q2

132 in fine in conclusion.
133 remiss 'not vigilant or cautious' (Johnson).
136 shuffling deceit. See notes to 3.3.61 and 3.1.67.
137 unbated unblunted. (Short for 'unabated'.)
137 a pass of practice 'practice' means a deliberate and malicious stratagem – as in 66 above and 5.2.297. Claudius is speaking of a thrust which is intended to kill. (The other possible meaning is 'a bout intended for exercise'.)
140 unction ointment.
140 mountebank disreputable, itinerant seller of medicines and cures.
142 cataplasm poultice, medicated dressing.

143 Collected Put together. Compare 3.2.233.
143 simples medicinal plants.
144 Under the moon Probably 'anywhere in the world' (though Thompson and Taylor recall Lucianus's recipe for poison at 3.2.231–6).
146 gall injure, wound.
149 fit us to our shape suit us for our design, the plan that we are fashioning. But there is a strong secondary meaning exploiting the word's theatrical senses (costume, disguise, hence role); i.e. fashion us into the parts we are going to play.
150 drift aim, purpose.
153 blast in proof explode in being tested (like a faulty cannon).

When in your motion you are hot and dry,
As make your bouts more violent to that end,
And that he calls for drink, I'll have preferred him
A chalice for the nonce, whereon but sipping,
If he by chance escape your venomed stuck,   160
Our purpose may hold there. But stay, what noise?

Enter GERTRUDE

How, sweet queen!
GERTRUDE One woe doth tread upon another's heel,
    So fast they follow. Your sister's drowned, Laertes.
LAERTES Drowned! Oh where?   165
GERTRUDE There is a willow grows askant a brook,
    That shows his hoar leaves in the glassy stream.
    Therewith fantastic garlands did she make,
    Of crow-flowers, nettles, daisies, and long purples,
    That liberal shepherds give a grosser name,   170
    But our cold maids do dead men's fingers call them.
    There on the pendant boughs her cronet weeds

---

157 that] Q2; the F   158 preferred] prefard Q2; prepar'd F   161 But … noise] Q2; *not in* F   162 How … queen] F;
not in Q2   164 they] Q2; they'l F   166 askant] ascaunt Q2; aslant F   166 a brook] F; the Brooke Q2   167 hoar] hore
F; horry Q2   168 Therewith] Q2; There with F   168 make] Q2; come F   171 cold] F; cull-cold Q2   172 cronet] Q2,
Ridley; Coronet F; crownet *Wilson*

158 preferred presented to, offered. The choice
between the readings of Q2 and F (prepar'd) is very
difficult, since both have strong claims. Claudius
plans either to have a chalice *made ready* ('prepared') for Hamlet when occasion demands, or to
offer one to him ('preferred').
159 for the nonce for that particular purpose or
occasion.
160 stuck thrust.
161–2 But stay… queen! See collation.
It seems necessary to conflate Q2 and F at this point.
165 Drowned! Oh where? This response has
been ridiculed as insensitive. Perhaps Laertes is
meant to express not so much shock and grief as
incredulity and amazement. He has just seen her
alive.
166–83 Gertrude offers an extended verbal picture of Ophelia's death. The details that she provides should not be taken to suggest that she stood
aloof at the scene, as an impassive eye-witness to the
drowning. Her speech is a functional account of
Ophelia's death. It has been suggested that the
queen's story is something of a 'cover-up' of
a deliberate act of suicide, but in view of other
inconsistencies it is better to say that Gertrude
steps out of her role to serve the purpose of the play.

166 askant F's 'aslant' gives yet another Q2/
F doublet. Both words are normally adverbs meaning 'obliquely' and neither was used, as here, as
a preposition.
167 hoar grey.
168 Therewith … make She made garlands
from the willow, interwoven with wildflowers and
weeds. F reads 'There with fantastic garlands did
she come.'
169 crow-flowers 'The crow-flower is called
wild williams, marshy gilly-flowers and cuckoo gilly-
flowers' (John Gerard, *The Herball* (London, 1597),
480–1).
169–71 long-purples … call them Generally
identified as the wild orchis, *Orchis mascula*, which
has a tall flower stem with a spike of purple flowers.
The 'grosser name' – something to do with testicles –
and 'dead men's fingers' apply to the shape of the
roots. (See NV and *OED* sv 'Dead men's fingers'.)
170 liberal free-spoken.
171 cold So F. Q2's 'cull-cold' looks like the
remnant of a Shakespearean false start.
172 cronet So Q2. '[C]ronet', 'crownet' and
'coronet' (which F gives) were all variant forms.
Ridley restored Q2's form, since the metre requires
two syllables, 'cronet weeds' means the garland of

Clamb'ring to hang, an envious sliver broke,
When down her weedy trophies and herself
Fell in the weeping brook. Her clothes spread wide,   175
And mermaid-like awhile they bore her up,
Which time she chanted snatches of old lauds
As one incapable of her own distress,
Or like a creature native and indued
Unto that element. But long it could not be   180
Till that her garments, heavy with their drink,
Pulled the poor wretch from her melodious lay
To muddy death.

LAERTES   Alas, then she is drowned?
GERTRUDE Drowned, drowned.
LAERTES Too much of water hast thou, poor Ophelia,   185
And therefore I forbid my tears. But yet
It is our trick; nature her custom holds,
Let shame say what it will. When these are gone,
The woman will be out. Adieu my lord,
I have a speech of fire that fain would blaze,   190
But that this folly douts it.   *Exit*
CLAUDIUS   Let's follow, Gertrude.

---

174 her] Q2; the F   177 lauds] laudes Q2; tunes F   181 their drink] Q2; her drinke F   182 lay] Q2; buy F   183 she is] Q2, Q1; is she F   190 of fire] F; a fire Q2   191 douts] *Knight*; doubts F; drownes Q2

---

willow and weeds which Ophelia had made.
   173 envious malicious.
   173 sliver a small branch or twig (though it is not a sliver until it has broken off). Compare *Lear* 4.2.34–5, 'She that will sliver and disbranch / From her material sap'.
   177 lauds hymns. So Q2; F gives 'tunes', as does Q1. '[L]aud' is an unusual word, not frequently used outside its technical reference to the second of the canonical hours in the Catholic breviary.
   178 incapable uncomprehending.

   179 indued adapted, conditioned.
   182 the poor wretch Gertrude used this phrase for Hamlet at 2.2.166.
   187 our trick a way we have.
   188 these i.e. his tears.
   189 The woman ...... out The woman in me will have finished.
   191 douts extinguishes ('folly' being his weeping).

How much I had to do to calm his rage!
Now fear I this will give it start again.
Therefore let's follow.

Exeunt

5.1 *Enter two* CLOWNS

CLOWN Is she to be buried in Christian burial, when she wilfully seeks
her own salvation?

OTHER I tell thee she is, therefore make her grave straight. The crowner
hath sat on her, and finds it Christian burial.

CLOWN How can that be, unless she drowned herself in her own   5
defence?

OTHER Why, 'tis found so.

CLOWN It must be *se offendendo*, it cannot be else. For here lies the
point: if I drown myself wittingly, it argues an act, and an act hath
three branches – it is to act, to do, to perform. Argal, she drowned   10
herself wittingly.

OTHER Nay, but hear you goodman delver –

CLOWN Give me leave. Here lies the water – good. Here stands the
man – good. If the man go to this water and drown himself, it is

---

Act 5, Scene 1 5.1] Q 1676   1 when she] Q2; that F   3 therefore] Q2; and therefore F   8 *se offendendo*] F; so
offended Q2   10 to act] Q2; an Act F   10 to perform] Q2; and to performe F   10 Argal] argall F; or all Q2

Act 5, Scene 1

5.1 There is a clearly marked gap of time
between the end of Act 4, in which we hear of
Ophelia's death, and the beginning of Act 5, when
they are digging her grave. The gap is meant to be
short, however; Hamlet spoke in his letter to the
king of seeing him 'tomorrow'.

0 SD Both Q2 and F give us the entry for 'two
clowns' and refer to them in the speech headings as
'Clown' and 'Other'. This is evidently
Shakespeare's designation. The First Clown, the
head gravedigger, is called by Hamlet and calls
himself the sexton (75, 137 below).

1–2 wilfully … salvation Probably
a malapropism, in which the Clown confuses salvation and damnation. As the following lines indicate,
he knows that suicide is forbidden by the church
and rules out the possibility of Christian burial. See
Introduction, 48–9.

3 straight straightaway. But he accidentally
implies that if it weren't Christian burial, she

would have a crooked grave.

3 crowner Common colloquial form of 'coroner', an officer whose chief function is to determine the circumstances of violent or accidental
deaths.

8 *se offendendo* Another malapropism. He
means *se defendendo*, in self-defence, a justifiable
plea in case of homicide.

9–10 an act … branches There is general
agreement with the suggestion made in the eighteenth century by Sir John Hawkins (see NV) that
Shakespeare had in mind the celebrated legal arguments of 1561–2 on the suicide of Sir James Hales,
who had walked into the river at Canterbury in
1554. In a suit over whether his lands were thereby
forfeit, there was much fine discussion on the nature
of the act, including the argument that an act con-
sisted of three parts, the Imagination, the
Resolution, and the Perfection. See Plowden's
Commentaries, 1761, 259.

10 Argal For *ergo* (therefore).

12 goodman delver master digger.

will he, nill he, he goes – mark you that. But if the water come to   15
him, and drown him, he drowns not himself. Argal, he that is not
guilty of his own death shortens not his own life.

OTHER But is this law?

CLOWN Ay marry is't, crowner's quest law.

OTHER Will you ha' the truth on't? If this had not been a gentlewoman,   20
she should have been buried out o' Christian burial.

CLOWN Why, there thou sayst – and the more pity that great folk should
have countenance in this world to drown or hang themselves
more than their even-Christen. Come, my spade; there is no ancient
gentlemen but gardeners, ditchers, and gravemakers; they hold up   25
Adam's profession.

OTHER Was he a gentleman?

CLOWN A was the first that ever bore arms.

OTHER Why, he had none.

CLOWN What, art a heathen? How dost thou understand the scripture?   30
The scripture says Adam digged. Could he dig without arms? I'll
put another question to thee. If thou answerest me not to the
purpose, confess thyself –

OTHER Go to!

CLOWN What is he that builds stronger than either the mason, the   35
shipwright, or the carpenter?

OTHER The gallows-maker, for that frame outlives a thousand tenants.

CLOWN I like thy wit well in good faith. The gallows does well, but
how does it well? It does well to those that do ill. Now, thou dost
ill to say the gallows is built stronger than the church; argal, the   40
gallows may do well to thee. To't again, come.

OTHER Who builds stronger than a mason, a shipwright, or a carpenter?

CLOWN Ay, tell me that, and unyoke.

OTHER Marry, now I can tell.

CLOWN To't.   45

---

20 on't] F; an't Q2   21 o'] a Q2; of F   24 even-Christen] euen Christen Q2; euen Christian F   28 A was] Q2; He was
F   29–31 Why … arms] F; *not in* Q2   37 frame] F; *not in* Q2

15 **will he, nill he** whether he will or no, willy-
nilly.

16–17 **he that is not guilty … life** i.e. only
suicides fail to live out their allotted spans.
The Clown's logic is a profound critique of the
reasoning of educated men.

19 **crowner's quest law** coroner's inquest law.

23 **countenance** permission, authorization.

24 **even-Christen** Collective noun for 'fellow
Christians' (see *OED* sv 'christen' and 'even-
Christian').

24–5 **there is no … Adam's profession** The
Clown, spurred by his recognition of the privileges of
'great folks', claims elite status for his profession on
account of its longevity, which reaches back to the
first man. His punning logic on 'bearing arms' continues through 31.

24 **ancient** i.e. of long standing.

33 **confess thyself** – 'Confess and be hanged'
was proverbial. See Tilley C587.

37 **frame** structure.

43 **unyoke** unyoke the oxen; finish the day's
work.

OTHER Mass, I cannot tell.

Enter HAMLET *and* HORATIO *afar off*

CLOWN Cudgel thy brains no more about it, for your dull ass will not
mend his pace with beating; and when you are asked this question
next, say a grave-maker. The houses he makes lasts till doomsday.
Go, get thee to Yaughan, fetch me a stoup of liquor.   50

[*Exit Second Clown*]

In youth when I did love, did love,   *Song*
Methought it was very sweet
To contract-o the time for-a my behove,
Oh methought there-a was nothing-a meet.

HAMLET Has this fellow no feeling of his business? A sings in   55
grave-making.

HORATIO Custom hath made it in him a property of easiness.

HAMLET 'Tis e'en so, the hand of little employment hath the daintier
sense.

CLOWN   But age with his stealing steps   *Song* 60
Hath clawed me in his clutch,
And hath shipped me intil the land,
As if I had never been such.

[*Throws up a skull*]

HAMLET That skull had a tongue in it, and could sing once. How the
knave jowls it to th' ground, as if 'twere Cain's jawbone, that did   65

---

46 SD] F; *Enter Hamlet and Horatio* Q2 *(after 54)*   49 he makes] Q2; that he makes F   50 get thee … fetch] F; get thee
in, and fetch Q2   50 stoup] stoupe F; soope Q2   50 SD] *Rowe; not in* Q2, F   51 SD *Song*] Q2; *Sings.* F   53 contract-o]
contract ô Q2; *contract* O F   53 for-a] for a Q2, F   54 there-a] there a Q2; *there* F   54 nothing-a] nothing a Q2; *nothing*
F   55 A sings] a sings Q2; that he sings F   55 in] Q2; at F   58 daintier] F; dintier Q2   60 SD *Song*] Q2; *Clowne sings*
F   61 clawed] Q2; *caught* F   62 intil] F; into Q2   63 SD] *Capell; not in* Q2, F; *he throwes vp a shouel* Q1   65 th'ground]
F; the ground Q2   65 'twere] twere Q2; it were F

---

46 SD So F. Q2 provides the entry at 54, which
conflicts with Hamlet's first remark that they have
been watching and listening.

50 **Yaughan** An eccentric spelling of 'Johann'.

50 **stoup** a large jar or pitcher.

51–4, 60–4, 79–82 **In youth when I did love**
The Clown sings a very free version of a popular
song printed, as by Thomas Vaux, in the anthology
now known as *Tottel's Miscellany*, 1557, 'I loathe
that I did love.' See a full discussion, with the
music, in Sternfeld, esp. 130–1, 151–5.

53–4 **contract-o … for-a … there-a …
nothing-a** The Clown is decorating his lyric.
For an accommodation to the music, see

Sternfeld, 155.

53 **To contract … behove** i.e. to pass away the
time to my own advantage.

57 **a property of easiness** 'a matter of indifference' (N. Alexander).

62 **intil** into. So F.

63 SD *Throws up a skull* Capell's SD reflects Q1,
'*he throwes vp a shouel*', where 'shouel' is presumably a compositor's misreading of 'skull', required
in 64.

65 **jowls** bangs (with a pun on 'jowl' = 'jaw').

65 **Cain's jawbone, that did** the jawbone of
Cain, who did … A further reminder of the story of
Cain and Abel (see Introduction, 2, 35, 44). There

the first murder. This might be the pate of a politician which this ass now o'erreaches, one that would circumvent God, might it not?

HORATIO It might my lord.

HAMLET Or of a courtier, which could say 'Good morrow sweet lord, how dost thou sweet lord?' This might be my Lord Such-a-one,   70 that praised my Lord Such-a-one's horse when a meant to beg it, might it not?

HORATIO Ay my lord.

HAMLET Why, e'en so, and now my Lady Worm's, chopless, and knocked about the mazard with a sexton's spade. Here's fine   75 revolution, and we had the trick to see't. Did these bones cost no more the breeding but to play at loggets with 'em? Mine ache to think on't.

CLOWN   A pickaxe and a spade, a spade,   *Song*
               For and a shrowding sheet,   80
               Oh a pit of clay for to be made,
               For such a guest is meet.

               [*Throws up another skull*]

HAMLET There's another. Why may not that be the skull of a lawyer? Where be his quiddities now, his quillets, his cases, his tenures, and his tricks? Why does he suffer this rude knave now to knock him   85 about the sconce with a dirty shovel, and will not tell him of his

---

66 This] Q2; It F   67 now o'erreaches] Q2; o're Of-/fices F   67 would] Q2; could F   70 thou sweet lord] Q2; thou, good Lord F   71 a] Q2; he F   71 meant] F; went Q2   74 chopless] Choples Q2; Chaplesse F   75 mazard] F; massene Q2   76 and] Q2; if F   77 'em] F; them Q2   79 SD *Song*] Q2; *Clowne sings*. F   82 SD] *Capell; not in* Q2, F   83 may] Q2; might F   84 quiddities] Q2; Quiddits F   84 quillets] F; quillites Q2   85 rude] F; madde Q2

is a curious English medieval tradition that Cain killed Abel with the jawbone of an ass (see the Old English *Solomon and Saturn*, ed. J. E. Cross and T. D. Hill (University of Toronto Press, 1982), 101–3). Since Skeat referred to this tradition in 1880 (*N & Q* 21 Aug.), it has often been supposed that the ass's jawbone is meant here, but of course it is Cain's skull – so contemptuously dropped – that Hamlet means. In view of the widespread appearance of the legend in medieval drama and iconography (see J. K. Bonnell, *PMLA* 39 (1924), 140–6) it seems certain that it was in Shakespeare's mind as he wrote, because of the 'ass' in 67.

67 **o'erreaches** A politician was a man who o'erreached, in the sense of duped, his pawns and enemies. Now the tables are turned as the gravedigger o'erreaches (i.e. handles) his skull.

74 **Lady Worm's** The skull of Lord Such-a-one now belongs to the worm (NV).

74 **chopless** The chops or chaps are the lower

jaw and the flesh about it.

75 **mazard** a drinking-bowl; here used facetiously for the skull or head.

75–6 **fine revolution** elegant overturning of social rank.

76 **trick** knack.

76–7 **Did these bones … loggets with 'em?** Was the value of bringing up these people so slight that we may justifiably play games with their bones?

77 **loggets** A country game in which wooden truncheons about 2 feet long were thrown at a fixed stake.

84 **quiddities … quillets** subtle distinctions, quibbles. One would expect a like-sounding pair, either quiddits/quillets, or quiddities/quillities. F's 'quiddits' could be the true reading.

84 **tenures** suits connected with the holding of land.

86 **sconce** Colloquial for 'head'.

action of battery? Hum, this fellow might be in's time a great buyer
of land, with his statutes, his recognizances, his fines, his double
vouchers, his recoveries. Is this the fine of his fines and the recovery   90
of his recoveries, to have his fine pate full of fine dirt? Will his
vouchers vouch him no more of his purchases, and double ones too,
than the length and breadth of a pair of indentures? The very
conveyances of his lands will scarcely lie in this box, and must
th'inheritor himself have no more, ha?

HORATIO Not a jot more my lord.   95

HAMLET Is not parchment made of sheepskins?

HORATIO Ay my lord, and of calves' skins too.

HAMLET They are sheep and calves which seek out assurance in that.
I will speak to this fellow. Whose grave's this sirrah?

CLOWN Mine sir.   100

(*Sings*)
Oh a pit of clay for to be made
For such a guest is meet.

HAMLET I think it be thine indeed, for thou liest in't.

CLOWN You lie out on't sir, and therefore 'tis not yours. For my part,
I do not lie in't, yet it is mine.   105

HAMLET Thou dost lie in't, to be in't and say 'tis thine. 'Tis for the

89–90 Is this ... dirt] F; *not in* Q2   90–1 Will his vouchers] F; will vouchers Q2   91 and double ones too] F; & doubles Q2   93 scarcely] Q2; hardly F   97 calves' skins] Calues-skinnes Q2; Caue-skinnes F   98 which] Q2; that F   99 sirrah] Q2; Sir F   101 SD *Sings*] Capell; *not in* Q2, F   101 Oh] *O* F; or Q2   102 For ... meet] F; *not in* Q2   104 'tis] Q2; it is F   105 yet] Q2; and yet F   106 'tis thine] F; it is thine Q2

87 **action of battery** lawsuit dealing with physical violence.

88 **statutes** securities for debts, mortgages.

88 **recognizances** bonds undertaking to repay debts or fulfil other legal obligations.

88–9 **double vouchers ... recoveries** Like fines, recoveries were fictitious suits to obtain the authority of a court judgement for the holding of land. A voucher, or *vocatio*, calls in one of the parties necessary in this action – a double voucher rendering the tortuous process even more secure (see the full account in Clarkson and Warren, *The Law of Property in Shakespeare*, 128–30).

89 **fine** conclusion.

90 **fine pate** subtle head.

91 **purchases** Technically, this refers to the transfer of property by other means than inheritance. But the word was widely used in Shakespeare's time to indicate, in a pejorative sense, acquisitions and enrichments of any kind. See note to 93 below.

92 **pair of indentures** Two copies of a legal

agreement would be made on the same sheet of parchment which was then cut in half by means of an indented or zig-zag line, as a precaution against forgery.

93 **conveyances of his lands** deeds relating to purchases of land for himself. This lawyer has feathered his own nest. See note to 'purchases' above (91).

94 **inheritor** He who has come to own all these lands has in the end only the space of his coffin, which is not big enough even for the documents of his canny dealings. A subtle joke because this lawyer is not technically an 'inheritor'. Like so many Elizabethan lawyers, he has come to his estates by 'purchase'.

98 **assurance** Parchment documents provide legal proof ('assurance') of material gains, but only fools would seek in them assurance, or security, against mortality.

103–4 'Hamlet uses the familiar *thee* and *thou* to the Sexton, but the Sexton uses the respectful *you* in reply' (Kittredge).

dead, not for the quick, therefore thou liest.

CLOWN 'Tis a quick lie sir, 'twill away again from me to you.

HAMLET What man dost thou dig it for?

CLOWN For no man sir.   110

HAMLET What woman then?

CLOWN For none neither.

HAMLET Who is to be buried in't?

CLOWN One that was a woman sir, but rest her soul she's dead.

HAMLET How absolute the knave is! We must speak by the card, or   115
equivocation will undo us. By the lord, Horatio, this three years
I have took note of it: the age is grown so picked, that the toe of
the peasant comes so near the heel of the courtier, he galls his kibe.
How long hast thou been grave-maker?

CLOWN Of all the days i'th'year, I came to't that day that our last King   120
Hamlet o'ercame Fortinbras.

HAMLET How long is that since?

CLOWN Cannot you tell that? Every fool can tell that. It was the very
day that young Hamlet was born, he that is mad and sent into
England.   125

HAMLET Ay marry, why was he sent into England?

CLOWN Why, because a was mad. A shall recover his wits there, or if
a do not, 'tis no great matter there.

HAMLET Why?

CLOWN 'Twill not be seen in him there. There the men are as mad as   130
he.

HAMLET How came he mad?

---

116 this] Q2; these F   117 took] Q2; taken F   118 heel of the] Q2; heeles of our F   119 grave-maker] Q2; a Graue-
maker F   121 o'ercame] o'recame F; ouercame Q2   123 the very] F; that very Q2   124 is mad] Q2; was mad
F   127–8 a … A … a] Q2; he … hee … he F   128 'tis] Q2; it's F   130 him there. There] him there, there Q2;
him, there F

107 **the quick** the living.

115 **absolute** precise, literal-minded.

115 **by the card** i.e. with the precision of
a sailor, navigating by his compass; 'card' could
mean either the seaman's chart, or the face of the
compass. In 5.2.103 below, 'card' probably means
'map'.

116 **equivocation** deliberate playing on language and double meanings. The rest of the conversation between Hamlet and the Clown
demonstrates that the Clown is adept at this kind
of wordplay.

117 **picked** fastidious, refined.

118 **galls his kibe** rubs his chilblain, a sore from
exposure to cold.

120–1 **our last … o'ercame Fortinbras** See
1.1.80–95.

123–4 **very day … born** The Clown connects
Hamlet's birth with his father's defeat of King
Fortinbras. Later (137–8), the Clown dates the
three events – his start as sexton, Hamlet's birth,
and King Hamlet's victory – to thirty years ago,
making clear that Hamlet is thirty.

CLOWN Very strangely they say.

HAMLET How, strangely?

CLOWN Faith, e'en with losing his wits.   135

HAMLET Upon what ground?

CLOWN Why, here in Denmark. I have been sexton here man and boy
      thirty years.

HAMLET How long will a man lie i'th'earth ere he rot?

CLOWN Faith, if a be not rotten before a die, as we have many pocky   140
      corses nowadays that will scarce hold the laying in, a will last you
      some eight year, or nine year. A tanner will last you nine year.

HAMLET Why he more than another?

CLOWN Why sir, his hide is so tanned with his trade, that a will keep
      out water a great while, and your water is a sore decayer of your   145
      whoreson dead body. Here's a skull now: this skull hath lien you
      i'th'earth three and twenty years.

HAMLET Whose was it?

CLOWN A whoreson mad fellow's it was. Whose do you think it was?

HAMLET Nay I know not.   150

CLOWN A pestilence on him for a mad rogue, a poured a flagon of
      Rhenish on my head once. This same skull sir, was Yorick's skull,
      the king's jester.

HAMLET This?

CLOWN E'en that.   155

HAMLET Let me see. [*Takes the skull.*] Alas poor Yorick! I knew him
      Horatio, a fellow of infinite jest, of most excellent fancy, he hath
      borne me on his back a thousand times – and now how abhorred

---

137 sexton] Sexten Q2; sixteene F   140 Faith] Q2; Ifaith F   140 a ... a] Q2; he ... he F   141 nowadays] now adaies
F; *not in* Q2   141 a] Q2; he F   144 a] Q2; he F   146 this skull] F; *not in* Q2   146–7 hath ... earth] Q2; has laine in the
earth F   147 three and twenty years] F; 23. yeeres Q2   152 This same ... Yorick's skull] *Pope (substantially)*; This same
skull sir, was sir *Yoricks* skull Q2; This same Scull Sir, this same Scull sir, was *Yoricks* Scull F   156 Let me see] F; *not in*
Q2   156 SD *Takes the skull*] Capell (at 154); *not in* Q2, F   158 borne] F; bore Q2   158 now how] Q2; how F

136 **ground** cause. But the Clown takes him to
mean 'land' or 'country'.

140–1 **pocky corses nowadays** diseased
corpses. The phrase reflects the frightening spread
of syphilis through sixteenth-century Europe.

141 **hold the laying in** last through the inter-
ment. (Compare *OED* Lay v^1 86.)

152 **Rhenish** Rhine wine.

152 **This same ... skull** This is an eclectic
reading put together from Q2 and F.

152 **Yorick** The name is so famous that we may
forget that this is where it was born. If Yaughan
stands for Johann, possibly Yorick is Shakespeare's
version of Jörg.

156 **Let me see** So F. Q2 omits, and it is likely
that the phrase was added in preparation for stage-
performance. The phrase is also in Q1.

158–9 **abhorred ... it is** i.e. to think of riding on
the back of one who is now a mouldy skeleton.

in my imagination it is! My gorge rises at it. Here hung those lips
that I have kissed I know not how oft. Where be your gibes now? your   160
gambols, your songs, your flashes of merriment that were wont
to set the table on a roar? Not one now, to mock your own grinning?
Quite chop-fallen? Now get you to my lady's chamber, and tell her,
let her paint an inch thick, to this favour she must come. Make her
laugh at that. – Prithee Horatio, tell me one thing.   165

HORATIO What's that my lord?

HAMLET Dost   thou   think   Alexander   looked   o'   this   fashion
i'th'earth?

HORATIO E'en so.

HAMLET And smelt so? Pah!   *[Puts down the skull]*

HORATIO E'en so my lord.   170

HAMLET To what base uses we may return, Horatio! Why may not
imagination trace the noble dust of Alexander, till a find it stopping
a bunghole?

HORATIO 'Twere to consider too curiously to consider so.

HAMLET No faith, not a jot, but to follow him thither with modesty   175
enough, and likelihood to lead it, as thus: Alexander died, Alexander
was buried, Alexander returneth to dust, the dust is earth, of earth
we make loam, and why of that loam whereto he was converted
might they not stop a beer-barrel?

            Imperious Caesar, dead and turned to clay,   180
            Might stop a hole, to keep the wind away.
            Oh that that earth which kept the world in awe
            Should patch a wall t'expel the winter's flaw!
But soft, but soft! Aside – here comes the king,

---

159 in my imagination it is] Q2; my imagination is F   162 Not one] Q2; No one F   162 grinning] Q2; Ieering F   163
chamber] F; table Q2   167 o'] F; a Q2   169 Pah] Q2; Puh F   169 SD] *Collier; not in* Q2, F   172 a] Q2; he F   174
consider too] Q2; consider: to F   176 as thus] F, *not in* Q2   177 to dust] Q2; into dust F   180 Imperious] Q2, Q1;
Imperiall F   183 winter's] F; waters Q2   184 Aside] F; awhile Q2

159 **gorge** contents of the stomach; i.e. he
retches with disgust.
  160–1 **gibes ... gambols** scoffs, jests, practical
jokes, rather than anything physical.
  162 **to mock ... grinning** i.e. to laugh at the
face you're making, 'grinning' is not a smile but
a facial distortion, generally of anger (a snarl) or
pain, but sometimes of a forced laugh.
  163 **chop-fallen** chap-fallen, with the chops or
chaps (the lower jaw) hanging down – figuratively,
dismayed or dejected.
  164 **paint an inch thick** apply cosmetics,
which Hamlet associates with both female sexuality
and 'the rot of death'. See Farah Karim-Cooper,
Cosmetics in Shakespeare and Renaissance Drama
(Edinburgh University Press, 2006), 194–5.
  164 **favour** appearance.

167 **Alexander** Alexander the Great, fourth-
century Macedonian conqueror of Greece and
lands stretching west and east.
  173 **bunghole** pouring hole in a cask or barrel.
  174 **too curiously** with excessive care, over-
elaborately.
  175 **modesty** moderation.
  178 **loam** a mortar or plaster made of clay and
straw, etc.
  180 **Imperious** So Q2 and Q1. F has 'Imperiall'.
Shakespeare uses both words interchangeably.
  183 **flaw** squall.
  184 **but soft! Aside** So F. Q2 has 'but soft
awhile'. Hamlet has obvious reasons both for moving aside and for choosing his own time to confront
the king; 'soft!' urges caution; see note to 3.1.88.

The queen, the courtiers.

Enter CLAUDIUS, GERTRUDE, LAERTES, *and a coffin,* [*with* PRIEST] *and*
LORDS *attendant*

                      Who is this they follow?   185
And with such maimèd rites? This doth betoken
The corse they follow did with desperate hand
Fordo it own life. 'Twas of some estate.
Couch we awhile and mark.   [*Retiring with Horatio*]
LAERTES What ceremony else?   190
HAMLET That is Laertes, a very noble youth. Mark.
LAERTES What ceremony else?
PRIEST Her obsequies have been as far enlarged
        As we have warranty. Her death was doubtful,
        And but that great command o'ersways the order,   195
        She should in ground unsanctified have lodged
        Till the last trumpet. For charitable prayers,
        Shards, flints, and pebbles should be thrown on her.
        Yet here she is allowed her virgin crants,
        Her maiden strewments, and the bringing home   200
        Of bell and burial.
LAERTES Must there no more be done?
PRIEST   No more be done.
We should profane the service of the dead

---

185 SD] *Enter K. Q. Laertes and the corse* Q2 *(margin)*; *Enter King, Queene, Laertes, and a Coffin, with Lords attendant* F *(after
king 184)* **185 this**] Q2; *that* F **188 of some**] Q2; *some* F **189** SD] *Capell; not in* Q2, F **193, 202** SH PRIEST] F;
Doct. Q2 **196 have**] F; *been* Q2 **197 prayers**] Q2; *praier* F **198 Shards**] F; *not in* Q2 **199 crants**] Q2; *Rites* F

185 SD Q2 gives us 'the corse' rather than a coffin
(Q1 gives a coffin). Neither Q2 nor F provides the
priest (Q1 does). The priest is '*Doct.*' in Q2 speech
headings. Dover Wilson argues that Shakespeare
had in mind a Protestant 'Doctor of Divinity'
(*What Happens in 'Hamlet'*, 69).
  186 maimèd mutilated, truncated.
  188 Fordo Destroy.
  188 it its. See note to 1.2.216.
  188 some estate considerable social
importance.
  191 Couch we Let us conceal ourselves ('couch'
suggests stooping or crouching to take cover).
  191 That is Laertes On the inconsistencies of
Horatio's familiarity at court, see note to 1.2.176.
But Wilson points out in his edition that Horatio
and Laertes have not met on stage.

  194 warranty authorization.
  194 Her death i.e. the manner of her death. For
questions surrounding Ophelia's death as a suicide,
see Introduction, 48–9.
  195 great command the commands of great
ones.
  195 the order the regular proceeding.
  197 For Instead of.
  198 Shards Broken pottery.
  199 crants garlands hung up at funerals, especially those of young girls. So Q2. F has 'rites'.
  200 strewments Another most unusual word,
meaning, presumably, flowers strewn on a coffin.
See 213 below.
  200–1 bringing home / Of bell and burial
bringing her to her last home with bell-ringing and
proper burial.

To sing sage requiem and such rest to her
As to peace-parted souls.

LAERTES   Lay her i'th'earth,   205
And from her fair and unpolluted flesh
May violets spring. I tell thee, churlish priest,
A ministering angel shall my sister be
When thou liest howling.

HAMLET   What, the fair Ophelia!

GERTRUDE Sweets to the sweet, farewell.   [*Scattering flowers*]   210
I hoped thou shouldst have been my Hamlet's wife.
I thought thy bride-bed to have decked, sweet maid,
And not t'have strewed thy grave.

LAERTES   Oh treble woe
Fall ten times treble on that cursèd head
Whose wicked deed thy most ingenious sense   215
Deprived thee of. Hold off the earth awhile
Till I have caught her once more in mine arms.

                    Leaps in the grave
Now pile your dust upon the quick and dead
Till of this flat a mountain you have made
T'o'ertop old Pelion or the skyish head   220
Of blue Olympus.

HAMLET [*Advancing*]   What is he whose grief
Bears such an emphasis? whose phrase of sorrow
Conjures the wandering stars, and makes them stand
Like wonder-wounded hearers? This is I,

---

204 sage] F; a Q2   210 SD] *Johnson*; not in Q2, F   213 t'have] F; haue Q2   213 treble woe] Q2; terrible woer F   214 treble] F; double Q2   217 SD] F; not in Q2   220 T'o'ertop] To'retop Q2; to o're top F   221 SD *Advancing*] *Capell*; not in Q2, F   221 grief] Q2; gricfes F   223 Conjures] Q2; Coniure F

204 sage requiem solemn funeral music. Many editors prefer Q2's 'a' to F's 'sage', but the word can mean 'grave' as well as 'wise'.

204 such rest i.e. invoke or pray for such rest.

205 peace-parted souls those who have died a natural death.

215 most … sense excellent intelligence (?).

217 caught her … in mine arms Since Q2 gives 'a corse' rather than 'a coffin' in the SD at 185 it may be that Shakespeare thought of a bier rather than a closed coffin, but Q1 confirms that the scene as played used a coffin, sealed or not. There is no evidence that Laertes raises the corpse, as in many productions he does.

220 Pelion A mountain in Thessaly. In Greek myth, giants attempted to climb to heaven by putting Pelion on top of Ossa.

221 Olympus The mountain in Thessaly where in Greek myth the gods lived, 'blue' because it reaches the sky.

222 emphasis … phrase Hamlet accuses Laertes of employing a rhetorician's 'emphasis' – vigorous or forceful expression – and of expressing sorrow in a conventional 'phrase', or formal style.

223 wandering stars planets.

224 wonder-wounded struck with amazement.

Hamlet the Dane.

LAERTES   The devil take thy soul. [*Grappling with him*]   225
HAMLET Thou pray'st not well.
I prithee take thy fingers from my throat,
For though I am not splenitive and rash,
Yet have I in me something dangerous
Which let thy wisdom fear. Hold off thy hand.   230
CLAUDIUS Pluck them asunder.
GERTRUDE   Hamlet, Hamlet!
ALL   Gentlemen!
HORATIO Good my lord, be quiet.
                    [*The Attendants part them*].
HAMLET Why, I will fight with him upon this theme
Until my eyelids will no longer wag.
GERTRUDE O my son, what theme?   235
HAMLET I loved Ophelia; forty thousand brothers
Could not with all their quantity of love
Make up my sum. What wilt thou do for her?

---

225 SD *Grappling with him*] *Rowe; not in* Q2, F   228 For though] Q2; Sir though F   228 splenitive] spleenatiue Q2,
F   228 and] F; *not in* Q2   229 in me something] Q2; something in me F, Q1   230 wisdom] wisedome Q2, Q1; wisensse
F*(uncorrected)*; wisenesse F*(corrected)*   230 Hold off] Q2, Q1; Away F   231 ALL Gentlemen] Q2; *not in* F   232 SH
HORATIO] *Hora.* Q2; *Gen.* F   232 SD] *Rowe; not in* Q2, F

---

225 **Hamlet the Dane** Hamlet asserts his title to the throne: see note to 1.1.15.

225 SD *Grappling* ... Q1 has Hamlet jump at this point into the grave, where the two men struggle ('*Hamlet leapes in after Leartes*'). Q2 and F are silent, so it is also possible that Laertes is meant to scramble out of the grave and rush upon the man who killed his father.

An anonymous elegy on Burbage (who died in 1618) says, 'Oft have I seen him leap into the grave / Suiting the person which he seemed to have / Of a sad lover with so true an eye / That there I would have sworn he meant to die' (Edwin Nungezer, *A Dictionary of Actors and of Other Persons Associated with the Public Representation of Plays in England Before 1642*, reprint (New York: Greenwood Press, 1968), 74 (spelling modernized). This is assumed to refer to Hamlet, but the sad lover meaning to die sounds more like Romeo. Granville-Barker, in

Prefaces, argued eloquently that Shakespeare intended Laertes to leap out of the grave and attack Hamlet, while Gurr and Ichikawa describe the important characterological and symbolic nature of Hamlet's jump in 'The Early Staging of *Hamlet*', 153–4.

228 **splenitive** quick-tempered, irascible.

230 **wisdom** So Q2. F's 'wiseness' is an attractive reading here, conveying a certain contempt or irony. '[W]isdom' is supported by Q1.

234 **wag** Simply 'move' or 'open and close'. Hamlet means he will fight while he has any muscular strength left, even if only to blink.

236–8 **I loved Ophelia ... my sum** Given Hamlet's previous treatment of Ophelia, these lines seem insensitive (Laertes was pompous and overbearing in 1.3, but he never behaved as cruelly to her as Hamlet did). MacDonald says 'Perhaps this is the speech in all the play of which it is most difficult to get into a sympathetic comprehension.'

CLAUDIUS Oh he is mad Laertes.

GERTRUDE For love of God forbear him. 240

HAMLET 'Swounds, show me what thou't do.
        Woo't weep, woo't fight, woo't fast, woo't tear thyself?
        Woo't drink up eisel, eat a crocodile?
        I'll do't. Dost thou come here to whine,
        To outface me with leaping in her grave? 245
        Be buried quick with her, and so will I.
        And if thou prate of mountains, let them throw
        Millions of acres on us, till our ground,
        Singeing his pate against the burning zone,
        Make Ossa like a wart. Nay, and thou'lt mouth, 250
        I'll rant as well as thou.

GERTRUDE   This is mere madness,
        And thus awhile the fit will work on him;
        Anon, as patient as the female dove
        When that her golden couplets are disclosed,
        His silence will sit drooping.

HAMLET   Hear you sir, 255
        What is the reason that you use me thus?
        I loved you ever – but it is no matter.
        Let Hercules himself do what he may,
        The cat will mew, and dog will have his day.   *Exit*

CLAUDIUS I pray thee good Horatio wait upon him. 260

                                  Exit Horatio

---

241 'Swounds] Q2; Come F   241 thou't] th'owt Q2; thou'lt F   242 woo't fast] Q2; *not in* F   243 eisel] *Theobald²*; E.sill Q2; *Esile* F   244 Dost thou] F; doost Q2   251 SH GERTRUDE] *Quee.* Q2; *Kin.* F   252 thus] F; this Q2   259–60 SD [*Exit / Exit Horatio*] *Pope; Exit Hamlet / and Horatio* Q2; *Exit* F*(259)*   260 pray thee] Q2; pray you F

242 **Woo't** Colloquial for 'wilt thou'.

243 **eisel** vinegar (to increase his bitterness).

243 **eat a crocodile** i.e. to increase the flow of hypocritical tears (the false crying of the crocodile is proverbial, see Tilley C831).

249 **the burning zone** the sun's orbit between the tropics.

250 **Ossa** See note to 220 above.

250 **and if.**

251–5 **This is mere madness … drooping** F gives this speech to Claudius, most inappropriately, and is supported by Q1.

254 **her golden couplets are disclosed** 'The pigeon lays two eggs, and the young, when

disclosed or hatched … are covered with yellow down' (Dowden).

255 **silence … drooping** i.e. his quietness resembles that of the patient dove not moving from her young and 'drooping' with lack of food for herself.

258–9 **Let Hercules … day** One of Hamlet's riddles. If, in his analogy, Laertes is figured by the cat and dog, then the rough translation is 'even Hercules could not stop Laertes from having his petty triumph'. If Laertes is figured by Hercules, and Hamlet by the cat and dog, then 'Laertes can carry on, but Hamlet will eventually get his turn.'

(*To Laertes*) Strengthen your patience in our last night's
    speech;
We'll put the matter to the present push. –
Good Gertrude, set some watch over your son. –
This grave shall have a living monument.
An hour of quiet shortly shall we see,   265
Till then in patience our proceeding be.

                         Exeunt

[5.2] *Enter* HAMLET *and* HORATIO

HAMLET So much for this sir, now shall you see the other.
    You do remember all the circumstance?
HORATIO Remember it my lord!
HAMLET Sir, in my heart there was a kind of fighting
    That would not let me sleep. Methought I lay   5
    Worse than the mutines in the bilboes. Rashly,
    And praised be rashness for it – let us know,
    Our indiscretion sometime serves us well
    When our deep plots do pall, and that should learn us
    There's a divinity that shapes our ends,   10

---

265 shortly] F; thirtie Q2 *(uncorrected)*; thereby Q2 *(corrected)*   **266** Till] F; Tell Q2   **Act 5, Scene 2**   **5.2]** *Rowe*   **1** shall you see] Q2; let me see F   **5** Methought] me thought F; my thought Q2   **6** bilboes] Bilboes F; bilbo Q2   **7** praised] praysd Q2; praise F   **8** sometime] Q2; sometimes F   **9** deep] Q2; deare F   **9** pall] Q2 *(uncorrected)*; paule F; fall Q2 *(corrected)*   **9** learn] Q2; teach F

261 in our last night's speech i.e. by remembering what we planned last night.

262 present push immediate operation.

264 living enduring – with a grim secondary meaning that Hamlet's death will be the memorial for Ophelia.

Act 5, Scene 2

1 So much … other A mid-conversation entry, 'this' referring presumably to the first part of the story and 'the other' to the rest of it.

2 circumstance details.

6 the mutines in the bilboes mutineers in their shackles.

6–7 Rashly … rashness 'rash' (etc.) in

Shakespeare means as often 'hasty', 'sudden', as it does 'unconsidered' or 'ill-advised'. The sense here is of a sudden, impulsive act without forethought.

7 let us know let us recognize, acknowledge.

8 indiscretion want of prudence and forethought (rather than a misguided act).

9 pall weaken, grow flat and stale (like wine that has gone off).

9 learn teach.

10–11 a divinity … we will i.e. there is a higher power in control of us, directing us towards our destination, however much we have believed in and asserted (often clumsily) our own power and control.

                    Rough-hew them how we will –
HORATIO   That is most certain.
HAMLET Up from my cabin,
            My sea-gown scarfed about me, in the dark
            Groped I to find out them, had my desire,
            Fingered their packet, and in fine withdrew   15
            To mine own room again, making so bold,
            My fears forgetting manners, to unseal
            Their grand commission; where I found, Horatio –
            O royal knavery! – an exact command,
            Larded with many several sorts of reasons,   20
            Importing Denmark's health, and England's too,
            With ho! such bugs and goblins in my life,
            That on the supervise, no leisure bated,
            No, not to stay the grinding of the axe,
            My head should be struck off.
HORATIO   Is't possible?   25
HAMLET Here's the commission, read it at more leisure.
            But wilt thou hear now how I did proceed?
HORATIO I beseech you.
HAMLET Being thus benetted round with villainies,
            Or I could make a prologue to my brains,   30
            They had begun the play. I sat me down,
            Devised a new commission, wrote it fair.
            I once did hold it, as our statists do,
            A baseness to write fair, and laboured much
            How to forget that learning; but sir, now   35

---

17 unseal] F; vnfold Q2   19 O] Oh F; A Q2   20 reasons] Q2; reason F   27 hear now] Q2; heare me F   29 villainies]
Capell; villainy *Theobald²;* villaines Q2; Villaines F   30 Or] Q2; Ere F

---

11 **Rough-hew** Give a preliminary shape to, make a first attempt or draft (*OED* 1, 2). A sense of crude botching is provided by Florio in a definition of *Abbozzare*: 'to rough-hew or cast any first draught, to bungle up ill-favouredly'. (See NV.)

13 **sea-gown** seaman's coat of coarse cloth, a duffle-coat.

13 **scarfed** wrapped loosely.

15 **Fingered** Filched, stole.

15 **in fine** in conclusion.

17 **forgetting** neglecting; i.e. causing him to forget.

20 **Larded** See 4.5.37.

21 **Importing** Appertaining to.

22 **bugs ... life** fantastic threats to be feared from my continued existence.

23 **supervise** viewing (of the commission).

23 **no leisure bated** i.e. no free time was to abate, or delay, the execution.

24 **grinding** sharpening.

29 **benetted round** i.e. trapped.

29 **villainies** Both F and Q2 agree in reading 'villains'. But this leaves the line metrically lame, and many editors find the abstract 'villanies' more apt here.

30 **Or** Before, ere. See note to 1.2.147.

30–1 **Or I could ... begun the play** i.e. his brains had put a plan into motion before he consciously or willingly gave them directions.

33 **statists** statesmen.

34 **baseness** something befitting people of low rank.

It did me yeoman's service. Wilt thou know
Th'effect of what I wrote?
HORATIO   Ay good my lord.
HAMLET An earnest conjuration from the king,
        As England was his faithful tributary,
        As love between them like the palm might flourish,   40
        As peace should still her wheaten garland wear,
        And stand a comma 'tween their amities,
        And many suchlike as-es of great charge,
        That on the view and knowing of these contents,
        Without debatement further, more, or less,   45
        He should those bearers put to sudden death,
        Not shriving time allowed.
HORATIO   How was this sealed?
HAMLET Why, even in that was heaven ordinant.
        I had my father's signet in my purse,
        Which was the model of that Danish seal;   50
        Folded the writ up in the form of th'other,
        Subscribed it, gave't th'impression, placed it safely,
        The changeling never known. Now, the next day
        Was our sea-fight, and what to this was sequent
        Thou know'st already.   55
HORATIO So Guildenstern and Rosencrantz go to't.
HAMLET Why man, they did make love to this employment.
        They are not near my conscience. Their defeat

37 Th'effect] Q2; The effects F   40 like] Q2; as F   40 might] Q2; should F   43 as-es] Assis F; as sir Q2   44 know-ing] Q2; know F   46 those] Q2; the F   48 ordinant] Q2; ordinate F   51 in the form of th'other] Q2; in forme of the other F   52 Subscribed] Subscrib'd F; Subscribe Q2   54 sequent] Q2; sement F   55 know'st] F; knowest Q2   57 Why ... employment] F; *not in* Q2   58 defeat] Q2; debate F

36 **yeoman's service** the service of a faithful attendant ('yeoman' in its earlier sense of a servant in a royal household).
38 **conjuration** solemn entreaty.
39 **As England ... tributary** See 3.1.163–4.
42 **a comma 'tween their amities** An odd phrase, but the language is meant to be affected. *OED* points to the definition of a comma given by Puttenham (*Art of English Poesy*, 1589, II.iv) as 'the shortest pause or intermission' between sections of speech. So the kingdoms are meant to be as near together as separate institutions can be, and what is between them is peace, not discord.
43 **charge** burden (punning on 'as-es' = asses).
45 **debatement further, more, or less** more discussion. Hamlet continues to ridicule official verbiage.
47 **shriving time** time for confession and absolution. Compare Hamlet's attitude to the death of Claudius, 3.3.73–95.
48 **ordinant** directing.
49 **signet** seal, ring with a seal.
50 **model of that Danish seal** A copy of the official seal of Denmark on the commission which Hamlet has handed to Horatio (26 above). Copy here does not imply something that comes after.
52 **Subscribed it** Signed it (with Claudius's name).
57 **Why man ... employment** This line is found only in F. See Textual Analysis, 260–4.
58 **defeat** destruction. Compare 2.2.523.

Does by their own insinuation grow.
'Tis dangerous when the baser nature comes   60
Between the pass and fell incensèd points
Of mighty opposites.

HORATIO   Why, what a king is this!

HAMLET Does it not, think thee, stand me now upon –
He that hath killed my king, and whored my mother,
Popped in between th'election and my hopes,   65
Thrown out his angle for my proper life,
And with such cozenage – is't not perfect conscience
To quit him with this arm? And is't not to be damned
To let this canker of our nature come
In further evil?   70

HORATIO It must be shortly known to him from England
What is the issue of the business there.

HAMLET It will be short. The interim's mine,
And a man's life's no more than to say 'one'.
But I am very sorry, good Horatio,   75
That to Laertes I forgot myself,

---

59 Does] Q2; Doth F   63 think thee] Q2; thinkst thee F   68–80 To quit ... comes here] F; *not in* Q2   73–5 It ...
mine, / And ... 'one'. / But ... Horatio,] *Hanmer;* It ... short, / The ... no more / Then ... *Horatio,* F   73 interim's] F;
interim is *Hanmer*

59 insinuation coming between Hamlet and
Claudius.

60 baser inferior in rank. See note to 34 above.

61 pass thrust. Compare 4.7.137.

61–2 pass ... opposites Hendiadys and transferred epithet. The fell (deadly) pass of the sword-
points of incensèd opposites (opponents).

63 Does it not ... stand me now upon Is it not
now incumbent upon me.

63 think thee bethink thee, please consider; F's
'thinkst thee' is a difficult impersonal construction,
meaning 'does it appear to thee'.

65 Popped in This is meant to be contemptuous, though not necessarily comic. For Hamlet's
accusation, compare 3.4.99–101.

66 angle fishing-line.

66 my proper life my very life.

67 cozenage cheating, fraud.

67 is't not perfect conscience is it not divinely
sanctioned.

68–80 This whole passage is absent from Q2. See

Textual Analysis, 263.

68 quit requite, punish.

68 is't not to be damned See Textual Analysis,
263–4. Hamlet sees a prospect of damnation not,
as before, in obeying a possibly fraudulent ghost
(2.2.556), or in suicide (3.1.78), but in failing to
rid the world of the evil represented by Claudius.

69 canker of our nature a cancerous growth in
humankind.

69–70 come / In enter into.

71–2 Horatio does not answer Hamlet directly,
but warns him that Claudius will soon hear of the
death of Rosencrantz and Guildenstern and is then
bound to act swiftly and decisively against Hamlet.

73 The interim's mine Deeply ironic, in view
of the plot against his life which has been prepared by
Claudius and Laertes, and which is now about to be
sprung. Interim = two syllables; the line is a foot short.

74 And a man's life ... one And in any case
one's whole life is only a short space of time. One's
death is never very far away.

For by the image of my cause, I see
The portraiture of his. I'll court his favours.
But sure the bravery of his grief did put me
Into a towering passion.

HORATIO   Peace, who comes here?   80

Enter young OSRIC

OSRIC Your lordship is right welcome back to Denmark.

HAMLET I humbly thank you sir. – Dost know this water-fly?

HORATIO No my good lord.

HAMLET Thy state is the more gracious, for 'tis a vice to know him.
He hath much land and fertile; let a beast be lord of beasts, and   85
his crib shall stand at the king's mess. 'Tis a chough, but as I say,
spacious in the possession of dirt.

OSRIC Sweet lord, if your lordship were at leisure, I should impart a
thing to you from his majesty.

HAMLET I will receive it sir with all diligence of spirit. Put your bonnet   90
to his right use, 'tis for the head.

OSRIC I thank your lordship, it is very hot.

HAMLET No believe me, 'tis very cold, the wind is northerly.

OSRIC It is indifferent cold my lord, indeed.

HAMLET But yet methinks it is very sultry and hot for my complexion.   95

OSRIC Exceedingly my lord, it is very sultry, as 'twere – I cannot tell
how. But my lord, his majesty bade me signify to you that a has
laid a great wager on your head. Sir, this is the matter –

---

78 court] *Rowe;* count F   80 SD *Enter young* OSRIC] F; *Enter a Courtier* Q2   81 SH OSRIC] *Osr.* F; *Cour.* Q2 *(& so throughout)*   82 humbly] F; humble Q2   86 say] Q2; saw F   88 lordship] Q2; friendship F   90 sir] Q2; *not in* F   90 Put] F; *not in* Q2   92 it is] Q2; 'tis F   95 But yet] Q2; *not in* F   95 sultry] soultry F; sully Q2   95 for] F; or Q2   97 But] F; *not in* Q2   97 a has] Q2; he ha's F

77–8 **by the image … of his** i.e. I recognize in my situation the essential features of his.

79 **bravery** extravagant display.

80 SD **young** OSRIC '*young Osricke*' (F) is only '*a Courtier*' in Q2. F brings forward his name from 171 and 231 below (where Q2 gives it as '*young Ostricke*').

82 **water-fly** 'the proper emblem of a busy trifler' (Johnson).

85–6 **let a beast … mess** i.e. if you own a lot of livestock, even though you are an animal yourself, you'll have a place at the king's table; 'crib' = manger.

86 **chough** Pronounced 'chuff'. A big black cliff bird, but the name seems to have been used for the jackdaw as well, and that is probably what is meant here, since the jackdaw chatters. Jenkins has revived the old arguments of Caldecott and Furness (see NV) that the word should be 'chuff', a country bumpkin, a coarse, rough fellow.

90–1 **Put your … use** Osric has taken his off in deference to Hamlet, who now tells him to put it back on.

91 **his** its.

94 **indifferent** moderately.

95 **complexion** temperament.

HAMLET I beseech you remember.

[HAMLET *moves him to put on his hat*]

OSRIC Nay good my lord, for my ease in good faith. Sir, [here is newly   100
come to court Laertes; believe me an absolute gentleman, full of
most excellent differences, of very soft society and great showing.
Indeed, to speak feelingly of him, he is the card or calendar of
gentry, for you shall find in him the continent of what part a
gentleman would see.   105

HAMLET Sir, his definement suffers no perdition in you, though I know
to divide him inventorially would dozy th'arithmetic of memory,
and yet but yaw neither in respect of his quick sail. But in the verity
of extolment, I take him to be a soul of great article, and his infusion
of such dearth and rareness as, to make true diction of him, his   110
semblable is his mirror, and who else would trace him, his umbrage,
nothing more.

OSRIC Your lordship speaks most infallibly of him.

HAMLET The concernancy, sir? Why do we wrap the gentleman in our
more rawer breath?   115

OSRIC Sir?

HORATIO Is't not possible to understand in another tongue? You will
to't sir, really.

---

99 SD] *Johnson; not in* Q2, F   100 good my lord] Q2; in good Faith F   100 my ease] Q2; mine ease F   100–25 here
is … Well sir] Q2; *not in* F   101 gentleman] Q 1611; gentlemen Q2   103 feelingly] Q 1611; fellingly Q2*(corrected)*;
sellingly Q2*(uncorrected)*   107 dozy] *Kittredge;* dosie Q2*(uncorrected);* dazzie Q2*(corrected);* dizzie Q 1611   108 yaw]
Q2*(uncorrected);* raw Q2*(corrected)*   118 to't] too't Q2*(uncorrected);* doo't Q2*(corrected)*

99 remember *OED* (1d) cleverly associates this
with the rather odd use of 'remember your courtesy'
or 'be remembered' to request someone to put on
his hat or cover his head. Perhaps this is right; but
perhaps Hamlet just asks him to remember what he
has said.

100–25 F here imposes a swingeing cut. Like the
cutting out of the Lord's part, 171–82 below, this is
clearly an attempt to shorten this very long build-up
to the final scene by cutting out material not essential to the plot. These lines are almost entirely fun at
the expense of Osric's diction.

102 excellent differences i.e. he excels in
a variety of different accomplishments. Delius suggested the ingenious gloss 'different excellences'
(NV).

102 soft society easy sociability.

102 great showing excellent appearance.

103 card or calendar map or standard.

104 gentry gentility.

104–5 the continent … would see the embo-
diment or container of any quality to which
a gentleman would aspire.

106 perdition loss.

107 inventorially by means of a detailed
account of his qualities.

107 dozy make dizzy. Kittredge restored this
quite common variant of 'dizzy' in 1939.

108 yaw swing off course.

108 neither after all.

108 in respect of in comparison with.

108–9 in the verity of extolment to praise him
truthfully.

109 of great article i.e. there would be many
articles to list in his inventory.

109 his infusion what is poured into him, his
nature.

110 dearth dearness, high price.

111 trace him follow him closely.

111 umbrage shadow.

114 The concernancy sir? What's all this
about? The word seems to be Hamlet's invention.

114–15 wrap … breath i.e. attempt to dress
him in the crudity of language.

117–18 Is't not possible … really
Paradoxically, Horatio's interjection is more

HAMLET What imports the nomination of this gentleman?

OSRIC Of Laertes?   120

HORATIO His purse is empty already, all's golden words are spent.

HAMLET Of him sir.

OSRIC I know you are not ignorant –

HAMLET I would you did sir, yet in faith if you did, it would not much
approve me. Well sir?]   125

OSRIC You are not ignorant of what excellence Laertes is.

[HAMLET I dare not confess that, lest I should compare with him in
excellence, but to know a man well were to know himself.

OSRIC I mean sir for his weapon; but in the imputation laid on him
by them, in his meed he's unfellowed.]   130

HAMLET What's his weapon?

OSRIC Rapier and dagger.

HAMLET That's two of his weapons, but well.

OSRIC The king sir hath wagered with him six Barbary horses, against
the which he has impawned, as I take it, six French rapiers and   135
poniards, with their assigns, as girdle, hangers, and so. Three of
the carriages in faith are very dear to fancy, very responsive to the
hilts, most delicate carriages, and of very liberal conceit.

HAMLET What call you the carriages?

HORATIO I knew you must be edified by the margent ere you had done.   140

---

126 Laertes is.] Q2; *Laertes* is at his weapon. F   127–30 HAMLET I dare … unfellowed] Q2; *not in* F   129 his weapon]
Q 1676; this weapon Q2   134 king … wagered] Q2; sir King ha's wag'd F   135 he has impawned] hee has impaund Q2;
he impon'd F   136 hangers] F; hanger Q2   136 and so] Q2; or so F   140 HORATIO I knew … done] Q2; *not in* F

obscure than the ridiculous colloquy which he
interrupts. Some think he asks Osric if he can't
understand his own jargon when another person
speaks it. Perhaps it is an appeal to start again in
a simpler language. 'You will to't' may mean (to
Osric) 'You will get there eventually.'

119 **What imports … gentleman?** What is the
purpose of naming this gentleman?

124–5 **not much approve me** i.e. it would be
little to my credit to have such a testimony from
you.

127–8 **I dare … know himself** If Hamlet were
to admit Laertes's excellence, he would have to
claim that same excellence for himself.

129–30 **in the imputation … by them** in what
people attribute to him.

130 **meed** merit (*OED* 3).

133 **but well** but never mind.

134 **Barbary horses** Arab horses, much prized,
and soon to be bred in England by James I.

135 **impawned** wagered (F's spelling,
'impon'd', may indicate pronunciation). This is
now Laertes's stake set up against the king's.

136 **poniards** daggers.

136 **assigns** accessories.

136 **hangers** the straps to hold the sword,
attached to the girdle or sword-belt.

136 **and so** and so on.

137 **dear to fancy** i.e. they please one's taste.

137 **very responsive** well adjusted to the hilts,
or handle.

138 **carriages** loop attached to the belt for holding a sword (see 141).

138 **liberal conceit** imaginative design.

140 **edified by the margent** made wiser by
a marginal gloss.

OSRIC The carriages sir are the hangers.

HAMLET The phrase would be more germane to the matter if we could
carry a cannon by our sides; I would it might be hangers till then.
But on, six Barbary horses against six French swords, their assigns,
and three liberal-conceited carriages – that's the French bet against   145
the Danish. Why is this impawned, as you call it?

OSRIC The king sir, hath laid sir, that in a dozen passes between yourself
and him, he shall not exceed you three hits. He hath laid on twelve
for nine. And it would come to immediate trial, if your lordship
would vouchsafe the answer.   150

HAMLET How if I answer no?

OSRIC I mean my lord, the opposition of your person in trial.

HAMLET Sir, I will walk here in the hall. If it please his majesty, it is
the breathing time of day with me. Let the foils be brought, the
gentleman willing, and the king hold his purpose, I will win for   155
him and I can. If not, I will gain nothing but my shame and the
odd hits.

OSRIC Shall I redeliver you e'en so?

HAMLET To this effect sir, after what flourish your nature will.

OSRIC I commend my duty to your lordship.   160

HAMLET Yours, yours.

                                                            [*Exit Osric*]

He does well to commend it himself, there are no tongues else for's
turn.

HORATIO This lapwing runs away with the shell on his head.

HAMLET A did comply with his dug before a sucked it. Thus has he,   165

---

141 carriages] F; carriage Q2   143 a cannon] Q2; Cannon F   143 it might be] F; it be might Q2 *(uncorrected)*; it be Q2
(corrected)   145 bet] Q2; but F   146 impawned] impon'd F; all Q2   147 laid sir] Q2; laid F   147 yourself] Q2; you
F   148–9 laid … nine] Q2; one twelue for mine F   149 it would] Q2; that would F   153 it is] Q2; 'tis F   156 and
I can] Q2; if I can F   156 I will] Q2; Ile F   158 redeliver … so] F; deliuer you so so Q2   161 Yours, yours] F; Yours
Q2   161 SD] *Capell, following Rowe; not in* Q2, F   162 He does] F; doo's Q2   163 turn] Q2; tongue F   165 A did] Q2;
He did F   165 comply] F; so sir Q2 *(corrected)*; sir Q2 *(uncorrected)*   165 a sucked] Q2; hee suck't F   165 has] Q2; had
F

142–3 **The phrase … sides** The term 'carriages' (= wheeled vehicles) would be more relevant
or appropriate if they were using large ammunition
like a cannon.

147–9 **The king sir … twelve for nine**
The terms of the bet are confusing and have puzzled
editors since Johnson. There are to be a maximum of
twelve bouts ('a dozen passes'). The bet, that Laertes
will not lead by more than three hits, can be construed
in two ways. Either Laertes must win three consecutive
bouts, or he must win three more bouts than Hamlet
out of the twelve, so that he wins as soon as he reaches
eight hits. Hamlet wins with five hits. 'He hath laid on
twelve for nine', which has been taken to mean that
Laertes must win twelve (rather than eight) bouts, or
that Laertes ('he') negotiated for a maximum of twelve
rather than nine bouts, may also be understood as the

'odds' on each of the combatants. See Evert
Sprinchorn. 'The Odds on Hamlet', *The American
Statistician* 24.5 (1970), 14–17.

150 **vouchsafe the answer** offer yourself as an
opponent.

154 **breathing** exercising.

158 **redeliver you** report back what you say.

159 **after what flourish** conforming to whatever embellishment.

160 **commend my duty** See note to 1.5.184.
Hamlet takes up the routine word 'commend' in its
meaning 'recommend'.

164 **This lapwing … head** A proverb for juve-
nile forwardness (Tilley L69).

165 **did comply with his dug** was polite to his
mother's (or his nurse's) nipple. '[C]omply' is given
in F; Q2 has 'so sir'.

and many more of the same bevy that I know the drossy age dotes
on, only got the tune of the time and outward habit of encounter,
a kind of yesty collection, which carries them through and through
the most fanned and winnowed opinions; and do but blow them
to their trial, the bubbles are out.   170

[*Enter a* LORD

LORD My lord, his majesty commended him to you by young Osric,
who brings back to him that you attend him in the hall. He sends to
know if your pleasure hold to play with Laertes, or that you will
take longer time.

HAMLET I am constant to my purposes, they follow the king's pleasure.   175
If his fitness speaks, mine is ready; now or whensoever, provided
I be so able as now.

LORD The king and queen, and all, are coming down.

HAMLET In happy time.

LORD The queen desires you to use some gentle entertainment to   180
Laertes, before you fall to play.

HAMLET She well instructs me.]

[*Exit Lord*]

HORATIO You will lose, my lord.

HAMLET I do not think so. Since he went into France, I have been in

---

166 many] Q2; mine F   **166** bevy] Beauy F; breede Q2   **167** outward] F; out of an Q2   **168** yesty] F; histy Q2   **169**
fanned and winnowed] *Warburton;* prophane and trennowed Q2; fond and winnowed F   **170** trial] Q2; tryalls F   **170-**
82 *Enter a* LORD ... instructs me] Q2; *not in* F   **171** Osric] *Rowe;* Ostricke Q2   **182** SD] *Theobald²; not in* Q2   **183** lose]
Q2; lose this wager F

166 the drossy age the people of these rubbishy times.

167 got the tune of the time has learned to perform according to the tastes of the time. The sense of external show versus internal emptiness is repeated in 'outward habit of encounter'.

168 yesty collection yeasty, frothy mixture or brew (see notes to 3.2.233, 4.7.143).

168 carries them through allows them (the bevy) to pass through.

169 fanned and winnowed Synonyms for sifted (as in grain that has had the chaff blown off). '[F]anned' is Warburton's emendation for F's 'fond'; Q2 has 'profane', which would shift the meaning of the phrase to 'vulgar and select'.

169–70 blow ... bubbles are out The image is of a frothy mass being refined into bubbles which can be blown away. The superficial qualities of people like Osric take them through the society of superior people, but they cannot last, and when they are tested, their hollowness reveals itself.

170 SD–182 SD Enter a LORD ... This passage is not found in F, which thus dispenses with an additional character not necessary to the play.

171 commended him to you sent his compliments to you (see note to 1.5.184).

175 I am constant to my purposes A grim double meaning here: Hamlet must also be thinking of his deeper resolve.

176 If his fitness speaks When his convenience names a time.

179 In happy time It is an opportune time.

180 use ... entertainment give a courteous reception. The queen's request complicates Hamlet's apology to Laertes at 198, as it makes unclear whether Hamlet is motivated by his own regret (5.2.75–7), his mother's insistence, or some combination of the two.

184 Since ... I have been Hamlet's claim to have been practising seems to contradict 2.2.280–1, where he says he has 'forgone' gentlemanly exercises. But the earlier statement may have been a ruse for Rosencrantz and Guildenstern.

continual practice; I shall win at the odds. But thou wouldst not   185
think how ill all's here about my heart – but it is no matter.

HORATIO Nay good my lord –

HAMLET It is but foolery, but it is such a kind of gaingiving as would
perhaps trouble a woman.

HORATIO If your mind dislike anything, obey it. I will forestall their   190
repair hither, and say you are not fit.

HAMLET Not a whit, we defy augury. There is special providence in
the fall of a sparrow. If it be now, 'tis not to come; if it be not to
come, it will be now; if it be not now, yet it will come – the
readiness is all. Since no man of aught he leaves knows, what is't   195
to leave betimes? Let be.

A table prepared, with flagons of wine on it. Trumpets, Drums and Officers
with cushions. Enter CLAUDIUS, GERTRUDE, LAERTES *and* LORDS, *with*
other Attendants with foils, daggers and gauntlets

CLAUDIUS Come Hamlet, come and take this hand from me.

[*Claudius puts Laertes's hand into Hamlet's*]

HAMLET Give me your pardon sir, I've done you wrong;
But pardon't as you are a gentleman.
This presence knows,   200
And you must needs have heard, how I am punished

---

185 But thou] F; thou Q2   185 wouldst] Q2; wouldest F   186 how ill all's] Q2; how all F   188 gaingiving] F;
gamgiuing Q2   190 obey it] Q2; obey F   192 There is] Q2; there's a F   193 If it be now] F; if it be Q2   195 of
aught . . . what is't] of ought he leaues, knowes what ist Q2; ha's ought of what he leaues. What is't F   196 Let be] Q2; *not*
in F   196 SD] *This edn; A table prepared, Trumpets, Drums and officers with Cushions, King, Queene, and all the state, Foiles,*
daggers, and Laertes. Q2; *Enter King, Queene, Laertes and Lords, with other Attendants with Foyles, and Gauntlets, a Table and*
Flagons of Wine on it. F   197 SD *Claudius . . . into Hamlet's*] *This edn; not in* Q2, F; *Gives him the hand of Laertes /*
Hanmer   198 I've] F; I haue Q2   199–200 But . . . knows] F; *as one line* Q2

---

185 **at the odds** given these particular odds.

188 **gaingiving** foreboding, apprehension.
Perhaps stronger than 'misgiving': Shakespeare
thinks of 'gain' as in 'gainsay' – indicating opposition. This is a singular use of an uncommon word.

192 **we defy augury** Hamlet rejects the pagan-
inflected notion of 'augury', the attempt to read
signs of future events and to take steps accordingly.

192–3 **There is … sparrow** '[S]pecial providence' is a theological term for a particular act of
divine intervention that fits God's plan for the individual in the ordering of the universe. '[T]he fall of
a sparrow' alludes to Matthew 10.29. Hamlet now
trusts in God's immediate concern and control, and
he will therefore accept the circumstances which present themselves and neither avoid nor accelerate them.

193 **If it be now** i.e. his own death. He knows the
king will be making a second attempt to murder him.

He must also have in mind the final confrontation
when he will 'quit' Claudius, even if it costs him his
life.

195–6 **Since no man … betimes?** Based on
Q2, with the sense that since no one has any knowledge of the life he leaves behind him, what does it
matter if one dies early? F's reading is simpler, closer
to 'you can't take it with you'.

196 **Let be** Do not try to alter the course of
things.

196 SD This is a conflation of Q2 and F. F does not
provide for trumpets and drums (i.e. trumpeters and
drummers), nor the cushions, nor the daggers. Q2,
on the other hand, does not have gauntlets nor does it
specify the flagons (= vessels containing drink, with
possible Eucharistic overtones).

200 **presence** assembly (suggesting a formal
court occasion).

With a sore distraction. What I have done,
That might your nature, honour and exception
Roughly awake, I here proclaim was madness.
Was't Hamlet wronged Laertes? Never Hamlet.   205
If Hamlet from himself be tane away,
And when he's not himself does wrong Laertes,
Then Hamlet does it not, Hamlet denies it.
Who does it then? His madness. If't be so,
Hamlet is of the faction that is wronged,   210
His madness is poor Hamlet's enemy.
Sir, in this audience,
Let my disclaiming from a purposed evil
Free me so far in your most generous thoughts,
That I have shot my arrow o'er the house   215
And hurt my brother.

LAERTES   I am satisfied in nature,
Whose motive in this case should stir me most
To my revenge; but in my terms of honour
I stand aloof, and will no reconcilement
Till by some elder masters of known honour   220
I have a voice and precedent of peace
To keep my name ungored. But till that time
I do receive your offered love like love,
And will not wrong it.

HAMLET   I embrace it freely,
And will this brother's wager frankly play.   225

---

202 a sore] Q2; sore F   212 Sir ... audience] F; *not in* Q2   215 my arrow] Q2; mine Arrow F   216 brother] Q2;
Mother F   222 keep] F; *not in* Q2   222 ungored] vngord Q2; vngorg'd F   222 till] F; all Q2   224–5 I embrace ...
play] F; *as prose in* Q2   224 I embrace] Q2; I do embrace F

203 **exception** sense of grievance.
204–11 **I here proclaim ... enemy** Hamlet's
emotional and mental stability during the closet
scene, when he killed Polonius, remains an open
question. But his remorse and regret now for how
he has harmed Laertes is presented as genuine.
206 **tane** taken.
210 **faction** party.
216 **in nature** so far as natural feeling goes.

217 **motive** prompting.
221 **voice** judgement.
221 **of peace** for reconciliation.
222 **my name ungored** my reputation
undamaged.
224 **And will not wrong it** A falsehood, since
Laertes is preparing to kill Hamlet.
225 **frankly** freely, with an unburdened mind.

Give us the foils, come on.

LAERTES   Come, one for me.

HAMLET I'll be your foil Laertes. In mine ignorance
Your skill shall like a star i'th'darkest night
Stick fiery off indeed.

LAERTES   You mock me sir.

HAMLET No, by this hand.   230

CLAUDIUS Give them the foils, young Osric. Cousin Hamlet,
You know the wager?

HAMLET   Very well my lord.
Your grace has laid the odds a'th'weaker side.

CLAUDIUS I do not fear it, I have seen you both.
But since he is bettered, we have therefore odds.   235

LAERTES This is too heavy, let me see another.

HAMLET This likes me well. These foils have all a length?

OSRIC Ay my good lord.

Prepare to play

CLAUDIUS Set me the stoups of wine upon that table.
If Hamlet give the first or second hit,   240
Or quit in answer of the third exchange,
Let all the battlements their ordnance fire.
The king shall drink to Hamlet's better breath,
And in the cup an union shall he throw
Richer than that which four successive kings   245
In Denmark's crown have worn. Give me the cups,

---

226 come on] F; *not in* Q2   233 has] Q2; hath F   235 betterd] better'd F; better Q2   238 SD] F*(237); not in* Q2   242 ordnance] Q2; Ordinance F   244 union] vnion F; Vnice Q2 *(uncorrected)*; Onixe Q2 *(corrected)*

227 **foil** Material used to set off or display some richer thing, as a jewel (with obvious pun).

229 **Stick fiery off** Stand out brilliantly.

233 **laid the odds** A puzzling phrase, which has generated much discussion. Either Claudius has backed the weaker contestant, or, more probably, he has kindly provided an advantage for Hamlet in the handicap he has given Laertes.

234–5 An extremely politic reply. Claudius says he does *not* think Hamlet is weaker, but because Laertes has *improved*, he has arranged the wager to give an advantage for Hamlet.

236 **let me see another** It has been suggested by Wilson that Osric is an accomplice, but whatever 'shuffling' is done to get the poisoned and unbated foil into Laertes's hand is done by himself.

237 **likes me** pleases me.

239 **stoups** the flagons mentioned in 196SD.

241 **Or quit ... exchange** Or, having lost the first two bouts, gets his revenge in fighting the third bout.

243 **better breath** i.e. he will drink to the increase of Hamlet's energy or power.

244 **union** a pearl of special quality and high value. So F. Q2 printed first 'Vnice', which was changed to 'Onixe' after correction. When F again has 'Vnion', at 305, Q2 again prints 'Onixe'. This is the poison that Claudius promised in 4.7.156–61.

246 **Give me the cups** The cups, or goblets, are not mentioned in 196SD. The wine from the flagons or stoups is to be poured into them and brought to Claudius. (There is a good deal of ceremonial fetching and carrying in this scene.) Claudius then explains just how his toast will be given. He does not drink until after the first bout (259).

And let the kettle to the trumpet speak,
The trumpet to the cannoneer without,
The cannons to the heavens, the heaven to earth,
'Now the king drinks to Hamlet!' Come, begin,   250
And you the judges bear a wary eye.

Trumpets the while

HAMLET Come on sir.
LAERTES Come my lord.

They play

HAMLET One.
LAERTES No.   255
HAMLET Judgement.
OSRIC A hit, a very palpable hit.
LAERTES Well, again.
CLAUDIUS Stay, give me drink. Hamlet, this pearl is thine.
Here's to thy health.

Drum, trumpets sound, and shot goes off

Give him the cup.   260
HAMLET I'll play this bout first, set it by awhile.
Come.

[*They play*]

Another hit. What say you?
LAERTES A touch, a touch, I do confess't.
CLAUDIUS Our son shall win.
GERTRUDE   He's fat and scant of breath.
Here Hamlet, take my napkin, rub thy brows.   265
The queen carouses to thy fortune, Hamlet.
HAMLET Good madam.

---

247 trumpet] Q2; Trumpets F   250 'Now ... Hamlet.'] *as reported speech in Capell; not differentiated in*
Q2, F   251 SD] Q2; *not in* F   253 Come my lord] Q2; Come on sir F   260 SD] *This edn; Drum, trumpets and shot.*
Florish, a peece goes off Q2 (*257*); *Trumpets sound, and shot goes off* F   261 set it by] Q2; set by F   262 SD *They play*] *They*
play again / Rowe; not in Q2, F   263 A touch, a touch] F; *not in* Q2   263 confess't] Q2; confesse F   265 Here ...
brows] Q2; Heere's a Napkin, rub thy browes F

247 **kettle** kettle-drum.
259–60 give me drink ... health The king
drinks to Hamlet's health while holding the 'pearl'
aloft. He then deposits the poisoned pellet in the
goblet while the drum, trumpet, and shot are
sounding off.
264 **fat ... breath** Scholars have resisted the
implication that Hamlet is corpulent, stuffed, or
gross (all synonyms for 'fat' and all available from
other uses of the word as an adjective or verb at

1.5.32, 2.2.531, 3.4.154 and 4.3.21–2). They look for
alternative meanings of the word: sweaty, though this
is not properly attested, or out of condition, which can
be associated with shortness of breath. Hamlet's musing on 'your fat king and your lean beggar' (4.3.22)
suggests that he does not see himself as fat, since he is
all too conscious that he is not the king.
265 **napkin** handkerchief.
266 **carouses** drinks a health.

CLAUDIUS Gertrude, do not drink!

GERTRUDE I will my lord, I pray you pardon me.

                            [Drinks]

CLAUDIUS *[Aside]* It is the poisoned cup. It is too late.   270

HAMLET I dare not drink yet madam, by and by.

GERTRUDE Come, let me wipe thy face.

LAERTES My lord, I'll hit him now.

CLAUDIUS   I do not think't.

LAERTES And yet it is almost against my conscience.

HAMLET Come, for the third, Laertes. You do but dally.   275

    I pray you pass with your best violence.

    I am afeard you make a wanton of me.

LAERTES Say you so? Come on.

                              Play

OSRIC Nothing neither way.

LAERTES Have at you now!   *[Wounds Hamlet]*   280

           In scuffling they change rapiers

CLAUDIUS Part them. They are incensed.

HAMLET Nay, come again.   *[Wounds Laertes]*

            [Gertrude falls]

OSRIC Look to the queen there, ho!

HORATIO They bleed on both sides. How is it my lord?

OSRIC How is't Laertes?   285

LAERTES Why, as a woodcock to mine own springe, Osric.

    I am justly killed with mine own treachery.

---

269 SD *Drinks*] Hanmer; *not in* Q2, F   **270** SD *Aside*] Rowe; *not in* Q2, F   **274** it is almost against] Q2; 'tis almost 'gainst
F   **275** You do but] Q2; you but F   **277** afeard] affear'd F; sure F   **278** SD] F; *not in* Q2   **280** SD *Wounds Hamlet*]
Laertes wounds Hamlet . . . / Rowe; not in Q2, F   **280.1** SD *In scuffling . . . rapiers*] F; *not in* Q2   **282** SD *Wounds Laertes*]
Rowe *(substantially); not in* Q2, F   **282.1** SD *Gertrude falls*] *Queen falls* / Capell; *not in* Q2, F   **284** is it] Q2; is't
F   **286** mine own springe] Q2; mine Sprindge F

274 And yet ... conscience Rowe made this an aside, and many editions follow. But it is possible that Laertes is speaking directly to the king.

276 pass thrust.

277 make a wanton of me indulge me as though I were a child.

279 Nothing neither way This is presumably the end of the third bout.

280 Have at you now! Laertes signals an attack on Hamlet in violation of the official structure of the duel.

280 SD In scuffling ... So F. There are no stage directions in Q2. The exchange of rapiers, given in F's stage direction, is confirmed by Q1, '*They catch one anothers Rapiers*'. The sense indicated by 'Have at you' is that Laertes lunges at Hamlet before he is ready and wounds him slightly with the unbated and poisoned foil. Realizing that there is some malpractice, Hamlet fights violently with Laertes, disarms him, picks up the deadly rapier and sees its unbated point. The fight resumes until Hamlet succeeds in wounding Laertes.

286 as a woodcock ... springe i.e. caught in my own trap. See 1.3.115.

HAMLET How does the queen?

CLAUDIUS   She sounds to see them bleed.

GERTRUDE No, no, the drink, the drink – O my dear Hamlet –
    The drink, the drink – I am poisoned.   [*Dies*] 290

HAMLET Oh villainy! – Ho, let the door be locked!
    Treachery! Seek it out!

                        [*Laertes falls*]

LAERTES It is here Hamlet. Hamlet, thou art slain,
    No medicine in the world can do thee good,
    In thee there is not half an hour of life –   295
    The treacherous instrument is in thy hand,
    Unbated and envenomed. The foul practice
    Hath turned itself on me; lo, here I lie,
    Never to rise again. Thy mother's poisoned –
    I can no more – the king, the king's to blame.   300

HAMLET The point envenomed too! Then, venom, to thy work!

                        Hurts the king

ALL Treason, treason!

CLAUDIUS Oh yet defend me friends, I am but hurt.

HAMLET Here, thou incestuous, murderous, damnèd Dane,
    Drink off this potion. Is thy union here?   305
    Follow my mother.   *King dies*

LAERTES   He is justly served,
    It is a poison tempered by himself.
    Exchange forgiveness with me, noble Hamlet.
    Mine and my father's death come not upon thee,
    Nor thine on me.   *Dies* 310

HAMLET Heaven make thee free of it! I follow thee.

---

290 SD *Dies*] *Queen dies / Rowe*; not in Q2, F   292 SD *Laertes falls*] *Capell*; not in Q2, F   293 Hamlet. Hamlet, thou] F; *Hamlet, thou* Q2   295 hour of life] F; *houres life* Q2   296 thy hand] F; *my hand* Q2   301 SD] F; *not in* Q2   304 Here] *Heere* F; *Heare* Q2   304 murderous] F; *not in* Q2   305 thy union] F; *the Onixe* Q2   306 SD] F; *not in* Q2   306–7 He … himself] F; *as one line* Q2   310 SD] F; *not in* Q2

288 **sounds** swoons.

297 **envenomed** poisoned.

297 **practice** plot.

302 **Treason, treason!** This reaction to the stabbing of Claudius suggests the support and acceptance that he has had at court. It thus gives some indication of what Hamlet all along has had to face in planning to kill the king for a crime unknown to the people. Notice also his concern (323–4) at not having been able to explain the reasons for his action.

305 **Drink off this potion** Hamlet forces the drink down Claudius's throat.

305 **thy union** In a double sense: the fake pearl and its poison, and the 'incestuous' marriage.

307 **tempered** mixed, prepared.

309 **come not upon thee** This is a wish or prayer rather than a statement: 'Let not these deaths be visited upon, or charged to thee!'

311 **make thee free** absolve thee.

I am dead, Horatio. Wretched queen adieu.
You that look pale, and tremble at this chance,
That are but mutes or audience to this act,
Had I but time, as this fell sergeant death   315
Is strict in his arrest, oh I could tell you –
But let it be. Horatio, I am dead,
Thou livest; report me and my cause aright
To the unsatisfied.

HORATIO   Never believe it.
I am more an antique Roman than a Dane.   320
Here's yet some liquor left.

HAMLET   As th'art a man,
Give me the cup. Let go, by heaven I'll ha't.
O God, Horatio, what a wounded name,
Things standing thus unknown, shall live behind me!
If thou didst ever hold me in thy heart,   325
Absent thee from felicity awhile,
And in this harsh world draw thy breath in pain
To tell my story.
        March afar off, and shot within
          What warlike noise is this?

OSRIC Young Fortinbras, with conquest come from Poland,
To the ambassadors of England gives   330
This warlike volley.

HAMLET   Oh I die, Horatio,
The potent poison quite o'ercrows my spirit.
I cannot live to hear the news from England.

---

318 cause aright] Q2; causes right F   322 ha't] hate Q2; haue't F   323 O God] O god Q2; Oh good F   324 shall live] F; shall I leaue Q2   328 SD] *Steevens; March afarre off, and shout within* F; *A marche a farre off* Q2 (Q2 *and* F *then give /* Enter Osrick)   330 To the] *Pope;* To th' Q2, F   330–1 To … volley] *as one line* Q2, F

313 **chance** mischance.

314 **mutes** Characters in a play with no speaking parts. Hamlet's remarkable view of himself as he dies, as being at the centre of a theatre-performance, is discussed by Anne Righter, *Shakespeare and the Idea of the Play* (New York: Barnes & Noble, 1962), 147.

315 **fell sergeant** Officer who summoned persons to appear before a court. '[F]ell' = deadly.

319 **unsatisfied** i.e. those who require an explanation.

320 **antique Roman** i.e. for whom suicide might be noble rather than damnable. Cato is the person the Elizabethans would chiefly have in mind in a context like this. Compare *Julius Caesar* 5.1.100–7.

329 OSRIC Both Q2 and F give an entry for Osric at this point. But it doesn't appear that he has left the stage. Perhaps Shakespeare meant him to go to the door as if to investigate, then return.

332 **o'ercrows** triumphs over (an image from cockfighting).

But I do prophesy th'election lights
On Fortinbras; he has my dying voice.   335
So tell him, with th'occurrents more and less
Which have solicited – the rest is silence.   *Dies*
HORATIO Now cracks a noble heart. Good night sweet prince,
    And flights of angels sing thee to thy rest. –
    Why does the drum come hither?   340

Enter FORTINBRAS *and* ENGLISH AMBASSADORS, *with drum, colours*
and Attendants

FORTINBRAS Where is this sight?
HORATIO   What is it you would see?
    If aught of woe or wonder, cease your search.
FORTINBRAS This quarry cries on havoc. O proud death,
    What feast is toward in thine eternal cell
    That thou so many princes at a shot   345
    So bloodily hast struck?
I AMBASSADOR   The sight is dismal,
    And our affairs from England come too late.
    The ears are senseless that should give us hearing,
    To tell him his commandment is fulfilled,
    That Rosencrantz and Guildenstern are dead.   350
    Where should we have our thanks?
HORATIO   Not from his mouth,
    Had it th'ability of life to thank you;
    He never gave commandment for their death.
    But since, so jump upon this bloody question,

---

336 th'] Q2; the F   **337** silence.] Q2; silence. O, o, o, o. F   **337** SD] F; *not in* Q2   **338** cracks] Q2; cracke F   **340** SD] F
(Ambassador); Enter Fortenbrasse, with the Embassadors Q2   **341** you] Q2; ye F   **343** This] Q2; His F   **345** shot] Q2;
shoote F   **346** SH I AMBASSADOR] I. E. Capell; Embas. Q2; Amb. F

334–5 th'election ... Fortinbras i.e.
Fortinbras will be chosen as the next king. See 65
above, and the note to 1.2.109.
  335 voice vote.
  336 occurrents more and less i.e. all the
happenings.
  337 solicited – prompted, brought forth.
  338 cracks a... heart The heart-strings were
believed to snap at the moment of death.
  340 SD ENGLISH AMBASSADORS The F direction
gives us only one ambassador, again reflecting the
theatre's scaling down of Shakespeare's generous
provisions.

  343 This quarry cries on havoc This heap of
bodies proclaims a massacre. A 'quarry' is literally
a heap of dead animals after a hunt. For 'cries on',
compare *Othello* 5.1.48, 'Whose noise is this that
cries on murder?'
  344 toward being prepared. Monosyllable,
'to'ard'.
  344 eternal Shakespeare occasionally uses this
word as if it meant 'damnable' or 'infernal'. See
Othello 4.2.130, 'some eternal villain'. (See *OED* 7,
and Schmidt.)
  354 jump immediately.
  354 question quarrel, dispute (compare 4.4.26).

You from the Polack wars, and you from England,   355
Are here arrived, give order that these bodies
High on a stage be placèd to the view,
And let me speak to th'yet unknowing world
How these things came about. So shall you hear
Of carnal, bloody, and unnatural acts,   360
Of accidental judgements, casual slaughters,
Of deaths put on by cunning and forced cause,
And in this upshot, purposes mistook
Fallen on th'inventors' heads. All this can I
Truly deliver.

FORTINBRAS   Let us haste to hear it,   365
And call the noblest to the audience.
For me, with sorrow I embrace my fortune.
I have some rights of memory in this kingdom,
Which now to claim my vantage doth invite me.

HORATIO Of that I shall have also cause to speak,   370
And from his mouth whose voice will draw on more.
But let this same be presently performed,
Even while men's minds are wild, lest more mischance
On plots and errors happen.

FORTINBRAS   Let four captains
Bear Hamlet like a soldier to the stage,   375
For he was likely, had he been put on,
To have proved most royal; and for his passage,

---

358 to th'yet] F; to yet Q2   362 forced cause] F; for no cause Q2   364 th'inventors] Q2; the Inuentors F   368 rights]
Q2; Rites F   369 now] Q2; are F   370 also] Q2; always F   371 on more] F; no more Q2   373 while] Q2; whiles
F   377 royal] royall Q2, Q1; royally F

360 **carnal ... acts** Claudius's deeds.
361 **accidental judgements** punishments
brought about fortuitously. Horatio no doubt has
Laertes in mind.
362 **put on** arranged, set up.
362 **forced cause** A cause created by the wrest-
ing of the truth into falsehood (compare *Winter's
Tale* 3.3.79, the 'forced baseness' which Leontes has
put upon Perdita). Horatio probably means the
instructions to the English king to execute
Hamlet. Some editors wrongly suppose 'forced' =
'compelled'.
363 **this upshot** the final issue, visible here
('upshot' is the deciding shot in an archery contest).
368 **rights of memory** Fortinbras asserts his
claim to the land lost by his father to Hamlet Sr.

369 **my vantage** my present advantageous
situation.
371 **his mouth ... more** Horatio will speak for
Hamlet, whose vote is likely to influence other
electors.
372 **presently** immediately.
373 **wild** lacking order, bewildered.
374 **On** Arising from.
376 **put on** put to the test.
377 **royal** So Q2. F's 'royally' gives the phrase
a different meaning. Q2 means that Hamlet, if he
had become king, would have turned out to be truly
royal. F means that Hamlet would have thrived in
true royal fashion.
377 **passage** i.e. from this world.

The soldier's music and the rite of war
Speak loudly for him.
Take up the bodies. Such a sight as this   380
Becomes the field, but here shows much amiss.
Go bid the soldiers shoot.

Exeunt marching, after the which a peal of ordnance are shot off

---

378 rite] right Q2; rites F   380 bodies] Q2; body F   382 SD] F; *Exeunt* Q2

378 **rite of war** F gives 'rites', but Shakespeare frequently uses the singular, e.g. 'the rite of May', *Midsummer Night's Dream* 4.1.133; 'rite of love', *All's Well* 2.4.41.

382 *a peal of ordnance* a salute of guns.

READING LIST

The phrase 'an embarrassment of riches' cannot do justice to centuries of important studies of *Hamlet*. Neither can a single list of recommended titles. Devised with the undergraduate in mind, the selection that follows represents some of the most significant, illuminating, or useful works or collections of literary, textual, and performance and adaptation criticism. The list is divided according to these categories, although there is, of course, significant overlap in these methods. Each section is arranged alphabetically.

LITERARY STUDIES

Adelman, Janet. *Suffocating Mothers: Fantasies of Maternal Origin in Shakespeare's Plays, 'Hamlet' to 'The Tempest'*. New York: Routledge, 1992.

Charnes, Linda. *Hamlet's Heirs: Shakespeare and the Politics of a New Millennium*. New York: Routledge, 2006.

De Grazia, Margreta. *'Hamlet' without Hamlet*. Cambridge University Press, 2007.

Edwards, Philip. 'Tragic Balance in *Hamlet*', *Shakespeare Survey* 36 (1983), 43–52.

Eliot, T. S. 'Hamlet and His Problems', in *The Sacred Wood: Essays on Poetry and Criticism*. London: Methuen, 1964 [1920], 95–103.

Empson, William. '*Hamlet* When New', *Sewanee Review* 61.1 (1953), 15–42.

Farley-Hills, D., ed. *Critical Responses to 'Hamlet' 1600–1900*, 4 vols., 1995–9.

Foakes, R. A. *'Hamlet' Versus 'Lear': Cultural Politics and Shakespeare's Art*. Cambridge University Press, 1993.

Frye, Roland Mushat. *The Renaissance 'Hamlet': Issues and Responses in 1600*. Princeton University Press, 1988.

Garber, Marjorie. '*Hamlet*', in *Shakespeare After All*. New York: Anchor Books, 2004, 466–505.

Granville-Barker, Harley. *Prefaces to Shakespeare: 'Hamlet'*. Princeton University Press, 1946.

Greenblatt, Stephen. *Hamlet in Purgatory*. Princeton University Press, 2001.

Jenkins, H. '*Hamlet* Then Till Now', *Shakespeare Survey* 18 (1965), 34–45.

Jump, John D. *Shakespeare: 'Hamlet': A Selection of Critical Essays*. London: Macmillan, 1968.

Kerrigan, John. *Revenge Tragedy: From Aeschylus to Armageddon*. Oxford: Clarendon Press, 1996.

Kerrigan, William. *Hamlet's Perfection*. Baltimore, MD: Johns Hopkins University Press, 1994.

Kinney, Arthur, ed. *'Hamlet': New Critical Essays*. New York and London: Routledge, 2002.

Levin, Harry. *The Question of 'Hamlet'*. New York: Oxford University Press, 1959.

Mack, Maynard, 'The World of *Hamlet*', *The Yale Review* 41 (1951–2), 502–23.

Shapiro, James. *1599: A Year in the Life of William Shakespeare*. New York: Faber & Faber, 2005.

Showalter, Elaine. 'Representing Ophelia: Women, Madness, and the Responsibilities of Feminist Criticism', in *Shakespeare and the Question of Theory*, ed. Patricia Parker and Geoffrey Hartman. London: Methuen, 1985, 77–94.

Weimann, Robert. 'Hamlet and the Purposes of Playing', in *Author's Pen and Actor's Voice: Playing and Writing in Shakespeare's Theatre*, ed. Helen Hughes and William West. Cambridge University Press, 2000, 151–79.

Wilson, John Dover. *What Happens in 'Hamlet'*. Cambridge University Press, 1935.

TEXTUAL STUDIES

Bourus, Terri. *Young Shakespeare's Young Hamlet: Print, Piracy, and Performance*. New York: Palgrave Macmillan, 2014.

Clayton, Thomas, ed. *The 'Hamlet' First Published (Q1, 1603): Origins, Form, Intertextualities*. Newark: University of Delaware Press, 1992.

Erne, Lukas. *Shakespeare as Literary Dramatist*. Cambridge University Press, 2003.

Lesser, Zachary. *Hamlet after Q1: An Uncanny History of the Shakespearean Text*. Philadelphia: University of Pennsylvania Press, 2015.

Marino, James. *Owning William Shakespeare: The King's Men and Their Intellectual Property*. Philadelphia: University of Pennsylvania Press, 2011.

Menzer, Paul. *The Hamlets: Cues, Qs, and Remembered Texts*. Newark: University of Delaware Press, 2008.

Stern, Tiffany. 'Sermons, Plays and Note-takers: *Hamlet* Q1 as a "Noted" Text', *Shakespeare Survey* 66 (2013), 1–23

Werstine, Paul. 'The Textual Mystery of *Hamlet*', *SQ* 39.1 (1988), 1–26.

PERFORMANCE HISTORY AND ADAPTATION STUDIES

Bevington, David. *Murder Most Foul: Hamlet Through the Ages*. Oxford University Press, 2011.

Burnett, Mark Thornton. '"I see my father" in "my mind's eye": Surveillance and the Filmic Hamlet', in *Screening Shakespeare in the Twenty-first Century*, ed. Mark Thornton Burnett and Ramona Wray. Edinburgh University Press, 2006, 31–52.

Dawson, Anthony B. *Shakespeare in Performance: 'Hamlet'*. Manchester University Press, 1995.

Escolme, Bridget. 'The Point or the Question: Text, Performance, *Hamlet*', in *Talking to the Audience: Shakespeare, Performance, Self*. New York; Routledge, 2005, 53–94.

Gurr, Andrew, and Mariko Ichikawa, 'The Early Staging of *Hamlet*', in *Staging in Shakespeare's Theatres*. Oxford University Press, 2000, 121–62.

Hapgood, Robert. 'Introduction', in *Hamlet, Prince of Denmark*. Shakespeare in Production Series. Cambridge University Press, 1999, 1–96.

Howard, Tony. *Women as Hamlet: Performance and Interpretation in Theatre, Film, and Fiction*. Cambridge University Press, 2007.

Kennedy, Dennis, ed. *Foreign Shakespeare: Contemporary Performance*. Cambridge University Press, 1993.

Kliman, Bernice W. *'Hamlet': Film, Television, and Audio Performance*. London and Toronto: Toronto University Press, 1988.

Lavender, Andy. *Hamlet in Pieces: Peter Brook, Robert La Page, Richard Wilson*. London: Nick Hern, 2001.

Litvin, Margaret. *Hamlet's Arab Journey: Shakespeare's Prince and Nasser's Ghost*. Princeton University Press, 2011.

Maher, Mary Z. *Modern Hamlets and their Soliloquies*. University of Iowa Press, 1992.

Mander, Raymond, and Joe Mitchenson. *'Hamlet' through the Ages: A Pictorial Record from 1709*. London: Rockliff, 1952.

Mills, John A. *'Hamlet' on Stage: The Great Tradition*. Westport, CT: Greenwood Press, 1985.

Peterson, Kaara L., and Deanne Williams. *The Afterlife of Ophelia*. New York: Palgrave Macmillan, 2012.

Rosenberg, Marvin. *The Masks of 'Hamlet'*. Newark: University of Delaware Press, 1992.

Scofield, Martin. *The Ghosts of 'Hamlet': The Play and Modern Writers*. Cambridge University Press, 1980.

Shattuck, Charles Harlen. *The Shakespeare Promptbooks: A Descriptive Catalogue*. Urbana: University of Illinois Press, 1965.

White, R. S. *Avant-Garde Hamlet: Text, Stage, Screen*. Madison, NJ: Fairleigh Dickinson University Press, 2015.

WEBSITES

Hamlet on the Ramparts: http://shea.mit.edu/ramparts

Hamlet Works: http://triggs.djvu.org/global-language.com/ENFOLDED/index.php

Ophelia and Web 2.0: https://sites.google.com/site/opheliaandpopularculture/home

APPENDIX 1 Textual Analysis

By Philip Edwards

Shakespeare's *Hamlet* appears to be a rewriting or a reworking of a well-known earlier play of unknown authorship. But what do we mean when we speak of 'Shakespeare's *Hamlet*'? The textual problem of the play is of great complexity. It may seem an exasperating coincidence that a play which is as perplexing and problematic for the critic as *Hamlet* should also have unusually severe textual difficulties, but in fact the ambiguities in the meaning of the play are closely connected with its lack of a clear and settled text. Both the prince and his play come down to us in more shapes than one. If the prince were not so mercurial the text would be more stable. It is Shakespeare's difficulty in containing *Hamlet* within the bounds of a play, and the theatre's difficulty in comprehending the working of Shakespeare's mind, that have led to the multiple and scarcely reconcilable variations in the play's language and structure.

Everyone who wants to understand *Hamlet*, as reader, as actor, or director, needs to understand the nature of the play's textual problems, and needs to have his or her own view of them, however tentative. Ideally, every theatre-goer should be aware of the issues, so that he or she can appreciate whose *Hamlet* is being presented.

In searching for a solution to the play's textual problems, we should not imagine that we are likely ever to find ourselves with a single definitive text. The study of the early texts of *Hamlet* is the study of a play in motion. Earlier editors of *Hamlet* may have thought that 'a complete and final version' of the play was the object of their search,[1] but nowadays we are more ready to accept what centuries of theatrical history tell us – that what is written for the theatre often undergoes considerable modification as it moves from the writer's desk towards performance on the stage and also during performance. We must be prepared for the possibility that the variations in the text of *Hamlet* are not alternative versions of a single original text but representations of different stages in the play's development. Then our task becomes to choose the moment at which we would try to arrest the movement of the play and say 'This is the *Hamlet* we want'; or even, if we dare, 'This is the *Hamlet* that Shakespeare most wanted.' Do we have enough evidence to describe the history of Shakespeare' *Hamlet* in its early days and put together a version of it as it existed at a given point in time, a version that we can call not a definitive text but in our view the *best* text?

It is this question which this textual analysis tries to answer. While it will be necessary to consider material evidence about printing and publishing and playhouse procedures, the reader will see that the important decisions about the text of *Hamlet*

---

[1] See, for example, Joseph Quincy Adams's introduction to his 1929 edition.

are in the end literary decisions: not a matter of technical demonstration but of literary and linguistic judgement. Just as no one can argue about Hamlet who is not aware of the problems of its text, so no one can argue about the text who does not have a watchful eye for the value of words and for the possible meanings of the play.

We possess three basic printed texts of *Hamlet*, and no manuscript. The first published text is dated 1603, 'The Tragicall Historie of HAMLET Prince of Denmarke. By William Shake-speare'. The title page claims this to be the play 'as it hath beene diuerse times acted' by Shakespeare's company 'in the Cittie of London: as also in the two Vniuersities of Cambridge and Oxford, and else-where'. The publishers were Nicholas Ling and John Trundell, the printer Valentine Simmes.[1] This publication, known as the first quarto (Q1), is generally recognized as a 'bad' quarto: a corrupt, unauthorized version of an abridged version of Shakespeare's play. It runs to 2,154 lines.[2] Only two copies of this publication survive.

The second publication is dated 1604 in some copies and 1605 in others. It has the same title, but carries the legend, 'Newly imprinted and enlarged to almost as much againe as it was, according to the true and perfect Coppie'. This publication, the second quarto (Q2), is not well printed, but is generally held to be based on Shakespeare's own manuscript, his 'foul-papers'; that is, the completed draft, as opposed to a fair copy, which he submitted to his company. This is the fullest of the three versions, 3,674 lines. It was printed by James Roberts for Nicholas Ling.[3] Roberts had entered the play in the Stationers' Register, as if intending to publish, as early as 26 July 1602. ('The Revenge of Hamlett Prince Denmarke as yt was latelie Acted by the Lo: Chamberleyn his servants'.)[4] A. W. Pollard believed that this was a 'blocking' entry organized by the acting company to prevent unauthorized publication.[5] If this was the case, the move was clearly a failure. Roberts may well have been securing his own right, with the company's consent, for publication at some later date. But again, it did not prevent Ling's 1603 publication, and, whatever the source of Ling's text, publication gave him rights in the play, so he shared with Roberts the venture of the authorized text in 1604.

The third basic text is that published in the posthumous *Comedies, Histories, and Tragedies* of Shakespeare in 1623, the First Folio (F). A number of passages found in the second quarto, amounting to 222 lines, are omitted, but five new passages, totalling 83 lines, are added, giving a total for the play of 3,535 lines. There are a great many variant readings, some of them trifling and some of them very important. There is no general agreement about the source of this text except that it shows the influence of the theatre.

[1] W. W. Greg, *Bibliography of the English Printed Drama*, vol. I, 1939, no. 197a. There are numerous reprints. A facsimile was published by the Scolar Press in 1969.

[2] For the length of the various texts I use the figures given by Alfred Hart in *Shakespeare and the Homilies*, 1934, 124–5, 148–9.

[3] Greg, *Bibliography*, no. 197b. There is a facsimile edited by W. W. Greg (1940), and another published by the Scolar Press (1969).

[4] Greg, *Bibliography*, I, 18.   [5] *Shakespeare Folios and Quartos*, 1909, 73.

These three texts are not wholly independent of each other. James Roberts's compositors,[1] while they were setting the second quarto, had in front of them not only a manuscript but a copy of the bad quarto of 1603 and they frequently copied its readings in the first act and possibly elsewhere.[2] The Folio compositors[3] may likewise have made use of a copy of the second quarto, though the extent of this use is extremely uncertain.[4] There is always a problem when our texts disagree, but the agreement of two texts on a particular reading can be the result of mere copying.

There can hardly be dispute about the view, orthodox since the publication of Dover Wilson's *The Manuscript of Shakespeare's 'Hamlet'* in 1934, that the manuscript used by the printer for the second quarto (Q2) was Shakespeare's own 'foul-papers'. The sheets must have been in a rough condition and must have presented considerable difficulties to the compositors in the way of bad handwriting, deletions and insertions. There are many quite extraordinary readings, as can be seen by looking at the collation in the present edition, for example 1.2.77, 2.2.391, 3.2.325, 4.7.22, 4.7.61. I shall argue also that by the time the MS. reached the printing house, several years after Shakespeare completed it, it must have become illegible in a number of places through wear and damage.

It is evident that on half-a-dozen occasions there is a muddle in the second quarto which was caused by Shakespeare having changed his mind as he wrote but not making his erasures or deletion marks so positive or clear that the compositors understood them.[5] Here are two small examples.

2.2.73   Q2:   Giues him threescore thousand crownes in anuall fee
            F: Giues him three thousand Crownes in Annuall Fee

2.2.493–4   Q2:   a speech of some dosen lines, or sixteen lines
            F: a speech of some dosen or sixteene lines

In the first example, Shakespeare may have started to write 'three score crowns', changed it to 'three thousand crowns' but failed to delete 'score' positively enough for the Q2 compositor to take notice of it. With 'score' retained, the line is metrically overloaded. Similarly, the casual phrase 'some dozen or sixteen lines' seems to have come after the false start of 'some dozen lines', but the first 'lines' has not been properly deleted.

It looks as though Shakespeare hesitated a good deal over the Player Queen's speeches in 3.2, perhaps not finding it easy to get exactly the right kind of prosy sententiousness without becoming positively tedious. Two of the couplets found in the second quarto are omitted in the Folio (3.2.152–3 and 199–200) and I think

---

[1] For the division of the texts between two compositors, see J. R. Brown, *Studies in Bibliography* 7 (1955), 17–40.
[2] *MSH*, pp. 158–62; Greg, *Shakespeare's First Folio*, 1955, 315–16; A. Walker, *Textual Problems of the First Folio*, 1953, 121; F. T. Bowers, *Studies in Bibliography* 8 (1956), 39–66; Jenkins, 46–52.
[3] C. Hinman, *Printing ... of the First Folio*, 1963, II, 208–75; updated in Jenkins, 53–4.
[4] Jenkins summarizes the previous debate in his discussion, pp. 65–73.
[5] Several Shakespearean texts contain material which clearly was meant to be deleted, e.g. *Love's Labour's Lost* and *Romeo and Juliet*. See Greg, *Shakespeare's First Folio*, 110, 220.

Shakespeare had marked them for excision. Concerning two more of the prosy couplets there is definite evidence of Shakespeare's hesitation.[1]

3.2.148   Q2:   For women feare too much, euen as they loue,
                And womens feare and loue hold quantitie,
                Eyther none, in neither ought, or in extremitie,

          F: For womens Feare and Loue, holds quantitie,
                In neither ought, or in extremity:

Evidently the first line in Q2 was given up; it is the first line of an uncompleted rhyming couplet. And evidently 'Eyther none' was meant to be deleted also; in the Folio version both sense and metre are completed. A little further on, the variants between Q2 and F again suggest that Shakespeare's corrections were not understood by the Q2 compositor.

3.2.203   Q2:   Both heere and hence pursue me lasting strife,
                If once I be a widdow, euer I be a wife.

          F: Both heere, and hence, pursue me lasting strife,
                If once a Widdow, euer I be Wife.

It looks as though Shakespeare cancelled the first 'I be' in the second line and the Q2 compositor nevertheless set it. All these false starts in the Player Queen's speeches suggest that Shakespeare did not find it easy to write stilted verse.[2]

The presence of unobserved deletion marks in the copy for Q2 has been widely accepted, though their possible extent has never been fully investigated.[3] The most ingenious argument that these marks existed and were ignored by the Q2 compositors was provided by Dover Wilson himself (*MSH*, p. 30) in discussing the following speech by Claudius, 4.1.39–45, which I give as it appears in the quarto, adding square brackets to indicate that part of the speech which is omitted in the Folio.

    And let them know both what we meane to doe
    And whats vntimely doone,
    [Whose whisper ore the worlds dyameter,
    As leuell as the Cannon to his blanck,
    Transports his poysned shot, may misse our Name
    And hit the woundlesse ayre,] ô come away,
    My soule is full of discord and dismay.

The passage as it stands in Q2 is clearly incomplete, since there is a grammatical as well as a metrical gap after 'whats vntimely doone' in the second line. The passage will make sense if we fill the gap with such words as those suggested by Theobald and Capell, 'so haply slander'. As one of his 'three alternative explanations' of the puzzle, Dover Wilson suggested

---

[1] Compare Greg, *Shakespeare's First Folio*, 314.
[2] Other possible examples in Q2 of false starts are mentioned in the notes to 3.2.335, 4.5.74–6, and 4.7.8.
[3] See J. M. Nosworthy, *Shakespeare's Occasional Plays*, 1965, 139.

that the lines in question were marked for omission in the original manuscript not by transverse
lines ... but by some kind of brackets or rectangular enclosure, an arm of which appeared to
delete the first half-line of the passage, so that the Q2 compositor set up all but that half-line.

It may well be that the section of the speech omitted in F, including the lost half line,
was one of the passages in the play which Shakespeare 'surrendered in the actual
process of composition', to use J. M. Nosworthy's phrase.[1] If Shakespeare, having got
as far as 'woundlesse ayre', begins to feel (as well he might) that he is meandering, and
strikes out all after 'vntimely doone', he will need to pick up the metre and complete
the imperfect line he is now left with. The line as given in the Folio provides a perfect
seam:

> And what's vntimely done. Oh come away,

A number of cuts made in the Folio version of Hamlet's speeches to Gertrude in Act
3, Scene 4 (53–88, 158–81) may all reflect Shakespeare's own tightening of his
dialogue as he wrote. With the Player Queen, Shakespeare's problem had been to
strike a balance between sententiousness and vapidity; in the closet scene, we have to
be made to feel that Hamlet goes on too much, and here the danger is that he will
merely seem prolix. Here is the passage 3.4.68–88 (modernized), first as it appears in
the Folio, and secondly as it appears in the second quarto (with brackets round the
additional material).

F: You cannot call it love, for at your age
     The heyday in the blood is tame, it's humble,
     And waits upon the judgement; and what judgement
     Would step from this to this? What devil was't
     That thus hath cozened you at hoodman-blind?
     O shame, where is thy blush? Rebellious hell,
     If thou canst mutine in a matron's bones,
     To flaming youth let virtue be as wax
     And melt in her own fire. Proclaim no shame
     When the compulsive ardour gives the charge,
     Since frost itself as actively doth burn,
     And reason panders will.

Q2: You cannot call it love, for at your age
     The heyday in the blood is tame, it's humble,
     And waits upon the judgement; and what judgement
     Would step from this to this? [Sense sure you have,
     Else could you not have motion, but sure that sense
     Is apoplexed, for madness would not err,
     Nor sense to ecstasy was ne'er so thralled,
     But it reserved some quantity of choice
     To serve in such a difference.] What devil was't
     That thus hath cozened you at hoodman-blind?
     [Eyes without feeling, feeling without sight,
     Ears without hands or eyes, smelling sans all,

---

[1] Nosworthy, *Shakespeare's Occasional Plays*, 140.

Or but a sickly part of one true sense
Could not so mope.] O shame, where is thy blush?
Rebellious hell,
If thou canst mutine in a matron's bones,
To flaming youth let virtue be as wax
And melt in her own fire. Proclaim no shame
When the compulsive ardour gives the charge,
Since frost itself as actively doth burn,
And reason panders will.[1]

If we put the two versions together in this order, our familiarity with the fuller version is less likely to obstruct our perceiving that the speech is much more effective when the cuts have been made. Each of the two passages cut from the Folio has an uncertainty of control about it which suggests a tentative exploration from which Shakespeare pulled back. It will be noticed that if Shakespeare, as he was composing the speech, stopped at 'Could not so mope' and decided to abandon the three-and-a-half lines he had just written, he must obviously continue with a new full line, which is what we have in the Folio:

O shame, where is thy blush? Rebellious hell,

But the second quarto, by printing the excised half line *and* the new full line, is left with half a line too much.

Could not so mope, O shame, where is thy blush?
Rebellious hell,

There are very many short lines in *Hamlet*, and they are not in themselves evidence that the text has been altered. But when these short lines appear in the quarto only, in association with passages omitted from the Folio, they suggest revision. Here is the second quarto's version (modernized) of 1.4.69–79, with brackets round that part of it omitted from the Folio.

HORATIO What if it tempt you toward the flood, my lord,
Or to the dreadful summit of the cliff
That beetles o'er his base into the sea,
And there assume some other horrible form
Which might deprive your sovereignty of reason,
And draw you into madness? Think of it.
[The very place puts toys of desperation
Without more motive, into every brain
That looks so many fathoms to the sea
And hears it roar beneath.]
HAMLET It waves me still. Go on, I'll follow thee.

Here again we can imagine Shakespeare stopping himself after running on too far. The impressiveness of this speech as it appears in the Folio is the emphasis laid on Horatio's fear that the Ghost may draw Hamlet into madness. This ominous

---

[1] For 'panders' Q2 reads 'pardons'.

introduction of the theme of the tainted mind is much weakened by the continuation of the speech as it appears above, in which Horatio says that the place, not the Ghost, puts the idea of suicide into people's minds. Hamlet doesn't need a cliff to put thoughts of suicide into his head. If Shakespeare marked the passage within square brackets for deletion, he would need to continue with a full line, which is what we have in Hamlet's reply. But once again, by printing both the excised half line and the new full line, the second quarto leaves us with the tell-tale half line 'And hears it roar beneath'. This stitching to retain the verse pattern is not always so neat; in the other much-altered speech in 3.4, lines 158–81, one of the cuts leaves the very short line 'Refrain tonight' (166); but in the following cut, the half line which is left hanging, 'To the next abstinence' (168), is completed by 'Once more good night' (171).

Is it possible that other passages which appear only in the second quarto had been cancelled by Shakespeare himself and were never meant to form part of his play? In *Shakespeare's Occasional Plays*, J. M. Nosworthy argued that two major Folio cuts, usually taken to be unintelligent theatre-cuts, were in fact 'composition cuts'. They are both reflective passages preceding an entry of the Ghost, and neither of them makes full sense as it stands. The first passage, 1.1.108–25, is largely Horatio's discussion of the portents before the death of Caesar. It is not a strong or necessary speech, and few would find the play worse for its absence. The second passage (1.4.17–38) is not so easily written off, being the speech in which Hamlet, after being indignant that Danish drinking habits besmirch the whole nation, reflects on 'the vicious mole of nature' which ruins the reputation of otherwise worthy men. The speech ends with the notorious 'dram of eale' crux. Nosworthy writes (p. 141), 'The simplest explanation of this crux is that the sentence is unfinished, the implication being that Shakespeare lapsed into incoherence and gave up the struggle.' Nosworthy found the whole 'lengthy meditation' sententious. Dover Wilson's defence of the speech, that it was needed 'to lull the minds of his audience to rest and so startle them the more with his apparition' (*MSH*, p. 25), is not much of a compliment. Though it is often maintained that the speech has an important choric value, as regards Hamlet himself, and affords a glimpse of Shakespeare's view of tragedy, both these contentions are disputable, and I doubt whether removing the speech decreases the effectiveness of the scene or diminishes our understanding of the play. It is quite possible that these two cuts are theatre-cuts, but there is in my opinion much to be said for the view that Shakespeare was dissatisfied with them as he wrote.

Jonson said of Shakespeare, 'He flowed with that facility, that sometime it was necessary he should be stopped. *Sufflaminandus erat*.'[1] The evidence of the second quarto of *Hamlet* shows both Shakespeare's facility and his awareness of the need to curb it. It is ironic that compositors may have unwittingly preserved a good deal of material which Shakespeare decided to dispense with. If that is in fact the case, they will have provided us with immensely valuable information about Shakespeare's methods of composition, but presented an editor with the formidable problem of whether he should put back into a play what Shakespeare had decided to leave out.

---

[1] *Discoveries*; in *Ben Jonson*, ed. Herford and Simpson, VIII, 1947, 583–4.

Although there is at least one more passage found in the second quarto only which may have been a 'composition cut' (4.7.99–101), I want now to consider two major passages which do not appear in the Folio text but which have none of those deficiencies, structural, thematic, or linguistic, which may suggest Shakespeare's discontent with them as he wrote. These are Hamlet's speech to Gertrude at the end of the closet scene, 3.4.203–11, about Rosencrantz and Guildenstern (hoisting the engineer with his own petar), and the long fourth soliloquy (4.4), 'How all occasions do inform against me', after Hamlet has seen Fortinbras's army. These are generally held to be playhouse cuts, but there are reasons for thinking that Shakespeare himself may have removed both speeches.

Here is the first passage, in modernized form, first as in the Folio and then in the fuller quarto version.

> F: HAMLET   I must to England, you know that?
> GERTRUDE   Alack,
>   I had forgot. 'Tis so concluded on.
> HAMLET   This man shall set me packing.
>
> Q2: HAMLET   I must to England, you know that?
> GERTRUDE   Alack,
>   I had forgot. 'Tis so concluded on.
> HAMLET   There's letters sealed, and my two schoolfellows,
>   Whom I will trust as I will adders fanged,
>   They bear the mandate. They must sweep my way
>   And marshall me to knavery. Let it work,
>   For 'tis the sport to have the engineer
>   Hoist with his own petar, an't shall go hard
>   But I will delve one yard below their mines
>   And blow them at the moon. Oh 'tis most sweet
>   When in one line two crafts directly meet.
>   This man shall set me packing.

Hamlet's speech in the fuller quarto version creates many problems. In the first place, though the audience has just seen Claudius instructing Rosencrantz and Guildenstern to accompany Hamlet to England, Hamlet has been given no means of learning that they are to go with him. And the audience has still to be told (it comes at 4.3.54) that Claudius is using the voyage to England to liquidate Hamlet. There are problems graver than these, however. One is the surprise of this new conviction in Hamlet that Rosencrantz and Guildenstern are accomplices in a plot to destroy him. The second is the definiteness of Hamlet's plans. In spite of the recent reappearance of the Ghost urging him to his main task of revenge, he here renounces the immediate prosecution of his mission, accepts the journey to England, and with cool pleasure undertakes to countermine Claudius's plots in his own good time, and to destroy Rosencrantz and Guildenstern.

The explicitness of this speech is surely remarkable. What Hamlet here outlines is what actually happens. Can Shakespeare have wanted Hamlet at this point to be so buoyantly in charge of his own destiny? It is a major factor in Hamlet's actions on board ship, as he narrates them to Horatio in 5.2, that the idea of entering the cabin of

Rosencrantz and Guildenstern was a sudden inspiration, a wild rashness, in which he saw the hand of Providence. It was by means of that unplanned move that Hamlet learned of Claudius's treachery, and it was as a consequence of that knowledge that Hamlet sent Rosencrantz and Guildenstern to their deaths. George MacDonald, in his 1885 edition of the play (p. 181), suggested that it was Shakespeare's original plan that Hamlet should board the vessel looking for an opportunity to outwit his companions, but that he altered the plan 'and represents his escape as more plainly providential'. The change in Hamlet's relationship with Rosencrantz and Guildenstern, now sent to their deaths on a sudden impulse, is surely reflected in a line which is found in the Folio but not in the second quarto, and which may therefore be an addition or an insertion into the original script. In reply to Horatio's pensive words, 'So Guildenstern and Rosencrantz go to't', Hamlet (in the second quarto) impatiently replies 'They are not near my conscience', as indeed he might have some justification in saying if they were accomplices of Claudius whom Hamlet had long decided must be got out of the way. But if they are no more than repulsive sneaks, royal toadies, who are unwitting agents in the king's plot, their grim punishment is a more sensitive affair. 'Why man, they did make love to this employment', says Hamlet in the Folio, 'They are not near my conscience.' In view of other important lines in Hamlet's communication to Horatio which are also found only in the Folio (and which I shall shortly discuss), it seems very likely that Shakespeare revised this passage. If so the new line, 'Why man, they did make love to this employment', etches in Hamlet's awareness of the unspoken accusation in Horatio's remark, and his wish to exculpate himself in the new moral context for the deaths of Rosencrantz and Guildenstern.

To return to the 'engineer' speech, we may feel that the value of the curt ending given to the closet scene in the Folio, no more than a sardonic recognition of the king's plan to get him out of Denmark and a consciousness that he, Hamlet, has now given Claudius the pretext which he wanted ('This man shall set me packing'), lies not only in avoiding a commitment to a delayed revenge but also in its complete silence about any plans whatsoever. The play is not the less eloquent for this silence. A great many possibilities are going through our minds about what may be going through Hamlet's. The Hamlet whose experiences and thoughts have been with us for three acts is lessened and limited by the plan and the threat which he issues in the quarto version of his speech. If it's bluster, of course, or the old 'procrastination', it would have a place in a credible total view of Hamlet, but a view I could not share. Shakespeare may have thought it best not to provide Hamlet with arguments for his acceptance of being sent off to England.

This question of his willingness to leave is at the forefront in the fourth soliloquy in 4.4, which is not given in the Folio at all. The core of the speech is self-reproach for not having done a deed which ought to have been done, and which could easily have been done. Hamlet finds his inactivity inexplicable.

Q2:   Now whether it be
       Bestial oblivion, or some craven scruple
       Of thinking too precisely on th'event –
       A thought which quartered hath but one part wisdom

> And ever three parts coward – I do not know
> Why yet I live to say this thing's to do,
> Sith I have cause, and will, and strength, and means
> To do't   (4.4.39–46)

This looks very much like an alternative to the 'engineer' speech we have been discussing. As Hamlet faces being sent to England, we are given first a demonstration of defiance and determination; then we are to see him in a state of nerveless drifting, bafflement, indecision, and inactivity. Again, a credible Hamlet can be made out, if we postulate a violent swing of mood, from blustering threats to guilt and self-questioning. But it is also possible to see the fourth soliloquy as a second attempt, a contradictory attempt, and a weaker attempt to provide a psychological bridge for this very difficult stage of the plot, Hamlet's departure for England.

Although entire theories of the prince have been built on this speech, it is not one of the great soliloquies; much less intricate, subtle, mobile and suggestive than the two great central soliloquies, 'O what a rogue and peasant slave' and 'To be or not to be'. But, more important, it is a speech which does not know all that has gone before it. Hamlet's thoughts and emotions have become far too complicated and deep for this simple self-accusation to make any sense –

> Sith I have cause, and will, and strength, and means
> To do't.

No, it is insufficient and inappropriate for Act 4 of *Hamlet*. We may agree with Ernst Honigmann[1] that when Shakespeare was writing a play he would not necessarily have begun with Act 1 and gone on to the end, but might have tried out speeches or scenes which would eventually find their place in the later parts of the play. Perhaps the fourth soliloquy was such a speech. But by the time we have reached the point at which it has been placed, Hamlet has become so immense in his mystery, so unfathomable, that the speech is scarcely adequate for the speaker.[2]

It seems to me the likeliest thing in the world that in creating a hero who is a tangle of conflicting tendencies Shakespeare would have written a lot of tentative material – passages relating to aspects of Hamlet and his mission which needed saying but whose final placing was uncertain – and that in the end some of this material would seem redundant or wrong, and not to belong anywhere. If 'How all occasions do inform against me' comes into this category, its removal at rather a late stage in the preparation of the play was a much bigger wrench than the removal of the 'engineer' speech, because we are left with an awkward fragment of a scene, just about enough to remind us of the existence of Fortinbras.

By omitting the engineer speech and the fourth soliloquy, the Folio version leaves Hamlet silent about being sent to England, except for his taunt about Claudius's purposes – 'I see a cherub that sees them' (4.3.45). This silence throws a great deal of

---

[1] *The Stability of Shakespeare's Text*, 1965, ch. 4.
[2] Compare W. Empson, '*Hamlet* When New', *Sewanee Review* 61 (1953), 15–42 and 185–205; also E. Prosser, *Hamlet and Revenge*, 1967, 207–8.

weight on to the explanations of his thoughts and actions which Hamlet gives to Horatio on his unlooked-for return, in 5.2, particularly about his loss of confidence in his 'deep plots' and his submission to the guidance of heaven. The heart of his explanation is a short passage which is for me the pivot of the entire play.

> And is't not to be damned
> To let this canker of our nature come
> In further evil?   (5.2.68–70)

These lines are found only in the Folio, and I find it hard to resist the conclusion that Shakespeare wrote them in at the time he cut out the two earlier speeches in 3.4 and 4.4. It is the destination to which a 'revised' Hamlet has come, and is all the evidence we need of the 'kind of fighting' in his heart between the reappearance of the Ghost in Gertrude's room and the return to Denmark.

This vital area of the play appears in the two texts as follows (modernized and corrected):

Q2: HORATIO So Guildenstern and Rosencrantz go to't.
     HAMLET They are not near my conscience. Their defeat
          Does by their own insinuation grow.
          'Tis dangerous when the baser nature comes
          Between the pass and fell incensed points
          Of mighty opposites.
     HORATIO   Why, what a king is this!
     HAMLET Does it not, think thee, stand me now upon –
          He that hath killed my king, and whored my mother,
          Popped in between th'election and my hopes,
          Thrown out his angle for my proper life,
          And with such cosenage – is't not perfect conscience?

                         Enter a COURTIER

F: HORATIO So Guildenstern and Rosencrantz go to't.
     HAMLET Why man, they did make love to this employment.
          They are not near my conscience. Their defeat
          Doth by their own insinuation grow.
          'Tis dangerous when the baser nature comes
          Between the pass and fell incensed points
          Of mighty opposites.
     HORATIO   Why, what a king is this!
     HAMLET Does it not, think'st thee, stand me now upon –
          He that hath killed my king, and whored my mother,
          Popped in between th'election and my hopes,
          Thrown out his angle for my proper life,
          And with such cosenage – is't not perfect conscience
          To quit him with this arm? And is't not to be damned
          To let this canker of our nature come
          In further evil?
     HORATIO It must be shortly known to him from England
          What is the issue of the business there.

HAMLET It will be short. The interim's mine,
   And a man's life no more then to say 'one'.
   But I am very sorry, good Horatio,
   That to Laertes I forgot myself,
   For by the image of my cause, I see
   The portraiture of his. I'll court his favours.
   But sure the bravery of his grief did put me
   Into a towering passion.
HORATIO   Peace, who comes here?

Enter young OSRIC

In the second quarto version there is obviously something missing at the end, after 'conscience'. It could be that Shakespeare has struck out some words similar to the Folio's 'To quit him with this arm' and inserted the all-important longer passage which appears only in the Folio, either in the margin where they were overlooked by the Q2 compositor, or on a separate sheet or slip which, in the four years or more elapsing between the completion of the manuscript and its use in Roberts's printing house, had somehow gone astray.

This matter of a separate slip or interleaved sheet is of course the purest speculation, but it might help to explain the existence in the Folio of another passage not found in the second quarto, the 'war of the theatres' passage, 2.2.313–33. If when he was completing his play in 1601 Shakespeare had indeed added this new material to an already written Act 2, Scene 2, and written it on an additional separate sheet, it may well have become separated or lost by 1604.

I have been suggesting that Shakespeare's 'foul-papers', which were used by Roberts in setting up the 1604/5 quarto, contained a certain amount of material which Shakespeare had decided he didn't want. Whatever cancellation marks he used were not observed or not understood by Roberts's compositors. The manuscript may also have contained insertions which again were either not seen or not understood by the compositors. As a result, the second quarto supplies us with some of Shakespeare's rejected first thoughts and fails to provide us with some of Shakespeare's second thoughts.

In addition, I have suggested that some major changes affecting the part of Hamlet in the last half of the play, reflected in the omission of two major speeches in the Folio, were possibly the result of a revision by Shakespeare. When might such a revision have taken place? Perhaps at the time when it became necessary to make a fair copy of the 'foul-papers'. We can only guess what happened when Shakespeare had a new play ready for his own company. Even Shakespeare, one assumes, had to have his play accepted. It must have been read and discussed. Perhaps it was given to Shakespeare to read out an untidy and unpunctuated manuscript. For all we know, alterations may have been talked about at this stage, and the revision may have taken place then. What looks certain is that at an early stage there would be the need to prepare a fair copy. There was an important discussion of this question of fair copies by Fredson Bowers in *On Editing Shakespeare* in 1955. Theatres normally required fair copies from their playwrights. Bowers suggested that Shakespeare's privileged position may have freed

him from the labour of making his own transcript, but, since a fair copy would be
essential for the preparation of the actors' parts and the promptbook, we have to think
it possible that the playhouse scrivener would 'make an intermediate transcript of
them [the foul-papers] for consideration, revision, submission to the censor, copying
of the parts, or sometimes for marking and cutting in preparation for the final promptbook' (pp. 20–1). Again, 'A temporary manuscript to serve as a basis for the copying of
the parts and for guiding rehearsal would be a practical necessity before the book-
keeper was ready to engage himself to the preparation of the final prompt-book'
(p. 113).

It is evident that the hypothesis of an intermediate scribal transcript of foul-papers
will serve to explain the source of the text of a number of Shakespeare's plays, which
exhibit the tell-tale features of neither foul-papers nor promptbooks.[1] It seems very
probable that the Folio text of *Hamlet* began its life as such a transcript, a fair copy of
Shakespeare's foul-papers, containing his latest revisions, before the play went into
production. This was the view argued by J. M. Nosworthy in *Shakespeare's Occasional
Plays*.[2] It runs counter to the view advanced with such brio by John Dover Wilson in
The Manuscript of Shakespeare's 'Hamlet' that the Folio text was based ultimately on
the theatre's promptbook. The promptbook theory never received more than cautious
acceptance. Nosworthy points out that Greg was always uneasy about it. Only his
respect for Dover Wilson seems to have kept him loyal to the theory.[3] A strong
argument against the Folio text being based on the promptbook is its length.
At 3,535 lines it is only 140 lines or so shorter than the second quarto, and as Greg
said it cannot 'suggest any serious attempt to shorten the play' (*Shakespeare's First
Folio*, p. 317). The average length of plays at the time was under 2,500 lines.[4] Plays
varied in length, of course, and it is clear that both Shakespeare and Jonson were given
to writing very long plays. Even so, there is no chance of a play of over 3,500 lines
being acted in full. If it is an acting version we are looking for, it will be something
nearer the length of *Macbeth*, or the first quarto of *Hamlet*.

In the next place, a text so deficient in its stage directions could never have served in
the theatre. The Folio follows the second quarto in omitting very many exits, and
some entrances too, and it actually leaves out some important exits which are present
in the quarto. It omits some of the quarto's directions for music, for properties, for offstage noises and onstage actions. (The parallel lists of stage directions in Dover
Wilson's *Manuscript of Shakespeare's 'Hamlet'* make a comparison of the two texts
a simple matter.) It is of course true that the Folio adds to and changes the stage
directions as found in the second quarto, but, essentially, the Folio's attention to
staging is fitful and patchy, and its concerns for properties almost nil. A working
promptbook would have regularized and filled out the mechanics of staging in

---

[1] E.g. *As You Like It*. See R. Knowles's introduction to the New Variorum edition, 1977, esp. 331–4.

[2] In his 1982 edition, Jenkins supports the idea of a 'pre-prompt' transcription; see 59, 64.

[3] 'On the whole it seems to be a rather queer prompt-book, if prompt-book it is, that lies behind F.'
(*Shakespeare's First Folio*, 323; see also 316.)

[4] Hart, *Shakespeare and the Homilies*, 86–9.

a consistent manner, and this would certainly be reflected in any printed version based on it.[1]

If the Folio text is not based ultimately on the promptbook of the play, it is also abundantly clear that its ultimate source is not a strict fair copy of Shakespeare's manuscript. The departures from the text of the second quarto, quite apart from the cuts already discussed, and making every allowance for the inaccuracy of the Q2 compositors, are too extensive for the phrase 'fair copy' to be allowable. Bowers's phrase 'intermediate transcript' is very helpful. A scrutiny of the differences between the stage directions in Q2 and F points us towards the special quality of the transcript that lies behind the Folio text, neither a straightforward copy of Shakespeare's manuscript nor yet a full production script developed from it.[2]

It will be quickly noticed that the variants in the stage directions and the staging which they imply are not spread evenly through the play. In the first act, though there are two alterations which I shall comment on, F tends to omit Q2's directions. Indications for 'Flourish' are generally omitted; the sound of the cannon at 1.4.6 is not mentioned; 'It spreads his arms' and 'The cock crows' are eliminated. Half way through the second act a change of attitude towards stage-business is discernible. Q2's directions are observed, altered and added to. Hamlet enters 'reading on a book' (2.2.165). At 2.2.338, Q2's 'Flourish' is recorded and expanded: 'Flourish for the Players'. By the middle of Act 3, F's attention to music is such that all Q2's directions are noticed (some of them altered), and new directions are being inserted.

By far the greater number of revisions to the stage directions occur in the last three acts. Of the 52 which are of special significance, only 19 occur up to the crucial moment of the king's exit from the play-scene (3.2), which is just slightly beyond the actual half-way point of the play. As concern with matters of staging develops in the Folio text, there is an increasing boldness in intervening and interfering with the text itself in connection with the changes. Nothing previous to 4.5.0 shows the temerity of cutting out the Gentleman who tells Gertrude about Ophelia's madness, and giving his lines (so inappropriately) to Horatio and Horatio's to Gertrude. Innovations of this kind begin a little earlier, at 4.3.0, where, by depriving Claudius of the 'two or three' who enter with him, a prepared public utterance is turned into an unsuitable worried self-communion.

It looks as though a scribe's conception of his task changed during the course of making a transcript. At the outset, he is providing a plain text on which the promptbook may be based. Flourishes are left out because the musical effects are to be decided later. But as the work of transcribing these untidy papers continues – and for all we know discussion about the staging of the play grows more detailed – the transcript begins to include proposals or decisions about the details of the staging and the size of the cast. We can suppose that the scribe is the book-keeper himself, the man

---

[1] The failure in F to carry out the act and scene division beyond the beginning of Act 2 is a further argument against prompt-copy. See Greg, *The Editorial Problem in Shakespeare*, 3rd edn, 1954, 35–6.

[2] This was the conclusion reached by T. M. Parrott and Hardin Craig in their 'critical edition' of the second quarto, 1938, p. 50: 'not the prompt-book, but, probably, the manuscript on which the final prompt-book . . . was based'.

responsible for preparing the promptbook and supervising the production.[1] His concern with practicalities of the theatre (including paying and costuming men and boys for walk-on parts) will become clearer if we now look at the character of the changes made in the Folio's stage directions.

In the first place, on a number of occasions the scribe was visualising what has to happen on stage more clearly than Shakespeare seems to have done. At 1.5.113, for example, Horatio and Marcellus, in pursuit of Hamlet, will need to cry 'My lord, my lord!' before and not after their entry on stage. At 2.2.489–97, Polonius cannot be left awkwardly on stage while Hamlet discusses the 'dozen or sixteen lines' with the First Player. In the graveyard scene (5.1), Hamlet and Horatio need to enter earlier, 'a farre off', in order to listen to the Clown before they comment on what he is doing.

Secondly, the scribe was intolerant of Shakespeare's vagueness about the names and functions of characters and how many there were in group entries. (It is interesting that the permissive entry of the 'two or three' kind must have had a definiteness for him.) So 'Enter the Players' becomes 'Enter foure or fiue Players' (2.2.384). 'Enter Horatio and others' becomes 'Enter Horatio with an Attendant' (4.6). 'Enter old Polonius, with his man or two' becomes 'Enter Polonius, and Reynaldo' (2.1). The scribe's need to identify and to number is very interestingly shown in the directions for the dumb-show in 3.2, with provision for 'Mutes' and 'a Fellow'. At 5.2.340, 'the Embassadors' becomes 'English Ambassador'.

The scribe's constant concern to reduce the number of minor characters throws into relief the strange lavishness, for a practical man of the theatre, with which Shakespeare produced additional characters, especially late in the play, who have little or nothing to say or do. Sometimes the reduction is quite deft, as at 4.5.111 where Laertes's militant followers, instead of entering as 'others', are made to remain shouting outside the doors. But sometimes the attempt to stanch the unending stream of supernumeraries is more damaging to the texture of the play. The Lord who invites Hamlet to the fencing match at 5.2.170 is cut out along with twelve lines of text. I have already mentioned the disfigurement caused by the removal of the 'two or three' who enter with Claudius at 4.3.0, and the removal of the Gentleman at 4.5.0. At 3.2.312 it would appear from the quarto that Shakespeare's idea was that the players should come on as a consort to play music. 'Enter the Players with Recorders' is reduced to 'Enter one with a Recorder', and the text has to be changed.

The three major entries of the full court at 1.2.0, 3.2.81, and 5.2.196 show considerable changes, with the Folio versions showing a special concern for the management of these important stage occasions, filling out the bare entries of the quarto with elaborate detail. The many alterations for the grand entry to witness the fencing contest in the final scene give an impression of being tentative and provisional.

If it is accepted that the changes in the stage directions in the Folio text are *notes towards a production* made while transcribing Shakespeare's foul-papers, and that the book-keeper included signals to the actors, and was ready to alter the text to

---

[1] For the book-keeper's duties, see Greg, *Shakespeare's First Folio*, 100.

accommodate his more frugal standards of numbers in the cast, then some other variants which have been taken to be 'actors' interpolations' or accretions to the text sanctioned by stage custom may also be seen as the work of the scribe.[1] At 5.1.152 the Gravedigger produces another skull, which he says was Yorick's. 'This?' asks Hamlet. 'E'en that', replies the Gravedigger. In Q2 Hamlet continues 'Alas poore *Yoricke*'. But in F he says 'Let me see. Alas poore *Yorick*'. Hamlet's 'Let me see' provides for the transferring of the skull from one actor to the other.

It is not in the least surprising that an experienced playhouse scrivener, accustomed to Shakespeare's script, should be able to give a more intelligent rendering of the foul-papers than the compositors in James Roberts's printing house, especially in following Shakespeare's marks for deletion and insertion. He has on many occasions preserved the true reading of the text when the second quarto has blundered.[2] Yet he would alter Shakespeare's text, as we have seen, and he too could blunder. There is at 5.1.251–5 a very bad misascription of a speech by Gertrude to Claudius. It is quintessentially a Gertrude speech, anxious, protective, sentimental, flowery, and there can be no reason except carelessness for giving it to Claudius. How do we know that this misascription in the Folio was the error of a scribe at an early date in the play's history and not the error of the Folio compositors? Because the 'bad' first quarto of 1603 also contains the erroneous ascription.

The first quarto gives us some of the strongest and clearest evidence of the nature of the manuscript which is the source of the Folio text, and helps to distinguish its various archaeological layers. Corrupt and adulterated though its text is, it demonstrates that an acting-text of *Hamlet*, based on the playhouse transcription of Shakespeare's foul-papers which we have been discussing, had become established in performance by 1603. When the Folio and the first quarto agree on readings which differ from the second quarto and are manifestly or arguably inferior to the second quarto, we may consider we have evidence of changes which the book-keeper made when copying out Shakespeare's manuscript, which changes were then transmitted to the promptbook and into performance, and so were established in the theatre-text corruptly 'reported' in the first quarto.

The invaluable tables of common and divergent readings given by Dover Wilson in *The Manuscript of Shakespeare's 'Hamlet'* show us on pp. 336–40 a number of occasions when the first quarto confirms an early weakening of Shakespeare's text. The second quarto's 'But who, a woe, had seene' (i.e. 'But who – ah woe! – had seen') was weakened to 'But who, O who, had seen' found in both the first quarto and the Folio (2.2.460). 'The Lady doth protest too much' was weakened to 'The Lady protests to[o] much.' An interesting change is at 4.7.177 where in the description of the death of Ophelia the first quarto confirms that Shakespeare's 'snatches of old laudes' (Q2) had been altered to 'snatches of old tunes' (F). Presumably the book-keeper thought 'lauds' altogether too outlandish or unfamiliar.

---

[1] See *MSH*, p. 79, and Jenkins in *Studies in Bibliography* 13 (1960), 31–47.
[2] E.g. the fretful, not the fearful porpentine (1.5.20), and scullion, not stallion (2.2.540).

Once the fair copy of Shakespeare's manuscript had been made, it would be necessary to prepare from it a shorter version for acting, the promptbook, from which in turn the actors' parts would be taken. Unfortunately we have no idea what the form of this acting version was, nor whether Shakespeare was involved in creating it. If he knew of some of the changes already made involving some of the minor characters in the later part of the play (which have just been discussed) he cannot have approved of them. Things already seem to be going forward without his co-operation; and it seems to me very unlikely that he was closely engaged in what to some extent must have been a mutilation of his work. *Macbeth*, of which we have only a single text of about 2,500 lines, is alone among the Histories and Tragedies in giving us what looks like an acting-text. What Shakespearean riches have been lost in achieving that brevity is beyond conjecture. With *Hamlet* it is the other way round. We have two texts, one authorial of great amplitude, and one which seems to contain authorial deletions and changes and also bears signs of the play being got ready for the stage. But we have no evidence of the shape of the play as it was eventually acted on Shakespeare's stage. Why in the first place Shakespeare should on this occasion as on many others have written a play manifestly too long for theatrical presentation is a far-reaching and unsettling question.

The one link we have with *Hamlet* as acted at the Globe Theatre is the first quarto of 1603, deriving as it must from a stage version based upon the transcript which we have postulated as lying behind the Folio text. The verbal links between the transcript and the first quarto have been noted, and there is further evidence of dependence in the fact that the passages deleted by the Folio (which appear in the second quarto) are all missing from the first quarto.[1] In trying to fill the great gap in our knowledge of the history of *Hamlet*, the shape of the play as given on Shakespeare's stage, we need to look closely at the first quarto.

The first quarto is a much-abbreviated as well as a much-debased version of Shakespeare's play as we know it from the second quarto and the Folio. The standard example of its quality is the opening of the 'To be or not to be' soliloquy (here modernized):

> To be or not to be, ay there's the point;
> To die, to sleep, is that all? Ay, all.
> No, to sleep, to dream; ay marry, there it goes,
> For in that dream of death, when we awake
> And borne before an everlasting judge,
> From whence no passenger ever returned,
> The undiscovered country, at whose sight
> The happy smile, and the accursed damned

The quality varies greatly, however, and in some parts of the play, especially near the beginning, there is an approximation to the standard text. There is little dispute that

---

[1] One or two phrases in Q1 seem to echo passages cut from F. It is not at all unlikely that in preparing the promptbook for the Globe some extra material from the foul-papers was added for clarification. See Chambers, *William Shakespeare*, 1930, I, 416, and Duthie, 273.

the first quarto is a 'reported' text, an attempt to put together the text of a play from memory without recourse or access to an authoritative manuscript. It is generally thought, in view of the superiority of the text whenever he is on stage, that the actor playing Marcellus, perhaps doubling as Lucianus in the play-within-the-play, was responsible for the piracy.[1]

While in the main the first quarto follows, to the best of its ability, an abbreviated version of the standard play, there are four substantial and interesting departures. The first is that Polonius has become Corambis. Secondly, the 'To be or not to be' soliloquy and the subsequent nunnery scene are placed earlier than in the standard text. Third, at the end of the closet scene Hamlet asks Gertrude to assist him in revenge, and she vows that

> I will conceal, consent, and do my best,
> What stratagem soe'er thou shalt devise.

The fourth change is a drastic reworking of Hamlet's return from the voyage to England. Horatio is given a new scene with the queen, in which he tells *her* the news that in the standard text Hamlet tells *him* of the king's plot on his life and the exchange of the commission which sends Rosencrantz and Guildenstern to their doom. There is no mention of the fight with the pirates.

Is it possible that these alterations represent a recognized version of Shakespeare's play as it was acted in London before 1603 when the first quarto was published? Some evidence that the shape of the first quarto was the conventional and accepted shape is provided by a curious German manuscript of 1710, now lost, which was printed in 1781: *Der bestrafte Brudermord oder Prinz Hamlet aus Dannemark* (sometimes known as *Fratricide Punished*).[2] This play may well be the descendant of a *Hamlet* taken by a travelling English company to Germany in the early seventeenth century. Details of such companies are given by E. K. Chambers in *The Elizabethan Stage* (ii, 272–92), and *Hamlet* is one of the plays acted. But, writes Bullough, 'generations of actors played havoc with the original text and doubtless changed incidents as well as dialogue' (*Narrative and Dramatic Sources*, vii, 21). However, it is possible to discern that the original text, while not dependent on the first quarto of *Hamlet*, shared many of its features. In particular, Polonius is Corambus, and the nunnery scene occupies the same early position as in the first quarto. But the first quarto scene between Horatio and the queen telling of Hamlet's escape is not repeated. Instead Hamlet gives the information to Horatio himself, as in the second quarto (though the circumstances of the escape have become altered out of recognition). So it seems possible that the change of name from Polonius to Corambis or Corambus, and the earlier placing of the nunnery scene, were established features of *Hamlet* as it was being acted before 1603; but that the other features of the first quarto – the complicity of the queen with *Hamlet* and the reworking of the news of Hamlet's escape – are peculiar to that text. It is

---

[1] This view was advanced by H. D. Gray in 1915 and accepted by Duthie.
[2] See Duthie, 238–70. There is a translation in Bullough, vii: 128–58.

a plausible suggestion that the new role for the queen is not new at all, but is a recollection of the old play of *Hamlet*.[1]

The transposition of the nunnery scene in the first quarto and in *Bestrafte Brudermord* invites further discussion for the light it may be able to shed on the matter of the fluidity of the text of *Hamlet*, with which we began this discussion.

In the first quarto, when Corambis has heard Ophelia's story of Hamlet bursting into her room and has decided that this is love-madness, he says 'Let's to the King', and in the following scene Ophelia enters with Corambis, though she has nothing to say while Hamlet's letter to her is read out and the 'Ophelia trap' is planned. Then Hamlet enters, with the king saying 'See where he comes, poring upon a book.' Corambis asks the queen to leave, gives Ophelia a book, and we launch into the 'To be or not to be' soliloquy and the nunnery scene. At the end of this, Hamlet goes out, Ophelia voices her distress, and the king and Corambis make their comments, all – very roughly – as in the standard text. But then Hamlet must enter again, and Corambis greets him to initiate the fishmonger scene. This runs on as usual to the 'rogue and peasant slave' soliloquy with Hamlet's resolve to test the king in a play. The 'Mousetrap' play follows almost at once, after the interposition of the equivalent of only the first 35 lines of 3.1.

It has often been noted[2] that in the standard text of *Hamlet*, Polonius like Corambis tells Ophelia to accompany him to the king.

> Come, go with me, I will go seek the king.   (2.1.99)

>   Come, go we to the king.
> This must be known.   (2.1.115–16)

But when he enters in 2.2 he is alone. Did Shakespeare once toy with – even try out – the idea of bringing Hamlet on after the long lapse of time that is supposed to follow the end of the first act, to show him meditating suicide? And of following that with the attack on Ophelia, which gives continuity with the earlier attack which we have just heard about from Ophelia herself? It is curious not only that we have the signs of an intention to bring on Ophelia in 2.2 but also that there is a noticeable 'join' in 3.1 to initiate the nunnery scene. At 2.2.158, in planning the Ophelia trap, Polonius says

> You know sometimes he walks four hours together
> Here in the lobby . . .
> At such a time I'll loose my daughter to him.
> Be you and I behind an arras then.

At 2.2.205, however, at the end of the fishmonger scene, Polonius says

I will leave him, and suddenly contrive the means of meeting between him and my daughter.

---

[1] Duthie, 196–206. There is a translation in Bullough, VII, 128–58.
[2] Especially by Harley Granville Barker in his *Preface*, 1937, an important contribution to which this discussion is indebted.

(This is the Folio reading: the second quarto omits most of this, and gives the obviously defective sentence: 'I will leave him and my daughter.') At 3.1.28, Claudius says

> Sweet Gertrude, leave us too,
> For we have closely sent for Hamlet hither,
> That he, as 'twere by accident, may here
> Affront Ophelia.

In the word 'closely', the normal sense of secrecy applies to Claudius's purpose and not to sending the message; he has sent for Hamlet under pretence of something other than the real reason. When Hamlet enters, however, he is deep in meditation, communing with himself, giving no indication whatsoever that he has been sent for. This is his usual lobby walk, and he is surprised when he sees Ophelia. We can see that his entry belongs to the original scheme prepared for by Polonius's words at 2.2.158, 'sometimes he walks four hours together / Here in the lobby ... / At such a time I'll loose my daughter to him.' Claudius's words are inconsistent with Hamlet's entry, and Polonius's words at 2.2.205 are inconsistent with Claudius's words. It is arguable that postponing 'To be or not to be' and the nunnery scene has led to a little gluing and patching; the defectiveness of the second quarto at 2.2.205 suggests problems with the manuscript arising from deletions or additions.

The positioning of 'To be or not to be' where it now finds itself is of profound importance for the ultimate meaning of the play. Yet it is easy to see that 3.1 is not the only place it could have gone. Shakespeare may well have hesitated about what Chambers calls 'the order of the tests by which the court endeavours to ascertain the reason of Hamlet's strangeness' (*William Shakespeare*, I, 416). Once it finds its final placing, it invites incomprehension. Hamlet has been given his mission, has cursed himself for his delay, has planned to test the Ghost's veracity with a play and – now what? Back to the beginning and the strain of the very first soliloquy, wishing he were dead and cursing the conscience that stops him from doing anything. A great many critics try to rescue Shakespeare from his decision to place 'To be or not to be' where it is by denying the plain truth of what the soliloquy says, that is, that death is better than life but that we haven't the courage to kill ourselves. From Dr Johnson onwards there has always been someone who tries to pull Hamlet out of the deep pit of pessimism he is in. Here at least we might agree with Rebecca West that critics misinterpret *Hamlet* because they cannot face its bleakness.[1] Would it therefore be surprising if actors of Shakespeare's day, with perhaps a Hamlet among them, had argued that the play would go with a greater swing if, when he has decided on his plan to test both the Ghost and Claudius, Hamlet were allowed to get on with it? The leap into Ophelia's grave shows us that Hamlet was allowed to do things on the stage that Shakespeare hadn't wanted him to do (see the note to 5.1.225SD). Possibly the players, possibly Shakespeare's own fellows, pushed 'To be or not to be' and

---

[1] *The Court and the Castle*, 1958.

the nunnery scene back to an earlier position which Shakespeare had originally tried out but later rejected. The whole history of the development of the playing text of *Hamlet* in the theatre shows not merely abbreviation of the play but an ironing out of its complexities. The refusal of the stage to meet the challenge of the personality that Shakespeare created may have begun very early.

Our postulated fair copy of Shakespeare's manuscript, having been used to create the promptbook and the actors' parts, would be carefully preserved in case a new promptbook were ever needed. When it became desirable to supplant the inferior first quarto with its outrageous claim to be the play that Shakespeare wrote, it was Shakespeare's own manuscript, now no doubt in a very messed-up condition, that was given to the printer. Little wonder that the compositors tried to get help from a copy of the first quarto. It seems very plausible that in the three years and more since Shakespeare completed his play wear and tear had made the manuscript less legible than it was when the book-keeper took it over to make his transcript. There is one particular area of the second quarto, from 5.2.145 to 170, where omissions and errors (by comparison with the Folio) are unusually deep and extensive. For example:

5.2.146	Q2:	why is this all you call it?
	F:	why is this impon'd as you call it?
158	Q2:	Shall I deliuer you so?
	F:	Shall I redeliuer you e'en so?
161–2	Q2:	Yours doo's well to commend it himselfe
	F:	Yours, yours; hee does well to commend it himselfe
165	Q2:	A did so sir with his dugge [corrected from 'A did sir']
	F:	He did Complie with his Dugge
166	Q2:	more of the same breede
	F:	more of the same Beauy
167	Q2:	and out of an habit
	F:	and outward habite
168	Q2:	a kind of histy collection
	F:	a kinde of yesty collection
169	Q2:	prophane and trennowed opinions
	F:	fond and winnowed opinions

An interesting feature of this series of misreadings is the uncharacteristic attempt to invent and supply words, like 'breede' and 'prophane'. This last is a less wild guess than it seems. The Folio's 'fond' is itself a misreading of 'fand' (= 'fanned'). If a tattered manuscript had what seemed to be (with the common mistake of final e for final d) 'fane', the compositor may have thought he had the tail-end of 'profane'. At any rate, it very much looks as though this page of Shakespeare's manuscript had become very difficult to decipher since it had been used for the theatre transcript some years before. It seems to me unlikely that Roberts's compositors would on their own initiative supply words like 'prophane'; they would have turned to a superior for help.

There are three other places in the second quarto where I think the extraordinary distance of the variant from the much stronger Folio reading indicates that the manuscript was no longer legible and that a guess was made in the printing house to remedy the deficiency. (The variant readings are discussed in the commentary as they occur.)

1.3.26   Q2:   As he in his particuler act and place
        F: As he in his peculiar Sect and force

3.3.79   Q2:   Why, this is base and silly, not reuendge
        F: Oh this is hyre and Sallery, not Reuenge

3.4.50   Q2:   With heated visage
        F: With tristfull visage

I have already suggested that two passages which appear in the Folio but are not found in the second quarto, namely the passage in 2.2 about the war of the theatres and the words of Hamlet in 5.2, 'Is't not to be damned . . . ', were late additions which either became detached or were overlooked. A third omission from the second quarto is the passage 2.2.229–56 which contains the reference to Denmark being a prison. It has often been suggested that by 1604 with Anne of Denmark as the king's consort this might have seemed a sensitive passage and so was cut out. This is the best explanation; possibly the printing house was where this self-censorship took place. If we could leave the text of *Hamlet* at this point, with only Roberts's compositors between us and Shakespeare's manuscript, and Jaggard's compositors (who set up the Folio text) between us and the book-keeper's transcript of the same manuscript, we should be fortunate indeed. It is certain, however, that the manuscript used by Jaggard for printing the Folio text was not the book-keeper's transcript itself but a careless and rather free copy of it. The copy was made sometime after 1606, and conceivably was made specially for the printing of the Folio (1623). The existence of a second scribe was argued by Dover Wilson in *The Manuscript of Shakespeare's 'Hamlet'*, and though I do not think we can accept the colourful rogue whom Dover Wilson believed he had driven into a corner (p. 56), an old actor and a fan of Burbage, who would write down what he had heard the actors say instead of relying on his copy, there can be no doubt of this agent of transmission. His existence is proved by the first quarto. When Q2 and Q1 agree in what appears to be the true reading, and they differ from F, then since Q1 has no access to the true reading except through the stage version which emanated from the book-keeper's transcript, that transcript must once have contained the true reading, and it must have been obliterated at a later stage. That 'later stage' in hundreds of minor cases must have been the setting up of the Folio text itself, but often the extent of the variation takes it far beyond a compositor's error. The tendency to substitute a word of similar sense often makes the Folio text a sort of paraphrase. Examples are 'just' for 'jump' at 1.1.65; 'day' for 'morn' at 1.1.150; 'gives' for 'lends' at 1.3.117; 'two' for 'ten' at 2.2.177; 'swathing' for 'swaddling' at 2.2.351; 'that' for 'yonder' at 3.2.339; 'claims' for 'craves' at 4.4.3; 'imperial' for 'imperious' at 5.1.180 (all these examples in modernized form). The concurrence of Q2 and Q1 in a good reading when the variant in F is also a good reading cannot prove that the F reading is a substitution by the second scribe, because the use by the Q2 compositors of a copy of Q1, particularly in the first act, can mean that the reading common to Q2 and Q1 is an error deriving from the latter. So the famous doublets in Act 1, where Q2 and Q1 agree against F, become no easier to solve. (E.g. lawless / landless, 1.1.98; sallied / solid, 1.2.129; interred / enurned, 1.4.49; waves / wafts 1.4.61; roots / rots, 1.5.33.)

A convincing demonstration can be made, by the use of the first quarto, of how Shakespeare's language was progressively weakened during the course of the two transcriptions lying between his foul-papers and the printing of the Folio.

1.1.161   Q2:   And then they say no spirit dare sturre abraode
          Q1:   And then they say, no spirite dare walke abroade
          F: And then (they say) no Spirit can walke abroad

The inference here is that the first scribe, the book-keeper, has made the no doubt unconscious substitution of 'walk' for 'stir' and this has found its way to the stage and thence eventually into the first quarto. The second scribe has weakened 'dare' to 'can'.

The Act to Restrain Abuses of Players of 1606 (see Chambers, *Elizabethan Stage*, IV, 338–9) forbade the use of the name of God, Jesus, the Holy Ghost or the Trinity in any play. It is clear that the second scribe made appropriate changes in his text when he remembered, but that he sometimes forgot. 'God' becomes 'Heaven' at 1.5.24 and elsewhere; 'By the mass' (2.1.50), ''Sblood' (2.2.337) and ''swounds' (2.2.528) are removed, but 'Gods bodkin' actually becomes 'Gods bodykins' (2.2.485). 'God a mercy' is smoothed to 'Gramercy' (4.5.194).

To summarize the foregoing discussion about a possible relationship between the three texts of *Hamlet*: the second quarto of 1604/5 was printed from Shakespeare's own manuscript, his 'foul-papers', as submitted to his company in 1601. This manuscript contained quite a number of passages which Shakespeare had marked for deletion. These deletion-marks were ignored or overlooked by the compositors, so that the second quarto – and consequently the received text of *Hamlet* – preserves much that Shakespeare had himself discarded. In the playhouse, an official fair copy was made of Shakespeare's no doubt untidy manuscript as a first stage towards preparing a text for the theatre. This fair copy did not include those false starts and unwanted passages which Shakespeare had marked for deletion. It also cut out two passages and added a third; these three changes can be considered as a multiple change of fundamental importance for the meaning of the play, and it is possible that the responsibility for these late changes was Shakespeare's. As the preparation of the fair copy went forward, the scribe made an increasing number of changes to his text, many of which stem from a determined effort to reduce the large number of minor and walk-on characters.

This conjectural fair copy eventually became the Folio text of 1623, but not directly. A transcript of the fair copy must have been made at some point after 1606 by a scribe with a cavalier indifference to the ethic of fidelity to one's copy. This second scribe did untold damage by casualness and rash improvement, and this damage is compounded by the usual carelessness and liberties of the Folio's compositors.

The first quarto of 1603, an abbreviated and adapted version in language which severely corrupts the original, inherits the cuts and changes made in the early playhouse transcript, and demonstrates that the transcript was in progress towards the Globe's official promptbook. It is not inconceivable that in spite of all its corruption it reflects the shortened acting version of Shakespeare's own theatre. The first quarto was used by the compositors of the second quarto, especially during the first act. It is also likely that the Folio compositors had available a copy of the second quarto.

This hypothesis of the relation between the texts may be represented by the following diagram.

The text of *Hamlet*

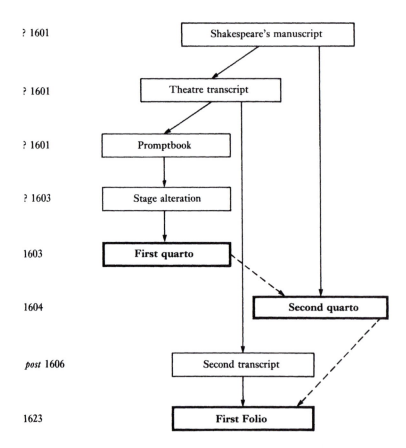

? 1601	Shakespeare's manuscript
? 1601	Theatre transcript
? 1601	Promptbook
? 1603	Stage alteration
1603	First quarto
1604	Second quarto
post 1606	Second transcript
1623	First Folio

I now return to the question with which I began. What do we mean by 'Shakespeare's *Hamlet*'? I believe there was a point when Shakespeare had made many alterations to his play, mostly reflected in cutting rather than adding material, some of which he may have made after preliminary discussions with his colleagues among the Chamberlain's Men. The play then became the property of these colleagues who began to prepare it for the stage. At this point what one can only call degeneration began, and it is at this point that we should arrest and freeze the play, for it is sadly true that the nearer we get to the stage, the further we are getting from Shakespeare. This ideal version of the play does not exist in either of the two main authoritative texts, the second quarto and the Folio, but somewhere between them.

However convinced one may be that the true history of the text of *Hamlet* is of the kind that has been described in this analysis, it is not always possible (as Hamlet found in the 'To be or not to be' soliloquy) to have the courage of one's convictions. To present readers with a lean and spare *Hamlet* lacking the 'dram of eale' speech and the soliloquy 'How all occasions do inform against me' might seem arrogance and eccentricity, even if the missing passages were supplied at the foot of the page. I have however wished to keep the different shapes of the second quarto and the Folio in front of the reader as much as possible. I have therefore marked all the second quarto passages which are cut in the Folio within square brackets. As for the main body of the text where the two early versions run parallel, the text of this edition will necessarily be an eclectic text, because neither version, in the case of any single variant, has a guaranteed superiority over the other. In some cases I have judged the Folio to be correct and in some cases the quarto.

With the stage directions, I have pursued a policy of compromise between the two texts. It is obvious (from the second quarto) that Shakespeare had not fully thought out the movements on stage and that the Folio provides necessary improvements. I have blended the two, to preserve an intimacy with Shakespeare's own pen, and also the greater clarity of the Folio's staging.

APPENDIX 2 NAMES

The names in *Hamlet* are a motley collection. Hamlet and Gertrude derive from the original names in Saxo Grammaticus, and an attempt to provide further Danish names can be seen in Rosencrantz and Guildenstern, in Voltemand (Valdemar), and also in Yaughan and Yorick (both mentioned in Act 5), and Osric (though as Jenkins points out this latter is also a good Anglo-Saxon name).

Laertes and Ophelia are from Greek, Laertes being the name of Ulysses' father. Claudius is very Roman, like Marcellus and Cornelius. Horatio, Francisco, Barnardo are run-of-the-mill playhouse names. (Horatio was the name of the murdered son in *The Spanish Tragedy*.) Fortinbras, with its Frenchness ('Strong-arm'), is an odd name for a Norwegian king and his son. Polonius is even more perplexing; Polonia was a regular name for Poland.

The forms of the names, like almost everything to do with the play, are very unstable. Gertrude, the established spelling of the queen's name, comes from the Folio, and is almost certainly not the way Shakespeare wrote it, for it appears in the second quarto as Gertrard (and once as Gertrad). The spelling Rosencrantz was not established until the eighteenth century. It looks as though the second quarto spelling Rosencraus is this time not Shakespeare's but a continued misreading of 'Rosencrans'; the regular form in the Folio is Rosincrance. It has been thought best to retain the established forms of Gertrude and Rosencrantz in this edition. Barnardo is a different matter; this is the spelling of both quarto and Folio, and there is no reason to follow the editorial form Bernardo.

The most striking change in naming takes place outside the two main texts. Polonius is Corambis in the first quarto, and his man is Montano. This change may reflect revision for performance by the Chamberlain's Men at the Globe. (This idea presumes that the text behind Q1 was composed after, and not before, the manuscripts behind Q2 and F.) If so, it is impossible now to say what led to the change. Perhaps there was the danger of some offence in the earlier name; perhaps someone thought it was odd to suggest that the Danish counsellor was a Pole. Whether the change was made by Shakespeare's company or not, it is interesting that the new name was certainly in Shakespeare's mind around the year 1603, for he included 'Corambus' in the rag-bag list of names of officers produced by Parolles in *All's Well That Ends Well* 4.3.161–5. But it looks as though Corambis was coined to suit the role of the Danish counsellor. Gollancz made the excellent suggestion that the name comes from 'crambe' or 'crambo', which, deriving from 'crambe repetita' (cabbage served up again), referred to silly verbal repetition. Apparently the form 'corambe' is occasionally found. (See Duthie, 223, and *OED* under 'crambe'.)

There are many minor variants in the spelling of names, and these are not usually taken account of in the collation. Reynaldo, for example, is the second quarto form; in the Folio he is Reynoldo. Elsinore appears regularly in the second quarto as Elsonoure, and in the Folio as Elsenour and Elsonower. Osric is called Osrick once in the quarto and on all other occasions Ostrick or Ostricke; in the Folio he is always Osricke.